The Waters Above:

Earth's Pre-Flood Vapor Canopy

The Waters Above:

Earth's Pre-Flood Vapor Canopy

Joseph C. Dillow

MOODY PRESS
CHICAGO

© 1981 by
THE MOODY BIBLE INSTITUTE
OF CHICAGO

All rights reserved. No part of this book may be reproduced in any form without permission in writing from the publisher, except in the case of brief quotations embodied in critical articles or reviews.

Unless otherwise indicated, all Scripture quotations in this book are from the *New American Standard Bible,* © 1960, 1962, 1963, 1968, 1971, 1972, 1973, 1975, and 1977 by The Lockman Foundation, and are used by permission. Other quotations are from the *King James Version* (KJV).

Library of Congress Cataloging in Publication Data

Dillow, Joseph C
   The waters above.
   Bibliography: p. 427.
   Includes indexes.
   1. Deluge. 2. Creation — Biblical teaching. 3. Bible. O.T. Genesis I-XI — Criticism, interpretation, etc. 4. Cosmology, Biblical. 5. Bible and science.
I. Title. II. Title: Earth's pre-flood vapor canopy.
BS658.D54   222'.1106   80-15339
ISBN: 0-8024-9198-7

Printed in the United States of America

*To Jane and Lloyd Thomas,
who first told me about Jesus Christ
and who loved me into His kingdom.
And to Bud Hinkson,
who first taught me that all Scripture is inspired,
and whose godly life has always been
a shining example of New Testament Christianity.*

Contents

CHAPTER	PAGE
Foreword	xiii
Preface	xvii
Acknowledgments	xxi
1. Science and the Bible	1
2. Biblical Evidence for the Water Heaven Theory	43
3. Other Scriptural Evidence for the Water Heaven	77
4. The Canopy in World Mythology	113
5. Scientific Evidence for the Vapor Canopy Model	135
6. Critique of Various Canopy Models	193
7. What the Pre-Flood Atmosphere Was Like	221
8. Some Problems with the Vapor Canopy Theory	267
9. Radiation and the Vapor Canopy	287
10. The Riddle of the Frozen Giants	311
11. The Laughter of the Gods	355
12. The Catastrophic Freeze	397
13. How It All Fits Together	421
Bibliography	427
Subject Index	461
Index of Persons	471
Index of Scripture	477

ILLUSTRATIONS

ILLUSTRATION	PAGE
1.1 The Critical View of Hebrew Cosmology	9
5.1 Semi-log Plot of Declining Longevity of Postdiluvian Patriarchs	161
6.1 Coordinate System and Nomenclature Used in Equations of Motion	205
6.2 The Diffusion of Water Vapor from the Canopy to the Surface of the Earth	220
7.1 Theoretical Canopy Atmosphere with No Clouds	235
7.2 Model of the Pre-Flood Atmosphere	242
7.3 Proposed Temperature Structure of the Pre-Flood Atmosphere and Vapor Canopy	243
7.4 Movement of a Parcel of Air into a Temperature Inversion	249
7.5 Taylor Vortices Between Two Concentric, Rotating Cylinders	251
7.6 Model of the Taylor Stability of the Ancient Atmosphere	252
7.7 Finite Difference Model with 70 Layers, Each 100 Meters Thick	261
7.8 Plot of the Flux of Water Vapor through the Nearest 100 Layer Beneath the Canopy As a Function of Time	262
9.1 Rayleigh Scattering and Beer's Law	292
9.2 The Effect of a Greater Zenith Angle on the Optical Path of a Light Ray	301
9.3 Angles above the Horizon at Which Stars of Various Magnitudes Would Come into View Under the Canopy	302
9.4 Section of the Pre-Flood Sky in Which Stars Were Visible	303
11.1 Plot of Dimensionless Excess Temperature $(1-\theta)$ Versus the Fourier Number, Fo, for Various Values of the Coordinate for a Cylinder	389
12.1 Development of Low Pressure Centers Prior to the Flood	411

TABLES

TABLE		PAGE
1.1	The Correspondence Between Days 1-3 and 4-6	24
2.1	From Chaos to Chaos, the Conceptual Tie Between Genesis 1:7 and 7:11	65
3.1	Yahweh's Control over Chaos	101
4.1	Parallels Between Greek and Hebrew Canopy Legends	121
4.2	Parallels Between the Indian and Hebrew Stories of the Water Heaven	123
5.1	Air Temperatures in the Cretaceous	143
5.2	The Principal Parameters of Pteranodon Ingens	147
5.3	The Ages at Death of the Postdiluvian Patriarchs	159
5.4	The Electromagnetic Spectrum	165
5.5	Radiation Exposures in the United States	167
6.1	Spherical Radius at Which All the Ice Will Melt, $L/D = 0$	208
6.2	Radius Ratios for Ice Entering from Roche's Limit	210
7.1	Constants Used in Radiative Heat Transfer Calculations	228
7.2	Canopy Temperature Profile	237
9.1	Relative Intensities of Visible Stars	289
9.2	Luminances and Visual Magnitudes of Standard Light Sources	291
9.3	Pre-Flood Adjusted Intensities Relative to Today	299
9.4	Angles above the Horizon at Which Stars of Various Magnitudes Would Become Visible under the Canopy Compared with Today	302
9.5	The Number of Stars of Each Magnitude Visible in the Pre-Flood Heavens	304
11.1	Progressive Decay of Gladiolus Flower Petals in a Solution of Stomach Juice at Various Temperatures (in Hours)	380
11.2	Variation of Thermal Conductivity (with Temperature) of Mammoth	384
11.3	Variation of Specific Heat (with Temperature) of Mammoth	385

11.4	Time in Hours to Bring the Temperature of the Stomach Contents Down to 40°F	390
11.5	Comparison of Cooling and Freezing Rates in a Cow and a Mammoth	394
11.6	Comparison of Cooling and Freezing of a Mammoth "Blast Frozen" and a Mammoth Buried in Ice	395
12.1	Reclassification of Geological Strata Along the Lines of Flood Geology	409

Foreword

THE "CANOPY THEORY," which postulates a primeval body of water surrounding the earth above its atmosphere, has been discussed by many writers and speakers throughout the past century. Identified with the "waters which were above the firmament" (Gen. 1:7, KJV), which were set in place by God on the second day of creation, these primordial waters were believed to have produced a marvelous climate for the original world. But they also served as one of the agents in its later destruction, descending in the form of global torrents of rain at the time of the great Flood in the days of Noah.

I first learned of the canopy theory in 1941 in a lecture by Dr. Irwin Moon in one of his famous Moody Bible Institute "Sermons from Science." His message made a profound impression on me and was one of the main events which triggered my own lifelong interest in the harmonization of the Bible and science. A passing reference to the idea in a paper by George McCready Price, two booklets by Vernon Kellog, and one by N. I. Saloff Astakhoff stimulated further study of the subject. My first book, *That You Might Believe* (Chicago: Good Books, Inc., 1946) consequently placed considerable emphasis on an antediluvian vapor canopy as the main physical system which provided a storm-free, mild climate for the "very good" world (Gen. 1:31) which God had created. It later condensed and precipitated through the "windows of heaven" (Gen. 7:11, KJV) to inundate the world with a great deluge.

The book *The Genesis Flood*, which I co-authored with Dr. John Whitcomb in 1961, was graciously used by the Lord as perhaps the main catalyst to set in motion the remarkable revival of scientific biblical creationism that has marked the past fifteen years. One of the models stressed in that book was the canopy theory, and we tried to place it on a reasonably sound scientific basis, at least in a qualitative sense. The idea of a pre-Flood vapor canopy seemed to correlate an abundance of both biblical and scientific data, and many evangelicals, both scientists and theologians, were persuaded of its validity and of its great value in strengthening faith in the historicity of the early chapters of Genesis.

Not surprisingly, however, a number of critics — both within and outside evangelicalism — soon began to find fault with the canopy theory at various points. This was true, of course, with other sections of The Genesis Flood as well. (I suppose there have not been many evangelical books of recent decades which stirred up more critics than this one did!) Many tried to destroy its influence by overt hostility; others tried to undermine it by "condemning it with faint praise." John Whitcomb and I could at least take comfort in reflecting that it is easier to tear down than to build, and that most books with a significant impact supporting biblical literalism must expect such critics to surface.

Of course we have always stressed that the scientific models in the book were subject to refinement, as long as the basic biblical doctrines (recent special creation of all things and a world-destroying flood) were not undermined. The canopy model, in particular, needed thorough quantitative analysis to support or modify our own qualitative analyses.

There have, in fact, been a number of scientists who have undertaken detailed scientific studies of the postulated canopy and its effects during the past decade. These have, unfortunately, become discouraged by the sheer magnitude of the calculations involved and have never really finished their studies.

But now, at long last, the Lord has raised up Joseph Dillow. A man of unusual persistence, as well as one with sound training in both science and Scripture, Dr. Dillow has produced this tremendously important study of the great canopy, analyzing its evidences, its physical nature, and its profound effects on the earth. He has also been able to draw on the expertise of numerous other scientists with whom he has consulted. The canopy model involves the sciences of physics, astronomy, meteorology, thermodynamics, optics, mechanics, dynamics,

Foreword

hydrology, cryogenics, and others. The breadth of the canopy model's impact is staggering, and no one person could, without aid from many others, ever hope to analyze it all. I believe the Lord raised up all these associates, as well as Dr. Dillow, to contribute to the tremendous synthesis accomplished in this volume.

In many sections the book will be difficult to follow, even for those with training in science and mathematics, but it is vital that these sections be included for those who may want to check their validity. The basic message will come through to everyone, however, and it is a thrilling message. The antediluvian vapor canopy and its global effects have, once and for all, been demonstrated to be sound both scientifically and historically. The historical accuracy of Genesis 1 — 11 is more solidly established than ever before.

This is not to say, of course, that all questions have been answered or that all aspects of Dr. Dillow's treatise are final. He points out the need for much further study, whether for verification or modification. The scope is so broad, and the range of topics so vast, that there are bound to be points of disagreement.

In fact, there remain a number of points with which I disagree. These are relatively minor, however, and I do not even want to discuss them for fear of detracting from the overall impact of this remarkable book. As a matter of fact, Dr. Dillow's study has already forced me to change a number of my own previous ideas.

This book is an example of scientific creationism at its best, and is a book we have needed for a long time. I am happy to commend it enthusiastically, confident that it will prove a great stimulus to the growing creationist revival of these latter days.

HENRY M. MORRIS, Ph.D.
Director, Institute for Creation Research
San Diego, California

Preface

IN 1961 one of the most controversial books of the middle twentieth century confronted the Christian scientific community — *The Genesis Flood* by Henry M. Morris and John C. Whitcomb, Jr. An analysis of the reviews by scientists and theologians in the years following its publication reveals a wide polarity of responses.[1] The authors argued for a total reconstruction of historical geology based on the literal exegesis of Genesis 1 — 11. It was refreshing to find a scientist and a theologian taking the biblical documents seriously as a framework of approach to prehistory.

The main thesis of the book was that the present geological column can be more adequately explained on the assumption of a global deluge described in the Bible and throughout all of ancient literature. An integral part of the deluge geology promoted by Morris and Whitcomb involved the existence of a pre-Flood vapor canopy from which the forty days of rain in the biblical record descended.

The implications of the earth's having been surrounded by such a canopy are vast. The assumption of its existence leads to a harmonization of many heretofore unexplained facts of the rock record. It also raises problems that evangelicals must seriously face in the interaction between science and Scripture, such as the legitimacy of extracting any kind of mechanistic science out of biblical language and the potential conflicts between interpretations based on biblical exegesis and historical science of today.

In that the vapor canopy was not the central thesis of *The Genesis Flood*, Morris and Whitcomb did not take the space to

1. Charles Albert Clough, "A Calm Appraisal of *The Genesis Flood*," pp. 1-172.

develop fully its scientific and physical implications. They wrote, "The physics and meteorology of such a vapor canopy, and its maintenance in the antediluvian atmosphere, may be difficult to delineate in detail."[2]

This book is an attempt to assume that burden and to delineate at least some of the details and physical implications of such a canopy.

One of the strong points of *The Genesis Flood* is the authors' attempt to lay out a careful exegetical foundation before beginning to make scientific conclusions. The same practice will be followed in this book. Before the science of such a canopy can be considered, it must first be established from the Bible exegetically that such a canopy existed. This leads us directly into the issue of the relationship between primitive mythologies and the elevated cosmology of the biblical records. Not only that, but also the perplexing question of scriptural language and modern science will have to be considered before plunging into the scriptural evidence for the existence of such a canopy.

The bulk of the book, however, will deal with the scientific implications of such a canopy. Serious scientists have often been discouraged from attempting a scientifically credible canopy model. In what follows, an attempt will be made to suggest a plausible mechanism of how such a canopy could have been supported above the ancient atmosphere as well as how the surface temperatures could have allowed the earth to be habitable with such a severe "greenhouse" effect. This canopy may conceivably be linked with antediluvian longevity, gigantism in the fossil record, and the origin of astrology. Its condensation offers a suggested mechanism for the enigma of the so-called Pleistocene extinctions and the accompanying burial and deep freeze of numerous mammoth carcasses found in the tundra muck of Russia.

This book is the first formal attempt to deal with the subject of the vapor canopy from an exegetical and scientific viewpoint. It is my sincere hope that this work will provoke many others to further research and analysis of many of the book's suggestions.

2. Henry M. Morris and John C. Whitcomb, Jr., *The Genesis Flood*, p. 240.

It is also my hope that those who read the book will gain an increased confidence in the God-breathed words of Scripture. With this in view, I offer this work to the reading public with the prayer that the Lord Jesus Christ might be honored and that He will use it for His purposes and for His glory.

Acknowledgments

AS THE LIST of *Personal Communications* in the Bibliography indicates, I have received help from numerous sources in the structuring of the vapor canopy theory. The research involved in this project often led to many fields in which I had no special training. As a result, I took great care to check specific points with specialists in those fields.

Several have given much of their time and counsel. In particular, I would like to thank Professor Roger Simpson of the Mechanical Engineering Department at Southern Methodist University. Dr. Simpson, while not necessarily agreeing or disagreeing with the entire model presented, nevertheless provided considerable help in many of the calculations related to thermodynamics as well as general counsel and advice in other areas.

Robert Newman, who holds a doctorate in astrophysics from Cornell University, was especially helpful in offering constructive criticism of many scientific and exegetical points. Dr. Newman's help is particularly appreciated because he does not hold to the canopy theory, yet willingly entered into interaction with me and made many helpful suggestions.

Meterologist Larry Vardiman was especially helpful in introducing me to the meteorology of the canopy. Dr. Vardiman took time from his busy schedule to quantify the decay of the canopy by molecular diffusion, a crucial point of the model. Clyde McKnight, Ed Holroyd, and John Burkhalter, all with doctorates in atmospheric science, graciously read the manuscript and made many helpful suggestions. Also, many thanks to Dr. Robert Whitelaw, who does not accept the canopy theory, but who helped sensitize me to the exegetical and scientific problems involved in it.

Since I was out of my geological depth, it was a great help to have a geologist, Kirby Anderson, who holds an M.S. in evolution from Yale University, to interact with me. He works with Probe Ministries in Dallas, Texas, and was personally involved with me in many of the questions relating to human and animal physiology and geology.

I would like to give special thanks to Dr. Klaus Potsch of Vienna, Austria, for his valuable help in the translation of certain Russian manuscripts and in some of the calculations involved in the canopy model. With his background in theoretical physics and thermodynamics he has been immensely helpful in the analysis of the radiation balance within the canopy. He has unselfishly given hours of his time to a computer model of the canopy and, more than anyone else, has helped me to understand the physics of the problem.

It was Roger Rusk, retired physics professor from the University of Tennessee, who inspired many of the thoughts that appear in this book. Much of the material in the book was originally presented as a Th.D. dissertation to the faculty of Dallas Theological Seminary. I would especially like to thank Dr. Charles Ryrie and Dr. Kenneth Barker for allowing me to pursue this study in connection with my doctoral work and the seminary for permission to publish the dissertation in book form.

My original interest in the canopy theory was aroused when I read *The Genesis Flood* by Henry Morris and John Whitcomb. Dr. Morris later graciously consented to be a reader of the dissertation and offered many helpful comments.

I am greatly indebted to my editor, William A. Shell, for the numerous corrections made in the original manuscript and for his excellent suggestions that have greatly improved many sections of the text. Any errors that remain, of course, are my responsibility.

I give special thanks to my wife, Linda, for her supportive attitude as I burned the midnight oil many months at a time in pursuit of what we came to call my "magnificent obsession."

Finally, the typing of such a manuscript demanded special care in view of all the scientific equations and extensive footnoting. Many thanks go to my typist supreme, Mrs. Laurence (Joyce) Allen.

CHAPTER 1

Science and the Bible

A WELL-KNOWN PROFESSOR of philosophy and logic, who believes in the inspiration of the Bible, was once approached by a skeptic who said, "Well, everyone knows, professor, that the Bible is not a textbook of modern science."

The professor replied, "Do you realize that you have just committed what we call in logic the fallacy of the false obversion?"

The man was somewhat taken aback and sputtered, "What's that?"

The dictionary defines a false obversion as "a form of inference in which a negative proposition is inferred from an affirmative or an affirmative from a negative."[1]

When a man says, "The Bible is not a textbook of modern science," he is usually implying, "Therefore the Bible contains scientific errors." A person can say something that has implications without stating the implications, and so feel exonerated. For example, a salesman in New England was once having difficulty selling white eggs. Only brown eggs sell well up there. So he put a sign in his grocery store window saying, "All of our eggs are guaranteed not to turn brown." Now, of course, white eggs can be kept on the shelf for six months without turning brown. But he wanted people to draw an inference that the brown eggs they were buying elsewhere were once white and had turned brown. He committed the fallacy of the false obversion.

In a similar way, it is often asserted that the Bible is not a textbook of modern science. Of course, this is so patently

1. *The Lexicon Webster Dictionary,* 1:655.

obvious that one wonders why the statement is ever made. Is the thought behind this statement that people who believe in the literal truth of the Bible believe that the Bible could be used as a textbook in quantum mechanics or biochemistry? Certainly not! Why, then, is this completely banal comment so frequently offered? Apparently it is a somewhat indirect way of saying that the Bible may possibly contain errors of fact about scientific matters in that it was not written to teach science. However, this involves another logical fallacy; it is the classic illustration of the non sequitur. The non sequitur is an incorrect conclusion drawn from a correct premise. The incorrect conclusion in this case is: the Bible contains scientific error. The correct premise is that the Bible was written primarily to teach religious truth. There is no obvious connection between the premise and the conclusion; it is a non sequitur. Certainly the fact that the Bible was written mainly to communicate religious truth does not logically imply in any way, "Therefore, it contains errors of scientific fact."

It is obvious that the Bible is not a scientific textbook in the sense of giving detailed technical descriptions and mathematical formulations of natural phenomena. But this is not an adequate reason for questioning the objective accuracy of the numerous portions of Scripture which do deal with natural phenomena and historical events. The Bible is not a mathematics text either, but we expect that Daniel understands sixty-nine weeks by the phrase, "seven weeks and sixty-two weeks" (Dan. 9:25). The Bible is not, strictly speaking, a historical textbook either, but we expect that when it alludes to things which can be historically verified, it should be accurate. Likewise, the Bible is not technically a textbook of modern science, but when it refers to things which can be measured or checked by modern science, it should be accurate.

THE BIBLE IS A "TEXTBOOK OF MODERN SCIENCE"

In what sense, then, is the Bible a "textbook of modern science"? In this way: the Bible gives the modern scientist a framework within which to perform his research into the geophysics of the ancient earth. It provides a general framework and starting presuppositions for him. Since science in the purest sense deals only with that which is reproducible and measurable in the laboratory, when the scientist launches out into the questions of earth history, he has taken a step of faith. There is no way that some ancient events can be reproduced in the laboratory. So the scientist correctly makes some initial faith assumptions which provide a framework for his investigation. These assumptions by nature are faith assumptions. He may assume the doctrine of uniformity, which postulates that present processes may be extrapolated indefinitely into the past or future and that, therefore, "all things continue as they were from the beginning of the creation" (2 Pet. 3:4, KJV). This old assumption of modern science has, of course, been radically modified so that it is now recognized that there have been serious variations in process rates in the ancient earth. The other assumption the scientist may begin with is that the Bible is true, and therefore what it teaches about creation, the age of the earth, the Flood, and other scientifically relevant events is accurate. If he embraces the latter alternative, he has an entirely different framework within which to investigate the ancient earth than if he started with some version of a radically modified uniformity principle. Either way, it is a faith decision. The scientist was not there in the geologic past to check and see if uniformity always held or to what degree it was modified.

This book assumes that the Bible is the inerrant, authoritative Word of God; therefore, it provides a framework for scientific investigation of the ancient earth. Only God was there when it all happened, so He is the only one who can tell us what it was "really like." Science is a valuable technique for gathering the data and interpreting it. However, the interpretation that the scientist places on his data depends on the assumption that he brings to the data. If he is an evolutionist, assuming that there was no creation and that matter is eternal, he will interpret the data of the radioactive clocks on that assumption — namely, that there were no created amounts of end products in the rock to begin with. If the scientist is a creationist, he will assume that there was a creation and that one cannot know anything certain about how much of each element, isotope, and so-called "decay products" the Creator may have put in the rocks to begin with. Hence the creationist will interpret the data differently than the evolutionist does.

The evolutionary geochronologist assumes by faith there was no creation and can only approximate the amount of end products in the rock to begin with. The creationist geochronologist assumes by faith there was a creation and therefore initial amounts are totally uncertain. For, "By faith we understand that the worlds were prepared by the word of God" (Heb. 11:3). So, for the Bible-believer, science as an investigative technique is used. However, science is rejected as an interpretive tool to reconstruct a world view. So the determining criteria for understanding the major outlines of ancient history are interpretive principles which govern the interpretation of the Bible. What the Bible teaches is what ancient history was really like.

At this point, the scientist who sincerely loves Christ and the Bible is confronted with a tension. Frequently, the apparently obvious interpretations of the Bible seem to contradict his scientific background. How is he to handle this? Because he is not trained in biblical exegesis and theology, all too often he is content to fall back on the fact that there are many different interpretations. So he often feels a freedom to select from the maze of options the one that happens to be most consistent with his particular scientific background. This raises the question as to which of these different possible interpretations will be taken as the correct one. Or more precisely, what criterion does one use to select the correct one from these possible interpretations? The tendency of many Christians, who are scientifically trained, seems to be to select the interpretations that best fit with their personal scientific convictions. So exegetical probability is ultimately determined not by biblical hermeneutics but by the autonomous science of the interpreter. Furthermore, there often seems to be a studied attempt to avoid probing too deeply into all these various interpretations. Just the fact that they exist seems to be sufficient basis for picking any one of them. Frequently, however, these varying interpretations are motivated by the desire to reinterpret the Bible to fit the latest theory of modern science. It is highly improbable that the Bible is as ambiguous as these various interpretations would lead us to believe. It is much more probable that many of these variations originated in the imagination of their interpreters.

Furthermore, continually reinterpreting Genesis into conformity with historical science has its own dangers. Discussing the American Scientific Affiliation's volume *Evolution and Christian Faith*, by Russel L. Mixter, a famous scientific (non-evangelical) historian said, "Maintenance of what these writers call 'verbal inspiration' is likely to prove possible only by continual reinterpretation of the Bible. In the long run, perpetual reinterpretation may prove more subversive of the authority of Scripture than would a frank recognition of the limitations of traditional doctrines."[2] Sometimes evangelicals holding the "middle" position suspect that Genesis, after all, cannot be interpreted any way one wishes. J. Frank Cassel, an American Scientific Affiliation leader, once reflected on how a Bible teacher will "fudge" his exegesis when he deals with Genesis 1 — 11. "I still wonder whether he's given me more time because I demanded it, or because it's really there. The same question applies to the days of Genesis 1 and to the universality of the Noahic flood."[3]

Along the same lines, ardent evolutionist T. H. Huxley reflected on how such constant reinterpretation casts doubt on the credibility of the Bible altogether. He said:

> If we are to listen to many expositors of no mean authority, we must believe that what seems so clearly defined in Genesis — as if very great pains had been taken that there should be no possibility of mistake — is not the meaning of the text at all.... A person who is not a Hebrew scholar can only stand aside and admire the marvelous flexibility of a language which admits of such diverse interpretations.[4]

Charles Clough, in his insightful analysis of this problem, has made it disturbingly clear that there are only three paths to follow:

2. John C. Green, *Darwin and the Modern World View*, p. 32.
3. J. Frank Cassel, "The Origin of Man and the Bible," *Journal of the American Scientific Affiliation* 12 (June 1960):15.
4. Cited by Oswald T. Allis, *God Spake by Moses*, p. 158.

(1) Evangelicals can uphold normal exegesis of Genesis 1-11 and, in faith that this is God's Word, conduct scientific re-evaluation along the lines of flood geology or some form of catastrophism. The wise man said, "The fear of the Lord is the beginning of knowledge," and he also said, "The fear of the Lord is the beginning of wisdom" (Proverbs 1:7; 9:10).

(2) Evangelicals can adopt a passive and non-committal interpretative stance in which Geneses 1-11 is made to conform to whatever happens to be the present reconstruction of historical science.

(3) One may take the path of liberalism, acknowledge that the Bible normally interpreted teaches things contrary to "modern science," and simply reject it.[5]

The first alternative is the only viable one for a Christian. The Bible does provide a perfectly sound basis for understanding not only religious truth but also physical processes. "It may very effectively serve as a 'textbook' of scientific principles within which we can satisfactorily explain all the data of science and history. Whether or not we choose to accept this framework is basically determined by whether or not we *want* to do so. Those who elect the evolutionary framework do so not because the facts of science require this, but because this is the philosophic thought-structure they desire."[6] As Paul said, "They did not *like* to retain God in their knowledge" (Rom. 1:28, KJV, itals. added).

The Bible with its perfect claim to authority based on the authority of Jesus Christ (Matt. 5:17-18; John 10:34-35) clearly establishes a framework of interpretation within which men are expected to formulate their understanding of the data of science. It is most reasonable and gracious of God to do so, since it would be impossible for man by the study of *present processes* to know anything for certain either about the ancient past or the distant future. Only God can *know* these things, and we are able to know the truth about these matters only through faith in

---

5. Charles Albert Clough, "A Calm Appraisal of *The Genesis Flood*," p. 170.
6. Henry M. Morris, *Studies in the Bible and Science*, p. 110.

Science and the Bible

God's statements concerning them. Therefore, the believing Christian goes to the Bible for his basic orientation in all departments of truth. The Bible is his textbook for science as well as his guide to spiritual truth.

Having made that basic commitment, we are immediately confronted with the problem of interpretatively determining exactly what that "framework" is. Moses, for example, has been accused of simply plagiarizing the framework of his heathen neighbors.

THE CRITICAL VIEW

How did Moses understand the structure of the universe? Did he share the primitive concepts of his Near Eastern contemporaries, or did he, through divine revelation, receive new information that lifted his writing far ahead of its time? Much ink has been spilt on both sides of this question, and it seems appropriate to highlight some aspects of this debate before considering the exegetical, mythological, and scientific considerations relating to the existence of a pre-Flood vapor canopy. In fact, some understanding of the interplay between early mythology and Moses' world view is necessary for coming to a correct understanding of his meaning when he spoke of the "waters above the firmament."

A cosmology is one's theory of the structure of the universe. Many have seen Moses' cosmology penned in the early chapters of Genesis as a mere adaptation and elevation of the primitive concepts rampant in the Middle East in the second millennium B.C. Edmond Jacob illustrates this viewpoint:

> In a general way, the Israelites shared the ideas common to the ancient world, conceiving the world as a three-story building, the heavens above, the earth below, and the waters under the earth (Ex. 20:4), a representation which rests as much upon observational data as upon certain mythological concepts.[7]

7. Edmond Jacob, *Theology of the Old Testament*, p. 145.

> The sky was considered solid, resting on pillars, and thus formed a dome over the earth. Because of its solidarity, this celestial vault can separate the terrestrial ocean from the celestial and its rupture would be equivalent to the return of primeval chaos.[8]

Above the celestial ocean, according to many critics, a high chamber is constructed, supported by beams, where God established His throne (Psalm 104:3). This celestial vault is often likened to a tent pitched by Yahweh (God's personal name, often incorrectly rendered Jehovah) (Job 9:8; Psalm 19:4; Isa. 40:22; 44:24), or to a mirror of molten metal (Job 37:18). The columns supporting the vault are the mountains and they can be shaken by thunder, which is Yahweh's voice (Job 26:11; Psalms 18:8; 29:5). The stars are behind the vault when they are invisible (Psalm 19:6; Hab. 3:11). Also, in Jacob's reconstruction of Hebrew thought, there are containers for certain atmospheric forces such as snow and hail (Job 38:22) which God opens for judgment (Isa. 28:17; 30:30). Rain passes through the celestial vault to the earth through the door and lattice window arranged in the vault (Gen. 7:11; Psalm 78:23-25; Isa. 60:8). The earth is flat, resting on pillars whose bases go down into the waters of the great ocean which feeds into the terrestrial oceans by means of subterranean conduits. As Eichrodt sums up, "Israelite cosmology exhibits, as is only to be expected, extensive agreement with the general ideas of the ancient world on the subject."[9] Figure 1.1 depicts this reconstruction."[10]

It is our thesis that these critical views are incredible. Only the most implacable insistence on making the Bible fit into ancient mythology could ever allow such a confusing and distorted view of Moses' cosmology. There is no such primitive cosmology in the Bible.

8. Ibid., p. 149.
9. Walther Eichrodt, *Theology of the Old Testament*, 2 vols., 2:93; see pp. 96-107, 113-17 for a profound discussion on the *difference* between Hebrew and pagan cosmology.
10. T. H. Gaster, "Cosmogony," in *The Interpreter's Dictionary of the Bible*, 1:703.

Science and the Bible 9

FIGURE 1.1

Fig. 1.1. — The Critical View of Hebrew Cosmology: (1) waters above the firmament; (2) storehouses of snows; (3) storehouses for hail; (4) chambers of winds; (5) firmament; (6) sluice gates; (7) pillars of the sky; (8) pillars of the earth; (9) fountains of the deep; (10) navel of the earth; (11) waters under the earth; and (12) rivers of the netherworld. From *The Interpreter's Dictionary of the Bible*, Volume 1, page 703. Copyright 1962 by Abingdon Press. Used by permission.

Many of the expressions that Jacob and Eichrodt refer to are figurative and should not be taken in such a crassly literal way as many critics insist. Furthermore, there are numerous passages of Scripture that would seem to teach that the Hebrews decidedly did not share the cosmology of their neighbors. E. W. Maunder cites Job 26:7 as proof: "He stretches out the north over empty space, and hangs the earth on nothing." Thus, he argues, the Hebrews must have considered the earth as a sphere because they acknowledged that the heavens appeared to rotate around the earth, and concluded that the earth must have been hung in empty space.[11] In this passage, the "north" is a reference to the northern circumpolar constellations, and Job sees them as stretched out over empty space. So he had no concept that the heavens rested on the earth or were borne up by mountains.

We should avoid two dangers in the interpretation of this kind of language.[12] On one extreme, we must avoid the attempt to find precise anticipations of modern scientific discoveries. This is because some of these descriptions are in popular language. On the other extreme, we must avoid the tendency to fit metaphorical language into a definite cosmology. For example, it is unfair of the critics to insist that the "firmament" ("heavens") is a solid vault or dome in which the sun and moon are hung as lamps. The firmament is sometimes spoken of as a curtain (Psalm 104:2; Isa. 40:22) and on another occasion as a scroll (Isa. 34:4). Following the interpretive principles of the critics, one would have to insist on the basis of these passages that the Bible teaches that the heavens are a composite of cloth curtains and literal paper scroll unrolled with all the stars painted on it.

Furthermore, the "windows of heaven" are mentioned as the source of rain (Gen. 7:11), but the Bible also tells us that rain comes from the clouds (Judg. 5:4; Job 36:27-28; Psalm 77:17). It may be true that the windows of heaven do not refer to clouds. In fact, in my opinion, they refer to the condensation of a pre-Flood vapor canopy. But either way, these passages do not teach that there is a dam made of wooden beams holding back the celestial ocean until windows were opened in it. It may teach that there was a vast vaporous canopy surrounding the pre-Flood earth that was restrained from collapsing, but it does so in the form of a metaphor, and is not to be taken literally.

11. E. W. Maunder, "Astronomy," in *The International Standard Bible Encyclopedia*, 1:315.
12. James Orr, "World," in *The International Standard Bible Encyclopedia*, 5:3108.

Certain biblical passages could be read to mean that the sun, moon, and stars are attached to the firmament (by a string, perhaps? [Gen. 1:14]), but far more frequently the sun is pictured as pursuing his free, rejoicing course around the heavens (Psalm 19:5-6; Job 31:26). The expanse of "firmament" was probably just what it means to people today — the atmospheric heavens.

However, all of this requires that the nature of scriptural language be briefly considered before moving on to the positive statement of the Hebrew cosmogony reflected in Genesis.

THE NATURE OF SCRIPTURAL LANGUAGE

Biblical passages with reference to cosmology and other areas of science are often difficult to interpret. Sincere men of both liberal and conservative persuasions have labored over these passages for centuries, and still no definite conclusions have been reached that would be satisfactory to all. One of the most helpful recent discussions of this problem is that of Bernard Ramm in his excellent book *The Christian View of Science and Scripture*.[13]

Dr. Ramm suggests that several things characterize the nature of scriptural language. First, it is often popular and phenomenal, not scientific.[14] A phenomenon of nature may be described in two ways — scientifically or "as it appears." The latter is the primary method of Scripture. When one says, "The sun sets," he is speaking "as it appears." In point of fact, the sun does not "set," that is, sink below the horizon, but the earth rotates on its axis. However, none would charge a twentieth-century scientist with error if he said, "The sun sets." He is using the language of appearance, and this is a universally recognized and accepted language usage.

13. Bernard Ramm, *The Christian View of Science and Scripture*. The title is informative; while the book is excellent, the views it contains are not the Christian view. Many of them certainly do not coincide with my views.
14. Ibid., p. 46.

Furthermore, phrases like "the sun sets" are frequently only language conventions. That is, they are accepted ways of saying things which have no intended scientific implications in the mind of the author. So it is perfectly conceivable that Moses could have believed that the sun actually disappeared into an ocean at the end of the world, yet not be reflecting such a belief when he said "the sun sets." It is highly improbable that Moses did believe that, but even if he did, due to language conventions, he could say the sun sets, yet not even be thinking of the sun sinking into the ocean. It could mean for him simply what it means for us: the day has ended and it is time to go to bed.

Second, biblical language is culturally conditioned.[15] This is one of the most important issues of the entire problem of Christianity and science, and one that is seldom discussed. The Bible does speak in terms of the culture in which its writers lived. Its theological and scientific truth is expressed in the garb of ancient cultural modes. The liberal critic is wrong to imagine that the Bible is full of mistakes simply because the language used in the Bible is the same as the language used in other primitive cultures. Likewise, the believer in inerrancy should be cautious in expecting to find modern science in the Bible. The true position, according to Ramm, "is that the revelation of God came in and through the Biblical languages and their accompanying culture. Coming through these cultures it became meaningful and relevant; and being inspired of God, the writers were restrained from error."[16]

Extracting Scientific Truth from Genesis

The real question raised by the above discussion boils down to this: how much scientific information can one legitimately extract from these ancient documents? Which parts are purely phenomenological ("observer true"), and which parts are mechanistic ("scientifically true")? How does one find the transcultural element in Moses' words? As suggested above, the transcultural meaning, that is, those statements which

15. Ibid., pp. 48 ff.
16. Ibid., p. 49.

imply a definite cosmogony of the biblical writer, cannot be in conflict with the facts as they really are or else the Bible is in error. Since we operate on the assumption of an inspired Bible, we have another reliable source beyond empirical science to give us some insight into the "world that then was." It may be different from our world today, but that does not necessarily mean it is wrong. In fact, it may be the key to understanding some of the most perplexing things in the geological record and of the geophysics of the ancient earth.

How, then, does one perceive the scientific truth in the biblical narrative? Because of the fact that much of the language is phenomenological and dressed in cultural garb, this is no easy task. However, one seemingly obvious assumption must be stated before specific criteria can be delineated. That is, we must not lose sight of the intent of the biblical writer. Yet, strangely, that intent has often been studiously neglected. Hirsch discusses this point brilliantly: "It is a task for the historian of culture to explain why there has been in the past four decades a heavy and largely victorious assault on the sensible belief that a text means what its author meant."[17] Or as Walter Kaiser puts it, "The primary task of the Biblical scholar is to unfold the meaning of the text of Scripture as it was originally intended to be understood by the writer of that text. Those ideas, meanings, and truth intentions which he had in mind are the first order of business."[18]

In other words, in answer to the question, "How much scientific truth can one extract from Genesis 1?" the answer must be: "One can extract only that which the writer himself, Moses, intended to teach." It could be that there are statements made in a biblical text that have significance for modern science, but significance must always be distinguished from the meaning of the writer and hence the "teaching" of the Bible. This point will be examined later.

At no point has modern society, including some evangelicals, resisted hermeneutical rules more strenuously than when

17. E. D. Hirsch, Jr., *Validity in Interpretation*, p. 1.
18. Walter C. Kaiser, Jr., "The Literary Form of Genesis 1 — 11," in *New Perspectives on the Old Testament*, p. 48.

the readers are asked to submit to the principle of the writer's will. In our era of post-Kantian relativism and existential interpretation the main interest of too many interpreters is to extract a meaning from the text that is related to "What speaks to me," "What turns me on," or "What can I get out of the text," rather than what a biblical writer had intended by his use of his words. As Kaiser has so aptly stated it, "When liberalism excused itself from this demand, it turned its back on the revelation of God. If evangelicalism continues to dabble in the text as we have been for several decades, substituting Bible surveys and 'what do you get out of it' type of pooled ignorance sessions for the hard work of exegesis, we will also pay the supreme price — there will be no answer from God (Micah 3:7)."[19]

So the present crisis in hermeneutics is rooted ultimately in the existential climate of the age. The meaning of any text is personal and subjective; application is all, and what the text means personally to the reader is what is important. If some "neat" spiritual insight "turns you on," then that is what the text must mean. By the same token, if some possible scientific principle "turns you on," then let us say that this is what the text means. In the meantime the original writer pleadingly cries, "But that is not what I meant!"

It may be true that Moses shared the primitive mythological views of his contemporaries (as the critics teach), or that he anticipated modern science in many of his incidental statements (as conservative interpreters insist). This may be, but how do we know? The only way we can answer this question is by directing our attention to the will of the writer. After all, a text has to represent *someone's* meaning — if not the writer's, then the interpreter's. Once the writer is banished as the determiner of the text's meaning, it becomes apparent that there is no adequate principle for judging the validity of an interpretation.

Due to the doctrine of inspiration (see 2 Tim. 3:16-17), however, the interpreter of the Bible starts from the premise that God ultimately is the author of the early chapters of Genesis.

19. Walter C. Kaiser, Jr., "Legitimate Hermeneutics," an essay given at the International Conference on Biblical Inerrancy, Wheaton, Ill., November 1978, p. 6.28.

Hence, technically, it is the Holy Spirit's meaning that we must seek, not that of Moses. (Moses may not have been the original author but only a compiler of earlier written or oral traditions. But the question is still this: What was Moses' intent in selecting these traditions, compiling them in this way? or, What was the original author's intent?) However, the Holy Spirit chose to express Himself through Moses, using his personality, world view, vocabulary, way of thinking, modes of expression, and writing motivations. Practically speaking, Moses' meaning and God's meaning are the same. But the fact that Moses wrote under inspiration justifies the belief that the Holy Spirit's statements through Moses in Genesis 1 can be interpreted in light of the Holy Spirit's statements through other writers elsewhere in Scripture. Hence, the fundamental principle of Protestant hermeneutics emerges: the analogy of faith. In other words, let Scripture interpret Scripture. While this principle is valid, its relevance must be severely scrutinized lest we become guilty of wrenching a meaning from Moses' writings based on a later statement of Scripture that may have been totally foreign to Moses' way of thinking. Furthermore, as will be discussed later, by analogy the prophets' incomplete understanding of their messianic predictions in no way justifies a treasure hunt into secondary or "fuller" senses of Moses' words in search for scientific possibilities.

So the intent of Moses must be our primary concern here. Assuming this obvious point, several general criteria may now be specified which give limited guidance for extracting science out of these early chapters of Genesis. These following factors are not exhaustive, only preliminary, but each has a direct bearing on certain interpretative stances to be taken later, and hence will lay a foundation for the use of the text of Genesis to support the thesis of earth's ancient vapor canopy.

THE PRINCIPLE OF AUTHORIAL WILL

The first principle involved in extracting scientific data from Genesis 1, as discussed above, involves an understanding of the intent Moses had in writing this chapter. Only when his purpose is known is the interpreter able to judge what kind of scientific information can be implied. For example, if Moses' purpose was to tell us the meaning of the creation story for our lives today and not to give any specific comment about a definite cosmology, it would be precarious of the interpreter to draw definite scientific implications from his words.

In fact, this is a common existential approach to these chapters. Karl Barth, for example, "when asked in Holland if he believed the serpent really spoke in Eden . . . replied that it was more important to pay attention to what the serpent said."[20] Or, as John Macquarrie expressed it, "The question is not, 'How did the world begin?' or 'Who made it?' but rather, 'What does it mean to the creature?' or 'How does it affect our understanding of ourselves and our world to believe that we and it are creatures of God?' "[21]

Who says these are the questions — Moses or Macquarrie and Barth? Macquarrie may be right, but until he can demonstrate that these were the questions Moses intended to deal with, any interpretations of Genesis following from such a premise must remain open to doubt.

The polemic intent of Genesis. The relevance of the principle of authorial will is to be illustrated as the discussion unfolds. Now this question must be discussed: What was Moses' intent in writing the early chapters of Genesis? What was *he* trying to accomplish?

While it may be difficult to arrive at a purpose statement that would adequately express all of the various themes of these chapters (that is, Gen. 1—11), there seems to be a growing consensus that a major theme, at least, was to supply a corrective to the surrounding pagan mythologies. In other words, Moses is writing a polemic to counter the mythology of Israel's neighbors. While the trend in Old Testament studies used to be to assert that the Hebrews borrowed wholesale from the mythology of their neighbors, it is now generally recognized

20. Paul K. Jewett, "Neo-Orthodoxy," in *Baker's Dictionary of Theology*, p. 377.
21. John Macquarrie, *Principles of Christian Theology*, p. 195.

that the differences between Hebrew and pagan cosmologies are striking.[22] Indeed, these differences are so significant that the problem now is how to explain them. We find a satisfactory answer in the thesis that Israel's higher theology is explained by divine revelation. Waltke summarizes:

> Where did Israel get this higher theology? Why did it not appear among any other people? All the world was steeped in mythical thought except Israel. Her religion was like the sun compared to the night. No umbilical cord attached the faith of Moses and his successors with the other religions of the ancient Near East . . . . Moreover, this religion did not arise from Israel itself. Over and over again they confess that they are stiffnecked and prone to conform to the religions around them. No, Israel's religion did not originate in the darkened mind and heart of man. Instead, as the prophets consistently affirm, it is a revelation from God.[23]

This fact, that the Hebrews viewed their faith as utterly distinct from that of surrounding paganism, suggests that their prophetic leaders may have, from time to time, desired to challenge the pagan mythologies and correct them. As the Hebrews were about to enter the promised land, it is probable that God wanted to prepare them in advance for the pagan mythologies they would encounter. Out of the millions of pages of material that God could have left in describing the creation of the universe, He inspired Moses to select the equivalent of a hundred or so verses. Why did God select only this material, and why did He omit so much? To ask this question is to focus on God's intent in this section. His purpose determines what He includes and what He omits. So there is more here than a mere narration

22. H. Frankfort, H. A. Frankfort, John A. Wilson, Thorkild Jacobsen, and William A. Irwin, *The Intellectual Adventure of Ancient Man;* also Eichrodt, *Theology of the Old Testament*, Vol. 1, pp. 38, 39, 41, 42, 43, 45, 46, 47, 48, 104, 132, 136, 145, 148, 151, 157, 164, 166, 167, 172, 173, 174 for numerous discussions of the utter uniqueness of the Hebrew faith in contrast to that of her neighbors.
23. Bruce K. Waltke, *Creation and Chaos*, p. 46.

of events as they occurred; there is also a selection of material according to some controlling intent of the divine and human authors. The topics listed in Genesis 1 are consistently found to be in direct contrast to prevailing pagan cosmologies. This consistency suggests the intent of the passage.

Gerhard Hasel has succinctly summarized a few of the factors that suggest that God may have had a "correcting" intent.[24]

First, the depersonalized use of "the deep." The Hebrew word $t^eh\hat{o}m$, translated "the deep" in Genesis 1:2, appears to have been derived from the same Semitic root from which the name of the Babylonian chaos monster Tiamat was derived. While it used to be asserted that $t^eh\hat{o}m$ was directly borrowed from Tiamat,[25] Heidel has shown that this derivation is very unlikely.[26] Hasel argues that both words may go back to a common root meaning "ocean." The great difference is, however, that the Babylonians deified the ocean into a goddess who does battle with their chief hero-god Marduk. Tiamat and Marduk engage in vicious battle, and only after overcoming Tiamat's resistance to his will does Marduk establish order out of the chaos which Tiamat represents. Yet the consistent use of $t^eh\hat{o}m$ in the Old Testament is always that of a depersonalized and inanimate body of water (see any concordance). In both the pagan and Hebrew accounts, creation begins with "the deep" as an unorganized mass. But the Hebrew deep is impersonal and completely under the will of Yahweh, whereas the pagan deep is personal and resists the creating god. Because our culture has embraced the Judeo-Christian world view in many respects, our reaction is simply to say, "Of course, it is impersonal." But such a presentation is utterly without parallel in all ancient Near Eastern literature and would have been immediately recognized by its readers as a jab and correction to the

24. Gerhard F. Hasel, "The Polemic Nature of the Genesis Cosmology," *The Evangelical Quarterly* 45 (April-June, 1974):81-103.
25. B. W. Anderson, "Creation," in *The Interpreter's Dictionary of the Bible*, 1:726.
26. Alexander Heidel, *The Babylonian Genesis*, 3rd ed., pp. 90, 100.

Science and the Bible 19

nature myths. It is only our cultural distance that hinders our ability to feel the impact.

Second, the impersonal, submissive "great sea monsters." On the fifth day God created (Heb., bārā') the "great sea monsters" (Gen. 1:21, Heb. tannînim). A cognate term related to tannîn is found in many of the Ugaritic texts in which the monster is a dragon with whom the creating god must do battle. In these myths, the dragons are somewhat parallel to the "sea" in their opposition to the victorious god. Yet, as Hasel shows, in the Bible the mythological character of these tannînim is completely lacking. The tannînim of Genesis 1:21 are mere creatures in the water, lacking any mythological power. (They may refer to the dinosaurs.) Furthermore, in verse 21, these tannînim are said to have been created (bārā'). This is the first time that this word, bārā', has been used since verse 1. In the Old Testament it is always used of a creative act of God. Since bārā' is not used in connection with the creation of the land animals (v. 25), it appears that Moses uses the word here to emphasize that the sea monsters were created by God in an effortless act.

> A polemic emphasis becomes transparent; the tannînim are aquatic creatures which were "created" by God; they are not pre-existent rivals of the Creator which needed to be conquered as in Canaanite mythology . . . the choice of the term tannîn in connection with the term bārā' emphasizing God's effortless creation of the large aquatic creatures appears as a deliberate attempt to contradict the notion of creation in terms of a struggle as contained in the pagan battle myths. It appears inescapable to recognize here again a conscious polemic against the battle myth.[27]

Third, the creation and function of the luminaries. After documenting the widespread astral worship prevalent all over the ancient Near East, Hasel reads Genesis 1:14-18 in a new light.[28] The sun in Genesis is not a deity that existed prior to

27. Hasel, p. 87; see Mary Wakeman, *God's Battle with the Sea Monster*, p. 22, which says that tannîn in "Gen. 1:21 is a deliberate effort to contradict the battle myth."
28. Hasel, p. 89.

creation as is the sun god Shamash in the Karatepe texts; it is simply a light giver with a definite beginning. In fact, the names of the sun and moon are not even given; they are simply "light." This aversion to ascribing names to them undoubtedly comes from the fact that common Semitic terms for "sun" and "moon" are used at times for pagan deities. So an obvious opposition to star worship is apparent. In the pagan myths, the stars and heavenly bodies are great gods who rule creation, but in Genesis they are mere luminaries whose only "ruling" is by serving as light bearers. They are simply inanimate "stuff," effortlessly brought into existence by the Word of God and are not personal deities as in the nature myths. Von Rad is surely correct when he says, "The entire passage vss. 14-19 has a strongly antimythical feeling."[29] A reader in the fifteenth century B.C. would have picked this up immediately and perceived a corrective intent in the words of Moses. It would be as if a twentieth-century evolutionist spoke in a fundamentalist church on creation, and he consistently made a point of emphasizing the very things he knew the congregation did not agree with, yet never once said the Bible was wrong. Selection of material betrays obvious intent. If anyone doubts this, just watch the evening news.

Fourth, the purpose of the creation of man. In the Sumerian creation epic, as in the Babylonian *Atrahasis Epic* and *Enuma elish*, the purpose for the creation of man was simply to relieve the gods from the tedium of working for a living.[30] This mythological picture which presents the creation of man as a kind of afterthought to provide a work force for the gods and supply them with food is totally contradicted by Genesis 1. Man is presented in Genesis as the pinnacle of creation and not an afterthought. He is the only one "blessed by God" (1:28), and he is not a servant of the gods but the vice-regent of *the* God to rule over the entire creation (1:28-29). In stating this, Moses is directly contradicting the pagan notion that man has no significance or meaning.

Fifth, the separation of heaven and earth. It is against this

---

29. Gerhard von Rad, *Genesis*, p. 55.
30. Hasel, p. 90.

background of the polemic intent of Genesis that the major text with which we are concerned must be viewed — Genesis 1:6-8. Here God divides the waters which are below the expanse from the waters which are above the expanse. As mentioned above, the pagan world has many battle myths. In Babylon, Marduk defeats the chaos monster Tiamat, divides her in two, and uses one half of her body to create the celestial ocean. He was victorious over chaos. Thus, while in Babylon the deity has to do battle with the chaos monster, cut her in half, and create the world (bring order out of chaos) out of her remains, God simply speaks: "Let there be . . ." and the waters (chaos, "without form and void," 1:2, KJV, a description of "the deep," $t^eh\hat{o}m$) respond and obey — no battle, no fuss. We see immediate obedience. God does not need to post a sentry to prevent the celestial waters from returning back to the earth and hence reintroducing chaos. He simply arches up the atmosphere and with a word of His mouth restrains the waters up there. There is no effort, no struggle. This is the nature of the true God. He is completely sovereign and omnipotent, and does not have to do battle with mythological monsters. As Hasel points out, "Inherent in the Biblical presentation of the separation of heaven and earth is an antimythical polemic. Separation takes place without struggle whatever. It is achieved by divine *fiat*. . . ."[31]

The above illustrations of polemical intent are only representative and could be expanded considerably.[32] They all point to a common motif of Yahweh's effortless victory over inanimate stuff versus the pagan god's struggle to overcome and restrain some kind of monster.

After examining myths from Sumer, Babylon, Anatolia, India, Mesopotamia, and Canaan, Mary Wakeman concluded that there is a threefold motif behind all of them: (1) a monster of some kind who attempted to restrain creation; (2) the defeat of this monster by the victorious god, who therefore released the forces necessary for life; and (3) the hero's final control over

31. Ibid., p. 88.
32. Mary Wakeman, *God's Battle with the Sea Monster;* Waltke, *Creation and Chaos,* pp. 43-52; D. F. Payne, *Genesis One Reconsidered,* pp. 19-23.

these forces.[33] The same thoughts are clearly seen in the Genesis record. Yahweh overcomes the $t^eh\hat{o}m$.[34] However, there is no effort, revealing the polemical intent. Finally, the waters of chaos are brought under Yahweh's control and maintained above and below the firmament by the Word of Yahweh, whereas Marduk of Babylon needs to build literal wooden sluice gates and post sentries to keep the upper waters in place.

The relevance of these concepts to the thesis of earth's ancient vapor canopy are now apparent. There is a conceptual tie between the waters of above the firmament and the "windows of heaven" (Gen. 7:11, KJV). The "windows of heaven" restrain the waters of chaos, $t^eh\hat{o}m$, and can only be opened by the Word of God.[35] That is to say, the waters of chaos are completely under God's control. There is no continuing struggle to maintain them up there as in Babylon. When they finally do crash down again to earth, a global deluge results, but it only happens as Yahweh allows it, and when He does, the waters above the firmament merge once again with the waters below.

Furthermore, since this is a polemical section, and his intent is to correct erroneous pagan doctrines, it will be of particular interest to see which parts of the pagan ideas Moses *does not* correct. If it is true that Moses had the pagan cosmologies specifically in mind when he wrote Genesis 1, and if his intent was to correct the errors in them, it can safely be assumed that anything in the particular aspect of the myth under discussion that he does not correct he probably accepts. One of the things he does not correct is the notion of a literal liquid ocean placed above the atmosphere. As fantastic as it seems, it would appear that Moses then accepted this notion. This is particularly evident because in the discussion of the "waters above the firmament" (Gen. 1:6-8, KJV), there are aspects of pagan mythology

33. Wakeman, pp. 4-6.
34. Whether the $t^eh\hat{o}m$ and the "unformed and unfilled" earth were in existence *prior* to Genesis 1:1 (see Waltke, *Creation and Chaos*), is not relevant. God's activity involved, after the creation of $t^eh\hat{o}m$, a giving of order to it.
35. To call waters "chaos" is, of course, a theological-philosophical designation and not a physical one.

Science and the Bible 23

that Moses *does* correct, that is, (1) the idea of struggle; (2) the personal nature of these waters as in the deified Tiamat in Babylon; and (3) the notion that the upper waters had to be restrained by wooden sluice gates and sentries.[36]

Authorial intent and the structural arrangement. The second aspect of the principle of authorial will has to do with the structural arrangement of the narrative and is very important to understanding the meaning of Genesis 1:6-8 and for extracting scientific information out of the words of Moses. For some time it has been observed that there is a definite literary structure around which Moses presents his polemic. In showing us how the God of the Hebrews is superior to the pagan gods, Moses tells us that His creative activity involved giving of structure to that which was "formless," and filling of that which was empty. The problem that Yahweh had to overcome was that the earth was "without form and void" (Gen. 1:2). Moses divides the acts of creation into two groups: the first three days correct the "without form" condition, and the second three days correct the "void" condition.[37]

36. Obviously the meaning of "the waters above the firmament" is not so easily settled, and there are many other exegetical factors which must be considered. This discussion is reserved for Chapter 2.
37. This observation was made by W.H. Griffith-Thomas, *Genesis, A Devotional Commentary*, p. 29, and is followed by Derek Kidner, *Genesis*, p. 46; U. Cassuto, *A Commentary on the Book of Genesis*, p. 17; Waltke, *Creation and Chaos*, p. 61.

TABLE 1.1

THE CORRESPONDENCE BETWEEN DAYS 1-3 AND 4-6

THE CREATIVE ACTS			
\multicolumn{2}{c	}{To correct the "without form" condition: three acts of *dividing*}	\multicolumn{2}{c}{To correct the "void" condition: three acts of *furnishing*}
1	light from darkness	4	luminaries
2	upper waters from expanse lower waters	5	fish and birds
3	lower waters from dry land	6	beasts and man

Waltke summarizes:

> The parallelism of the last three days with the first three is apparent. Whereas on the first day there is light, on the fourth day the light is localized into luminaries; whereas on the second day there is separation of water and sky, on the fifth day there are created the fish to fill the seas and the birds to fill the skies; whereas land and vegetation were created on the third day, on the sixth day the land animals and man are formed who live on the land and are sustained by its vegetation.[38]

This literary structure of Genesis 1 reveals to us that Moses intended to tell us something as to the "structuring" of that which was formless on the first three days and the filling up of that which was empty (Heb. *bōhû*, "void," empty) on the second three days. This observation of the literary structure helps resolve an apparent difficulty in taking the *above* in a literal, mechanistic sense in verse 7, yet switching to an "observer

---

38. Waltke, p. 61.

true" sense when interpreting *in* in verse 15, "Let them be for lights *in* the expanse of the heavens...." Robert Whitelaw has argued, "Those who insist on ultra-literalism in 1:7-8 to teach a specific body of water above the firmament, should be equally literal in vs. 14-17 where God puts the sun, moon and stars *in* (not above) this same firmament. Taken literally then, if the canopy is taught here it lies beyond the stars."[39]

Buy why should one who is literal in verses 7-8 in regard to the *above* be "equally literal" in verses 14-17 in regard to *in*? Whitelaw does not say. Literature is full of illustrations of authors using both "observer true" and "mechanistically true" language in the same paragraph. There is no known precedent for Whitelaw's assertion. Context must determine such things and not some arbitrary, inflexible principle. Furthermore, in this particular section, the principle of authorial will (the context) informs us that Moses himself may have had just such a distinction in mind. Structuring the unformed by "dividing" is the emphasis on the first three days, and "filling" the empty is the force of the last three. Since the intent of the placing of the stars is for observation, it seems justifiable to press for an "observer true" use of *in* in verse 15. But the purpose of the expanse was to divide between two bodies of liquid water in verse 7; hence, a mechanistic use of *above* is probable.

If the *same* "firmament" is referred to in verses 7 and 14 (that is, the atmospheric heavens), then in verse 7 the text speaks of water which is actually above the "firmament" (mechanistically true), and in verse 14 it speaks of lights which "appear to be in" the firmament (observer true). On the other hand it may be that the heavens of verse 7 are atmospheric and the heavens

---

39. Robert Whitelaw, "The Canopy Theory and the Rift-Drift-Shift Theory in the Light of Scripture and Physical Facts," unpublished paper, personal communication 29 February 1976. Dr. Whitelaw is Professor of Nuclear and Mechanical Engineering at Virginia Polytechnic Institute and State University. See also, James E. Strickling, "The Waters Above the Firmament," (Letters to the Editor), *Creation Research Society Quarterly* 12 (March 1976):221 for a discussion of this objection.

of verse 14 are intergalactic. It is clear that the Hebrews *did* sometimes use the word *shāmayim* for intergalactic space. The phrase, "heaven of heavens," or the uppermost of the *created* heavens, distinguished it from the lower heavens just as the "holy of holies" is distinct from the "holy place." The heaven of heavens is not the abode of God in that it was created (Neh. 9:6; Psalm 148:4), and God does not dwell there (1 Kings 8:27). The phrase is used seven times (Deut. 10:14; 1 Kings 8:27; 2 Chron. 2:6; 6:18; Neh. 9:6; Psalms 68:33; 148:4). Also, if 2 Corinthians 12:2 speaks of the abode of God (that is, the *third* heaven), what is the *second* heaven? Would it not refer to intergalactic space?

Furthermore, a glance at Table 1.1 reveals another clearly delineated structural feature mentioned above: a movement in both sets of three days from heaven to earth. A spatial sequence is implied. God first creates light somewhere "out there" above the earth. Next in the spatial sequence are the waters above the expanse, then the expanse and the waters below the expanse (Gen. 1:7-8). Finally, *below* the "waters above" and *below* the expanse, is the earth. Clearly the sequence suggests that the "waters above" of the second day are *below* the light created on the first day and *above* the earth created on the third. If this is granted from the apparent structural intent of the author, then would it not follow that the luminaries of the fourth day which correspond to the light of the first day are, like that light, also *above* the "waters above"? This would reinforce the "observer true" interpretation of the *in* of verse 15, while allowing the "mechanistically true" interpretation of the *above* in verse 7. This is reinforced by the apparent correspondences between days two and five (fish and birds "fill" expanse and lower waters); and between days three and six (man, animals, and vegetation "fill" the dry land).

In conclusion, what may be said about the principle of authorial will and its relevance to the question of the extraction of mechanistic science out of Genesis 1? In view of the fact that Moses seems to be engaging the battle myths which purport to give a correct creation story, it seems likely that he intends more than a moral of "How are we to live?" in these chapters. He intends to correct erroneous mechanistic constructions, and he does so by offering the divine mechanistic reconstruction of some of the events of that first week. Also, in specific reference to the question of the "waters above," he only bothers to correct the mythological aspects of the water heaven myth but leaves this mechanistic construction intact. The fact that he speaks of "dividing" (that is, the giving of structure) seems to indicate that a definite scientific cosmogony with clear mechanistic implications is in the back of his mind. It may be concluded, therefore, that the liberal critics are wrong in their assertion that there are no scientific implications to this text. Furthermore, it seems that Ramm may have gone too far in ascribing so much of this passage to the "observer true" category. Much of it is mechanistically intended. In fact, there were no "observers" during that week. All that God gave us is a report of what He did during that week.

THE PRINCIPLE OF SHARABLE IMPLICATIONS

A second principle that will give the interpreter guidance in extracting scientific information out of the cultural and phenomenological language of the Bible is the principle of sharable implications.

By "implication of a text" we mean those legitimate inferences that can be drawn from a narrative which are possible aspects of the author's meaning. For example, if one were to say, "The tree is green," what are the implications of the word *tree*? Does tree imply *roots*? Does tree imply *bark*? Does tree imply *photosynthesis*? One who is trained in plant physiology would say yes to all of those things. So if Moses says "every shrub of the field," does he therefore imply roots, bark, and photosynthesis? It is a fact that trees and shrubs have roots. Does this mean that roots are implied every time someone uses the word *tree*? Obviously, a distinction must be made between the meaning of the text (the willed intent of the author) and the subject matter (all that might be known about a subject under discussion). When a six-year-old boy says, "There is a tree in our backyard," his willed meaning is that there is a "thing" with branches for tree houses that is fun to climb. When a plant physiologist says, "We are investigating trees," his willed meaning may include many scientific aspects such as photosynthesis rates and carbon dioxide concentrations necessary to promote the most rapid growth.

The reason for this discussion is that often interpreters of the Bible have assumed that the Bible teaches all kinds of things related to modern science because they were drawing inferences from the text and were not distinguishing the subject matter from the meaning. For an implication to be truly a part of the willed meaning of the author, it is necessary that the author and interpreter have mutually shared experiences of the meaning.[40] It would be invalid in the above illustration when talking to the little boy about a tree to assume that the little boy implies roots by his use of the word tree. It is not part of his "shared experience" with the interpreter. He does not even know that roots exist. A root would be part of the significance of the word tree but not part of the little boy's meaning or an implication of his meaning. It is perfectly proper to discuss the significance (for plant physiology) of the little boy's statement, but it would be improper to assert that the little boy "teaches" that trees have roots.

Now it is obvious that a distinction between the subject of trees and what Moses specifically intended to teach about them is necessary. But there is a definite boundary to the specific things that Moses may have intended to imply about trees. Only the implications of the word tree that lie within that boundary can legitimately be regarded the teaching of the Bible concerning trees.

What, then, determines the boundary? Two things are involved. First, and most important, is authorial will. Was the writer who used the word tree using it in a context where he was intending to discuss the photosynthesis rates in coniferous pines? If so, such implications as carbon dioxide concentrations, temperature, and light intensity could conceivably be ascribed to the writer's knowledge and could be included in his teaching regarding trees.

The second factor in determining the boundary of the class tree is the possibility of sharability. In order for an implication to be acceptable as the teaching of the writer, it must be possible that

---

40. Hirsch, p. 66.

the reader of his words has had some point of mutually shared experience of the thing, *tree* as in the illustration of the little boy's perception of tree and that of the plant physiologist mentioned above. As Hirsch puts it, "For it to lie in the boundary it has to be sharable."[41]

Anything lying inside the boundary delineated by these two criteria is a possible teaching of the writer. Anything lying outside this boundary may be valid in terms of its truth, but it cannot be said to represent the meaning and teaching of the writer.

The relevance of this to the subject of extracting mechanistic science from biblical statements should be obvious. For example, as mentioned above, it would exclude the association of the brooding of the Spirit over the waters (Gen. 1:2) with de Broglie's undulatory theory of matter.[42] It would have excluded the idea that wireless telegraphy is taught in Job 38:35, or that the atomic theory of matter is seen in Hebrews 11:3. Nuclear fission would not have been read into Genesis 1:4, airplanes into Isaiah 31:5, or radio into Ecclesiastes 10:20.[43] Nor can the water of Genesis 1:6-8 be equated with "plasma."[44] These things are all outside the boundary of the possible class because none of them are possible sharable items of consciousness or knowledge between the writer and the readers. They are to be excluded on many other grounds as well, but this one principle justifies their rejection.

41. Ibid., p. 94.
42. In 1924 L. de Broglie suggested that the behavior of electrons within atoms could be better understood if it were assumed that the motion of an electron depends on some sort of accompanying wave. This suggestion led to the development of quantum mechanics by Schrodinger, Heisenberg, and others. See "Electron Theory," in *Van Nostrand's Scientific Encyclopedia*, p. 930.
43. All of these illustrations are cited with disapproval by R.M. Page, "Science in the Bible," in *Zondervan Pictorial Encyclopedia of the Bible*, 5:295.
44. James Reid, *God, the Atom and the Universe*, chapter 6.

The relevance of this principle to the thesis of this book is more in the area of those things which lie outside the class, outside the boundary of the writer's possible meaning, and hence are not in the teaching of the Bible. Things which lie outside the boundary defined by this principle may fall into the category of the "significance of the text."

Perhaps a further illustration is in order here. This principle of sharable implications would also rule out many of the theories of modern science as being "consistent with" the early chapters of Genesis. For example, Robert Newman and Herman Eckelman have recently published an intriguing book in which they argue that the early chapters of Genesis are consistent with the theories of modern astrophysics which teach that the solar system condensed out of a rotating nebula.[45] To do so they must ascribe the meaning "gaseous cloud" floating in interplanetary space made up of H_2 and O_2 to the Hebrew words *mayim* ("waters") and *tᵉhôm* ("deep"). They must also see Moses as understanding that this cloud was the earth of Genesis 1:1 and that it later condensed and formed the solid earth. A lexical study of *'ereṣ* ("earth"), *mayim*, and *tᵉhôm* reveals that *'ereṣ* is always solid, *mayim* never means H_2 and O_2, and *tᵉhôm* never means an interplanetary gaseous cloud. It is inconceivable that such a conception of the universe was sharable between Moses and his contemporaries.

Three arguments have been presented in refutation of the principle of sharable implications.

First, it is claimed that, since the Holy Spirit is the author and not just Moses, a fuller sense than what Moses intended is allowable.[46] This is, of course, true; but the problem is, since God knows everything, then virtually all possible implications of a text could be allowed as teachings of the text because God knows all of the possible implications. Unless these possible implications are limited by some controlling factors, the Bible can be made to teach anything that God might have known about the particular subject under discussion. Since God chose

45. Robert C. Newman and Herman J. Eckelman, Jr., *Genesis One and the Origin of the Earth*.
46. Robert Whitelaw, personal communication, 25 May 1977.

to reveal Himself through human authors, it would seem that He considered that means adequate. If He had wanted to communicate something that was beyond the sharable implications of those writers, He could easily have done so by providing additional information. But unless He specifically tells us something beyond the normal meaning of the words in their cultural context, the exegete must limit His possible meanings to those which were sharable between Moses and his contemporaries.

Second, it has been argued from analogy with biblical prophecy that a greater sense beyond that of the original writer is often intended by God. Often, the appeal is made to 1 Peter 1:11 to show that the prophets did not understand all that was intended by their prophecies. However, Peter only referred to the fact that the prophets did not understand *when* the kingdom would be established. The reason they did not know these things is because God never revealed it to them in sufficient detail to give certainty. The text does not teach that there was a deeper or fuller meaning in the prophetic texts beyond what was sharable between the prophet and his contemporaries.

The "deeper meaning" idea is based on an incorrect translation of the Greek phrase *eis tina ē poion kairon* ("for what or what sort of time"). The *New American Standard Bible*, for example, renders the phrase "what person or time," when there is no mention of "person." The Greek particle *tina* is most naturally rendered simply "what" in this context. Then the quest of the ancient prophets to whom Peter refers becomes the same as that of the disciples of Jesus when they asked Him about His second coming, "When will these things be, and what will be the sign when all these things are going to be fulfilled?" (Mark 13:4) In other words, they were asking what the time of Jesus' arrival would be ("when") and what kind of time element would be involved ("the sign").

A misunderstanding of the nature of typology is often behind the prophetic analogy. When Matthew's typological interpretation of Hosea 11:1 (Matt. 2:15) or Peter's application of Psalm 16 to Christ (Acts 2:25-28) is used as proof that a fuller sense, beyond that which was mutually sharable, was intended by the Holy Spirit in Genesis 1, a confusion between type and allegory is present. Ramm defines allegorical interpretation as follows: "Allegorical interpretation is the interpretation of a document whereby something foreign, peculiar, or hidden is introduced into the meaning of the text giving it a proposed deeper or real meaning."[47] Hoskyns and Davey note that the "allegory expresses the relationship between certain persons and things by substituting a whole range of persons or things from an entirely different sphere of experience."[48]

Typological interpretation, on the other hand, does not import something into the text beyond *that which may be derived from the organic unity of the testaments.* "Typological interpretation is specifically the interpretation of the Old Testament based on the fundamental theological unity of the two testaments whereby something in the Old shadows, prefigures, adumbrates something in the New. Hence what is interpreted in the Old is not foreign or peculiar or hidden but arises naturally out of the text due to the relationship between the two testaments."[49]

To find Christ and the atonement in the sacrificial system, or to see the history of Messiah in the history of His people (Hos. 11:1) or in David's life (Psalm 16) is typological. However, when Philo, Origen, or Clement of Alexandria find Platonic philosophy in the Old Testament, that is allegory. So for the New Testament apostles to see Jesus in the Old Testament types due to the organic unity between the testaments is one thing, but to see a rotating nebula in Genesis 1:1-2 is entirely another.[50] There are simply no controls on such exegesis. Types are controlled by the New Testament revelation, but the supposed scientific sense beyond the knowledge of the Old Testament writers is not limited by anything but the fertile imaginations and autonomous science of the modern interpreter. To quote Ramm again, "Dana states that the difference is that the

47. Bernard Ramm, *Protestant Biblical Interpretation*, p. 204.
48. Edwyn Hoskyns and Noel Davey, *The Riddle of the New Testament*, p. 127.
49. Ramm, *Protestant Biblical Interpretation*, p. 204.
50. Newman and Eckelman, *Genesis One and the Origin of the Earth*, p. 71.

typological method is based on the theological connectedness of the two Testaments, whereas allegorical interpretation is 'assigning to Scripture an assumed meaning different from its plain literal meaning, derived deductively from some abstract or philosophical conception.' "[51]

Therefore, to those who would challenge the principle of sharable implications on the basis of dual authorship of Scripture (human and Divine) and the typological use of the Old Testament by the New, we would ask, "How is your method different from Philo?" "What controls do you offer?"[52]

While a fuller *sense* is never intended by the divine author above that which was immediately sharable between a prophet and his contemporaries, a fuller significance may be implied.[53]

Some evangelical interpreters argue that allegorical interpretation was used by the New Testament writers. Scripture itself, some claim, recommends this method by giving us two examples of "mild allegory."[54] These are Galatians 4:19-26 and 1 Corinthians 9:8-10. The principal argument is drawn from the former passage, and to it Walter Kaiser has replied concisely:

51. Ramm, *Protestant Biblical Interpretation*, pp. 205-6.
52. It is interesting to note that those who feel too much constraint is imposed by the principle of sharable implications are often those who tend to import their convictions concerning the interpretation of prophecy into their exegesis of Genesis 1. One who feels at ease finding a scientific sense beyond that which was sharable by the human authors and their readers is one who is comfortable with spiritualization of much of Old Testament prophecy as being fulfilled in the church. Catholic interpreters long insisted on this fuller sense: see Bruce Vawter, "Fuller Sense," *Catholic Biblical Quarterly* 26 (January 1964):92. For a good discussion of interpretation of prophecy by New Testament writers, see Paul Lee Tan, *The Interpretation of Prophecy*, pp. 193-236.
53. By fuller significance we mean a broader or different area of application, not a different or fuller *meaning* (sense).
54. Richard Longenecker, *Biblical Exegesis in the Apostolic Period*, p. 126.

(1) In Galatians 4:20, Paul confesses that he is somewhat hesitant as to just how he should address the Galatians, but he will now explain a point to them in their own way *(allaxai tēn phōnēn mou)*, using the Genesis story of Sarah and Hagar as an illustration to suit more their rabbinical tastes, for as Ellicott observed, (2) Galatians 4:24 warned that Paul merely borrowed the Old Testament for his illustration; he was not exegeting it, for he clearly said, *"all which class of things"* (hatina) viewed in the most general way "may be put into an allegory" *(estin allēgoroumena).*[55]

So there is no basis in this text for a supposedly allegorical, deeper sense beyond the sharable world views of the writer and his readers.

Third, it is sometimes argued that, since we use archaeology (a secular science) to help us interpret the Old Testament, certainly it is legitimate to find a fuller sense by the use of the other sciences, such as geology and astrophysics.[56] In other words, since we interpret the Bible by means of archaeology, why not by means of astrophysics? This line of thinking ignores fundamental distinctions. When archaeology is used to illuminate or better interpret the Old Testament, the interpreter is not going beyond the sharable implications but is using archaeology to understand what those sharable implications were. Archaeology informs the modern interpreter of what the writers and readers of the biblical record already understood at that time. However, when modern astrophysics is used, one is beyond what they could have understood, and it is therefore not sharable and hence not a possible meaning of the writer. That, of course, does not mean that the theories of modern astrophysics are necessarily wrong or even inconsistent with Genesis 1. In fact, they may dovetail nicely into it. However, it is certain that Genesis 1 does not "teach" these theories because they are beyond the sharable implications of Moses and his readers.

55. Kaiser, "Legitimate Hermeneutics," p. 6.9.
56. Robert Newman, personal communication, June 1977.

THE PRINCIPLE OF SIGNIFICANCE OF THE TEXT TO SCIENCE

By significance, the "meaning to" the text is meant and not the "meaning in."[57] The verbal meaning can be related to every conceivable state of affairs — historical, linguistic, psychological, physical, metaphysical, personal. It differs from an implication in that an implication is part of the writer's willed meaning while significance is not. This is important because frequently in this book the subject under discussion will be the significance of certain texts for modern science without any claim being made that the Bible teaches these things. For example, it will be shown that the Bible teaches the existence of a literal ocean of water above the pre-Flood earth. That is the willed meaning of Moses in Genesis 1:7 when he speaks of the waters above the firmament. However, the significance of that is great in relation to known scientific law. One might suggest that God arranged that water in a vapor form because that is the only way it could be maintained without a special miracle. But that is a significance of the text for modern science and is not the meaning of Moses, and it is not an inference that one could draw from the text. Furthermore, one might imply that, as a result of such a vapor canopy, the pre-Flood earth was heated by a greenhouse effect. But a vapor canopy and a greenhouse effect are part of the significance of the text and are not what the Bible teaches. To some extent it is like the difference between interpretation and application.

While it is true that the significance of the text for modern science is not the intended meaning of the writer, nevertheless it is quite possible that from a discussion of that significance one can reconstruct at least some of the climatic conditions that then prevailed, even if it was not Moses' intention to comment on them. Perceptive interpreters are always looking for clues in the text that lie outside the writer's willed meaning but nevertheless give us an insight into his background, beliefs, attitudes, knowledge, and other such things. For example, one could infer from Solomon's numerous comments on the ants,

57. Hirsch, p. 63.

evaporation and precipitation, botany, and psychology that he was a well-read man, somewhat of a scientist, and a profound student of human nature. Yet it is never his willed meaning to tell us these things. These are observations that come from the clues he leaves in the text. To discuss these things falls under the category of significance and not the teaching of Proberbs about Solomon, but it is necessarily valid.

Luke's comments about medicine and his scholarly style of Greek betray that he was probably a physician and was certainly an educated man. (He never tells us this; Paul does.) Yet one could read Luke or Acts, discern these clues, discuss the significance of them, and correctly conclude with a high degree of probability that Luke was a scholar and a doctor. By examining the pyramids, we can conclude something of the mathematical skill of the ancient Egyptians. By reading in the Talmud that one cure for illness is to carry the ashes of an ostrich egg during the summer in a linen bag and in winter in a cotton bag, we can begin to get some clues about the state of Jewish medical knowledge of the time. We could validly affirm that it was seriously deficient in at least some areas, even though it was not the willed meaning of the authors of the Talmud to inform us of this.

When David speaks of the "breath" of his enemies (Psalm 104:29), it is perfectly valid to conclude from our knowledge of human physiology today that in David's day there was oxygen in the atmosphere, even though there was no willed intent on David's part to communicate this in the psalm. When Job speaks of experiencing the "weight" of the "wind" (Job 28:25), one might infer that in his day there were pressure differentials caused by thermal disequilibrium, even though Job had no idea what caused winds, and was not intending to teach on the subject. When Micah speaks of "showers on vegetation" (Mic. 5:7), it is perfectly appropriate to conclude that in his day the processes of photosynthesis were going on, even though he knew nothing about photosynthesis and certainly did not intend to teach on it. Nevertheless, the presence of grass necessarily means there was photosynthesis. Now, just as David did not intend to tell us there was oxygen in the atmosphere, and Micah did not intend to tell us that photosynthesis was going on in his day, neither did Moses intend to tell us what the pre-Flood climatic regime was. However, just as surely as Luke, David, and Micah did tell us some of these things, so did Moses, even though it was not part of his willed meaning.

This point needs special emphasis because it is exactly in this area that the warning "the Bible is not a textbook of modern science" is so frequently raised. Numerous references in the book of Genesis have tremendous significance as clues for reconstructing the climatic regime of the ancient earth that are not explicitly taught in the text, nor are they part of the writer's willed meaning. It is, nevertheless, valid to infer from these references that certain conditions must have been *necessarily* present. For example, if Moses comments that there was a liquid ocean of water placed up above the atmosphere on the second creative day, it is necessary to infer that this liquid was arranged by God into some form that could be maintained by natural law. It would naturally turn to water vapor in view of low vapor pressure and the solar radiation, unless God supernaturally intervened and prevented it from doing so. Hence, the area of significance, cautiously applied, *and with the assumption that present-day laws of nature applied then*, can give us a "scientific textbook" look at the world that used to be. A reconstruction based on such inferences must be tentative and does not have the certainty of a reconstruction based on direct statements.

THE PRINCIPLE OF THE PRIORITY OF
NON-METAPHORICAL STATEMENTS

Another principle for extracting scientific information out of biblical statements is that the Bible's clear non-metaphorical statements about cosmology must take precedence over the statements dressed in cultural garb or figurative language. These direct statements then become the basis for interpreting the figurative ones. For example, Job specifically says that the earth "hangs on nothing" (Job 26:7), and that it is a sphere (Job 22:14; see also Prov. 8:27; Isa. 40:22). So when the Bible also speaks of the heavens as a curtain (Psalm 104:2), we are not to imagine a solid material dome, supported by pillars, and with the earth riding on the back of a great turtle. When the Bible directly teaches that rain comes from clouds (Judg. 5:4; Job 36:29; Psalm 77:17), there is no need to interpret the "windows of heaven" of Genesis 7:11 as sluice gates made of solid wooden beams.

Figurative or culturally common expressions are not always to be identified with the world view of the surrounding nations. Their point of similarity is frequently in cultural usage or in phenomenal description (that is, the "sun sets" in both the Ptolemaic and Copernican systems of astronomy). Based on the authority of Christ and the apostles, the Old Testament is free from error (Matt. 5:17-18; 2 Tim. 3:16-17; 2 Pet. 1:21-22). So we may assume that in these figurative expressions there is a meaning that is correct in terms of science, even if we are not able to penetrate it entirely.

When Milton speaks of "Jove," we do not believe he really believes in the existence of Jove. He has borrowed from the cultural vocabulary of his language. The problem in many of the biblical texts is not of borrowed concepts, but of borrowed images.[58] Certain cultural expressions are often based in primitive world views, but, due to repeated usage, they become conventions of the language and no longer have any scientific implications. For example, today, we in America speak of Europe as the "West." That is scientifically inaccurate. Europe is east of the United States. It is a cultural convention meaning the nations aligned against the communist bloc and to the west of the Soviet Union. In fact, its original meaning was simply the nations west of Russia. Likewise, the Hebrews may have borrowed many terms from their surrounding cultures and used them as figures of speech. They might speak of the "windows of heaven" and not be thinking of the cosmogony of the Babylonians which involved literal sluice gates holding back the celestial waters. It was simply a figure of speech for a source of rain, that is, the sky, without any longer carrying a specific scientific or cosmogonic implication. Likewise, the "pillars of

58. See Waltke, *Creation and Chaos*, pp. 13-15, for a discussion on this. Also Ron Allen, "The Leviathan-Rahab-Dragon Motif in the Old Testament," p. 63.

Science and the Bible 39

the earth" are simply the mountains, even though long ago the Babylonians, and perhaps, the Hebrews, considered them as supports for a metallic sky dome. It is a borrowed figure of speech for mountains, and it is perfectly conceivable that Moses could have used the term and not have been thinking of any definite cosmogony at all, just as we now speak of the West without thinking of the fact that Europe is really east of us.

THE PRINCIPLE OF DETERMINING THE LITERARY FORM

We cannot determine which aspects of scriptural teaching are transcultural until we first determine the literary form in which they are presented. If the literary genre is clearly poetry (most of the psalms or some of the speeches in the book of Job) or parabolic (as, for example, the story of Naboth's vineyard), then we must be careful about extracting historical or scientific details from them. If, however, the literary form is clearly historical, then scientific statements made within that framework can be considered transcultural if they fit the other principles listed above.

For example, the literary form of Genesis 1—11 is clearly that of a historical narrative, hence its statements relating to scientific fact or historical detail must be given serious attention. We can see that Genesis 1—11 is a historical narrative because the entire book is organized around the statement "These are the generations [histories] of _____ ." The expression is used four times in Genesis 12—50 to mark the four major histories of the narrative, and is used six times in Genesis 1—11. Since the latter part of the book is clearly historical and its histories are introduced by this phrase, it would follow that the histories introduced by the same phrase in Genesis 1—11 are likewise historical. Thus, we can seek real, factual, scientific detail from that portion of Scripture.

THE PRINCIPLE OF DETERMINING HOW THE SCRIPTURAL WRITERS USE FACTUAL DATA

Is something being merely described or is it being assumed as true? Is it described or taught? The general rule is that unless there are contextual indicators to the contrary, incidental scientific and historical details should be considered as the factual understanding of the biblical writers. We might, for example, be justified in assuming that the Bible teaches that lambs which mate by white striped rods (Gen. 30:37-39) will produce striped offspring were it not for the fact that the context tells us that Jacob conceded that this was due to the special intervention of God, that is, a miracle (Gen. 31:7-12).

We cannot dismiss such details as being real facts or prematurely embrace them as the teaching of God. We must carefully study the context and discover the way the terms are being used in it. The incidental historical and scientific references in Genesis 1—11 are so vast that to adopt either procedure, a priori, is extreme.

THE PRINCIPLE OF DISCERNING THE DIFFERENCES FROM NEAR EASTERN PARALLELS

Everything the people of Babylonia believed about the origin of the world (cosmogony) and the laws which govern its present processes (cosmology) was not necessarily wrong even if it contradicted what modern science says. When scriptural writers used words and phrases which are paralleled in the ancient Near Eastern texts, we must determine the type of similarity and the use Scripture makes of it. As argued above, the use of terms such as Leviathan and Rahab are clearly examples of borrowed imagery, not borrowed mythology. We see this from the theological stance of the biblical writers if from nothing else. Sometimes, however, there is no necessary theological conflict and no obvious intent to correct the myth in question. In such instances we must give serious attention to the possibility that the scriptural writers accepted this aspect of pagan belief as correct. The references to a "water heaven" are a good illustration.

THE PRINCIPLE OF ACCURATE DETERMINATION OF FIGURES OF SPEECH

Evangelicals and liberals alike have been guilty of superficial hand-waving arguments ("It's a figure of speech!") with regard

Science and the Bible 41

to the language of Genesis 1—11. Yet the determination of whether or not a certain text contains a figure of speech "is as exacting and as subject to hermeneutical controls as any analysis of a piece of prose text, for the figure of speech must be named, the definition given, and the case for its presence in the verse noted and the function and meaning of the figure in this context explained."[59] A classic work on this subject is *Figures of Speech Used in the Bible*,[60] which would greatly assist anyone wanting to find out what parts of the Bible are figurative and which parts are not. Once the figure is determined, then and only then can the discussion of the scientific truth implicit in the figure be undertaken. With the help of Bullinger's massive book, we can identify the figure of speech, see how it is used in other contexts, and be prepared to comment on the scientific issues.[61]

In summary then, we are to come to the cultural and figurative language and assume that Moses did not share the primitive world view of the past, and so inquire how these expressions could refer to scientific truth we know today. Any advanced Hebrew understanding must be credited primarily to divine revelation. This approach could lead to revolutionary insight into the history of the ancient earth. Too often evangelicals have capitulated by trying to "get Moses off the hook" by saying that language is only cultural or descriptive. While that is true, it avoids the basic problem of what Moses understood by that language and what, therefore, was his cosmology.

Insofar as the subject in this book is the pre-Flood vapor canopy, attention must now be directed to that particular issue. The entire world view of the Hebrews is not under consideration, but we will now undertake a careful examination of the phrases *firmament, waters above the firmament,* and *windows of heaven.*

59. Kaiser, "Legitimate Hermeneutics," p. 6.27.
60. E. W. Bullinger, *Figures of Speech Used in the Bible.*
61. Many of the ideas contained in these last four principles were derived from the discussion by Kaiser in "Legitimate Hermeneutics."

CHAPTER 2

Biblical Evidence for the Water Heaven Theory

Then God said, "Let there be an *expanse* in the midst of the waters, and let it separate the waters from the waters." And God made the expanse, and separated the waters which were below the expanse from *the waters which were above the expanse;* and it was so. And God called the expanse heaven. And there was evening and there was morning, a second day (Gen. 1:6-7).

In the six hundredth year of Noah's life, in the second month, on the seventeenth day of the month, on the same day all the fountains of the great deep burst open, and *the floodgates of the sky* were opened. And the rain fell upon the earth for forty days and forty nights (Gen. 7:11-12).

The italicized phrases in the above passages are the subject of this chapter. To what does the "expanse" refer ("firmament," KJV)? To what do "the waters which were above the expanse" refer ("the waters above the firmament," KJV)? What are "the floodgates of the sky" ("the windows of heaven," KJV)?

THE FIRMAMENT

The translators of the *New American Standard Bible* correctly render this term as "expanse," implying a vast open area, or the atmospheric heavens. The King James version translated it "firmament" (from the Latin Vulgate), implying something "firm," the celestial vault of ancient mythology. Several considerations have led some to assume that the idea of a solid domelike vault is what Moses had in mind. In fact, the translators of the *Jerusalem Bible* (1966) and *The New English Bible*

(1970) substitute the word "vault" for firmament, reflecting this opinion of Hebrew cosmology.

THE VERBAL FORM OF THE HEBREW ROOT

Frequently in Hebrew the meaning of a noun can be more clearly understood by an examination of the meaning of the verb form of that noun. The noun *rāqîa'* ("expanse") is derived from the verb *rāqa'*. This verb is used eleven times in the Masoretic text of the Old Testament. It is used of "spreading out" in the sense of "pounding" (2 Sam. 22:43) or "stamping" (Ezek. 6:11; 25:6); in fact, this is its basic meaning: "to spread out, stamp, beat out."[1]

Because the verb is sometimes used of hammering out strips of beaten metal (see Exod. 39:3; Num. 16:39; Jer. 10:9), some have postulated that the noun *rāqîa'* "harks back to the conception of the sky as a mirrorlike surface," as in Homer's "brazen heaven" (*Iliad*, 5.504).[2] Because of this possible verbal meaning, Moses has been accused of believing in the primitive, upside down, domelike celestial vault of ancient mythology.[3] Sometimes Job 37:18 is cited as proof of this: "Can you, with Him, spread out the skies, strong as a molten mirror?" Here the verb form *rāqa'*, "to spread out," is used and not the noun *rāqîa'* of Genesis 1:6-7. Supposedly God is here presented as stamping out the metallic dome of the firmament.[4] But the noun receiving the action in the Job passage is not the firmament (*rāqîa'*) but "sky" (*shaḥaq*), to which the lexicon ascribes the major meanings of "dust" or "thin cloud."[5] Fluffy clouds hardly refer to a

1. Francis Brown, S. R. Driver, and Charles A. Briggs, *A Hebrew and English Lexicon of the Old Testament*, p. 955.
2. T. H. Gaster, "Firmament," in *The Interpreter's Dictionary of the Bible*, 2:270.
3. Brown, Driver, and Briggs, p. 956.
4. Paul H. Seely, "The Three-Storied Universe," *Journal of the American Scientific Affiliation* 21 (March 1969):1.
5. Brown, Driver, and Briggs, p. 1007. In numerous passages the meaning "cloud" is much better (see 2 Sam. 22:12; Psalm 77:17; Isa. 45:8).

solid dome of the ancients. Furthermore, the verse is not even talking about creation; it is referring to meteorological phenomena of the present era. Finally, as Udd points out,[6] the point of similarity between the molten mirror and clouds is obviously not solidarity but susceptibility to spreading or expansion. Also, both reflect light and are "bright." Both clouds and molten metal mirrors are easily spread out and are bright.

So it is clear that the verb rāqa', on which the noun rāqîa', "firmament," is built, simply means to expand or to spread out. The result of the action of the verb does not necessarily produce an object that is solid. If metal is being spread out, then a solid would result. If clouds or atmosphere are being spread out, then an open expanse would result. Something solid is not in the meaning of the verb.

It appears that a possible verbal meaning, which sometimes involves the spreading out of metals, has incorrectly been forced into the noun usage in Genesis 1:6-8. It is a noun that is found in Genesis 1:6-8 and not a verb.[7] The noun usages are frequently of an expanse or an open empty space (see Ezek. 1:22, 23, 25, 26; 10:1).

THE PARALLELS WITH ANCIENT MYTHOLOGY

The fact that the word in its verbal form can mean to hammer out something solid (and given the presupposition that the Hebrews merely copied the mythology of the ancients) causes the critics to assume that Moses simply shared in the primitive mythology of his second millennium B.C. contemporaries. However, as Ramm observes, "It is typical of the radical critics to play up the similarity of anything Biblical with the Babylonian and to omit the profound differences or gloss over them."[8]

6. Stanley V. Udd, "The Canopy of Genesis 1:6-8," *Creation Research Society Quarterly* 12 (September 1975):90.
7. For an extensive discussion of raqîa', demonstrating its meaning as "expanse, atmosphere" in Genesis 1:6-8, see Stanley V. Udd, "The Early Atmosphere," pp. 15-39.
8. Bernard Ramm, *The Christian View of Science and Scripture*, p. 69.

The first chapter dealt with this tendency and that ground need not be gone over again.

THE SEPTUAGINT TRANSLATION

About 270 B.C. the Greek-speaking Jews in Alexandria in Egypt translated the Hebrew Scriptures into Greek. By that time Greek had become the common language of the Jewish people living in the dispersion. They translated the Hebrew word rāqîa' by the Greek word stereōma, which was used in classical Greek to express a solid body and not an empty expanse.[9] It had the idea of a vault of heaven as an embossed bowl.[10] However, the choice of the Septuagint translators in using stereōma for rāqîa' simply reflects the Alexandrian cosmology of the third century B.C., not necessarily the Hebrew cosmology of the fifteenth century B.C. The Greeks of the third century B.C. believed that the universe was composed of a succession of solid crystalline spheres, each carrying a planet.[11] So this argument from the Septuagint usage seems doubtful.

THE FIRMAMENT HAS FOUNDATIONS, PILLARS, AND WINDOWS

The terms "firmament" (rāqîa') and "heavens" (shamayim) are used interchangeably in the Old Testament. Yet we are told that the foundations of the heavens shake (2 Sam. 22:8), its pillars tremble (Job 26:11), and it has windows and doors (Gen. 7:11; Psalm 78:23; Mal. 3:10). The shaking of the foundations is supposedly a vibration of the earth's surface in which the supporting pillars are planted, the trembling pillars imply that the physical supports of the vault are shaking, and the windows are "obviously" literal holes in the celestial dome. Only the crass-

9. Henry George Liddell and Robert Scott, *A Greek-English Lexicon*, p. 1427.
10. G. Bertram, "Stereos," in *Theological Dictionary of the New Testament*, 7:609.
11. E. W. Maunder, "Astronomy," in *The International Standard Bible Encyclopedia*, 1:315.

Biblical Evidence for the Water Heaven Theory

est literalism can use this as an argument to prove that the firmament in Hebrew thought was a literal dome.

Newman has pointed out that "although 'pillar' in English has a strong connotation, 'upright support,' the Hebrew word is often used for standing objects which support nothing."[12] For example, two pillars (Heb. 'ammûd) were located on the porch of Solomon's temple, but they supported nothing (1 Kings 7:15-22). Likewise, the Israelites were led in the wilderness by a "pillar of cloud" during the day and a "pillar of fire" at night (Exod. 13:21-22), but these "pillars" supported nothing. The Bible also speaks of a "pillar of smoke" (Judg. 20:40). So the Hebrew word 'ammûd "can often be translated merely 'column' or 'upright' in agreement with the verb 'āmad, 'to stand,' from which it is derived."[13] The "pillars of the earth," then, could simply refer to the upright mountains which rise from the earth with no implication that they hold up the metallic dome of the sky. Pillars of heaven would be so designated simply because they point toward the sky, or heaven. As for Hannah's statement, "The pillars of the earth are the Lord's, and He set the world on them" (1 Sam. 2:8), the Hebrew word māṣûq, translated "pillars," is used here in the sense of "how it appears." It is only a poetic way of saying that the earth is firm and solid.

The shaking of the foundations is simply a figure of speech for an earthquake which causes the mountains (the pillars of heaven) to shake. When a violent rainstorm hits, it is as if heaven has opened its windows. This is how it appears to the eye of the observer. Moses is simply using the language of description. Only crass literalism tries to force a cosmology out of these descriptions. It would be like hearing a twentieth-century scientist refer to the "sun setting" and then insisting that he really believes that the sun sinks into the ocean at the end of the world at the twilight.

So on the first day of creation, God separated the waters which were below the expanse (the atmospheric heavens) from the waters which were above the atmospheric heavens. But to

12. Robert Newman, "The Biblical Teaching of the Firmament," p. 39.
13. Ibid.

what does Moses refer when he speaks of the "waters which were above the expanse"?

THE WATERS ABOVE THE EXPANSE

When God separated the waters which were under the expanse from the waters which were above the expanse, an obvious miracle was involved. The radical critic never tires of seeing this as a reference to the celestial ocean resting on top of a metal dome that is found in much ancient mythology. In particular, the parallel is often drawn between the Babylonian account of creation and that of the Hebrews. In that account Marduk slays the chaos monster Tiamat, the goddess of the world ocean. He then cuts her carcass in half horizontally and out of one half makes the heavens and the celestial waters. Yet as Cassuto, the great Jewish commentator, observes:

> It is true that in the Pentateuch, too, reference is made to the division of the primeval world-ocean into two halves, situated one above the other, but the entire mythological picture is completely erased. Here we have neither war nor weapons; a body is not carved up, nor are its segments used for construction; a simple process of physical unfoldment takes the place of the mythical train of events described in the pagan legends.[14]

There seem to be two basic options in understanding the meaning of "the waters above."

CLOUDS IN THE ATMOSPHERE

The usual and oldest view is that the reference is to the clouds in the sky.[15] Kidner (following Edwyn Bevan) argues that the division in the waters referred to in Genesis 1:6-8 is the division between the liquid water on the surface and the "enveloping cloud" which surrounded the world at the end of the first day of

14. U. Cassuto, *A Commentary on the Book of Genesis, From Adam to Noah*, p. 32.
15. John Calvin, "Genesis," in *Calvin's Commentaries*, 1:5.

creation.[16] Leupold pictures a similar situation: "Apparently, before this firmament existed, the earth waters on the surface of the earth and the cloud waters as we know them were contiguous without an intervening clear air space. It was a situation like a dense fog upon the surface of the waters.... These clouds constitute the upper waters."[17]

Newman sees confirmation of this idea in several references in the Old Testament where waters are clearly associated with clouds, or at least with the heavens.[18]

> When He utters His voice, there is a tumult of waters in the heavens, and He causes the clouds to ascend from the end of the earth (Jer. 10:13; 51:16).
>
> Also with moisture He loads the thick cloud; He disperses the cloud of His lightning (Job 37:11).
>
> For He draws up the drops of water, they distill rain from the mist which the clouds pour down, they drip upon man abundantly. Can anyone understand the spreading of the clouds, the thundering of His pavilion? (Job 36:27-29).
>
> The clouds poured out water; the skies gave forth a sound; the arrows flashed here and there (Psalm 77:17).
>
> He wraps up the waters in His clouds; and the cloud does not burst under them (Job 26:8).

At first glance, these passages would seem to settle the issue in favor of the cloud interpretation. Clearly, the Hebrews understood that clouds and water were associated, and could have conceived "waters above" as clouds above. Also, this interpretation has the advantage of simplicity, avoids the mythological parallels with the surrounding nations, and fits well with the observed appearance of the heavens.

In spite of its apparent simplicity, however, if the plain language of the text is to stand, it is clearly impossible that the

16. Derek Kidner, *Genesis*, pp. 47, 55.
17. H. C. Leupold, *Exposition of Genesis*, 1:59-60.
18. Newman, p. 59.

"waters above" could refer to clouds. It is impossible for two reasons.

First, the text clearly states that the division in the midst of the waters was a division in the midst of the waters of the deep (Gen. 1:2). The "deep" clearly refers to the ocean, hence a division in the midst of the ocean is meant, not a division between the ocean and the clouds, mists, or fogs that are contiguous upon it.

Second, there were no clouds or mists mentioned in the text that could have been divided from the ocean waters. Where does the passage mention clouds? Where is the idea of mists or clouds enveloping the earth and contiguous with the surface of the waters stated? This must be read into the text in order to justify a pre-determined interpretation that has assumed that clouds must be meant.[19] If it be granted that the "expanse" refers to the atmospheric heavens (Gen. 1:7), then it follows that the atmosphere was not "made" until the second day. At the end of the first day only an empty watery world existed with no atmosphere, clouds, mists, or anything else mentioned as being above it. This world knew light and darkness, and was supernaturally preserved by God under the "moving" of the Spirit of God (Gen. 1:2). Since clouds are considered as being part of the atmospheric heavens, how could they be lifted above the atmospheric heavens on the second day when they had not yet been created? No, the text says that the raqîa' divided the waters of the deep which were created on the first day and hence were available to be divided. It simply does not allow that clouds and

19. Job 38:9 seems to refer to "clouds" ('ānān) and "thick darkness" ('ărāpel) that surrounded the primeval earth. Yet this language is so figurative that it is precarious to press it to mean clouds. Clouds, of course, simply could not exist without light to supply heat. Furthermore, 'ānān is often a symbol for "gloom" (Ezek. 30:18; 32:7; Zeph. 1:15; Ezek. 34:12; Joel 2:2). This would complement by parallelism the NASB translation of 'ărāpel as "thick darkness" which might imply the world as already in existence and being under judgment (Jer. 13:16 "darkness") and misery (Isa. 60:2, "darkness").

mists created on the first day were separated from the waters of the deep on the second.

A LITERAL LIQUID CELESTIAL OCEAN

In view of the principle of sharable implications discussed in the first chapter, the only other possible meaning of the text would be of a literal liquid ocean. It is clear that the Hebrews were aware of the literal liquid ocean concept from the surrounding myths, and that they were aware of clouds as a source of water. So any notion of an ice canopy or a vapor canopy is probably beyond their experience or knowledge.

For several reasons it seems preferable, in order to do justice more fully to the plain language of the text, to assume that the "waters above" refer not to clouds, but to a vast reservoir of liquid water, sufficient to supply forty days and nights of rainfall (Gen. 7:11-12).

The primary meaning of the preposition "above" is "upon." The preposition ‘al is used "of the substratum upon which an object in any way rests."[20] It can mean "over" or "above" (Gen. 1:20, the birds fly "over," ‘al, the earth and not in it), but it is never used of "in" or "within" or "among."[21] The term translated "above" is made up of two prepositions: "from" and "upon," (mē‘al).[22] "Above" is a good translation, but the meaning is more nearly "beyond it."[23] Thus, the literal language of the text would lead us away from the notion of clouds "in" the expanse to a concept of water "above" the expanse.

Edward Young has correctly observed, "I am unable to accept the opinion that the waters above the expanse refers to the clouds, for the position does not do justice to the language of the text which states that these waters are *above* the expanse."[24]

20. Brown, Driver, and Briggs, p. 752.
21. Ibid., pp. 752-59.
22. min + ‘al = mē‘al, see Ludwig Koehler and Walter Baumgartner, *Lexicon in Veteris Testamenti Libros*, p. 704.
23. E. J. Young, *Studies in Genesis One*, p. 90.
24. Ibid.

Newman, an advocate of the cloud interpretation of the "waters above," has attempted to blunt the force of this preposition by citing parallels which show that the word can mean "toward." He argues, first of all, that an Exodus passage gives a possible parallel use of *'al* with *shamayim* ("heavens") that could suggest that *'al*, when connected with *shamayim*, could mean either "toward" or "upon" but at the same time "within." "Now the Lord said to Moses, 'Stretch out your hand *toward* the sky, that hail may fall on all the land of Egypt' " (Ex. 9:22). Newman comments,

> Especially interesting are the four occurrences of *'al* with "heaven" in Exodus (9:22, 23; 10:21, 22). These are all alike, and the King James Version translates the first: "Stretch forth thine hand *toward* heaven." It is not likely that Moses is lifted up to hold his hand out over the dome! Therefore, either *'al* may mean "toward" when used with *shamayim*, or "heaven" includes the air and Moses' hand is "upon" it when he holds it aloft.[25]

The former is much more likely. "Heaven" here does not mean "atmosphere"; it simply is observer true language for "sky." Later on, Newman summarizes the possible interpretations of Genesis 1:7 (the "waters *above* the firmament") which he thinks may be suggested by the usages of *'al* in Exodus.

> We have shown in chapter three that the preposition *'al* is used with "heaven" (Ex. 9:22-23, 10:21-22) in a sense which must either mean "toward heaven" if this "heaven" is not the atmosphere, or "upon heaven" if it is. In the former case, we could translate Gen. 1:7 as the "waters which are toward the firmament" and Psalm 148:4 similarly. In the latter case, which seems more cogent, the waters would be "upon" the firmament or heaven, just as Moses' hand was upon the air, that is, suspended in it.[26]

Newman is confused on several points. First, the preposition used in Genesis 1:7 is a compound of *'al* — it is *mē'al*. The

25. Newman, p. 32.
26. Ibid., p. 57.

phrase in Exodus 9:22, is 'al-shamayim, while the phrase in Genesis 1:7 is mē'al-shamayim. The lexicon lists no usage of mē'al that can mean "toward."[27] In fact, even the use of 'al as "toward" in Exodus 9:22 is "not common,"[28] hence one should be careful about reading it into Genesis 1:7 unless there are clear contextual indicators that require it. There are no such textual indicators in Genesis 1. Newman's real point, however, is that since the 'al-shamayim of Exodus 9:22 can mean "upon and yet within," so can the mē'al-shamayim of Genesis 1:7. But it is highly unlikely that Moses implied that his hand was resting "on the air," that is, suspended "in it." Moses makes a simple statement that he was to point "toward the heavens," and to read mechanistic implications concerning the fact that his hand was resting upon the air seems improbable. The Exodus passage is simply saying in observer true language that Moses pointed toward the sky, with no mechanistic implications of "air" being included in the word "heavens." So unless Newman can demonstrate a likelihood of 'al meaning "upon" in the sense of "on and within" in Exodus 9:22, he has no right to read this unlikely meaning into Genesis 1:7. Such a use of 'al is clearly without parallel in the Old Testament unless the Exodus passages cited by Newman are such parallels, and to this writer's mind, they are not. Furthermore, as mentioned, it is mē'al-shamayim and not 'al-shamayim that was used in Genesis 1:7 anyway. So even if 'al-shamayim does mean "upon and yet within" in Exodus 9:22, what relevance does that have to Genesis 1:7?

Later Moses says, "Then God said, 'Let the waters teem with swarms of living creatures, and let birds fly above the earth in the open expanse of the heavens'" (Gen. 1:20). In the phrase "in the open expanse of the heavens," Newman finds additional support for his notion that 'al can carry the connotation of "upon and yet within." He says,

> This use should be compared with the phrase 'al-peney, "upon the face of," used in Gen. 1:20 for birds flying "upon the face of the heavens."

27. Brown, Driver, and Briggs, pp. 758-59.
28. Ibid., p. 757.

According to the dome view, the birds are seen in projection on the dome of the firmament, but I have found no examples of '*al-peney* which mean "projected against something from below." I suggest the phrase means the birds are flying "upon" the air, just as chaff is carried "before" the wind.[29]

However, the lexicon classes '*al-p^enê* as an altogether different preposition than '*al*.[30] Its usages are so distinct that it is not even included under the compound uses of '*al*. Furthermore, the same preposition is used in Genesis 1:2 of the Spirit of God's brooding "upon the face of" the deep. Surely, the Spirit of God is not "in" the deep or being "supported by it." The Spirit of God is above the surface. While it may be possible to read the theological concept of immanence into the passage to get some idea like "upon and yet within," this would seem to violate the plain statement that the Spirit of God was upon the *face* (that is, the top) of the waters. He is not "within the top" of the waters. Similarly, the birds are "below" the "surface" of the sky. It is the language of appearance. As one looks up, he sees the birds "in the sky" or "against the face of the sky." Cassuto observes,

> *In front of* (literally, "on the face of") *the firmament of the heavens.* The attempts that have been made to explain this phrase are not satisfactory. It seems to reflect the impression that a person receives on looking upward: the creatures that fly about above one's head appear then to be set against the background of the sky — in front of the firmament of the heavens.[31]

Neither is this observer true interpretation of '*al-p^enê* characteristic only of those who hold the dome view of the firmament. It is common among those who hold the cloud interpretation of the "waters above" and who view the firmament as the atmospheric heavens.[32]

29. Newman, "Biblical Teaching on the Firmament," p. 58.
30. Brown, Driver, and Briggs, pp. 818-19.
31. Cassuto, p. 49.
32. Kidner, p. 49; Leupold, p. 79.

The atmosphere is said to be "in the midst of" the waters and to divide between the waters. The atmospheric heavens are said to be in the midst of the waters. The waters are clearly those of Genesis 1:2 and are, therefore, in liquid form. The word translated "in the midst of" is *bᵉtôk*. It generally means, "in the midst of,"[33] and here seems to mean "in between." It is used of the bisection of animals (Gen. 15:10), but it does not always refer to the precise middle.[34] Thus, it does not, in Genesis 1:6, precisely tell where the division in the waters occurred, and it does not in any way say that half of the ocean was placed up above the earth and half of the ocean was left on the surface.[35] The preposition emphasizes that the firmament was in the midst of the waters, and not, as the cloud interpretation would have it, the waters in the midst of the firmament.

Furthermore, the task assigned to the firmament was to divide between the waters. As Udd observes, "The preposition *bên* meaning 'between,' would indicate the relative positions of the atmosphere and the waters. The layering would be first water, then atmosphere, and finally water. There were to be no intervening gaps. The atmosphere was to form an interface with the water at both of its extremities."[36]

Rain came from clouds in the expanse. The Hebrews were aware that rain came from clouds in the expanse (see Judg. 5:4; Job 36:28; Psalm 77:17), yet Moses speaks of a source of water above those clouds which were in the atmosphere. Consider Jeremiah's statement in this regard, "When He utters His voice, there is a tumult of waters in the heavens, and He causes the clouds to ascend from the end of the earth" (Jer. 10:13). Here the waters "in" (*bên*) the heavens are associated with the clouds. Moses, however, speaks of waters "above" (*'al*) the heavens (Gen. 1:7). Since they knew of waters "in," perhaps Moses' use of *'al* signifies another source of waters, that is, the heavenly ocean.

33. Brown, Driver, and Briggs, p. 1063.
34. Ibid.
35. See Udd, "The Early Atmosphere," pp. 43-45, for a discussion on this.
36. Ibid., pp. 44-45.

The expanse effected a separation of water in its liquid form. Not only does the cloud interpretation of the "waters above" suffer from the fact that there is no mention of clouds or mists in the text, but it contradicts the clear statement of the text that the division was a division in the midst of an oceanic mass. The question is, "What is being divided?" Clearly the division referred to is a division in the midst of the deep (Gen. 1:2), that is, in the midst of the primeval ocean. It was a division in water in its liquid phase as an oceanic mass; not between liquid droplets (clouds) and liquid ocean, but between liquid ocean and liquid ocean.

This separation was the task assigned to the atmosphere. Apparently God simply planted the expanse in the midst of the primeval ocean and it arched up, leaving an ocean above the atmosphere as well as an ocean below the atmosphere.[37] The parallelism would lead one to expect that if the waters below are an oceanic mass, so are the waters above. Furthermore, it is difficult to see how Moses could have counted the waters below (Gen. 1:2), which are clearly not in liquid droplets, as any different than the waters above (Gen. 1:7), which obviously came from them. The word "water" is used with no specific qualifications. A normal reading of the text as it stands here would, therefore, lead one to believe that Moses believed in a literal ocean of liquid H_2O (oceanic mass) that surrounded the ancient earth. Cassuto agrees:

> Thus as soon as the firmament was established in the midst of the layer of water, it began to rise in the middle, arching like a vault, and in the course of its upward expansion if lifted at the same time the upper waters resting on top of it. This marked a considerable advance in the marshalling of the components of the universe. Above now stands the vault of the heaven surmounted by the upper waters; beneath stretches the expanse

---

37. Although no such movement of the firmament in the sense of "arching" is mentioned, a movement like this may be implied in the verb "divide."

of lower waters, that is, the waters of the vast sea, which still cover all the heavy, solid matter below. The universe is beginning to take shape.[38]

The suggestion has been made that, since clouds contain water in liquid droplets, the cloud interpretation would still satisfy the language of the text.[39] It should be obvious, however, that Moses is talking about the waters (Gen. 1:2), which are not liquid droplets but are a vast ocean.

It is only our modern scientific knowledge that causes us to recoil at the notion of the earth actually surrounded by a literal ocean of liquid water. An entirely different set of natural laws would have had to have been in operation for such a state to have been maintained. However, we must not let our notions about what is possible determine what God was capable of doing during the week of creation.

The words for cloud are not used. While it is clear from the Old Testament that water is associated with clouds (see Job 26:8), of the more than 500 usages of "water" there are none which could refer to clouds except in context where they are clearly associated with clouds and a word for cloud is used. In other words, water (*mayim*), always means a water mass like a lake, river, bucket, or ocean in the Old Testament unless there are some specific contextual references tying it into clouds. No such contextual indications are given in Genesis 1; hence, according to usage, it should be assumed that the "waters above" here refers to liquid water, not to droplets or clouds.

Goppelt discusses the use of *mayim* ("water") in the Old Testament. He notes, "The ideas connected with water are not restricted to the concept itself but are also developed with the help of specific qualifications."[40] Genesis 1:7 contains none of

38. Cassuto, pp. 31-32. By "vault," Cassuto does not mean the solid dome of the critics but the atmosphere. Neither is he assuming a flat earth interpretation by his use of the word "arching."
39. Robert Newman, personal communication, May 1976.
40. Leonhard Goppelt, "Hudōr," in *Theological Dictionary of the New Testament,* 8:317.

the "specific qualifications," but is a simple reference to water.[41]

The Hebrews had six different words for cloud,[42] and none of them are used in Genesis 1:7. If Moses wanted to convey that he meant clouds by "waters above," he had ample vocabulary to do so. Instead, he used the usual word for water that always means water in the liquid phase (not droplets or clouds) unless there is a contextual reference connecting it with clouds. So to interpret "waters above" as clouds is, by usage, quite unlikely.

Argument from Moses' polemical intent. We know that the entire ancient Near East was full of creation myths which involved a literal liquid ocean that was formed out of the remains of the chaos monster whom a hero-god conquered (to bring order out of chaos). As we saw in the first chapter, Genesis 1 seems to be a polemic against these myths. If it be granted that Moses intended to correct the myths, then it is of great importance to consider aspects of a particular myth that he did *not* correct. Now the myth of the celestial ocean had four essential ingredients: (1) the ocean was formed out of the corpse of the defeated chaos monster Tiamat; (2) the hero-god had to struggle and battle to defeat this monster; (3) once the monster had been defeated and half of it turned into the heavenly ocean, wooden sluice gates had to be constructed and sentries posted in order to keep the waters of chaos from crashing back down to earth; and (4) the upper waters were considered to be a literal liquid ocean. Now in Moses' polemic, he clearly countered the first three aspects of the myth: the ocean was formed out of lifeless water in the deep, not a monster; there was no struggle, simply a spoken word; there were no sluice gates, simply the will of God to sustain the heavenly ocean. Why did Moses allow the fourth point to stand? Since he apparently had the upper waters aspect of the battle myth specifically in mind, and since it was his intent to correct the error in it, the only reason he would have left one aspect apparently uncorrected is if he accepted it as fact. The proof that he left it uncorrected is simply that the idea

41. Udd, "The Early Atmosphere," p. 50.
42. George V. Wigram, *The Englishman's Hebrew and Chaldee Concordance of the Old Testament,* p. 1419.

of "upper waters," which all his readers would have connected with the heavenly ocean in this kind of polemic against the battle myth (a specific context), was left to stand while the other parts were obviously modified.

Peter's commentary on Genesis 1:6-8. The Apostle Peter was confronted with "scoffers" who thought the idea of a second coming of Christ was silly. He answered their mocking in his second epistle (2 Pet. 3:3-13). The premise on which their argument was built was that "all continues just as it was from the beginning of creation" (3:4). Peter responded by reminding his readers that all has not continued as it was. In fact, the world before the Flood was completely devastated and changed by a flood. Similarly, the present world will one day be completely changed by a judgment of fire (3:7).

In describing how the old world order was changed, he informed his readers how it came into existence in the first place, then alluded to its destruction: "For when they maintain this, it escapes their notice that by the word of God the heavens existed long ago and the earth was formed out of water and by water, through which the world at that time was destroyed, being flooded with water" (2 Pet. 3:5-6).

We find three crucial phrases in this passage. First, Peter says that the earth *was formed* out of water and through water. The verb "was formed" *(sunistēmi)* carries the idea of "to be composed," "compounded," or "exist."[43] So the earth was composed or existed out of water and through water.

In what sense did the earth exist out of water *(ex hudatos)*? This seems to be a reference to the gathering together of the waters under the firmament so that the dry land appeared (Gen. 1:9). So the earth came into existence "out of" *(ex)* the water. As Alford puts it,

> ... *ex hudatos*, because the waters that were under the firmament were gathered together into one place and the dry land appeared: and thus water was the material, *out of* which the earth was made."[44]

43. W. F. Arndt and F. W. Gingrich, *A Greek-English Lexicon*, p. 798.
44. Henry Alford, *The Greek Testament*, 4:414.

But to what does the phrase "through water" (*di' hudatos*) refer? The precise meaning is vague, but if the phrase *ex hudatos* refers to the "waters below," then it would follow that *di' hudatos* might be intended by Peter to complete the description of the waters of Genesis 1:6-8 and, hence, refer to the "waters above." In what sense, then, could it be said that the earth consists or exists "through the waters above the firmament?" The *dia* here should be rendered "by means of." Therefore, Peter would be saying that the "world at that time," the world before the flood, existed "by means of" the "waters above the firmament."

Peter obviously knew that the world before the Flood was in some way different from the world order in his time. For one thing, he knew that prior to the Flood men lived an average of 900 years (see Gen. 5). He knew it was watered by "mists" and that there were no seasons, rainbows, or rain. Perhaps he understood that the pre-Flood world order was maintained or "existed" "by means of" the "waters above the firmament." That old world order, maintained by these two bodies of water, was destroyed (*kataklustheis*) by the merger of these two bodies of water once again, resulting in the global flood. This is apparently his meaning when he says, "through which the world at that time was destroyed, being flooded with water" (2 Pet. 3:6). The phrase "through which" cannot refer to the Word of God because the "which" in Greek is a plural, not a singular. Thus, it refers either to waters, or as this interpretation suggests, the *two* bodies of water alluded to above.[45]

The third time that water is mentioned in this passage, it refers to the water of the Flood (3:6). So the term is used three times, the first and third usages are clearly of a liquid ocean, that is, water in liquid and not droplet or cloud form. Udd summarizes, "The fact that the word "water" is used in the text three times, and that twice the word must be understood to

45. A later discussion will argue that the liquid upper ocean was changed to water vapor as part of the creative act. Thus it was partially by the upper waters that the earth was flooded, but they were in vapor form at the time of the Flood.

Biblical Evidence for the Water Heaven Theory 61

mean *liquid* water, would strongly suggest, if not indeed establish, that the third occurrence be also understood in that manner."[46]

The "deep," not the clouds, was placed in heavenly storehouses. The psalmist specifically informs us that the deep was placed up into the heavenly storehouses.

> By the word of the Lord the heavens were made,
> And by the breath of His mouth all their host.
> He gathers the waters of the sea together as a heap;
> He lays up the deeps in storehouses.
> Let all the earth fear the Lord;
> Let all the inhabitants of the world stand in awe of Him.
> For He spoke, and it was done;
> He commanded, and it stood fast (Psalm 33:6-9).

Once again, Yahweh is pictured as totally sovereign over chaos in creation. He simply speaks and the waters obey. There is a specific polemic intent to this section of the psalm. The phrase "He gathers the waters of the sea together as a heap" has been variously interpreted. Clericus, an 18th-century French Protestant commentator, sees it as a reference to the creation week when the waters were "gathered together" that the dry land might appear.[47] Others see it as a reference to the *present* containment of the sea in the ocean basins.[48] However, it is clearly a creation context: "By the word of the Lord the heavens were made." So the former view is to be preferred.

Of particular interest, however, is the phrase "He lays up the deeps in the storehouses." While it may simply be synomous parallelism and refer to the containment of the ocean basins it may be synthetic parallelism and refer to something beyond

46. Udd, "The Canopy and Genesis 1:6-8," p. 92. The three bodies of water are: (1) the liquid ocean of the second day which later changed to vapor; (2) the water of the Flood; and (3) the lower waters.
47. Clericus, cited by J. J. Stewart Perowne, *The Book of Psalms*, 1:296.
48. Perowne, 1:296.

that — the placing of the waters in the heavenly storehouse. There is no question as to the meaning of "the deeps." It is the plural of "the deep" (tᵉhôm) of Genesis 1:2. During the creation week, the psalmist tells us, the "deeps," — the waters of Genesis 1:2 — were placed in the "storehouses" ('ōṣār). The word 'ōṣār is used many times in the Old Testament, usually of the treasuries of a king, of the temple, or of a grain storage bin. However, the lexicon recognizes a certain class of usages related to cosmology in which it refers to the storehouses of heaven from whence come snow, hail (Job 38:22), wind (Jer. 10:13; 51:16), and rain (Deut. 28:12).[49] So the "deep" of Genesis 1:2 was placed into the heavenly storehouses according to the psalmist. Note that it was not clouds that were placed up there, but the "deep" (tᵉhôm), the liquid ocean. Such is the psalmist's understanding of Genesis 1:6-7.

In the surrounding nature myths it was believed that the heavens contained a literal wooden storehouse, outfitted with sluice gates to restrain the waters of chaos. Note the lack of mention of this idea in any of the cosmological uses of 'ōṣār in the Old Testament. The imagery is borrowed, and it is used as a figure of the heavenly reservoir for the ocean above, but the crassly literal remnants of the nature myths are dropped. In fact, the whole point of the quotation was that no such wooden reservoir or storehouse was necessary, for Yahweh of the Hebrews simply "spoke, and it was done; He commanded, and it stood fast" (Psalm 33:9). It was maintained in these heavenly storehouses by the word of Yahweh and under His total control.

Fearful of paralleling the Bible with the nature myths, conservative interpreters have generally viewed the storehouse as the ocean basins and not the heavenly storehouse of the myths.[50] However, by Old Testament usage of the word "storehouse" ('ōṣār), this interpretation is clearly unlikely.

49. Brown, Driver, and Briggs, pp. 69-70.
50. See Perowne, 1:296; Franz Delitzsch, *Psalms*, 1:403; Thomas J. Conant and Carl Bernhard Moll, *The Pslams* in Lange's *Commentary on the Holy Scriptures*, 5:231; A. R. Fausset, "The Book of Job" in *A Commentary on the Old and New Testaments*, 3:170.

Biblical Evidence for the Water Heaven Theory

When used in connection with water, creation, and cosmology (as it is here), it always refers to *heavenly* reservoirs and not earthly ocean basins;[51] in fact, nowhere is it ever used of ocean basins (see a concordance).

The Hebrews simply viewed the "storehouse" as the place in the heavens from which the waters, snow, wind, and other elements came. But during the creation week, the liquid ocean of Genesis 1:2 was placed up there and not the clouds. Today, only rain, snow, and hail remain. The imagery recalled to the psalmist's mind the victory of Yahweh in creation — a victory without effort, without struggle, without battling dragons. It was a victory accomplished by His spoken word; so, "Sing for joy in the Lord, O you righteous ones" (Psalm 33:1). Yahweh is King; He can be our "help and our shield" (33:20).

The amount of rain in the flood. A final reason for understanding the "waters above" as a heavenly ocean and not as clouds is that only such an ocean of water could have supplied sufficient water to maintain a forty-day global rainfall. Those who insist on the cloud interpretation of "waters above" would do well to ask, "Where did the water come from that supplied a forty-day rainfall?" It is easily demonstrated that the maximum amount of water that can be maintained in clouds in our entire present atmosphere is only about 10.54 cm for a saturated atmosphere with a sea level temperature of 28 degrees Celsius.[52] That amounts to 4.14 inches or a forty-day rainfall rate of 0.00431 inches per hour — hardly a torrential downpour.

However, with an ocean of water maintained up above the firmament, there is adequate water to fit the description of the great rain of Genesis 7. The precise mechanism for maintaining this heavenly reservoir will be examined in a later chapter.

There seems to be little doubt that Moses saw the waters above (Gen. 1:6-8) as the source of the water that came through the "windows of heaven" (Gen. 7:11). In view of the polemic intent of the writer, there seems to be a conceptual tie between

51. See Deut. 28:12; Job 38:22; Psalms 33:7; 135:7; Jer. 10:13; 51:16.
52. Horace Robert Byers, *General Meteorology*, p. 113.

these two passages. That tie is in the notion of the restraint and release of chaos. The "deep" ($t^eh\hat{o}m$) is placed up above the firmament and cannot come down until God says so. The waters are totally under God's control. In the nature myths, the worshipers had to reenact the victory of their hero-god over the waters of chaos every new year in order to secure the restraint and continued victory over these waters. As mentioned before, wooden sluice gates were used along with military sentries to keep these waters back. In the Bible all this is lacking. God simply speaks, and it is done. The waters are controlled by His decree. No sluice gates or sentries are needed. The waters above the firmament merge once again with the waters below only at the bidding of Yahweh. Many interpreters have seen this connection. For example, commenting on Genesis 7:11, Kidner says, "We can infer from the statement about the great deep and the windows of heaven a vast upheaval of the seabed, and torrential rain; but the expressions are deliberately evocative of chapter 1: the waters above and below the firmament are, in token, merged again, as if to reverse the very work of creation and bring back the featureless waste of chaos."[53] Indeed, when the rainfall had subsided, the entire earth had reverted to a situation similar to that described in Genesis 1:2. Water again covered the entire surface of the planet. Chaos reigned once more, but only under Yahweh's permission as a tool to judge man.

The connection in thought tracing the movement from chaos of Genesis 1:2 to the chaos of the Flood (Gen. 7:19-24) can be seen more clearly in Table 2.1.

If this be granted, then there must have been enough rainwater lifted above the atmosphere (Gen. 1:7) to have supplied a global rainfall for forty days.

---

53. Kidner, p. 91.

TABLE 2.1

FROM CHAOS TO CHAOS, THE CONCEPTUAL TIE BETWEEN GENESIS 1:7 AND 7:11

1:2	1:7	7:11	7:19-24
C	waters below the firmament	fountains of the great deep	C
H			H
A (separation)			A (merger)
O	waters above the firmament	floodgates of the sky	O
S			S

Now, how much rain is required? One certainly gets the "feel" that the division in the waters involved more than the skimming off the surface of the top four inches which would have to be assumed by the cloud theory (a *global* cloud cover could contain only about four inches of water). Yet, as pointed out above, it is not necessary to posit that one half of the ocean was lifted up there either. In view of the suggested conceptual tie outlined above, it seems best to say that only enough water was "divided" and raised up into the celestial ocean as was needed to supply forty days of rain. All of this gets rather involved and needs separate discussion.

THE AMOUNT OF RAIN IN THE FLOOD

THE FLOODGATES OF THE SKY

In order to estimate the amount of water in the celestial ocean, we must first understand the meaning of the phrase, "the floodgates of the sky" (Gen. 7:11).

At the inception of the forty days and nights of the flood of Noah, Moses exclaimed that "the windows of heaven were opened" (Gen. 7:11 KJV). The critics force this Hebrew expression into the mythology of the ancient world. "The firmament, or celestial dam, was believed to be punctuated at intervals by grilles or sluices through which the rain was released in due measure."[54] However, as Maunder insists, "It seems to show some dullness on the part of an objector to argue that this expression involves the idea of a literal stonebuilt reservoir with its sluices. Those who have actually seen tropical rain in full violence will find the scriptural phrase not merely appropriate but almost inevitable."[55]

This is clearly a poetic figure and does not imply the idea of the heavens as a solid mass.[56] This kind of comparison is technically known as hypocatastasis.[57] A hypocatastasis is an implied resemblance or representation. If a wife were to say, "My husband is *like* a beast," she is using a simile (a comparison using *like* or *as*). If, instead, the wife said, "You *are* a beast," she has now used a metaphor. Notice the comparison is more forceful. However, if she simply said, "You beast," she is now using a hypocatastasis. The comparison is implied but not stated. This figure is therefore calculated to arouse the mind and attract and excite the attention to the greatest extent.

So if Moses had said, "This downpour is as if the windows of heaven were opened" (Gen. 7:11), he would have been using a simile. No one would have charged him with equating the windows of heaven with the floodgates of mythology. If he had said, "This downpour is the opening of the windows of heaven," he would have been using a metaphor, and none of the critics would have raised an eyebrow. But when Moses said, "The windows of heaven were opened," he used a hypocatastasis, and so he has been accused of borrowing from the pagan myths. Moses chose a hypocatastasis instead of a metaphor or simile because he was trying to arouse the emotions and excite the mind of his readers to the greatest extent. It is just like the

54. T. H. Gaster, "Heaven," in *The Interpreter's Dictionary of the Bible*, 2:551.
55. E. W. Maunder, *The Astronomy of the Bible*, p. 49.
56. C. F. Keil and F. Delitzsch, *The Pentateuch*, 1:52.
57. E. W. Bullinger, *Figures of Speech Used in the Bible*, pp. 744-47.

Biblical Evidence for the Water Heaven Theory

wife who says, "You beast" (hypocatastasis) instead of "You are like a beast" (simile). She is trying to inject more emotion into the figure. Likewise, Moses is calling our attention to the violence of this rainstorm. It just was not a gentle Sunday afternoon drizzle. As Jamieson says:

> This Hebrew term denotes windows or apertures closed with lattice, not with glass (cf. Gen. 7:16; Ex. 12:3; Isa. 60:8), and hence they are represented as "opened" so that the waters from the clouds, instead of oozing slowly and gently, as through a piece of compact network, were poured down as through sluices or spouts (LXX, *katarraktai*; cf. 2 Kings 7:2,19; Isa. 24:18; Mal. 3:10). The language is highly figurative, intended to convey a vivid idea of the awful inundation.[58]

The lexicon defines *'ărūbā* as "lattice, window, sluice."[59] The word is used nine times in the Bible. In the Genesis account it is used in connection with rain (Gen. 7:11). However, the word is directly paralleled in the Ugaritic texts by the word *'urbt* which means "lattice."[60] This word illustrates the cognate use of *'ărūbā* in 2 Kings 7:1-3. In that passage the king was angry with Elisha because of a terrible hunger in the land and he believed that Elisha could change the situation. So he sent a messenger to Elisha with orders to put him to death. Elisha responded by predicting a sudden plenty in Samaria. "Then Elisha said, 'Listen to the word of the Lord; thus says the Lord, "Tomorrow about this time a measure of fine flour shall be sold for a shekel, and two measures of barley for a shekel, in the gate of Samaria" ' " (2 Kings 7:1). In other words, Elisha predicted that the next day the Lord would pour out a great blessing on the starving land. Crops would become so plentiful that they would be sold at very cheap rates. This raised considerable skepticism in the mind of one of the king's captains, so he

---

58. Robert Jamieson, "Genesis," *Commentary on the Old and New Testaments*, 1:95.
59. Brown, Driver, and Briggs, p. 70; see Maunder, 1:315.
60. Leah Bronner, *The Stories of Elijah and Elisha*, p. 73.

leaned over and expressed his doubt in the king's hearing. "And the royal officer on whose hand the king was leaning answered the man of God and said, 'Behold, if the Lord should make windows in heaven, could this thing be?' " (2 Kings 7:2) The captain was clearly thinking in Ugaritic terms. One of the Ugaritic texts deals with the building of Baal's house. Bronner observes, "The function of the window in Baal's house was to enable him to pour forth rain on to the earth. The windows were closely connected with the function of supplying rain."[61] Baal was supposed to open clefts in heaven and rain forth blessing to the earth through the window in his house in the sky. So the captain asked, Would God do this? Would He give rain to the earth? It was as if to say, "Is it possible to believe that the Lord would open windows in heaven and send down from it not rain, as usual, but fine flour and barley?" He thought of God's raining barley through these windows just as Baal is said to rain oil or honey through them. In the Ugaritic texts this simply means that, because rain falls, the earth yields produce in abundance. Thus, windows of heaven is a figure for rainfall.

Cassuto observes that "the term *windows of heaven* was used in their [Ugaritic] language to denote the source of rain."[62] The idea of "lattices" is not necessarily found in the usage of the Hebrew word in the Old Testament, but seems to be derived from its cognate '*urbt* in the Ugaritic texts.[63]

The other usages of '*ărūbā* do not necessarily refer to rain (except Gen. 8:2, and probably Mal. 3:10).[64] But it clearly does in Genesis 7:11 and 2 Kings 7:2. The latter passage is particularly instructive because it provides such a precise parallel to the Ugaritic.

The word as used in the Bible has none of the connotations found in the myths of a literal wooden sluice gate. Rather, it is

61. Ibid. In the Ugaritic texts the verb *pth* ("opened") and the noun '*urbt* (Heb. '*ărūbā*) are found in Tablet II AB, column vii, lines 17-18.
62. Cassuto, p. 87.
63. Ibid., p. 86.
64. See Gen. 7:11; 8:2; 2 Kings 7:2, 19; Eccles. 12:3; Isa. 24:18; 60:8; Hos. 13:3; Mal. 3:10.

used figuratively of an awful inundation. It was, indeed, a great rain.

THE RAINFALL RATE DURING THE FLOOD

According to Moses,

"In the six hundredth year of Noah's life, in the second month, on the seventeenth day of the month, on the same day all the fountains of the great deep burst open, and the floodgates of the sky were opened. And the rain fell upon the earth for forty days and forty nights" (Gen. 7:11-12).

The two sources of water for the Flood were the "floodgates of the sky" and the "fountains of the deep." As pointed out above, the expression "floodgates of the sky" is a hypocatastasis for a violent downpour of rain. Furthermore, the word translated "rain" (geshem) carries the notion of a "pouring rain" in distinction from the other words for rain — (māṭār)[65] or môreh, "a sprinkling rain." The word geshem is used of a "plentiful rain" (Psalm 68:9), and a "heavy rain" (1 Kings 18:41). So one is led to conceive not of a gentle rainfall, but of a torrential downpour. This is confirmed by the hypocatastasis "windows of heaven" referred to above. It pictures a violent rain.

What, then, constitutes a torrential downpour? Perhaps by observing contemporary rainfall rates we can determine some of the limits within which to interpret the rainfall rate of the flood. Cloud theorists may reject such pursuits as meaningless speculation, and, to a degree, they are correct. However, some kind of limits are certainly possible. There is no indication in the text of Scripture that the rainfall rate was beyond comprehension, just that it was heavy.

In New Orleans a rainfall rate of 4.7 inches per hour was reported on April 25, 1953.[66] In July 1862 in Cherrapunji, India, in 31 days it rained 366.14 inches, an average rate of ½ inch per

65. Keil and Delitzsch, 1:145.
66. Ray K. Linsley, Max A. Kohler, Joseph L. H. Paulhus, *Hydrology for Engineers*, p. 43.

hour.[67] On July 14, 1911 it rained 79.12 inches in 63 hours in Baguio, Philippines, about 1.25 inches per hour.[68] At Silver Hill, Jamaica, in the West Indies, rainfall for a four-day period during the passage of a hurricane amounted to 96.5 inches, about 1 inch per hour.[69] Monsoons in India are known to result in rainfall rates of 22 inches per hour, and rainfalls of up to 75 inches per hour have been reported.[70] Present data would then suggest that a torrential downpour would be more than a Sunday afternoon rain shower. It seems that a figure of several inches per hour to even 20 inches per hour could be used to fit well into the Genesis data of the great rain. For the purposes of a tentative model, let us pick a conservative rate, between 0.5 and 2 inches per hour. If it rained at that rate for 40 days and nights, between 40 and 160 feet of water would fall.

This certainly seems much more reasonable than Patten's estimate of a total of 18 to 36 inches of rainfall.[71] Over a 40-day period, 36 inches of rainfall would only amount to a rate of 0.036 inches per hour, hardly a "torrential downpour." In today's atmosphere, there is only about 2 inches of water.[72] Above the pre-Flood atmosphere there must have been at least 40 feet of water in the celestial ocean. Thus, the sheer amount of water necessary to sustain a torrential downpour for 40 days required a massive amount of water in the "waters above" and hence argues strongly for the liquid water rather than the cloud interpretation.

There are only three possible ways of avoiding this conclusion.

67. Ibid., p. 41.
68. Ibid.
69. Hunter Rouse, *Engineering Hydraulics*, p. 242.
70. Linsley, Kohler, and Paulhos, p. 41. This was a rate of 1.23 inches for one minute. Under flood conditions it would be conceivable that this rate could be maintained for hours, although it is impossible today.
71. Donald W. Patten, *The Biblical Flood and the Ice Epoch*, p. 204.
72. C. S. Fox, *Water*, p. xx.

Biblical Evidence for the Water Heaven Theory

The water was re-supplied through evaporation. It might be argued that during the rainfall, the waters were re-evaporated and cycled around and around, thus maintaining a torrential downpour rate for 40 days but without the necessity of 40 feet of water to do it. However, unless some unusual heat source was present, there could not have been any evaporation process going on during the rain to replenish the "waters above," because the atmosphere immediately above the earth was already at saturation level. The normal hydrologic cycle would, therefore, have been incapable of supplying the tremendous amounts of rain that the biblical record describes.

Other sources supplied the "waters above." As pointed out above, this appears to be an unlikely option. It seems that Moses intended to say that the only source of water that came through the windows of heaven was the water placed there on the second day (Gen. 1:6-7). However, cloud theorists and others who see the scientific difficulties of maintaining a literal ocean above the firmament have suggested several alternative explanations for the source of the rainfall. It should be emphasized here that the problem under discussion is not the source of water for the *Flood.* Presumably the majority of the flood waters came from the "fountains of the great deep" and from the ocean basin uplifts that spilled the oceans over the continents. The problem that is under consideration is only the source of the rain of the Flood — not the source of the flood waters themselves. As soon as the "waters above" are denied as the source, only two options remain: an extra-terrestrial source or a terrestrial source.

(1) Several have suggested that the source of the rain came from beyond planet earth. Patten, for example, suggested that an inter-planetary invader carrying an "ice-moon" came close enough to the earth for the "ice-moon" to be disintegrated. The ice particles then fell through the cloud cover canopy, precipitated it, and contributed to the rainfall of the flood.[73] While there may have been an ice planet, again exegesis requires that

---

73. Patten, p. 196.

the source of the rain was the waters in the heavenly ocean rather than outside invaders.

Reginald Daly proposes the fantastic suggestion that the water for the rain came "from heaven — beyond the edge of the universe." The great wind (Gen. 8:1) supposedly blew it off the earth again after the Flood and returned it to its original place above the heavens.[74]

(2) More commonly it is argued that the rain was recycled from terrestrial sources, that is, volcanoes. Since it is likely that the eruption of the fountains of the deep triggered violent volcanic activity, it is sometimes felt that volcanic water and surface water vaporized by lava were the main sources of the rainfall. Robert Whitelaw says, "The opening of the volcanic fountains throughout the great deep filled the heavens well into the stratosphere with steam and dust which quickly enveloped the globe, and rain began to fall as never before, rain that was continuously replenished by the continuous eruptions from beneath the seas."[75]

Perplexed by the problem of where the rain came from (since he does not believe in the canopy theory), Rehwinkel says, "How could the clouds form fast enough and continue to form and to produce those quantities of water required for a rain as described in Gen. 7:12? What produced the necessary evaporation? This is another of those questions for which we have no completely satisfactory answer."[76] In answer to this problem, he suggests that volcanic activity may provide the solution. He cites the fact that Mount Etna spewed out water at a rate of 4,600,000 gallons a day for 100 days when it was an active volcano. "And then imagine hundreds and thousands of volcanoes in furious activity all over the earth and in the seas, and the cloud-forming possibilities at once appear as beyond calculation."[77]

74. Reginald Daly, *Earth's Most Challenging Mysteries*, pp. 104-6.
75. Robert Whitelaw, "The Canopy Theory and the Rift-Drift-Shift Theory," personal communication, February 1976.
76. Alfred M. Rehwinkel, *The Flood*, p. 98.
77. Ibid., p. 100.

Biblical Evidence for the Water Heaven Theory

Now, the "cloud-forming possibilities" are not at all "beyond calculation." A simple approximation of the amount of water that could be contributed by the activity of volcanoes is easily presented.

Assuming the conservative rainfall rate of 0.5 inches per hour, one that has been observed for 31 days in India, this means that a total of 40 feet of water would fall during the global rain. This amounts to a volume of 2.2×10^{17} feet^3 or 1.37×10^{19} pounds of water. Rehwinkel suggests that thousands of volcanoes the size of Mount Etna could have supplied the necessary rain. Let us assume that 10,000 volcanoes (one volcano for every 140 x 140 miles plot of land and sea area of the earth) were spewing out 4,600,000 gallons of water per day and 100% of it was thrown into the rain cycle every day for 40 days. This would amount only to 1.534×10^{13} pounds of water or 0.000112% of the total rain needed.[78]

If 10,000 volcanoes were erupting at the same time, the earth would probably introduce many poisonous gases into the atmosphere. There are an estimated 1,400 volcanic cones on the floor of the ocean[79] and 516 known active volcanoes in the world today.[80] Normally, only a few volcanoes erupt every century and when they do, the effect on the earth's temperature is sufficient to reduce it by 4° F. for a number of years.[81] So unless all of that volcanic dust washed down in the canopy rain, the notion of 10,000 volcanoes going off at the same time during the Flood would unleash a catastrophe that could conceivably render the earth uninhabitable for Noah and his immediate descendants. However, let us maintain this fantastic figure in the following calculations.

78. These calculations are based on an assumed radius of the earth = 3,959 miles; the density of water = 62.4 pounds per cubic foot; and the weight of water = 8.337 pounds per gallon.
79. William A. Springstead, "Monoglaciology and the Global Flood," *Creation Research Society Quarterly*, 8 (December 1971):180.
80. Gordon A. MacDonald, *Volcanoes*, p. 450.
81. W. J. Humphreys, *The Physics of the Air*, p. 599.

A volcano could throw additional water into the rain cycle and hence, theoretically, contribute to the rain of the Flood in two ways: by steam emission and by evaporation of surface water due to heat. If the total heat emitted by a volcano is known, it is possible to estimate how much surface water it could evaporate. The heat of the volcano would be used in raising the temperature of the surrounding water from its initial temperature, T (assumed to be 80° F.), to boiling (212° F.) and then to vaporize that water once it has reached the boiling point. The equation for the total heat necessary to vaporize a given amount of water is:

$$Q = C_W M(T_S - T) + ML_W$$

$T_S = 212°$ F.; Q is the total heat in BTUs; C_W = the specific heat of water, 1 BTU/lb° F; M = the amount of water that would be turned to steam in pounds; and L_W is the latent heat of vaporization of water, 1075 BTU per pound at 0°C. Thus, if Q is known, it is a simple matter to solve for M.

Values of Q, total heat, for many different volcanoes have been estimated. Krakatoa (1883) emitted a total energy of 10^{25} ergs and Tambora (1815), the largest ever recorded, emitted 8.4 x 10^{26} ergs or 7.967 x 10^{16} BTUs.[82] Generally this volcanic heat is dissipated over a period of 3 to 30 years.[83] However, let us assume that 100% of the heat energy of 10,000 volcanoes all the size of Tambora was expended in 40 days. Furthermore, let us assume that all 10,000 of these volcanoes spewed out steam at a rate of 4,600,000 gallons a day like Mount Etna did. Finally, let us assume that 100% of the heat was applied to vaporizing water to put it into the rain cycle, and 100% of the steam was placed into the rain cycle. What percentage of the total water needed would this mechanism supply?

Granting these assumptions (all of which are impossibly favorable to the theory of the volcanic origin of the rain water), and assuming a moderate rainfall rate of 0.5 inches per hour for 40 days, 10,000 of these monster volcanoes would throw 1.534 x 10^{13} pounds of water into the rain cycle through steam and

82. MacDonald, p. 60.
83. Fred M. Bullard, *Volcanoes*, p. 62.

6.601 x 10^{17} pounds into it by vaporization of surface water, for a total of 6.601 x 10^{17} pounds. This amounts only to 4.8% of the total water needed. So even with these favorable assumptions, we can see that volcanic water would have had no significant bearing on the rainfall of a global deluge.

We need to note that the dissipation of heat energy from a volcano is exponential as a function of time. So much heat is dissipated at the first and the rate of dissipation gradually slows down over a period of many years. A volcano the size of Tambora, or any large volcano known for that matter, will take at least 30 years to dissipate all of its heat. Only a small percentage of that heat would be dissipated in the first 40 days. If one were to assume that 50% of the total energy was dissipated in the first 40 days (that is, in 0.365% of 30 years), these volcanic mechanisms would provide only 2.2% of the total water needed. Even this percentage is much too high because it is built on the assumption that 100% of the heat was used in vaporizing surface water, whereas most of it would be used up in simply heating the ocean water and the ground. Neither is it possible to assume that 100% of the water spewed forth as steam goes immediately into the rain cycle. Most of it would have been re-absorbed by cooling into the ocean waters before it ever escaped the surface of the ocean. Taking all of these factors into consideration, *it seems unlikely that volcanic activity could contribute more than 0.1% of the total water needed!*

Thus, this suggestion, like many which seem plausible until seriously quantified, is without basis. Volcanic waters and heat simply could not supply a sufficient amount of water to account for the amount of rain that fell during a 40-day rainfall of 0.5 inches per hour.

Besides the above arguments from the Scriptures regarding the existence of the water heaven, there are a number of indirect indications or "circumstantial" evidences of a climate that would be characteristic of a world surrounded by such a canopy. This circumstantial evidence is discussed in the next chapter.

CHAPTER 3

Other Scriptural Evidence for the Water Heaven

The presence of a water heaven above the earth would result in a markedly different climate than that which presently prevails in our world. Seasonal variations would be insignificant, rainbows would be absent, rainfall would not occur, and the earth would be watered by mists. Such a climate would be mild and Edenic. It would be interesting if there were indications in Scripture that such a unique climate characterized the antediluvian world.

No Rain but a Mist (Gen. 2:5-6)

Moses, in his record of creation, made an interesting comment relevant to pre-Flood climatology: "This is the account of the heavens and the earth when they were created, in the day that the Lord God made earth and heaven. Now no shrub of the field was yet in the earth, and no plant of the field had yet sprouted, for the Lord God had not sent rain upon the earth; and there was no man to cultivate the ground. But a mist used to rise from the earth and water the whole surface of the ground" (Gen. 2:4-6).

This passage is commonly taken among canopy theorists as a text indicating that prior to the Flood it did not rain.[1] Such a situation on a global basis would have been a natural result of

1. Issac Newton Vail, *The Deluge and Its Cause*, p. 66; Henry M. Morris and John C. Whitcomb, Jr., *The Genesis Flood*, pp. 215, 241; Donald W. Patten, "The Pre-Flood Greenhouse Effect," *A Symposium on Creation*, 2:25; Howard W. Kellogg, *The Canopied Earth*, p. 12.

an earth surrounded by the celestial ocean or a thermal vapor blanket. In such an environment a greenhouse effect would have resulted and the temperature differentials would be negligible, resulting in only minor wind movements, and hence, no rain.[2] Instead, the earth was watered by a "mist." During the cool of the day, the temperature would drop a few degrees and the water vapor in the atmosphere would condense out as a mist.[3] Hence, a mild, gentle climate would prevail with little erosion, no floods, or any of the other violent things associated with today's climatic regime.

Whether or not it would be possible for a world to exist without rain if there was a vapor canopy above the atmosphere is a question reserved for a later chapter. The question here is, Does Moses teach that prior to the Flood there was no rain?

The passage is fraught with difficulties, and few commentators see it as evidence of a no-rain climate prior to the Flood.[4]

AN APPARENT CONTRADICTION IN THE PASSAGE

Among the problems presented by this difficult passage, perhaps none has exercised the ingenuity of interpreters as has the apparent contradiction between two of the statements (Gen. 2:5 and 2:6). First, it is inferred that there was no vegetation "because" (*kî*) there was no moisture (2:5), yet it is then stated

2. A. James Wagner, "Some Geophysical Aspects of Noah's Flood," pp. 6-7.
3. This notion was generally confirmed by Edmond W. Holroyd, III, Ph. D. atmospheric science, Bureau of Reclamation, Boulder, Colorado, personal communication, 15 April 1977: "How to get normal rain out of an atmosphere with a canopy is an interesting problem. Dew and fog are going to be easier to derive than rain."
4. U. Cassuto, *A Commentary on the Book of Genesis*, 1:104; Harold G. Stigers, *A Commentary on Genesis*, p. 65; George Bush, *Notes on Genesis*, 1:53; John Peter Lange, "Genesis," *Lange's Commentary on the Holy Scriptures*, 1:202; C. F. Keil, *Genesis*, Biblical Commentary on the Old Testament, p. 78.

that the earth was watered by a "mist" ('ēd, 2:6). Competent scholars have suggested numerous solutions.

The two statements are contemporaneous. If they are contemporaneous, it might appear that they are contradictory.[5] Cassuto solves the difficulty by suggesting that particular plants only are referred to. The "shrub" (śîaḥ) cannot grow without rain, and the "plant" ('eśéb) cannot grow without a man to cultivate the field. Since thorns and thistles are connected with the curse (Gen. 3:18) and since it mentions 'ēśeb, he concludes that śîaḥ (2:5) refers to thorns which only grow up after a rain.[6] The dispensing and withholding of rain are thus connected with the dispensing of blessing for obedience and judgment for disobedience. While other plants were indeed in existence (at the time of 2:5), thorns (śîaḥ) and cultivated plants ('ēśeb) awaited judgment, rain, and the farmer (Adam), all of which were present by the fall. He concludes that it rained after the fall but not before. However, the connection of śîaḥ with the thorns (3:8) is gratuitous. (Why was not the word śîaḥ used in 3:18?) Furthermore, why cannot śîaḥ grow without rain? If the land was watered by a mist ('ēd), plenty of moisture was available.

Also, assuming the contemporaneous nature of the two statements (2:5 and 2:6), Paul Trudinger suggested a novel solution. He would translate ṭerem ("not yet") as "newly" and kî ("for") as "though," yielding the following translation, "In the day that the Lord God made the earth and the heavens, and every plant of the field was newly in the earth and every herb of

5. Skinner, for example, sees these verses as a confusion of sources: one from an arid country and one from a moist country. John Skinner, *A Critical and Exegetical Commentary on Genesis*, The International Critical Commentary, p. 56.
6. Cassuto, p. 102; also, Stigers, p. 65. Arthur Lewis similarly maintained, "This implies only the absence of field-crops, not the state of the earth before the day's work when all forms of vegetation were created." In "The Localization of the Garden of Eden," *Bulletin of the Evangelical Theological Society* 11 (Fall 1968):170.

the field had just begun to spring up, though the Lord God had not caused it to rain upon the earth and there was no man to till the ground; but a mist came up from the earth and watered the whole face of the ground."[7]

However, the translation of *kî* as "though" is rare, and the connection of *terem* with "fresh" or "recent" as its basic root is quite debatable.[8]

The second statement (2:6) is subsequent to the first (2:5). In order to avoid the apparent contradiction between these statements, others have suggested that the latter (2:6) is an event that occurred subsequent to the former (2:5).[9] McClellan summarizes, "If vegetation had not yet appeared for lack of moisture, it would be contradictory to say that anything sufficed 'to water all the surface of the soil' at the same time, unless there was too much water."[10] Meredith Kline, who shares this view, sees the mist (2:6) as answering, at a later time, the need for water expressed earlier (2:5), and the need for a farmer later (2:7).[11]

Even if one were to argue that the events of 2:6 are subsequent in thought if not in grammar,[12] some serious problems arise when an attempt is made to locate the precise time of 2:6 in the creation week. What day in the "day" of creation does 2:5 refer to? It cannot be before the third day because only water pre-

7. L. Paul Trudinger, " ' Not Yet Made' or 'Newly Made,' A Note on Genesis 2:5," *The Evangelical Quarterly* 47 (April-June 1975):68.
8. Francis Brown, S. R. Driver, and Charles A. Briggs, *A Hebrew and English Lexicon of the Old Testament*, p. 382; they say the root is unknown.
9. Franz Delitzsch, *A New Commentary on Genesis*, 1:117.
10. W. H. McClellan, "The Newly Proposed Translation of Genesis 2:5-6," *The Catholic Biblical Quarterly* 1 (1939):108.
11. Meredith G. Kline, "Because It Had Not Rained," *Westminster Theological Journal* 20 (May 1958):150.
12. The word order of 2:6 with the subject first followed by a verb in the imperfect normally indicates a disjunctive circumstantial clause contemporaneous with 2:5.

vailed, and no vegetation could have grown anyway. It cannot be later than the third day because all of the vegetation was created then ('ēśeb, 1:11). If 2:6 is subsequent to 2:5, this creates a ridiculous situation. God, on the morning of the third day, hesitates to create vegetation because there is no rain, and moisture will not be available until that afternoon (2:6). Even if śîaḥ and 'ēśeb refer to particular kinds of vegetation not created in 1:11, still it would appear that the plants could not await moisture for several days; but all plants customarily do so today.

The two statements are limited to the Garden of Eden. A third solution to this problem assumes that both statements refer only to unique conditions that existed in the Garden of Eden.[13] The thought would then be that there were no śîaḥ or 'ēśeb in Eden because it was not rain country; but there was rain elsewhere, because rainfall is normally considered to be global in nature. R. Laird Harris, who takes this view, sees the 'ēd as "river overflow."[14]

In justification for limiting these verses only to the Garden of Eden, it is often pointed out that by so doing it also solves another "contradiction" in the order of creation in Genesis 1 (vegetables *before* man) and Genesis 2 (man *before* vegetables).[15] Also, the thrust of the entire context is on the Garden of Eden, not on the world outside (2:7 ff.). Furthermore, verse 10 is very similar to verse 6 and might explain it.

> "A river went out of Eden to water the garden." The word for "river" is the usual Hebrew word used and the word "to water" is identical with the verb "watered" in vs. 6. It should be concluded that the watered

13. R. Laird Harris, "The Mist, the Canopy, and the Rivers of Eden," *Bulletin of the Evangelical Theological Society* 11 (Fall 1968):178; Keil, *Genesis,* p. 77. For discussion of the worldwide nature of the Edenic conditions, see Morris and Whitcomb, *The Genesis Flood,* pp. 454-73; for a contrary view, see Lewis, "The Localization of the Garden of Eden," pp. 169-75.
14. Harris, pp. 178-79.
15. Ibid., p. 178.

"garden" of vs. 10 is parallel to the watered "ground" of verse 6. Verse 6 does not refer to the whole globe at all. The whole passage refers only to Eden and it informs us that it was not a rain country; it was rather a territory watered by river overflow and irrigation.[16]

Beside the fact that it is highly unlikely that the conditions of the two statements can be limited to Eden, this explanation does not solve the apparent contradiction between these verses anyway. If plants in Eden cannot flourish because they lack moisture (2:5), why is the presence of moisture there (2:6)?

But the usage of 'ereṣ ("earth") renders the limitation to Eden quite unlikely. The word is used five ways in the Old Testament: earth, ground (similar to 'adāmâh), underworld, land (a circumscribed territory), and Canaan. Ottosson insists, "When 'ereṣ means a specific land it is always qualified by a genitive of direction, a topographical statement, etc., except in the case of the land of Canaan."[17] There are no such qualifying statements in Genesis 2:5-6.

Furthermore, Moses says the 'ēd rises from the 'ereṣ and waters the *whole surface* of the ground ('adāmâh). This word change would suggest that 'ereṣ has its common usage of the whole surface of the planet (1:1; 2:4 — immediate context!), that is, land *and* sea surface, while 'adāmâh is limited to the whole surface of the land in contrast to the land and sea. So the 'ēd rises from the land and sea surfaces and waters the 'adāmâh.

Finally, the subject of a localized Eden is not brought up until later (2:8). It would appear that the writer is moving from the general global situation in the "day" God made earth and heaven (2:4b-6) to the particular situation in Eden (2:7 ff.).

'Ēd refers to the deep. A final solution to this problem has been suggested by Derek Kidner.[18] He assumes the 'ēd means "a flood" and refers to the deep of Genesis 1:2. Thus, Moses began

16. Ibid.
17. Magnus Ottosson, "'Ereṣ," in *Theological Dictionary of the Old Testament*, 1:400.
18. Derek Kidner, "Genesis 2:5,6: Wet or Dry?" *Tyndale Bulletin* 17 (1966):112-13.

again by describing the situation on the first day of creation when the deep covered the earth (2:4 ff.). The 'ēd watered the earth in the sense of inundating it.

Several objections, however, might be raised. First, why is the order of 2:6 and 2:5 reversed? If Moses intended simply to start over, would it not have been more appropriate to begin with the 'ēd ("deep") and then go on to mention the lack of vegetation? That, at least, is the order of presentation in Genesis 1.

Second, the word shāqâh, "to water," is never used in the sense of a flood. It is used of irrigation by man (Deut. 11:10) and by a spring (Isa. 27:3), but always with a connotation of "refreshment." Kidner errs when he insists that the word can "denote any degree of watering."[19] He argues from another passage that the water can go "as far as the mountains" (Ezek. 32:6). However, this is a figurative statement for the land drinking *blood*, not water. The literal usages of shāqâh always carry the gentler sense of "to refresh, to give a drink" (Gen. 24:19), and never carry the catastrophic connotations of the judgmental flooding of the tᵉhôm (1:2). A global sea does not "water" or "refresh" the ground; it utterly inundates and buries it. The tᵉhôm (1:2) clearly speaks of the chaotic earth to which God gave form in the following verses.[20] Completely different concepts and nuances lie behind the word. Shāqâh would be singularly inappropriate to describe the tᵉhôm.

Finally, the Hebrews had several other words that clearly *do* refer to a flood, so why would Moses use one that never does if he intended to indicate a global inundation? The noun *mabbûl* (Gen. 7:6,7,10) would have been much more appropriate. In fact, if it be granted that there is a conceptual tie between the tᵉhôm ("chaos," 1:2) and the *mabbûl* ("flood," 7:6), which Kidner acknowledges,[21] would it not have been an even better choice? The verb nāhār (Job 22:16) would also be better for "flooding."

---

19. Ibid., p. 112.
20. See the discussion in chapter 1.
21. Derek Kidner, *Genesis*, p. 91.

All of the above solutions have weaknesses. However, before we suggest another solution to the apparent contradiction between the two passages, it is necessary to discuss the meaning of śîah haśśādeh, "shrub of the field;" 'ēśeb haśśādeh, "plant of the field;" and 'ēd, "mist."

THE SHRUB OF THE FIELD AND THE PLANT OF THE FIELD

In order to counter the common assertion that there is a contradiction between the order of creation in Genesis 1 (man *after* vegetables, 1:11) and Genesis 2 (man *before* vegetables, 2:7-8), it is often suggested that the vegetables (2:5) refer to a particular kind of vegetation that needed the cultivation of man and thus was not created on the third day (1:11).[22] Cassuto, Stigers, and Lange have all stressed that the "plant of the field" is a special category not mentioned on that day (1:11).[23] Keil follows this interpretation also, arguing that "field" (śādeh) refers not to the earth in general but to cultivated land.[24]

The word śîah ("shrub") is used only four times in the Old Testament.[25] In each case it refers to a desert shrub or a wild plant. The lexicon accordingly renders it as "bush, shrub, plant."[26] It is never used of thorns in particular and is never associated in context with the presence or absence of rain as a token of divine blessing or judgment. Therefore, Cassuto's equation of śîah with "thorns and thistles" (3:18) seems unfounded. It appears to be a general term for the undomesticated or wild plants of the earth.

The 'ēśeb, on the other hand, seems to be a general term for plants yielding food — domesticated plants. It is used eight times as a general term for vegetation;[27] six times as a figure of

22. For discussion of this "contradiction," see Skinner, p. 51, and S. R. Driver, *The Book of Genesis*, p. 35.
23. Cassuto, 1:101; Stigers, p. 65; and Lange, 1:200.
24. Keil, p. 77.
25. Genesis 2:5; 21:15; Job 30:4,7.
26. Brown, Driver, and Briggs, p. 967.
27. Exod. 10:12; Deut. 29:22 (Heb.); 32:2; Psalm 106:20; Isa. 42:15; Jer. 12:4; 14:6; Zech. 10:1.

speech;[28] seven times as a general term for food;[29] six times for crops;[30] and three times for plants yielding seed.[31] The distinction between crops, plants yielding seed, and food is not always precise, and these usages could, perhaps, be grouped as "cultivated vegetation." The lexicon renders it as "herb, herbage."[32]

In view of its usage in Genesis 1:11, 12, 29 (and perhaps 30), it seems unlikely to limit it to cereals or grain-producing plants as Cassuto does by paralleling 2:5 with 3:18. It is more likely that 'ēseb is simply another general term for vegetation that is the opposite of śîaḥ. Thus it refers to the domesticated plants in contrast to śîaḥ, which are wild undomesticated plants. No point can be made out of the fact that śîaḥ and 'ēseb are of the śādeh ("field"). While śādeh can mean "cultivated ground," its more common usage is simply "open field" or "country."[33] Besides, śîaḥ is never used of a cultivated or domestic plant. Śādeh clearly means "open field" in 2:19 where the phrase "beasts of the field" seems to parallel 1:25, "beasts of the earth" ('ereṣ), and refers to the wild animals of the open country. Thus, śādeh in 2:5 is a general term as it is in 2:19 and 1:25.

We conclude then that there is no clear basis for the common assumption that śîaḥ haśśādeh and 'ēseb haśśādeh are particular plants not mentioned on the third day (1:11). They are most naturally taken as broad terms for the two general categories of vegetation, wild and domesticated. Indeed, the only reason for arguing otherwise is simply that it would supposedly solve the apparent contradiction between 1:11 and 2:5 in the order of creation.

28. 2 Kings 19:26; Job 5:25; Psalms 72:16; 92:8; 104:14; Isa. 37:27.
29. Gen. 1:30; 9:3; Exod. 9:22, 25; Deut. 11:15; Psalm 106:20; Prov. 27:25.
30. Gen. 2:5; 3:18; Amos 7:2; Psalms 104:14; 105:35; Mic. 5:7 (NASB).
31. Gen. 1:11, 12, 29.
32. Brown, Driver, and Briggs, p. 793.
33. Ibid., p. 961.

A MIST USED TO RISE FROM THE EARTH

Many canopy theorists have believed that Genesis 2:6 provides a striking bit of circumstantial evidence for the existence of the ancient water heaven. Such a world would indeed be watered by mists and would be without rain. However, the Hebrew word 'ed ("mist,") is of uncertain meaning and has been translated in at least six different ways.

Spring. The LXX translated 'ēd as pēgē, "spring." McClellan summarizes, "Pēgē in the LXX, fons in the Vulgate, mabbua in the Pesitta, and epiblusmos in Aquila, all amount to 'spring' or 'fount.' "[34] However, we would expect the Hebrew word 'ayin if spring were meant.

Subterranean water. Albright has argued that the word is to be derived from the Sumerian river deity, Id: "It is to the Id, the subterranean source of fresh water, that the 'ēd of Genesis 2:6 must be traced."[35]

Inundation, overflow of a river. Speisor suggests that the word is derived from the Sumerian edu which means a flood or river overflow.[36] Harris, Kline, and others follow this view.[37]

Canal water. McClellan cites Deimal, Sachsse, and Theiss as deriving 'ēd from the Sumerian id, but rendering it "canal" rather than "subterranean water."[38]

The primeval sea. This older interpretation[39] has recently been adopted by Kidner.[40] He connects it with the t^{e}hôm (1:2).

34. McClellan, p. 110.
35. William F. Albright, "The Predeuteronomic Primeval," *Journal of Biblical Literature* 58 (1939):103.
36. E. A. Speisor, " 'Ed in the Story of Creation," *Bulletin of the American Schools of Oriental Research* 140 (December 1955):9-11.
37. Harris, "The Mist, the Canopy," p. 178; Kline, "Because It Had Not Rained," p. 150.
38. McClellan, p. 111.
39. Ibid., p. 110.
40. Kidner, "Genesis 2:5,6: Wet or Dry?," p. 110.

The unlikely nature of this suggestion has already been discussed.

Mist. This is the traditional rendering. According to McClellan, it was so translated by the Samaritan Targum, the Aramaic Targum of Onqelos, the !uthorized and Revised Versions, the Jewish Publication Society version, by the versions of Moffat and Meek in English, and of Fillion and Crampon in French; by the commentators Mariana, Malvenda, Calmet, Houbigant, Rosenmuller, Lamy, Hammelauer, Dillman, Hoberg, Spurrell, Procksch, Murillo, Hetzenauer, and Eduard Konig; also in the latter's Hebrew lexicon, and in Cowley's grammar.[41] It is accepted by Keil,[42] Leupold,[43] Lange,[44] Bush,[45] Calvin,[46] and Jamieson.[47] It has also been accepted by Driver,[48] Delitzsch,[49] and the lexicon of Brown, Driver, and Briggs.[50]

With such weighty traditional support behind the translation "mist," as well as its general acceptance by modern translators, we should look carefully before seeking to contradict it. Because the word is used only two times in the Old Testament, and because the root of the word is of uncertain origin, it appears that until we discover some extra-biblical Hebrew usages, the true meaning may never be known with precision. However, any translation of 'ēd should satisfy three criteria.

41. McClellan, p. 111.
42. Keil, p. 78.
43. H. C. Leupold, *Exposition of Genesis*, p. 113.
44. Lange, 1:102.
45. Bush, 1:53.
46. John Calvin, "Genesis," 1:17.
47. Robert Jamieson, "Genesis," in Robert Jamieson, A. R. Fausset, and David Brown, *A Commentary Critical, Experimental and Practical on the Old and New Testaments*, 1:34.
48. Driver, p. 37.
49. Delitzsch, p. 117. He connects it with the Arabic *ijad-atm*.
50. Brown, Driver, and Briggs, p. 15, where they suggest the doubtful derivation from the Arabic "be strong," hence that which provides protection or shade, that is, a "cloud." But also note p. 1119, where this derivation is labeled very dubious and the Akkadian *edu* is suggested as a possibility.

(1) *The nature of the "watering."* As pointed out above, shāqâh has the gentle notion of "refreshment" rather than the catastrophic notion of a flood or judgment. Hence the meaning "primeval sea" is doubtful. Mist, river, canal, or subterranean waters would be quite appropriate.

(2) *Comparative philology.* In the North East Semitic or Akkadian languages (2500-600 B. C.) we find two words which are apparently loan words from the ancient Sumerian (3000-2500 B. C.): *edu* and *id*. Albright connected *'ēd* with *id* and translated it as "subterranean source of fresh water."[51] Speisor argues against the identification of *'ēd* with *id* on the grounds that the Sumerian logogram in question was generally read in Akkadian as *naru*, "river," and normally would not have led to the Hebrew *'ēd*.[52] Furthermore, Albright's translation of "subterranean source of fresh water" lacks contextual justification.

The Akkadian *edu* is defined as "onrush of water, high water."[53] While this could have been carried over into Hebrew as *'ēd*, it would normally be *'edāh* or *'ēdē* (an original longer form could have led to *'ēd*). Furthermore, the dictionary connects it with sea waves, a raging tide, or a huge flood. "The phenomenon referred to by *edu* is a rare and catastrophic event."[54] One does not "refresh" the land with a "catastrophic flood." Moses also describes a recurrent phenomenon (the frequentive imperfect, "to water") and not a rare one (Gen. 2:6).

So while the etymology is certainly tempting, there is nothing particularly compelling about it. Carrying a root meaning in one language over into another is always precarious, particularly when there is obvious difference of scholarly opinion as to

51. Albright, p. 103.
52. Speisor, " *'Ed* in the Story of Creation," p. 9. Eugene Merrill has observed that the "Sumerian *id* could lead to *'ēd* on phonetic grounds, but it is impossible to prove etymologically and unlikely semantically." Professor Eugene Merrill, professor of Old Testament, Dallas Theological Seminary, personal communication, 27 March 1978.
53. Ignace J. Gelb et al., *The Assyrian Dictionary of the Oriental Institute of Chicago*, p. 35.
54. Ibid., p. 36.

Other Scriptural Evidence for the Water Heaven

which is the true root. The primary source of information on word meaning is usage in the Hebrew Bible. That should always take precedence over proposed root derivations in cognate languages. However, there is only one other place in the Old Testament where the word is used: Job 36:27.

(3) *Usage in Job 36:27.* Those who accept the derivation of *'ēd* from *id* or *edu* typically say that the meaning of *'ēd* in this passage is "inconclusive,"[55] "a guess,"[56] "too obscure to afford us much light."[57] The passage reads as follows:

> For He draws up the drops of water,
> They distill rain from the mist,
> Which the clouds pour down,
> They drip upon man abundantly (Job 36:27-28).

While it is true that the meaning here is not conclusive (it is not), yet it is not at all obscure. In fact, the most obvious and natural meaning is clearly "mist." It seems that those who are committed to the Akkadian derivation have simply thrown up a cloud of dust and then complained, "We cannot see!"

Marvin Pope states dogmatically, "The conjectured meaning 'mist' is certainly erroneous."[58] He then cites Albright and Speisor in support of his interpretation of *'ēd* as "subterranean cosmic reservoir," and makes no attempt to integrate this meaning of *'ēd* into the context. How do raindrops distill rain (or "into" rain) out of a subterranean cosmic reservoir?

We find no synonymous parallelism between the two lines (verses 27a and 27b). This is clear from the fact that "draws" (verse 27a) is third person singular while "distill" (verse 27b) is third person plural. So there is no necessary parallel of drawing up water from below (27a), and distilling rain upward from below (27b). If one were to think of distilling rain upward from below, perhaps some kind of an idea of "from a flood" or surface water would be appropriate. Even if the verses were in synonymous parallelism, the verb *gāra'* ("draws") does not

---

55. Speisor, p. 9.
56. Kidner, "Genesis 2:5,6: Wet or Dry?", p. 110.
57. McClellan, p. 110.
58. Marvin H. Pope, *Job*, The Anchor Bible, p. 235.

mean to draw "up." It simply means to "withdraw" with no reference to direction; and it can even mean "restrain."[59] The piel imperfect could therefore be translated, "He restrains the drops of water."

A problem arises with the third person plural verb (verse 27b). How do drops of water distill rain from the 'ēd? The Revised Standard Version solves it by arbitrarily changing the plural to a singular without evidence of manuscript corruption, and renders it: "he distils his mist in rain." A simpler solution is to take the māṭār ("rain") as the remote object of the verb and render, "they distill into rain."[60]

The verb zāqaq, "distill," means to "refine," as in the extraction of gold and silver out of ore (Job 28:1).[61]

As to the meaning of 'ēd, the most natural meaning is "mist." This is followed by Fausset,[62] Dhorme,[63] Delitzsch,[64] Zockler,[65] and many others. Pope's insistence that 'ēd mean "the flood" results in the following translation: "He draws the waterdrops that distill rain from the flood, that trickle from the clouds." Rowley is correct when he says, "This is not lucidly expressed, and the conception is not very convincing."[66]

It is quite natural to see the passage as describing the successive steps in the formation of rain.[67] First, the ascent of water drops in evaporation (verse 27a); second, the distilling of rain

59. Brown, Driver, and Briggs, p. 175.
60. Otto Zockler, *The Book of Job*, in John Peter Lange, ed., *A Commentary on the Holy Scriptures*, p. 148.
61. Brown, Driver and Briggs, p. 279.
62. A. R. Fausset, "The Book of Job," in Robert Jamieson, A. R. Fausset, and David Brown, *A Commentary Critical, Experimental and Practical on the Old and New Testaments*, 3:88.
63. E. Dhorme, *A Commentary on the Book of Job*, p. 553.
64. F. Delitzsch, *The Book of Job*, Biblical Commentary on the Old Testament, p. 288.
65. Zockler, p. 148.
66. H. H. Rowley, *Job*, p. 299.
67. Zockler, p. 586. Contrary to Pope, p. 236, there is nothing "fanciful" about this conception at all.

out of the mist which the evaporated water drops produced (verse 27b); and third, the fall of the rain to the earth (verse 28). This is the traditional view, and makes much better sense than any construction in which *'ēd* is rendered "flood."

A correct translation might go something like this:

> For He draws up the drops of water
> They distill into rain from the mist,[68]
> Which the clouds pour down,
> They drip upon man abundantly.

Because *'ēd* is used in only one other place in the Old Testament (beside Genesis 2:6), we can draw no certain conclusions as to its meaning. However, it is clearly perferable to interpret it as "mist" or "cloud" in Job 36:27. When translated "flood," it is not nearly as lucid.

The translations derived from *edu* or *id* do not satisfactorily meet the three criteria listed above and are debatable anyway. Since the traditional interpretation makes at least as good sense in Genesis 2:6 and much better sense in Job 36:27 than the new translations, there seems to be no compelling reason for abandoning it. Thus, tentatively, "mist" will be maintained in this discussion as the correct translation of *'ēd*.

A SUGGESTED SOLUTION TO THE APPARENT CONTRADICTION
BETWEEN THE TWO PASSAGES (2:5 AND 2:6)

The key to unraveling this difficult problem has been suggested by Leupold.[69] The *waw* ("and") which begins the passage (2:5-6) is not sequential, whereas the *waws* in chapter 1 are. In other words, it is to be translated with a sense of "also" rather than "next." The writer's choice of sequential *waws* in chapter 1 indicates his intention to stress sequence. As a result, there is no conflict between chapters 1 and 2 in the order of creation because no sequence is intended in chapter 2.

68. The *lāmed* in front of *'ēd* may be translated "from," see C. H. Gordon, *Ugaritic Textbook*, 10:1.
69. Leupold, p. 108.

What, then, is the reason for abandoning the *waw* consecutive in chapter 2? Is it not that Moses intended a thematic or topical arrangement in chapter 2? He is moving quickly into the account of God's work in the creation of man. The details of the general creation are unimportant here and are included only to provide a backdrop for the creation of man.

We should also remember that there is a particular "situation in life" into which this account was first applied.[70] The Hebrews were in the desert, without rain and without farmland. As they grumbled about no water, no figs, and no food, Moses reminded them that there was a time in which there was no rain, no vegetation, and no cultivation of fields. But God created vegetation, watered the world with a "mist," and, after creating man, provided a paradise for him. In the same way, they were now about to enter Canaan, a land that would have water and farmland, and the same God who solved the "no water — no form" problem on a worldwide basis in the original creation would certainly provide for them during their wanderings and conquest. So without reference to particular sequence, he simply described a "time" in which many of the things they presently lack (1440 B. C.) were not in existence at all; but the God of creation had provided once before — He would do it again. So Genesis 2:5-6 might be paraphrased this way:

> This is the account of the heavens and the earth when they were created, in the day that the Lord made earth and heaven. Now there was a time when there were no wild plants in the earth and when no domesticated plants had yet sprouted, indeed the Lord had not sent rain upon the earth; and there was no man to cultivate the ground. But a mist used to rise from the entire land and sea surface and water the whole surface of the land.

Note in the above paraphrase that *kî* ("for") is translated as "indeed" instead of as "for" in the sense of "because."[71] Much

---

70. This suggestion was made by Dr. Kenneth Barker, professor of Old Testament, Dallas Theological Seminary, personal communication, May, 1977.
71. Brown, Driver, and Briggs, p. 472.

Other Scriptural Evidence for the Water Heaven

of the difficulty in harmonizing the two statements in the passage has been that the cause for the lack of śîah and 'ēseb was assumed to be the lack of rain and of a farmer. This created needless complications, which are resolved simply by translating kî as "indeed" in accord with the general thematic notion of the context that "there was a time" when certain things known in 1440 B. C. did not exist at all. Conditions were once much different than they were then; indeed there was no rain and a mist watered the land.

No rain before the Flood. After listing the "time" in which there was no śîah haśśādeh or 'ēseb haśśādeh, or man, or rain, Moses goes on to mention the creation of vegetation (1:11; 2:8), the creation of man (2:7), but there is no mention of the creation of rain. In fact, only an explanatory statement was offered clarifying how the world was watered in the absence of rain. There was no rain but a mist. All of the items mentioned as absent (2:5) are soon brought into existence, but there is no mention of rain until the Flood (7:4). When it is mentioned, the same expression is used: māṭar ("to rain"). Both carry the notion of "to send rain" (hiphil). Since there are several Hebrew expressions for "to rain" (yārāh, gāsham) it may be significant that the same word, māṭar is used in both passages.

In a book of beginnings it is fair to assume that a first mention may be a first occurrence. Also, if the conceptual tie between "the waters above" and the "windows of heaven" be granted, this would further support the notion of no rain prior to the Flood. There was no rain until the waters above returned to the earth as rain when the windows of heaven were first opened.

NO RAINBOWS PRIOR TO THE FLOOD (GEN. 9:13)

When Noah got off the ark, God established a covenant with the human race through Noah in which He promised that He would never again destroy the planet by water. He also gave a sign of that covenant.

> And God said, "This is the sign of the covenant which I am making between Me and you and every living creature that is with you, for all successive generations; I set My bow in the

cloud, and it shall be for a sign of a covenant between Me and the earth. And it shall come about, when I bring a cloud over the earth, that the bow shall be seen in the cloud, and I will remember My covenant, which is between Me and you and every living creature of all flesh; and never again shall the water become a flood to destroy all flesh. When the bow is in the cloud, then I will look upon it, to remember the everlasting covenant between God and every living creature of all flesh that is on the earth" (Gen. 9:12-16).

Our first impression in reading this is that it refers to the first appearance of the rainbow in the heavens after the Flood. If this were true, it would have relevance to the canopy theory. Charles Clough has observed[72] that complete rainbows can form only when there are water droplets greater than 0.30 millimeters in the atmosphere.[73] This droplet size approaches that of falling rain rather than cloud droplets.[74] The optical phenomenon of the rainbow is thus intimately tied in with the existence of rain. If there are no droplets large enough to fall as rain, there will be no rainbow. Water droplets less than the size necessary to produce rain would be "mist," so the connections between no rain, mist, and no rainbows prior to the Deluge mutually reinforce one another as the probable interpretations.[75]

However, there are two possible ways of reading Genesis 9:13: "It may convey either (a) the unscientific idea that the rainbow was *created* after the Flood, or (b) the idea that the rainbow, already created, was then appointed to have a new significance as a symbol of mercy. Those who regard the narra-

72. Charles Albert Clough, "A Calm Appraisal of *The Genesis Flood*," p. 62.
73. Red fades out for droplets below this diameter. See John C. Johnson, *Physical Meteorology*, p. 184.
74. Shower rain has been observed to range from 0.50 to 4.00 mm. in diameter. Ibid., p. 220.
75. Merrill F. Unger, *Archaeology and the Old Testament*, p. 62; Donald Wesley Patten, *The Biblical Flood and the Ice Epoch*, p. 197.

Other Scriptural Evidence for the Water Heaven

tive as strictly historical can of course adopt only the latter of these views."[76] Several objections have been raised against the idea that this text teaches that the rainbow was created after the Flood.

First, as Patrick has mentioned, this is considered scientifically impossible.[77] However, it is only scientifically impossible if there was rain before the Flood; but a water heaven would preclude rain and we have already shown that there is good evidence that, according to the Genesis account, there was no rain, only mists. It is scientifically impossible if there was no vapor canopy, but since the canopy's existence is assumed here, this difficulty is removed.

Second, Cassuto has argued that since the verb *nātan* ("to make" or "to place") is in the present tense in verse 12 and in the perfect tense in verse 13, a deliberate contrast must be intended between the presently instituted sign in verse 12 and the past created rainbow in verse 13.[78] It is hard to see how this objection can be entertained seriously. The perfect tense would only mean that the rainbow was created sometime before it was appointed as a sign but says nothing about how long before. (It could have been one second!) Apparently it appeared in the heavens right after the Flood. It was a sign at that time of God's promise never again to inundate the earth. However, it had not yet been explained to Noah. In this passage God explains that the rainbow has been instituted as a sign of the covenant.

Third, Taylor Lewis has argued that, since the rainbow is designated as "My bow," this "shows that there was something to Him so called from the beginning."[79] But it obviously could have been called God's bow simply because He placed it in heaven after the Flood as a sign of the covenant.

Finally, it is often argued that God has frequently taken common practices like circumcision and baptism and invested them with special significance.

76. James Patrick, "Rainbow," in *Hastings' Dictionary of the Bible*, 4:196.
77. Ibid.
78. Cassuto, 2:138.
79. Taylor Lewis, note in Lange, 1:328.

> It was not the covenant itself, but only the token of that covenant; and just as the baptismal application of water, and the use of bread and wine in the Lord's Supper, both of which were adopted from existing usages, were constituted the symbols of spiritual blessings, so the rainbow was now consecrated to God to be a sign and seal of that covenant by which He pledged Himself that the water "should not be any more a flood to destroy the earth" and that upon the sight of it, He would remember His covenant.[80]

However, this is clearly an invalid analogy. While it may be true that God has used common practices like baptism or passover, and later invested them with new meanings, there is no evidence of His doing so in the early chapters of Genesis. The time periods labeled "for signs and for seasons" (Gen. 1:14) certainly did not exist prior to their first mention, and neither did the mark which the Lord appointed as a sign for Cain (Gen. 4:15). Prior usage, therefore, suggests that the introduction of an item as a sign amounts to the introduction of the item itself.

Also, this analogy breaks down in that the rainbow is an entirely different kind of sign than baptism, circumcision, or the Lord's Supper. These other signs are things done by man and made by man, but the rainbow is made by God alone. Jacob observes:

> The rainbow as a sign of the covenant has no parallels. Other signs are made by man, and remind him of a covenant with God as they are based on a commandment of His, e.g., the circumcision or the sanctification of the Sabbath .... The blood of the passover lamb in Egypt will be seen by God, but the Israelites shall put it on the doorposts. Man however does not make the rainbow nor shall he look upon it as a reminder of an obligation.[81]

The other signs remind man of an obligation — the rainbow reminds God of one; thus, it is a different category of sign. When God establishes a sign for Him to remember, He does not adopt a human procedure and invest it with new significance.

80. Jamieson, "Genesis," 1:106.
81. B. Jacob, *The First Book of the Bible: Genesis*, p. 66.

Other Scriptural Evidence for the Water Heaven

But even if it be granted that the usage of signs in other areas was sometimes built on the prior existence of the phenomenon now invested with new significance, it does not automatically follow that this is the situation here (Gen. 9:13). There has to be a first time for everything. However, it is reasonable and logical to assume that the first mention of such a sign would be its first occurrence, even if it cannot be proved.

But there are several reasons for considering that Genesis 9:13 does indeed refer to the post-diluvian origin of the rainbow.

First, the previous parallels with the sign of Cain (Gen. 4:15) and the stars for signs (Gen. 1:14) suggest that first mention of a phenomenon created directly by God refers to its first actual existence.

Second, the verb *nātan* is customarily translated "to put" or "to set."[82] While the usage "to appoint" is well established (Num. 14:4; 1 Kings 2:35), we get the immediate first impression on reading the passage that God "placed" the rainbow in the sky rather than "appointed" it as a sign. God would have said, "I appoint My bow in the cloud *as* a sign," rather than "I appoint My bow in the cloud and it shall be a sign."

Third, the independent meteorological correlation is striking. The independently deduced exegetical phenomena of no rain, no rainbow, and a world watered by a mist are precisely what the meteorology of situation would predict. Yet this knowledge of meteorology and of the optical properties of water drops was certainly beyond Moses.

Fourth, if the rainbow was a common phenomenon observed by men since creation, it is doubtful that its appearance in the heavens would provide much assurance that God would never again send a flood. Bush has summarized this quite well:

> The grand import which God intended to convey by this sign was that of *assurance of security* against the occurrence of another deluge, and had not the phenomenon been new, had men been familiar with it in past ages, it is not altogether easy to see how it could have been efficacious

---

82. Brown, Driver, and Briggs, p. 678.

enough to overcome the doubts and fears which it was intended to remove. "What guaranty does this afford us," they might say, "that we shall not be deluged again, since we have often beheld this sight, and were deluged notwithstanding?"[83]

It can hardly be argued that God's verbal promise made their security certain enough, because then it must be asked, "What need was there of any outward sign at all? Was not His word as certain without a sign as with it?"

Thus, we agree with Keil that "the establishment of the rainbow as a covenant sign of the promise that there should be no flood again presupposes that it appeared then for the first time."[84] This is the natural impression produced on the mind of anyone who reads the narrative without reference to any particular theory of prehistory. "And no one can doubt that the effect upon Noah's mind would have been far more vivid and striking had this been the first time the splended sight had met his eye."[85]

A bow, bent but without a string, and pointing toward the sky and not toward men, was a fitting symbol for this promise.

No Seasons Prior to the Flood (Gen. 8:22)

Seasons are mentioned for the first time as markers of climate changes (Gen. 8:22). This could mean that they began after the Flood. If so, another independent, yet physically related phenomenon can be deduced from the text. A lack of seasons would suggest a very slight pole-equator temperature difference. With no temperature differences, air masses would be of the same density and pressure and there would therefore be only minor air movement and little rainfall.[86] This would be a likely effect of a water vapor canopy.

83. Bush, 1:157.
84. Keil, 154.
85. Bush, 1:157.
86. A. James Wagner, "Some Geophysical Aspects of Noah's Flood," pp. 6-7.

However, if the canopy suddenly condensed, the greenhouse effect would be lost and seasonal variations would have been introduced for the first time.

It is, of course, impossible to prove that this text gives us the introduction of seasons. However, the lack of seasons correlates well with a no rain, no rainbow climate and a world watered by a mist. The mutual interdependence of these independently deduced exegetical data is impressive. Also, it is certainly reasonable to assume, as in the case of the rainbow, that first mention is first existence.

Some have objected, however, that seasons are mentioned on the fourth day of Creation (Gen. 1:14). But the seasons there are not climatic seasons but are for marking periods of time. It is not till this passage (Gen. 8:22) that there is any mention of such variations as summer, winter, cold, and heat.

This passage climaxes the theme of God's control over chaos. During the Flood year, God released His restraint on the waters of chaos, and disorder reigned. Now the uniformity of nature is being established by the divine will. Chaos is once again under Yahweh's control. God conquers chaos, restrains chaos, releases it to do His bidding, and then imposes His control over it once again whenever He chooses. This assurance is the basis for the Christian's confidence in the uniformity of nature. It is why the Christian accepts one of the basic precepts of modern science, that is, that nature is predictable. When a scientist performs an experiment in the laboratory and it is repeated later, he will get exactly the same results if he follows the same procedure. The secular scientist has no solid basis for his belief in this principle; the Christian does — God's providence.

The text, then, implies that seedtime and harvest, cold and heat, were introduced for the first time, and, in the words of Walter Brueggeman: "They are rather the assurance that disruptions which break up the orderly, peaceful, reliable foundations of life, which all may be referred to as "chaos," have now been dispelled from life or at least brought under effective control."[87] This situation stands in sharp contrast to the Flood,

87. Walter Brueggeman, "Kingship and Chaos," *The Catholic Biblical Quarterly* 33 (July 1971):320.

where death and disorder reigned (Gen. 7:22ff.). Now there is life and order. The text is a kind of "royal decree" which asserts the re-establishment of the kingship of Yahweh over the chaos of the Flood.[88]

In Greek, the opposite of "chaos" (disorder) is "cosmos" (order). Our word "cosmetics" comes from the Greek verb *kosmeō*, which means "to make order out of chaos."[89] That is what God did here (Gen. 8:22).

Note that this situation of imposed order was to last "while the earth remains." Would not this suggest that never again would a total disruption of the earth occur until the Second Coming? If so, it would tend to rule out theories of extensive post-Flood catastrophes as an explanation of the geologic column.[90]

It is worth noting that in confirmation of the "control over chaos" theme suggested above, that the last line of the promise reads, "Shall not cease" (Gen. 8:22), where "cease" is the Hebrew verb *shābat*, from which "Sabbath" is derived. This parallels the conclusion of the story of creation where Moses says, "He [God] rested on the seventh day" (Gen. 2:2-3). The use of the same verb at the end of both accounts points to a similar theme: God's work is finished. He is through creating, and He is through "re-creating," that is, setting up the *new* order. Just as the old order could not be changed unless God permitted it, neither can the seasonal variations of the new order be interrupted unless God permits it. All is under His control even when He rests. The pagan deities, on the other hand, never rested; they were in a continual struggle.

---

88. Walter Brueggeman, "Weariness, Exile, and Chaos," *The Catholic Biblical Quarterly* 34 (January 1972):19.
89. Henry George Liddell and Robert Scott, *A Greek-English Lexicon*, p. 835.
90. Immanuel Velikovsky, *Worlds in Collision*; other creationist writers like Donald Patten, who see a series of post-Flood catastrophes in *The Long Day of Joshua*; and the writings of Bernard E. Northrop.

So the first eight chapters of Genesis are unified around the theme of the conquest and restraint of chaos in which an antimythical motif prevails.[91] This may be diagrammed as in Table 3.1.

TABLE 3.1

YAHWEH'S CONTROL OVER CHAOS

CREATION	ADAM TO NOAH	FLOOD	POST-FLOOD
Conquest of Chaos	Restraint of Chaos	Release of Chaos	Restraint of Chaos
Gen. 1:1 2:4	2:5 7:11	7:12 8:21	8:22

IT WAS VERY GOOD (GEN. 1:31)

This combination of texts concerning the rainbow, no rain, and the seasons leads us to the conclusion that the Bible teaches that prior to the Flood the earth enjoyed a mild climate, was without storms, and was watered by a mist. Furthermore, as far as the physics of the situation are concerned, it is possible to construct a model that would result in a moderate, universally warm climatic regime due to the effects of a vapor canopy.

Another passage has some bearing on this question. Moses wrote, "And God saw all that He had made, and behold, it was very good" (Gen. 1:31). It seems justifiable to raise the question as to whether the present day climatic regime could, by any stretch of the imagination, be considered "good" for man or beast. Today, nearly 60 percent of the earth's surface is not suitable for human habitation. Vast areas of the planet are covered with arctic barrens and arid deserts. Hurricanes and earthquakes regularly wrench a terrifying death toll and cause immense human suffering. Are these things "good"? Is the present climate and all that comes with it, both good and bad, really what the loving Creator originally intended? Actually,

---

91. D. F. Payne, *Genesis One Reconsidered*, p. 22.

according to Rehwinkel, only 40 percent of the land surface is really suitable for man's existence, even though he can survive in other areas.[92] Could not one imply from this reference that the ancient earth was much more suitable to human habitation? Such mild conditions would be a result of a water heaven.

Ancient Longevity

We must now give some consideration to the references to the longevity of life of the antediluvian patriarchs (Gen. 5). Certainly such incredibly long lifespans suggest that *something* was different. A TV documentary some years ago suggested that 90 percent of cancers are caused by environmental factors. Perhaps there could be other factors related to our general climate and environment that were conducive to longevity in the pre-Flood world, and when they were taken away, longevity declined. It is certainly significant that it was after the Flood (that is, after the "waters above" had crashed down to earth) that longevity began to decline (see Gen. 11). Could these "waters above" have contributed in some way to ancient climatology so that the antediluvians could live an average of 912 years?

It may well be that the ancient climate was much milder and more suitable to human life. At least these two passages (Gen. 1:31; 5:1-31) could strongly suggest it. Such a climate modification would have been the result of an earth surrounded by a vapor canopy with its protection against the sun's actinic (shortwave) radiation and the damper on storm systems that would certainly have resulted.

Noah's Drunkenness (Gen. 9:21)

"Then Noah began farming and planted a vineyard. And he drank of the wine and became drunk" (Gen. 9:20-21). The question of how the only righteous man on the face of the earth (Gen. 6:5-9) — the one who *alone* was righteous (Gen. 7:1); who had just witnessed the most amazing intervention of God in

---

92. Alfred M. Rehwinkel, *The Flood in the Light of the Bible, Geology, and Archaeology,* pp. 1-4.

Other Scriptural Evidence for the Water Heaven 103

history and had experienced his miraculous preservation through a holocaust (Gen. 8:1); who walked with God and built altars for worship (Gen. 8:20); and who had just talked with the Lord as the Noahic Covenant was established (Gen. 9:9-17) — could possibly immediately afterward sin by getting drunk, has perplexed many interpreters. Furthermore, there is no indication of a rebuke or moral condemnation from the Lord of his activity.

There is a possible explanation of this uncharacteristic behavior that provides circumstantial evidence for the existence of the water heaven. Assuming a water heaven of 40 feet or more of precipitable water, as discussed in the previous chapter, the surface atmospheric pressure would be 2.18 atm. This would increase the partial pressure of carbon dioxide (CO_2) by a multiple of 2.18. This, in turn, would slow down the rate of fermentation of grapes. Louis Pasteur discovered the basic chemical reaction involved:[93]

$$C_6H_{12}O_6 \rightarrow 2CO_2 + 2C_2H_5OH$$

The equation describes the conversion of glucose to alcohol and carbon dioxide gas. The reaction can only proceed as the CO_2 is allowed to escape, and a higher atmospheric pressure will result in a higher partial pressure of CO_2 which, in turn, will retard the escape of CO_2. In the ancient world it would have taken longer for the wine to be produced under the conditions of a doubled partial pressure of CO_2. Once the canopy had condensed, the rate of formation of the alcohol in the wine would be speeded up, and Noah was simply caught off guard. There was more alcohol in that wine than there would have been in grapes fermenting for the same length of time under the water heaven.

A second factor that may have caught Noah off guard was that drunkenness occurs much more rapidly at lower pressures. If he had been used to an atmospheric pressure of 2.18 and drank wine under new conditions, he could have unintentionally gotten drunk. In altitude tests on a study of fifty-four human

---

93. "Fermentation," in *Van Nostrand's Scientific Encyclopedia*, p. 1014.

subjects, it was found that blood alcohol detention for subjects receiving a high dosage of alcohol yielded significantly higher levels of blood alcohol for subjects at 20,000 feet than for lower altitudes.[94]

So another piece of seemingly unrelated biblical data dovetails into the water heaven theory.

ARE THE "WATERS ABOVE" STILL PRESENT TODAY? (PSALM 148)

In Psalm 148 the psalmist calls on the "waters that are above the heavens" to give praise to God. Coffin maintains that since the psalmist lived long after the Flood and is still referring to the "waters above the heavens," the parallel phrase in Moses' account (Gen. 1:7) cannot refer to a liquid ocean (or a vapor canopy) because that would imply it was still up there in the psalmist's time; so the Genesis passage must refer to clouds.[95]

1. Praise the Lord!
   Praise the Lord from the heavens;
   Praise Him in the heights!
2. Praise Him, all His angels;
   Praise Him, all His hosts!
3. Praise Him, sun and moon;
   Praise Him, all stars of light!
4. Praise Him, highest heavens,
   And the waters that are above the heavens!
5. Let them praise the name of the Lord,
   For He commanded and they were created.
6. He has also established them forever and ever;
   He has made a decree which will not pass away.
7. Praise the Lord from the earth,
   Sea-monsters and all deeps;
8. Fire and hail, snow and clouds;
   Stormy wind, fulfilling His word;

94. Arnold E. Higgins et al., *The Effects of Alcohol at Three Simulated Aircraft Cabin Conditions*, pp. 1-17.
95. Harold G. Coffin, *Creation — Accident or Design*, p. 22.

9. Mountains and all hills;
    Fruit trees and all cedars;
10. Beasts and all cattle;
    Creeping things and winged fowl;
11. Kings of the earth and all peoples;
    Princes and all judges of the earth;
12. Both young men and virgins;
    Old men and children (Psalm 148:1-12).

Psalm 148 falls naturally into two divisions. In verses 1-6 the psalmist gives us his praise of God "from the heavens," and his focus is on the glories of the creation — the creation of the sun, moon, stars, angels, and hosts. In verses 7-12 the psalmist shouts his praises to the Lord "from the earth," and his focus is on God's sovereign control over wind, fire, beasts, cattle, kings, old men, and children. In verse 4 the psalmist declares, "Praise Him, highest heavens, and the waters that are above the heavens!" The phrase "waters that are above the heavens" is similar to the phrase, "the waters above the expanse" (Gen. 1:7). These waters are associated with the *heavens*, and are declared to be above them. Furthermore, they are set in contrast with the hail and snow, that is, water elements which are associated with his praise of the Lord "from the earth" in verses 7-12. In verse 8, he says, "Fire and hail, snow and clouds;[96] stormy wind, fulfilling His word." The "waters above the heavens" of the creation week seem to be distinct in the psalmist's mind from the hail and snow of earth which God sovereignly controls today.

In regard to the phrase "the waters that are above the heavens" (v. 4) Perowne says, "This is usually explained of the clouds, though the form of expression cannot be said to favour such an interpretation, nor yet the statement in Genesis, that the firmament or expanse was intended to separate the waters above from the waters below. Taken in their obvious meaning,

---

96. The word "clouds" (*qîṭôr*) is usually used of "smoke" (see Gen. 19:28; Psalm 119:83). Perowne sees it as chiastic with "fire." J. J. Stewart Perowne, *The Book of Psalms*, 2:482.

the words must point to the existence of a vast heavenly sea or reservoir."[97]

Typically, liberal commentators tend to see this text as proving that the psalmist believed in the existence of the vast heavenly reservoir. Dahood observes, "Above the visible vault of heaven there was believed to be a reservoir, the source of rain."[98] Conservative commentators generally take the traditional view that both Genesis 1:6-8 and Psalm 148:4 refer to clouds.[99] One difficulty with the cloud interpretation of this passage is that it contradicts a normal exegesis of Genesis 1:6-8. On the other hand, if the critical view, that is, a heavenly sea, is valid, then it would follow that not only did the Hebrews believe in a celestial ocean prior to the Flood, but they also embraced the world view of the metallic dome and present existence of the celestial sea held by the Canaanites. The latter view contradicts the inerrancy of Scripture and fails to note the differences in Israel's cosmology mentioned in chapter 1.

In favor of the cloud interpretation of Psalm 148:4 (and therefore by implication, Genesis 1:6-8) is the fact that the "waters that are above the heavens" are called on *in the psalmist's time* to praise God. So the psalmist, it is argued, must have assumed their present existence or he would not have asked them to give praise. However, to press this highly figurative language to imply *present* existence of the heavenly ocean simply because this ocean is being addressed in the present and called to do something, that is, praise God, in the present is clearly unwarranted. Technically, this figure of speech is called an "apostrophe," that is, "a turning aside from the direct subject-matter to address others."[100] A characteristic of this figure of speech is

97. Ibid.
98. Mitchell Dahood, *The Psalms,* The Anchor Bible, 3:353; Arthur Weiser, *The Psalms,* p. 838; Charles Briggs, *The Book of Psalms,* The International Critical Commentary, p. 539.
99. William Plummer, *Studies in the Book of Psalms,* p. 1202; E. W. Hengstenberg, *Commentary on the Psalms,* 3:550.
100. E. W. Bullinger, *Figures of Speech Used in the Bible,* p. 901.

that the person or thing being addressed and called on to do something in the present may not exist in the present, but may have existed in the past or may exist in the future. For example, David laments over the departed Saul and addresses him as if present (2 Sam. 1:24-25). The prophet Ezekiel addresses some hailstones that are to come on the false prophets in the *future* as if those hailstones existed right then (Ezek. 13:11). Poetic language is characterized by "license." The poet is free to address anyone from the past as if he is present right now and to call on him to do something. The point of such a figure must be determined by who is called on and what it is he (or "it," in this case) is asked to do. By examining that question, we find clues that reveal the intent of the writer in using the apostrophe.

Now in Psalm 148:4 it is quite clear that the actual presence of the "waters above" is irrelevant. They represent the chaos that God conquered, a theological designation. As those who have done battle with Yahweh and lost, they are called on now to praise His name! (This is similar to:"That at the name of Jesus every knee should bow," Phil. 2:10). In the battle myths, the chaos monster never praised her conqueror, but the chaos of creation has no choice — order has been imposed.

It has also been asserted that the fact that it says that God established these waters above "forever and ever" and "made a decree which will not pass away," suggests that if "waters above" refers to a celestial reservoir, then why did they "pass away" at the Flood? The phrases "forever and ever" and "a decree which will not pass away" (Psalm 148:6) are commonly understood in the biblical mentality to refer to God's providential control of creation. So they will not pass away or change unless God permits them, for all is under His control. As Briggs says, "He established His law in the heavens. . . . all have to submit to it. This is the nearest approach to immutable laws of nature that is known to Hebrew literature."[101] Hengstenberg points out that this decree "excludes all change in what has been made, that would be contrary to the will of the Creator, from whom the different parts of creation can never emancipate

---

101. Briggs, p. 539.

themselves to all eternity."[102] The fact that the Hebrew word 'ad ("forever and ever") often means a long period of time (or until God decides to change the situation) is well established.[103] So the fact that these waters are described as lasting forever does not necessarily mean that the temporary waters of the water heaven theory cannot be meant. It should also be pointed out that, ultimately, clouds will not last "forever and ever" either. This is highly poetic and metaphorical language.

The statements in Psalm 148:6 seem to parallel Genesis 8:22, and a chronological sequence is implied. The psalmist takes us from the first created beings, the angels (Psalm 148:1), through the creation week with the creation of the sun, moon, and stars (148:2-3), and the "waters above" (148:4); then, he pronounces the final decree establishing the uniformity of nature after the Flood (compare Gen. 8:22 and Psalm 148:6). At that point, he turns his attention to the present era and begins praise of the Lord *from the earth.*

Several factors seem to weigh in favor of this interpretation.

(1) The psalmist tells us that the first six verses describe a creation context: "For He commanded and they were created" (148:5). So he is telling us of the creation of the heavens and the imposition of order on them.

(2) The psalmist clearly distinguishes between the "waters that are above the heavens" (148:4) and the hail and snow which is connected with the waters found in the clouds (148:8).

(3) This view allows us to take the phrase "the waters that are above the heavens" in its normal literal force of a heavenly reservoir without requiring its continued presence in the psalmist's time, and so harmonizing it with a normal exegesis of Genesis 1:6-8.

Conclusion

We have argued in chapters 2 and 3 that a straightforward exegesis of Genesis 1:6-8 related to other Scriptures yields the teaching that at the end of the second creative day, a vast

102. Hengstenberg, 3:550.
103. See Job 19:24; 20:4; Psalms 9:5; 21:5, 7; 37:29; Hab. 3:6.

celestial ocean resided above the ancient atmosphere. This conclusion is based on the following arguments.

(1) The primary meaning of the word "above" leads us to the concept of water beyond and on the atmosphere, not within it as the cloud interpretation requires.

(2) The atmosphere is clearly said to be "in the midst of the waters" and to divide between the waters. The waters are not said to be "in the midst of" the atmosphere.

(3) The Hebrews knew the difference (from the battle myths) between water which came from clouds "in" the atmosphere and water "above" the atmosphere. Moses speaks of water above the atmosphere.

(4) Most important, the task assigned to the atmosphere was to divide between waters in the liquid form and not droplets or clouds. Clearly the division is in the midst of the deep (Gen. 1:2) and hence of a liquid ocean.

(5) Furthermore, the Hebrews had six different words for clouds and several words for vapor. Moses, however, does not use any of those words. Instead he uses the customary word for water when he wants to describe the waters above. While it is true that water is associated with clouds in the Old Testament, it is only so associated in contexts where clouds are specifically mentioned. In Genesis 1 there is no mention of clouds, mists, or fogs, therefore it is unacceptable to assume their presence. There simply is no reference to clouds contiguous with the surface of the water that the atmosphere could divide from the water.

(6) It is significant in view of the fact that Moses is attempting to correct the nature myths, that in the midst of the very myth he is attempting to correct, that is, the myth of the celestial ocean, he corrects all other aspects of it but leaves the notion of the heavenly ocean without comment or correction. In view of this polemic intent, one is therefore justified in assuming that Moses accepted this aspect of the battle myth as true.

(7) The apostle Peter seems to comment on the text under consideration in 2 Peter 3:3-13. Here Peter refers to the waters three times. On one of those occasions he makes an apparent reference to the waters above the firmament. Since in the other two references, water is clearly in a liquid form (an oceanic

mass, not cloud droplets), it should be assumed that Peter intends it to be understood that the waters above were also in liquid form, unless he specifically qualified otherwise. He did not so qualify.

(8) The psalmist clearly tells us that it was the "deep" that was placed in the heavenly storehouses (Psalm 33:7) and not clouds. This is a clear reference to the ocean referred to in Genesis 1:2.

(9) Only with the assumption of a celestial ocean could enough rain water have been supplied to sustain a forty-day-and-night rainfall. It is clear that Moses intends to convey to us that the source of rainfall was the "waters above" (Gen. 1:7) and not extra-terrestrial sources or volcanic waters. Furthermore, volcanic water recycled into the rain cycle could at best account for only less than 0.1% of the water needed if a moderate rate of flood rainfall of 0.5 inches per hour is assumed.

(10) The circumstantial evidence presented in this chapter gains its force largely from the fact that many of the incidental details mentioned in the Genesis account are surprisingly characteristic of a world surrounded by a water canopy. When we read Genesis 2:5-6 for the first time, it would probably be granted by most that the first impression is of an antediluvian world characterized by a diurnal dew regime and no rain. It would also be granted by most that the first mention of the rainbow seems to suggest in context that this was also the first existence of the phenomenon itself. However, first impressions are not always valid. In fact, a more careful examination of each of these passages reveals that there are no compelling exegetical reasons for insisting on any of the interpretations adopted in this chapter. To some extent, attempts to consider other interpretations than the ones arising from a first impression come from the apparent meteorological difficulties and other scientific improbabilities that these interpretations imply.

In a conversation with a professor of meteorology at Cornell University the canopy idea was presented to him. His first comment was, "This seems highly unlikely because it would mean that there would have been no rain." He was then directed to Genesis 2:5. His next comment was, "Well, it would seem that under such conditions, the earth would have had a rather heavy diurnal dew regime." When he read Genesis 2:6, his interest began to rise.

Is it not unusual that these phenomena which are deduced independently of the text of Genesis but from the atmospheric physics of the situation are specifically referred to in the text? So while each of them is not adequate in itself to suggest evidence of such a canopy, when taken together, our conviction increases that the first-impression interpretation is the correct one. This is further enforced by the statements that the ancient world was "very good" in contrast to today's climate, and at least the suggestion of a radically different environment affecting longevity and, perhaps, fermentation rates of wine.

The physics required to sustain such a literal liquid ocean are, of course, unknown. However, that should not necessarily determine whether or not the Bible teaches its existence. It could well have been maintained supernaturally from Adam till Noah. The phase in which it remained will be discussed in a later chapter, but what we maintain here is that Genesis teaches us that it was in a liquid ocean phase and not cloud, ice, or water vapor. It may have changed into some other phase, but if it did, the Bible is silent on this.

If such a vast canopy surrounded the ancient earth, it would be surprising if there were no references to it in the cultural memories of mankind. In fact, there are numerous such references in ancient myths to some kind of canopy and of a time when the earth's climate was considerably milder. A survey of these myths is the subject of the next chapter.

CHAPTER 4

The Canopy in World Mythology

The science of cultural anthropology has added some possible evidence for the existence of the pre-Flood celestial ocean. In nearly every culture there is an account of a great flood that inundated the earth and destroyed all mankind. In those stories a man or a family or a couple were saved by a canoe, an ark, or by climbing a mountain. In many of the accounts there are references to a climatic regime and even to a water heaven that offers striking parallels to the Genesis record.

Evidence of this kind must be handled with care, and not too much can be made of it. However, where scholars once tended to write off these accounts as primitive myths, now there is growing recognition of a possible historical basis that gave rise to them. Opinions differ and nothing can be said with certainty, but the evidence found in these myths is so widespread and so similar to the Genesis account that it seems appropriate to give it brief comment. We must remember, however, that this evidence is not the basis for belief in a pre-Flood canopy or in the fact of a global deluge. That evidence rests primarily on the biblical statements examined in the preceding chapters. These myths can be viewed only as offering a possible supplementary confirmation.

Assuming the reliability of the biblical account, we can give a plausible explanation for the origin of these stories. Obviously, in the years following the Flood, Noah and his sons would have shared the events of that fateful year of the Deluge many times with their descendants. They would have drawn attention to the differences between conditions that existed in the pre-Flood world and those of their generation. The decreasing longevity would also have caused some alarm and comment.

When their children asked, "What was it like before the Flood?" their answers would have been taken by these children and passed on to others through their own children. In the process the stories would have been mythologized, distorted, exaggerated, added to, and modified, until the original became only a faint memory. In the following pages we will analyze some of these "cultural memories" of an antediluvian water heaven. These do not represent eyewitness accounts, but reports passed on through Shem, Ham, and Japheth to their posterity.

The most comprehensive compilation of global flood stories is that by Sir James George Frazer in his three-volume *Folk-Lore in the Old Testament*.[1] He cites evidence of Flood accounts from the Indians in North America to the Indians of India. Hawaii, Alaska, Indonesia, Europe, Asia, Australia, and Mesopotamia all have Flood accounts. Needless to say, as the tribes migrated farther and farther from Ararat, the stories became more and more distorted. In fact, this point has been carefully documented by John Warwick Montgomery.[2] This impressive evidence would seem to substantiate the view that these stories *do* have a common origin and are not exaggerated tales of local catastrophes, as some have maintained.[3]

THE CANOPY IN ANCIENT MYTHOLOGY

After an analysis of numerous mythological accounts of the ancient earth, Kellogg concludes that many of them tell of a

1. See Sir James George Frazer, *Folk-Lore in the Old Testament*, 1:104-361. For other compilations of various Flood stories see Frederick Filby, *The Flood Reconsidered*, pp. 37-38; Theodore H. Gaster, *Myth, Legend and Custom in the Old Testament*, pp. 82-131; Stephen Herbert Langdon, *The Mythology of All Races*. Vol. 5, *Semitic Mythology*, John MacCulloch, ed., pp. 203-33.
2. See *The Quest for Noah's Ark*, p. 30, for a graphic presentation of the growing distortion of the Flood accounts the more geographically removed they are from Ararat.
3. Frazer, 1:360.

visible water heaven scintillating with light.[4] This heaven was the home of the gods, and it obstructed the power of the sun god. One day this water heaven was banished, and the sun came riding through as the conqueror of heaven and master of the wind and rain. One who believes the biblical account of primeval vapor canopy is tempted to see ancient allusions to the new burst of "sun power" that was undoubtedly unleashed when the canopy condensed during the rainfall of Noah's Flood. The ancients took this as the victory of the sun god over the watery heaven. Isaac Vail noted a similar theme in many myths, "We will find the ancient heaven represented as a screen. We will find the sun concealed — a slave or subaltern to an overmastering power; you will find the sun finally exalted through elemental conflict with Titan and Giant vapor, or tempest enemies, into immortality."[5]

It is interesting that many of the words for "heaven" in ancient manuscripts in some cases seem to have an etymology that suggests the idea of a celestial ocean. For example, in Akkadian and Arabic, the cognate words for "heaven" are used by metonymy to mean "rain." In this mythology it refers to the upper part of the cosmic ocean that enveloped the earth and is made of water.[6] The Greek word for heaven, *ouranos*, is probably derived from *ou*, "there," and *rainó*, "to sprinkle"; hence the "there waters."[7] Interestingly, it was located above the ether, or upper air.[8] So it parallels the Hebrew idea of waters *above* the expanse and not *in* them. The phrase is often found in the Orphic writing of the cosmic egg, which bursts open. The upper shell became the envelope of the world.[9] In Homer, a

4. Howard W. Kellogg, *The Coming Kingdom and the Re-Canopied Earth*, p. 23.
5. Isaac Newton Vail, *The Deluge and Its Cause*, p. 147.
6. T. H. Gaster, "Heaven," in *The Interpreter's Dictionary of the Bible*, 2:551-52.
7. Henry George Liddell and Robert Scott, *A Greek-English Lexicon*, p. 1356.
8. Ibid., p. 1094.
9. Helmut Traub, "Ouranos," in *Theological Dictionary of the New Testament*, 5:498.

brazen, iron, starry heaven resting on pillars served as the habitation of heavenly beings.[10] In the Magic Papyri, too, the term *ouranos* is common: as the firmament that includes the heavenly ocean.[11] Some have seen the etymology of the Hebrew word *shāmayim* as coming from *shām*, "there," and *mayim*, "waters"; hence, like the Greek *ouranos*, we again have the "there waters."[12] Others believe this Hebrew etymology is erroneous.[13]

EASTERN ASIA

Numerous accounts of a Flood and of a celestial vault are reported from eastern Asia. The Karen of Burma, for example, believe that the water of the great Flood came down from the "celestial vault."[14] This seems to be an idea similar to the celestial ocean held up by a metallic dome found in other myths.

BABYLON

In the Babylonian creation account, *Enuma Elish*, there are a number of references to a celestial ocean. As the story goes, Marduk went to war against the Babylonian chaos monster Tiamat, the salt water ocean. In this account there are three types of water. Apsu represents the sweet water ocean, Tiamat the salt water ocean, and Mummu the fog, the mist, and the clouds, which rose from Apsu and Tiamat and hovered over them. Thus Tiamat was considered the primeval ocean that surrounded the universe, whereas Apsu was the subterranean waters that fed the springs and rivers.[15] Possibly Apsu is paral-

10. Ibid.
11. Ibid., 5:500.
12. Walter Baumgartner, ed., *Lexicon in Veteris Testamenti Libri*, p. 986; also A. Cohen, *The Socino Chumash*, 1:3.
13. Traub, 5:502.
14. Frazer, p. 208.
15. Mary K. Wakeman, *God's Battle with the Sea Monster, A Study in Biblical Imagery*, p. 21.

The Canopy in World Mythology

leled by the waters of the deep (Gen. 7:11) that supplied most of the water for the Flood. When Marduk overcame Tiamat, he cut her body in half vertically. With one half of her body he formed the earth and with the other half he formed the sky (*Enuma Elish*, IV:138). Thus half of the primeval ocean was now up in the sky. This seems to parallel the "waters above the firmament" motif of Genesis. After this water was placed in the sky, a crossbar was fixed, and guards were posted and commanded to prevent the celestial waters from escaping (IV:139; see IV:128-45 [the "windows of heaven" of Genesis 7:11 perhaps?]). Marduk used these waters to construct the sky. They had to be prevented from falling back to earth.[16] The text reads:

> He cleft her [Tiamat] like a fish, in two halves;
> From the one half he made and covered the heaven.[17]

In the Babylonian parallel to the biblical Flood account, *The Gilgamesh Epic*, we find a number of references which, when viewed in the light of the Genesis record, have some interesting implications. Genesis speaks of the Flood being caused by the break-up of the fountains of the deep and by torrential rains. *The Gilgamesh Epic* records that "the land he broke like a pot" (the break-up of the fountains of the deep?).[18] Furthermore, torrential rains and destructive winds (the "great wind" of Genesis 8:1?) accompanied by lightning and thunder are the cause of the Flood (XI:96-131). Dikes, canals, and reservoirs burst open (XI:90-131).

A BUDDHIST ACCOUNT

The Buddhist account of Creation involves a vague and confusing reference to a "creative cloud" from which poured the waters that began to rotate in a "water circle." Out of this came

16. Alexander Heidel, *The Babylonian Genesis*, p. 115.
17. Owen C. Whitehouse, "Cosmogony," *Hastings' Dictionary of the Bible*, 1:505.
18. XI:107, see Alexander Heidel, *The Gilgamesh Epic and Old Testament Parallels*, p. 85.

the earth.[19] This creative cloud began to pour out gold, water, precious stones, iron, and other elements on the earth. The Buddhists seem to have conceived the early earth as covered by some kind of vaporous cloud canopy. It is not difficult to conceive of a vague memory of the "waters" above narrated by Noah's sons.

EGYPT

In ancient Egypt the heaven was regarded as an ocean parallel with that on earth.[20] The sun god traveled in a barge through this ocean which "surrounds the world."[21] This watery heaven was the god Canopus whose symbols were a water vase and the serpent. His very name is a memorial to the vapor canopy.[22] According to the legend, only the ocean existed in the beginning; an egg appeared on it, out of which issued the sun god. From himself he then bore four children, Shu, Tefnut, Geb, and Nut.[23] Nut was the sky goddess. In primordial times she was embraced by the earth god Geb, until Shu and Tefnut, the gods of the atmosphere, separated them by elevating Nut high above the earth and placing themselves beneath her.[24] In a modified version Re, the sun god, sprang from the union of Geb and Nut. He travels by day across the celestial ocean in a boat.[25] When night comes, he transfers to another boat, descends to the netherworld, and continues his voyage. In the account of Shu and Tefnut, the representatives of the atmosphere, thrusting themselves between Geb and Nut and raising Nut into the heavens, we have an obvious reference to the separation of the

19. L la Vallée Poussin, "Cosmogony and Cosmology (Buddhist)," *Encyclopedia of Religion and Ethics*, 4:131.
20. W. M. Flinders Petrie, "Cosmogony and Cosmology (Egyptian)," *Encyclopedia of Religion and Ethics*, 4:145.
21. Wakeman, p. 16; see Coffin texts, spell 160, John A. Wilson, *Ancient Near Eastern Texts*, p. 12.
22. Isaac N. Vail, *The Waters Above the Firmament*, p. vi.
23. James Henry Breasted, *A History of Egypt*, p. 56.
24. Charles F. Pfeiffer, *Old Testament History*, p. 137.
25. Whitehouse, *Hastings' Dictionary of the Bible*, 1:502.

waters below the expanse from the waters above the expanse of Genesis. The Egyptians received the story from Noah's sons through many generations and recounted the reference to a literal liquid water ocean above the atmosphere.

GREECE

The myths of Hellas have captivated the imaginations of men for centuries. Perhaps none of them are more moving than the majestic epic poetry of Hesiod. Born in 846 B.C., this farmer-turned-poet composed many poems, among which his *Theogony* is most famous. In it he gives the readers a "Genealogy of the Gods."[26] In the beginning, Hesiod says, was Chaos, and the *Theogony* traces the development from chaos to cosmos just as the biblical account in Genesis does.[27] From Chaos was born Erebus ("misty," "black night"); and from Erebus came Aether and Day. Aether is the "bright, untainted upper atmosphere, as distinguished from Aer, the lower atmosphere of the earth."[28] Above the Aether was Ouranos ("heaven"). As pointed out above, this heaven may be etymologically derived from "there waters." At any rate, in the Magic Papyri the term *ouranos* is common for the firmament, which includes the heavenly ocean.[29] Ouranos, or Uranus,[30] mated with the earth, and she bore the Titans, one of which was Cronos.[31] Cronos is *not* the god of time as is popularly conceived.[32] His precise nature is unclear, but he prevents his father, Ouranos (the "water heaven"), from ever mating with his mother again by castrating him. Uranus is no longer mentioned in Greek

26. Will Durant, *The Life of Greece*, p. 98.
27. Hesiod *Theogony*, lines 116ff, in *Hesiod The Homeric Hymns and Homerica*, trans. Hugh G. Evelyn-White, p. 87.
28. *Theogony*, lines 125 ff.
29. Traub, 5:498.
30. Michael Grant and John Hazel, *Gods and Mortals in Classical Mythology*, p. 413.
31. *Theogony*, line 137.
32. Harry Thurston Peck, ed., *Harper's Dictionary of Classical Literature and Antiquities*, p. 431.

mythology as a god to whom worship is ascribed.[33] This enforced separation between Ouranos and the Earth seems to parallel the battle between Marduk and Tiamat. The castration would suggest the conquest of Tiamat, her being cut in two, and her restraint up above the firmament. When Cronos comes to the throne, the water heaven has already been restrained.

During the reign of Cronos a golden age prevailed. Men lived without sorrow, were free from toil and grief, and also enjoyed longevity of life.[34] Interestingly, there were two suns — Hyperion and Helios. While Cronos reigned and men enjoyed the golden age, Hyperion was the sun that shone on this planet.[35] Hyperion was the son of Gaia ("earth") and Uranus (the sky, or "water heaven") before his castration.[36] In a later age, under Zeus, Hyperion is displaced by his son, Helios, and a new sun takes over.

The fall of Cronos and the golden age came through the rise of Zeus, the son of Cronos. The myths present Zeus as the weather god. He was particularly responsible for rain, hail, snow, and thunder. Thunderbolts were his constant and irresistible weapons, and one of his most common Homeric epithets was "Gatherer of Clouds."[37]

It is easy to see how this bizarre cosmogony could reflect an extremely distorted version of the true situation described by the sons of Noah to their descendants. Under the canopy the earth would have enjoyed a "golden age" such as Hesiod describes. Furthermore, a gathering of clouds, rain, and thunder must have marked the end of that "golden age" in the Bible, with the collapse of the canopy and the Deluge. Zeus, the cloud gatherer, may reflect the cloud canopy from which the rain of the Deluge fell. He was the god of weather and rain, and it was rain that ended the "golden age."

Under the canopy a dimmer sun would have been observable in the antediluvian heavens. Could not the Greek myth reflect

33. Grant and Hazel, p. 413.
34. Hesiod *Works and Days*, lines 110 ff.
35. Grant and Hazel, p. 240; *Harper's Dictionary*, p. 1588.
36. *Theogony*, line 134.
37. Grant and Hazel, p. 418.

this in the transfer of power to the new sun, Helios, when Hyperion lost power as the "golden age" ended? Table 4.1 illustrates some possible parallels with the biblical account. Admittedly, the parallel is not as precise as the table indicates. Zeus, for example, did not end the "golden age" with a deluge (although his name is associated with a plot to destroy the human race by flood[38]). Also, the Greeks continued to believe in the existence of the water heaven and the solid dome until at least the third century B.C. However, the parallels are close enough to suggest a common source. Perhaps both Genesis, the true account, and the Greek myth, the distorted account, go back to a report passed on through Noah.

TABLE 4.1

PARALLELS BETWEEN GREEK AND HEBREW CANOPY LEGENDS

		In the Beginning	Conquest of Chaos	Canopy Era	Deluge	Post-Flood
GREEK		Chaos	Ouranos and Gaia separated	Longevity Golden Age Ouranos Hyperion	Zeus, god of weather	Silver, bronze, and iron age; new sun; Helios
HEBREW		The Deep	Division of waters	Longevity "it was good" "waters above"	"windows of heaven"	Longevity declines

INDIA

Indian religious literature is full of references to a water heaven that could possibly be interpreted as the liquid ocean of the Hebrew records. In the *Vedas* and in the *Avesta* the idea of an upper or heavenly sea is frequent.[39] Originally, the upper waters were ruled by Varuna, the guardian of the "sea of heaven" from which he sent rain.[40] He acquired his position as "lord of the waters" after the great god Indra conquered the

---

38. Ibid., p. 422.
39. Whitehouse, *Hastings' Dictionary of the Bible*, 1:502.
40. Veronica Ions, *Indian Mythology*, p. 79.

Chaos monster Vritra, who, like Tiamat in Babylon, restrained the release of creative forces until conquered by Marduk. When Vritra was defeated by Indra, her belly was slit open and the cosmic waters were driven to their place in the atmospheric ocean where Varuna was installed as their ruler.[41] Subsequently (the chronology is ambiguous), Varuna was ousted from her position as the guardian of the atmospheric waters and made guardian of the terrestrial waters.[42] Indra took over as the god of the atmosphere. Varuna now resides in the netherworld at the roots of the world tree and near to (or in) the subterranean cosmic waters.[43] Today, Indra is the god of nature, a kind of Hercules with the characteristics of Zeus. He rules the sky, and when he thunders, he lets loose the rain. He is called "lord of heaven," or "rider of the clouds," or "the thunderer."[44]

We also find an interesting myth that relates to the sun. During the reign of Varuna, the water heaven, the sun was Ahura-Mazda. Varuna ruled, and the divinity of light, Mithras, was subordinate to him. During this reign Mithras was not the sun; he was simply the god of the upper air.[45] "But somehow, somewhere, he became the central deity in an almost new religion."[46] In the new religion Mithras, the new sun, was born from a rock, that is, the sun rising above the mountains. Mithras was a kind of ally with Ahura-Mazda. Apparently, there was a problem with darkness, so Ahura-Mazda instructed Mithras to solve the difficulty. Mithras promptly killed the wild bull that was responsible for the darkness, and light reigned. As a result, Ahura-Mazda yielded up supremacy to Mithras. A new sun now reigned. In other stories the darkness tried to destroy the human race by a flood, and Mithras, the new sun, rescued mankind.[47]

41. Wakeman, p. 11; see *Reg Veda*, I, 32.
42. Ions, p. 79.
43. F. B. J. Kuiper, "The Basic Concept of Vedic Religion," *History of Religions* 15 (November 1975):114.
44. *New Larousse Encyclopedia of Mythology*, p. 326.
45. John Ferguson, *The Religions of the Roman Empire*, 47.
46. Ibid.
47. Ibid.

The Canopy in World Mythology

The similarity of these myths to the Hebrew account is striking. Both begin with a situation of chaos that is overcome by the conquering god. The waters of the chaos monster are ruled in a heavenly ocean by Varuna, the sea of heaven. While Varuna reigns, Ahura-Mazda is the sun. With Varuna's ouster (the condensation of the canopy?), a new sun is installed, Mithras (a former subordinate of Varuna's), and darkness has been overcome. Certainly, just prior to the Flood, the world was enveloped in semidarkness due to the clouds. When the canopy condensed, a "new sun" with greater brightness and slightly differing optical appearance would have appeared in the postdiluvian heavens.[48] The god who overcame this darkness, ousted the water heaven, was the god of the storm, weather, rain, and clouds — Indra. In some of the stories, the birth of the new sun is connected with his saving the world from the global Deluge, precisely the parallel predicted by the collapse of the Genesis canopy and subsequent Flood. The nature of these parallels with the Hebrew account can be easily seen in Table 4.2.

TABLE 4.2

PARALLELS BETWEEN THE INDIAN AND HEBREW STORIES OF THE WATER HEAVEN

	Beginning	Conquest of Chaos	Restraint of Chaos	Release of Water Heaven
INDIA	Chaos "Vritra"	Indra slits Vritra's belly and drives the waters into the atmospheric ocean	Rule of Varuna, the water heaven Old sun	Varuna ousted Indra, the storm god, supreme New sun, Mithras Flood (in some stories)
HEBREW	Chaos "The Deep"	The division of the waters	Canopy	"The windows of heaven were opened" Flood

48. The optical effects of the canopy will be quantitatively considered in Chapter 9.

PERSIA

In the Persian sacred book the *Zend-Avesta* a deluge legend is told.[49] For 900 winters the sage Yima (the first mortal with whom the creator conversed) reigned over the world under the divine superintendence. During all that time there was neither cold wind nor hot wind (that is, a temperature equilibrium such as would be produced by a vapor canopy greenhouse effect), nor disease or death (longevity of life?). Because of the favorable climatic conditions, mankind and animals apparently increased at such an alarming rate that the earth had to be enlarged three times to accomodate them. The creator decided that a flood was the answer to overpopulation and proceeded to destroy them all. He informed Yima that fatal winters were going to fall on the material world, and that he would bring a fierce, foul frost. Such a situation would be expected with the collapse of the vapor canopy. A new climatic regime would be introduced. There would be a sudden deep freeze in many parts of the world, even in presently tropical regions.[50]

POLYNESIA

The islands of the South Pacific are rich in traditions that speak of a flood and possibly of a concept of a water heaven. Among the Ifugoo in the Philippines, for example, it is said that the sky used to be so close to the earth that it interfered with the sharpening of one's spear.[51] The Manobo of Mindanao say that the sky was once very close to the earth, and that while a woman was pounding with her pestle, she accidentally hit it, causing the heavens to ascend to a great height.[52] In Borneo the story is that six suns reigned in succession while the sky hung low; with the advent of the seventh sun, the sky retreated to its

49. Frazer, 1:180 ff.
50. The physical causes of this phenomenon will be analyzed in a later chapter.
51. Roland B. Dixon, *Oceanic Mythology*, 9:178.
52. Ibid.

present position. Similar tales are found in many of the islands.[53]

Again we find the theme of a new sun as would be predicted by the collapse of the Genesis canopy. The seventh sun is the most intense because the obstructing heavenly waters have been removed.

A Maori legend describes a division of the waters in a way similar to the Genesis account:

> And now a great light prevailed
> Io then looked to the waters, which composed him about,
> And spake a fourth time saying:
> "Ye waters of Tai-kam, be ye separate, heaven must be formed."
> Then the sky became suspended.[54]

Note that the division of the waters here occurred *after* the creation of light, just as in Genesis.

The famous Roman poet Ovid (43 B.C. to A.D. 18) compiled many ancient Roman myths in his magnum opus *Metamorphoses*. These fifteen "books" published in A.D. 7 recounted in engaging hexameters the renowned transformations of inanimate objects, animals, mortals, and gods. Since almost everything in Greek and Roman legend changed its form, the scheme permitted Ovid to range through the whole realm of classical mythology from the creation of the world to the deification of Caesar.[55] One of his themes involves the four ages of the world. Here he traced the traditions of ancient Roman mythology, which depict the earlier stages of the ancient earth. The first age was the golden age:

> The earth itself, too, in freedom, untouched by the harrow and wounded by no ploughshares, *of its own accord produced everything*; and men, contented with the food created under no compulsion, gathered the fruit of the arbute-tree, and the strawberries of the mountain, and cornels, and blackberries adhering to the prickly bramble-bushes, and acorns which

53. Ibid.
54. H. Hongi, "A Maori Cosmogony," *Journal of Polynesian Studies* 16 (1907):113.
55. Will Durant, *Caesar and Christ*, p. 256.

had fallen from the wide-spreading tree of Jove. Then it was *eternal spring*; and the gentle Zephyrs, with their soothing breezes, cherished the flowers produced without any seed. Soon, too, the Earth unploughed yielded crops of grain, and the land, without being renewed, was whitened with the heavy ears of corn. Then, rivers of mile, then, rivers of nectar were flowing, and the yellow honey was distilled from the green holm oak.[56]

Here is an interesting mythological description of a time in which the earth brought forth abundant crops; there were no seasons, only an "eternal spring," or uniformly subtropical temperature regime. This seems to parallel closely the conditions predicted from Genesis, that is, the greenhouse effect of earth's ancient water heaven.

During the golden age Saturn reigned. Saturn was an ancient rustic god equated with the Greek Cronos.[57] During the reign of Saturn life was easy and happy. He taught men to farm and how to enjoy the gifts of civilization. His name is derived either from *satur*, "stuffed, gorged," or *sator*, "a sower." If *sator* is the root of the name, then it would indicate his connection with the abundance of the golden age.[58] Saturn took over the rule from Coelus, Rome's most ancient deity. Coelus is roughly equivalent to the Greek Uranus or water heaven.[59] When Saturn took over, the water heaven was under his control and a golden age prevailed. It is not difficult to see here the subjugation of the waters theme from Greece where the waters of chaos are restrained as in the Genesis record. Saturn was deposed by Jupiter just as Cronos of Greece was deposed by Zeus. Jupiter is related to Zeus and was thought to be responsible for all kinds of weather, especially lightning and rain.[60]

The next age, according to Ovid, was the silver age. "Jupiter shortened the duration of the former spring, and divided the year into four periods by means of winters, and summers, and

---

56. Ovid *Metamorphoses*, trans. Henry T. Riley, Book 1, fable 3, p. 18.
57. Grant and Hazel, p. 360.
58. *New Larousse Encyclopedia of Mythology*, p. 205.
59. *Harper's Dictionary*, p. 1418.
60. Grant and Hazel, p. 255.

The Canopy in World Mythology

unsteady autumns, and short springs. Then for the first time, did the parched air glow with sultry heat, and the ice, bound up by the winds, was pendant."[61]

If, as the first chapters of this thesis have attempted to demonstrate, the earth was indeed once surrounded by a canopy of water or vapor, one would predict a relatively insignificant seasonal variation. Furthermore, such a lack of seasonal differences may be implied in Genesis 8:22. With the collapse of the canopy, drastic seasonal differences would have been introduced for the first time. This is the situation noted in the Roman myths.

SUMER

In ancient Sumer, the oldest known civilization, we also find accounts of the water heaven. The Sumerian creation epic recounts the ancient theme of the separation of the water heaven from the earth:

> After heaven had been moved away from earth,
> After earth had been separated from heaven. . . .[62]

This separation was effected by the air god Enlil.[63] The Sumerians believed that the waters above were maintained there by a solid metal vault. The composition of that vault may have been, in their thinking, tin, inasmuch as the Sumerian term for tin is "metal of heaven."[64] Heaven and earth were originally created by Nammu, a symbol for "sea,"[65] thus the heavens were watery. According to the Sumerians, inside this upside-down vault the sun, the atmosphere, the stars, and the planets were to be found. "Surrounding the 'heaven-earth' on all sides, as well as top and

---

61. Ovid, Book 1, fable 4, p. 19.
62. See Tablet #14068 in the Nippur Collection, cited by Samuel Noah Kramer, *Sumerian Mythology*, p. 37.
63. Ibid., p. 40.
64. Samuel Noah Kramer, *The Sumerians*, p. 113.
65. Kramer, *Sumerian Mythology*, p. 39.

bottom, was the boundless sea in which the universe somehow remained fixed and immovable."[66]

So in a garbled form we can detect the Hebrew idea of the waters above being formed out of the waters of the primeval sea.

The Sumerian Deluge story is also similar to the Hebrew. "All the windstorms, exceedingly powerful, attacked as one. The deluge raged over the surface of the earth seven days and seven nights. And the huge boat had been tossed about on the great waters."[67]

An Analysis

Interpreting these ancient myths is a tricky business. We find so many unknowns about what the ancients really believed that we cannot make certain statements about the details. Did they really believe, for example, in wooden sluice gates (Babylon)? An air god separating heaven and earth (Sumer)? A metallic dome for the heavens? That rain came through the windows in Baal's house (Canaan)? Much of the confusion exists because the ancients viewed all of nature as personal. They did not seem to draw the subject-object distinction between human beings and nature itself. They did not personify nature, that is, ascribe human characteristics to it, but they actually perceived nature as personal and of the same "stuff" as human beings. It was all united in one large unified being. Hence, to speak of sentries posted at the heavenly sluice gates did not necessarily mean little men in uniform standing guard. The restraining forces, whatever they were, were personal and may have only been conceptualized as particular humans.[68]

However, many seem to believe that there may be some mechanistic basis for the myths. Guirand summarizes: "Some have interpreted the noisy quarrels of Zeus and Hera as a mythological translation of storms or the struggle of the

---

66. Kramer, *The Sumerians*, p. 113.
67. Kramer, *Sumerian Mythology*, p. 39.
68. H. Frankfort, H. A. Frankfort, John A. Wilson, Thorkild Jacobsen, and William A. Irwin, *The Intellectual Adventure of Ancient Man*, pp. 3-27.

meteors and atmospheric disturbances in revolt against the sky. ... They were only translating the emotions they felt in the face of nature's great mysteries into gracious and poetic forms."[69]

Frequently these myths are simply a romanticized form of natural phenomena; sometimes they are allegorized accounts of historical facts.

For these reasons, it is always dangerous to try to read too much into these stories. However, the parallels to the Genesis record of a water heaven are frequent, interesting, and precise. This suggests either that one borrowed from the other, that they arose independently, or that both were derived from a common, more ancient source.

How are the accounts of a flood to be explained? Cultures from Babylon to South America report flood legends that closely parallel the details of the Genesis record. Furthermore, as argued above, we find widespread accounts of an ancient water heaven. Although this evidence could be explained in many ways, it is specifically predicated on the basis of a normal exegesis of the Genesis account and the assumption of its truthfulness. If there were a water heaven that condensed and resulted in a global deluge, we would expect to find a universal flood and water heaven traditions — and this is exactly what we do find. This tends to supply circumstantial evidence for a universal flood.

Secular anthropologists today, of course, simply say that Genesis borrowed and slightly purified these grotesque myths. The existence of these legends, instead of being evidence for a global deluge, are said to be evidence that Moses borrowed these stories from Babylonia. If, on the other hand, there were no such traditions, what would the secular anthropologist say about the Genesis tradition? "Would they not use this very lack of circumstantial evidence as a weighty objection to the veracity of the Biblical account?"[70] The presence of the legends serves to condemn the biblical account, and their absence would probably do the same.

69. Felix Guirand, *Greek Mythology*, p. 28.
70. Henry M. Morris and John C. Whitcomb, *The Genesis Flood*, p. 52.

The use of these legends as evidence for a universal flood (or water heaven) has been severely questioned by modern scholars. Sir James George Frazer says:

> Formerly, under the influence of the Biblical tradition, inquirers were disposed to identify legends of a great flood, wherever found, with the familiar Noachian deluge, and to suppose that in them we had more or less corrupt and apocryphal versions of that great catastrophe, of which the only true and authentic record is preserved in the Book of Genesis. Such a view can hardly be maintained any longer.[71]

Frazer's conclusion, however, is too hasty. We need to examine the two reasons he gives for rejecting the common source hypothesis.

First, he argues that many of the flood stories are too "diverse, often quaint, childish, or grotesque" to be copies of a single human original. Now Frazer may be right in his assertion that the flood stories do not come from a common source, but it is hard to see how his first objection to such a view can be taken with any seriousness. These kinds of distortions are exactly what we would expect if they did all descend from a common source. Frazer seems to think that by simply making a statement that they cannot be copies of a distant original is proof of the statement.

Second, Frazer argues that modern research has "proved" that the supposed divine original in Genesis is not an original at all, but a comparatively late "purification" of a much older Babylonian, or rather Sumerian, version. As we have pointed out in chapters 1 and 2, not only has modern research failed to prove this, but in fact it has proved exactly the opposite. Within fifteen years of the publication of Frazer's book (1918), archaeological investigations in the Near East totally overturned much of the testimony on which his statement was made.[72]

Furthermore, recent excavations at Tell Mardikh (Ebla) in Syria have revealed a creation account, dated hundreds of years before the Babylonian one, that is already "purified." It has

71. Frazer, *Folk-lore*, 1:334.
72. See the discussion in chapter 1, and William F. Albright, *Archaeology and the Religion of Israel*.

none of the polytheistic absurdities of the *Epic of Atrahasis* or the *Enuma Elish*. So the Hebrew account is more like this older version than the Babylonian.[73]

Not only is Frazer's case not proved, but he also apparently has represented a "straw man" of what the conservative evangelical position really is. No one today maintains that the Genesis account was the original one and that everything in ancient mythology was copied from it. What is asserted is that the Genesis account itself is an accurate representation of the ancient source whereas the pagan myths are distorted versions of the same source.[74] We do not know whether Moses received this information about the Flood by direct revelation or through divinely preserved oral tradition. But unless we assume the impossibility of revelation or at least the impossibility of its coming to Moses, Frazer's argument hardly carries any weight. Ultimately that is the very point in question, and we do not need to concede the validity of his point.

Having already rejected the notion that the ancient flood stories could be authentic cultural memories of the account described in Genesis, Frazer is then left with the perplexing problem of explaining the origin of these stories. If they did not arise from the account of the Flood passed on by Shem, Ham, and Japheth to their descendants, where did they come from? Frazer makes four points in regard to this.[75]

(1) His first point and his controlling assumption is that the stories of a global inundation must be false because modern geology says it is impossible. His certainty rests ultimately on the interpretation of the geological strata offered by the contemporary historical geologist. This interpretation, however, is open to serious challenge. In fact, there seems to be rather convincing evidence that it is the modern geologist's interpre-

73. Clifford Wilson, *Ebla Tablets: Secrets of a Forgotten City*, pp. 47-54; see also William Sanford LaSor, "Further Information About Tell Mardikh," *Journal of the Evangelical Theological Society* 19 (Fall 1976):265-70.
74. See Merrill F. Unger, *Archaeology and the Old Testament*, p. 37, and Bruce K. Waltke, *Creation and Chaos*, pp. 45-47.
75. Frazer, 1:342-61.

tations of fossil strata that are "impossible," not the fact of a global deluge. Convincing evidence is being presented by many creationist scientists that a global deluge may be the only way the geologic strata can be adequately explained.[76] More important, God has clearly revealed in His Word that just such a deluge did take place, and such a direct revelation of past conditions must take precedence over the finite inductive science of the historical geologist.[77]

(2) Since modern geology has "proved" that there cannot have been a global flood, these stories of such a global flood must represent local catastrophes which, in passing through the medium of popular tradition, have been magnified into worldwide catastrophes (unless, of course, these accounts are positive evidence for a global catastrophe!). He then cites stories of violent floods in Holland and other places around the world as evidence of local catastrophes that could have been magnified in transmission into global flood stories. However, even though this could certainly have happened, and probably has, in none of the local catastrophes he cites does he say that they were ever so magnified. He has hardly proved his point.

Furthermore, the "magnified local affair" theory suffers from its inability to explain the numerous similarities. In many of the accounts that Frazer himself documents, such details as the sending forth of the dove, the salvation of eight people, an ark, and two of every kind are present. John Bright has rejected this view for similar reasons: "It is difficult to believe that so remarkable a coincidence of outline as exists between so many of

76. For an excellent discussion on this see N. A. Rupke, "Prolegomena to a Study of Cataclysmal Sedimentation," in *Why Not Creation?*, ed. Walter Lammerts, pp. 147-79. Also see the massive geological comment in Morris and Whitcomb, pp. 116-330.
77. For a thorough development of the exegetical arguments for a geologically universal flood see Morris and Whitcomb, pp. 1-35. Their exegesis was carefully analyzed and generally validated by Charles Clough, "A Calm Appraisal of *The Genesis Flood*," pp. 1-177.

these widely separated accounts can be accounted for in this way."[78]

Frazer, of course, has a ready answer for these striking similarities. He says they are the result of the preaching of Christian missionaries.[79] Such a suggestion with respect to many of these stories is incredible. Byron Nelson has effectively refuted this thesis with several observations.[80] First, there are no universal legends of other great miracles recorded in the Bible, such as the crossing of the Red Sea. Why were only the Flood and "water heaven" legends dispersed? Second, why are there so many differences in detail and in emphases in all these legends if missionaries are the common source? Third, Whitcomb and Morris have observed that it seems highly unlikely that Christian missionaries would have ever reached all these tribes, and, if they did, they would hardly have wasted their time describing the Flood; they would have presented the gospel.[81] It would be a knowledge of Christ that would be found in these tribes if Christian missionaries had truly been there.

(3) Frazer's third objection is more substantial. He points out that the flood stories which come from islands or from sea coast communities and tribes ascribe the Flood to rising water and not to rain. Assuming his evidence is correct, this would tend to suggest that the stories were indeed local catastrophes that were magnified. In those island and sea coast communities floods were generally caused by earthquakes at sea that sent tidal waves roaring over the island. Since in the global flood stories of these communities only this kind of causative agent is described, it logically appears that they simply took a common local catastrophe and magnified it. Frazer's point here seems to have some force, but there is another possibility. Frequently in the transmission of ancient stories and legends the details have been modified to fit circumstances with which the local com-

78. John Bright, "Has Archaeology Found Evidence of the Flood?" *The Biblical Archaeologist* 5 (December 1942):56, 58, 59.
79. Frazer, 1:329-32.
80. Byron Nelson, *The Deluge Story in Stone*, p. 168.
81. Morris and Whitcomb, p. 54.

munity was more familiar. An obvious example of this is the custom of Medieval artists to depict Old Testament characters in Italian robes. Furthermore, it is common for local circumstances to become woven into any ancient story.[82] This is particularly noticeable in the tendency to bring ancient heroes and gods into the primitive stories.

The myths of the Egyptians are full of this tendency. As an original story from the city of Memphis is passed on to the city of Thebes, the local deity at Thebes takes the place of the deity at Memphis, or the theology is slightly modified to accommodate both. It could be that the islands and sea coast peoples lost the notion of rain as a causative agent during the transmission because they wanted to account for the Flood in terms of the causative agent with which they were most familiar — rising tides produced by earthquakes at sea.

(4) Finally, Frazer argues that since the earthquakes at sea can explain the coastal flood stories, then why cannot heavy rains explain the inland flood stories? Could be? Maybe? Might have been? This point is obviously based on the same difficulties as the preceding.

The simplest way to account for the universal testimony to a water heaven and a global flood is to assume that they represent a genuine cultural memory of a situation described by Noah's sons to their descendants. Although the case for a pre-Flood vapor canopy does not rest on this kind of data, it is certainly strikingly confirmed by it. The invention of writing, the excellent memories of ancient peoples, and the tendency of kings and other individuals to preserve their records in writing have led many anthropologists to believe that behind all legends there is an element of historical truth.[83]

---

82. Filby, p. 37.
83. Ibid., p. 38.

CHAPTER 5

Scientific Evidence for the Vapor Canopy Model

Something as stupendous as a vast thermal vapor blanket would undoubtedly have left an imprint on the geophysics of the ancient earth. At one presentation of the canopy hypothesis before a group of secular college students and professors, an anthropologist objected that there was no scientific evidence for the existence of such a canopy. Actually, the scientific evidence is sizable, if not conclusive; yet it is often difficult to present a "provable" case for any events of the geologic past. How, then, do we analyze the past?

One way is to design a model. From this model we can make certain predictions about such items as climate and the rock record. If an investigation of the rock record affirms those predictions, then we have to conclude that the proposed model is plausible. It must be admitted that it is impossible to prove the existence of such a canopy in a purely scientific sense. That is true of the theory of evolution, the theories of the ice ages, or almost any other reconstruction made by scientists about the ancient earth.

Another way a scientist goes about his job is to reproduce certain experiments in the laboratory over and over again, make observations about his results, and from those results draw conclusions and principles. However, in events of geological history, the crucial element of reproducibility is missing. How can one reproduce the ice age, the fracture of the continents, or the climatic regime of the paleozoic earth? Obviously this is impossible. Yet it is possible to construct scientific theories about the causes and effects of these events. We do this by designing a plausible model of "how it might have been," then making certain predictions on the basis of the model. When the predictions are confirmed by the evidence, the model rises in status.[1]

For example, the planet Pluto was discovered when a scientist observed some unusual perturbations in the orbit of the planet Neptune. Those perturbations led him to believe that there might be another planet beyond Neptune responsible for them. He constructed a model in which the orbit of that planet might be described, basing it on the limited data gathered from observing Neptune's orbit. From that model he predicted certain fluctuations in the future in Neptune's orbit and that this planet would be found in a certain quadrant of the sky at a certain time in the future. Sure enough, the predicted fluctuation in Neptune's orbit occurred, and the planet was discovered in the predicted quadrant.[2] The model was confirmed.

In the following pages we will make reference to various strata designations derived from historical geology. When *Cambrian* is mentioned, for example, what is meant is that type of strata designated by historical geology as being about 500 million years of age. These dates are, of course, not accepted by the creationist scientist.

THE VAPOR CANOPY MODEL

We will follow the same procedure in this analysis of the pre-Flood vapor canopy. The following is a proposed description of the model:

MODEL DESCRIPTION: The pre-Flood earth was enveloped in a thermal vapor blanket capable of precipitating many feet of water which condensed in the recent geological past in 40 days due to volcanic eruption, resulting in a geographically universal flood.

1. George Shortley and Dudley Williams, *Principles of College Physics*, 1:5.
2. This example is not exact because Pluto *was* found, but the vapor canopy never will be. Neither will evolution in the past ever be observed.

Notice the six key points in this model:

(1) The earth was surrounded by a vapor blanket. This is based on the evidences suggested in the previous chapters. In particular we focus on the statement of Genesis 1:6-7 of the celestial ocean. It is "inferred" that this ocean turned to vapor by the fourth creative day due to lower pressure and higher temperatures. We admit that the text does not explicitly say this, but that has little effect on either the model or the predictions.[3]

(2) This pre-Flood atmosphere contained sufficient water vapor to sustain a 40-day-and-night rainfall of about 0.5 inches per hour as discussed in chapter 2. This amounts to about 40 feet of water and, hence, 2.18 atmospheres of atmospheric pressure on the pre-Flood earth (Gen. 7:11-12).[4]

(3) The condensation of this canopy was recent. A strict chronology in the genealogies of Genesis 10 would suggest that the date of the Flood was around 2500 B.C. Furthermore, this notion of "recent" implies that the days of Genesis are literal 24-hour days. The day-age theory is not considered exegetically probable.[5]

3. The rationale for this switch from liquid to vapor will be explained in chapter 7.
4. One foot of water at 4° C = 0.029499 atm: *Handbook of Chemistry and Physics,* p. F-301. Therefore 1 atm = 33.8 ft. of water.
5. For a discussion of the day-age view see Gleason Archer, *A Survey of the Old Testament Introduction,* pp. 174-78. The rationale for the literal 24-hour-day view is presented by Henry Morris in *Biblical Cosmology and Modern Science,* pp. 56-71. For a discussion of the "no gap" view of the genealogies of Genesis 5 and 11 see H. David Clark, "The Genealogies of Genesis Five and Eleven." The classic argument for the gap theory of the genealogies may be found in William Henry Green, "Primeval Chronology," in *Classical Evangelical Essays in Old Testament Interpretation,* pp. 13-28 and in Benjamin B. Warfield, "On the Antiquity and Unity of the Human Race," in *Biblical and Theological Studies,* pp. 238-61.

(4) The "canopy" condensed in 40 days during the rainfall of the Flood of Noah (Gen. 7:12). This "sudden" condensation reduced the atmospheric pressure on the surface of the earth from 2.18 atmospheres to its present level.

(5) The cause of the condensation of the canopy was apparently the action of volcanoes in hurling volcanic ash into the atmosphere, providing condensation nuclei for the rain to form on (Gen. 7:11; Psalm 18:7-15).[6]

(6) The massive amounts of rain that descended produced a geographically universal deluge (Gen. 7:11-12; see vv. 6-8).[7]

These six characteristics of the vapor canopy model were determined by exegesis of the biblical text or by probable deductions from such exegesis. This exegesis and these deductions give us a "framework" for examining some of the phenomena of the ancient earth. This does not give us an exhaustive biblical model of ancient prehistory — only of one aspect of it, though a major one at that. These six items give us the sense in which the Bible *is* a textbook of modern science. They give us the faith framework within which scientific investigation of the ancient earth can profitably be carried on.

Now, based on this model, certain predictions could be made. Should the predictions be confirmed by the field data, then the model is probable. In this, the "scientific" evidence for the existence of earth's pre-Flood vapor blanket rests.

The Predictions

Assuming the validity of the model, at least ten predictions could be made about the geophysics of the ancient earth directly from the model. They are:

(1) A greenhouse effect
(2) High present-day concentration of He_3

6. It is debatable, of course, that Psalm 18 refers to Flood events. It is being assumed here that the catastrophic imagery of the psalm reflects the Deluge regardless of its specific application to local historical events.
7. However, most of the water of the Deluge came from the fountains of the deep (Gen. 7:11).

Scientific Evidence for the Vapor Canopy Model

(3) Increased atmospheric pressure
(4) Shielding from cosmic radiation
(5) A global flood
(6) Volcanic ash mixed with glacial ice
(7) A sudden and permanent temperature drop in the polar regions
(8) Fewer meteorites in pre-Flood strata
(9) Residual amounts of water in the stratosphere today
(10) A changed appearance of the heavenly bodies

Obviously, several different mechanisms could explain some of the above phenomena. In fact, for some of them the present day geologist has perfectly acceptable mechanisms based on his own models. However, if a model could be found that accounts for all of them with one simple assumption — a vapor canopy — then a highly probable model has been established.

The efficiency of any theory is equal to the number of facts correlated divided by the number of assumptions made.[8] If, in making just this one assumption, it is possible to correlate many divergent and seemingly unrelated facts, then the theory moves from possibility to probability. This is preeminently the case with the vapor canopy hypothesis, and it is on this fact that the "scientific" evidence for the existence of that canopy is based. Why, then, do these particular predictions naturally arise from a consideration of a vapor canopy model, and what is the evidence that these predictions are confirmed in the rock record?

PREDICTION 1: A GREENHOUSE EFFECT

Gilbert Plass gives us a helpful illustration of a greenhouse effect:

> A familiar instance of the "greenhouse effect" is the heating up of a closed automobile when it stands for awhile in the summer sun. Like the atmosphere, the car's windows are transparent to the sun's visible radiation which warms up the upholstery and metal inside the car; and the materials in turn re-emit some of their heat as infrared radiation. Glass, like

8. Provided there is not an equally long list of phenomena which do not fit the model.

CO_2, absorbs some of this radiation and thus traps the heat, and the temperature inside the car rises.[9]

Nearly one hundred years ago Isaac Vail suggested that just such a condition may have existed on the pre-Flood earth due to a ringed ice canopy.[10] That would have tended to put the entire earth in a temperature equilibrium, hence there would have been no violent winds or rainfalls.[11] It would have been a gentle climate, moderate at both poles.

Due to the canopy, a larger percentage of the sun's energy would have been absorbed and uniformly distributed over the earth than at present. This would have tended to inhibit atmospheric circulation and winds. One might, therefore, propose that the pre-Flood atmosphere would have had few particles of dust and salt stirred up by winds.

Geologists have long been aware of the evidence in the rock record that at one time the entire earth seems to have been uniformly tropical. Often this has been explained on the basis of an increase in solar radiation in the past. However, this is only one factor that controls climate on a worldwide basis. No evidence exists that changes have taken place in the radiation of the sun, but it is not necessary that there have been a change in the sun. If there were a change in the heat-absorbing capacity of the atmosphere, that would accomplish the same thing.[12] It seems equally possible that the worldwide warm climate was not due to an increase in solar radiation, but rather to an in-

9. Gilbert N. Plass, "Carbon Dioxide and Climate," *Scientific American* 201 (July 1959):41.
10. Isaac N. Vail, *The Waters Above the Firmament*, p. 86.
11. Preliminary data from Venus tends to support this. At high altitudes wind velocities of 224 mph were observed, while at 6 miles altitude velocities of only 4.5 mph prevailed, a gentle breeze: Richard B. Noll and Michael B. McElroy, "Engineering Models of the Venus Atmosphere," *Journal of Spacecraft and Rockets* 11 (January 1974):23.
12. See Henry M. Morris and John C. Whitcomb, *The Genesis Flood*, p. 252. These authors have developed this theme extensively, quoting much geologic literature establishing the existence of a former tropical climatic regime.

crease in the radiation absorption capacities of the atmosphere. The most likely means of accomplishing this would be through the increase in water vapor in the upper atmosphere.

What, then, is the evidence of a tropical climate on the ancient earth such as the vapor canopy model would predict?

Limestone deposits in the higher latitudes in the Cambrian indicate that they were deposited in warm or temperate waters, much warmer than today's.[13] Temperature determinations by the 0-18 method throughout Mesozoic strata indicate higher temperatures than today. For example, in Scotland, during the Jurassic, the Mesozoic temperature was 17-23° C, whereas today it is 7-13° C. In England, during the Cretaceous, this method yielded temperature values of 16-23° C compared to today's 5-15° C.[14] Palm tree fossils have been found in early Tertiary strata in Alaska. Crocodiles were prolific at that time in New Jersey and in England. They are present only in tropical climates today.[15] Eocene London was at a temperature of 20° C compared to today's 10° C. During the Pliocene (25 million years ago), Frankfurt, Germany, had a temperature of 14° C compared to today's 9° C. All of these temperature determinations are based on the 0-18 method which is very uncertain. However, it at least indicates a considerably warmer climate in comparison to today.[16]

The evidence indicates that in Europe and North America, a warm climate prevailed into the high latitudes from the Cambrian to the end of the Tertiary, a period of over 500 million years.[17] Most of the Mesozoic was tropical. "In those days the earth had a tropical or sub-tropical climate over much of its land surface, and in the widespread tropical lands there was an abundance of lush vegetation. The land was low and there were no high mountains forming physical or climatic barriers."[18]

13. Ibid., p. 244.
14. A. E. M. Nairn, *Descriptive Paleoclimatology*, p. 267.
15. Ibid., p. 268.
16. Ibid., p. 270.
17. Ibid., p. 256.
18. E. H. Colbert, "Evolutionary Growth Rates in the Dinosaurs," *Scientific Monthly* 69 (August 1949):71.

Explorer Edward Toll reported finding a fallen ninety-foot fruit tree with ripe fruit and green leaves still on its branches in the frozen ground of the New Siberian Islands. The only tree vegetation that grows there now is the one-inch-high willow.[19] This suggests that the climate in Siberia was once tropical and suddenly changed to a freezing temperature. In Antarctica large fossil leaves of tropical plants have been found in Permian sandstone 250 miles from the South Pole. The coal and fossil wood deposits there testify to a favorable climate in the past.[20] Furthermore, fossil trees with thirty-four well-defined rings were found, which indicates rapid growth in a temperate climate.[21] A once swampy, humid environment is indicated by the lush vegetation found in Antarctica. Right after the Devonian, a severe climatic change occurred, and continental glaciation set in. Could this be related to the Flood?

Near Cairo, Egypt, broad-leaf forests were suddenly entombed and petrified, indicating that at one time the climate was lush and humid. Today, Cairo's average annual rainfall is three to four inches.[22] In the arid American West, we find petrified forests containing broad-leaf deciduous trees, conifer trees, and even palm trees. The tree rings suggest that they were large and fast growing. All of this suggests a sudden change in humidity, which is what one would expect if the earth's pre-Flood vapor canopy condensed in forty days, thus radically altering the temperature equilibrium and climate regimes all over the planet.

19. Charles Hapgood, "The Mystery of the Frozen Mammoths," *Coronet* (September 1960):74; Bassett Digby, *The Mammoth and Mammoth Hunting Grounds in Northeast Siberia*, pp. 150-51.
20. George A. Doumani and William E. Long, "The Ancient Life of Antarctica," *Scientific American* 207 (September 1962):169.
21. Ibid.
22. Donald W. Patten, "The Pre-Flood Greenhouse Effect," in *A Symposium on Creation, II*, p. 19.

It is estimated that the difference of air temperature between pole and equator was only 43° F during the Cretaceous, compared with 86° F today. Table 5.1 shows a typically assumed temperature distribution.[23]

TABLE 5.1

AIR TEMPERATURES IN THE CRETACEOUS

Latitude/Degrees	Mean Sea-level Air Temperature (Cretaceous)/°F	Mean Sea-level Temperature (today)/°F
0	88	82
20	84	77
40	73	61
60	57	39
80	48	3.2
90	45	−4

One of the major difficulties of the canopy explanation for the tropical regime of the ancient earth is the apparent existence of local ice ages in the Permian, a time when, on our present model, the canopy would still be surrounding the pre-Flood earth. Vast glaciation has been observed in the equatorial areas of Africa, South America, and India. It is, of course, possible that the Permian strata are post-Flood, and hence no particular difficulty would be involved. In fact, the Flood would then be an explanation for the existence of glaciers at the equator.

Some geologists have accounted for this Permian glaciation as well as the tropical fossil material at the South Pole by the Gondwanaland concept. Gondwanaland is said to be the southern part of a vast supercontinent that existed long ago. When continental drift began, Gondwanaland broke off from the land mass and supposedly migrated around the South Pole while

23. Cherrie D. Bramwell and G. R. Whitfield, "Biomechanics of Pteranodon," *Philosophical Transactions of the Royal Society of London, B. Biological Sciences* 267 (11 July 1976):564.

being periodically glaciated and then moving back up to the tropics. However, there are serious difficulties with this explanation.

> For example, there is little evidence that climatic belts existed in the earlier history of the earth; yet climatic zonation, both latitudinal and vertical, is clearly apparent in all parts of the earth today. This anomalous situation is difficult to explain. It is impossible to reconstruct a super-continent which could lie entirely within one climatic regime. Any rotating planet, orbiting the sun on an inclined axis of rotation, must have climatic zonation. It is obvious, therefore, that climatic conditions in the past were significantly different from those in evidence today.[24]

Even if the earth's axis were not tilted, there should still be climatic zonation belts. Their absence suggests a uniform moderate climate on the ancient earth, the precise prediction of the canopy model.

It is also possible that the supposed evidences for this glaciation do not really suggest ice at all. The evidence for Permian glaciation rests on the existence of tillites and striation. Tillites are hardened tills, which are non-sorted aggregations of gravel, sand, and some boulders in a clay matrix. Striations are scratch marks supposedly carved by the ice in the rock beneath. Morris has pointed out that there are many other agencies that could have left these things. In a catastrophe such as the biblical Deluge, it seems easy to imagine that violent currents carrying such items as boulders and sediments at fantastic speeds could have left much evidence of striations and tillites completely unrelated to ice.[25]

Supposedly, gouge marks in softer soil, buried and filled in later, are evidence that a glacier passed by. However, a Cana-

24. Edgar B. Heylmun, "Should We Teach Uniformitarianism?" *Journal of Geological Education* 19 (January 1971):36; see also M. J. Budyko, "The Effect of Solar Radiation Variations on the Climate of the Earth," *Tellus* XXI, 5 (1969):611.
25. Morris and Whitcomb, pp. 247-48. For an extensive discussion of the so-called Permian glaciation and the geological evidence against it, see Harold W. Clark, *Fossils, Flood, and Fire*, pp. 106-10.

dian expedition using specially insulated diving equipment has been studying the action of icebergs (not glaciers) scraping along the bottom of the ocean. One of the men concerned said, "When you look behind, you find the sea floor gouged out as though a giant ploughshare had gone through."[26] Could not this suggest something about gouge marks commonly attributed to glaciers during the ice age? Could not the gouge marks, which supposedly give evidence of Permian glaciation in India and elsewhere, be the results of icebergs floating on the top of the receding flood waters in a later era? When the canopy condensed, sudden cooling would have resulted in many areas, producing icebergs that floated in the post-Flood waters.[27] As they floated toward the equator they would have melted.

PREDICTION 2: HIGH PRESENT DAY CONCENTRATION OF HE_3

In our present atmosphere there is an unusually high concentration of He_3. Whitcomb and Morris first called attention to this as a possible evidence that the earth's troposphere may have once been surrounded by a water vapor canopy.

> In addition to the formation of Carbon 14 from nitrogen in the atmosphere by cosmic-ray neutrons, these neutrons also react with deuterium (heavy hydrogen, the hydrogen isotope in heavy water), which would undoubtedly have been present in substantial amounts in such a canopy, to form tritium, a still heavier isotope of hydrogen. Tritium is unstable and decays rapidly by beta decay to an isotope of helium, He_3. But it turns out that there is too much He_3 in the atmosphere to be accounted for by this process operating at present rates during geologic time.[28]

26. *The Kingston* (Ontario) *Whig-Standard*, 21 September 1970, p. 3.
27. The factors producing such a temperature drop will be analyzed in a later chapter. For thorough discussion of the problems related to interpreting till, drift, and striations as an evidence of glaciation, see Sir Henry Howorth, *The Glacial Nightmare and the Flood* and *Ice or Water*, a two-volume sequel. These works are summarized by Douglas E. Cox, "Problems in the Glacial Theory," *Creation Research Society Quarterly* 13 (June 1976): 25-34.
28. Morris and Whitcomb, p. 375.

Deuterium is always present in water at a ratio of about 1 part deuterium for every 6,000 parts ordinary hydrogen.[29] Thus, the more water present in the atmosphere, the more deuterium present. This would result in much more tritium, which is formed by the bombardment of deuterium by cosmic-ray neutrons. Therefore, since tritium decays to He_3 with a half life of 12.5 years, much greater amounts of He_3 would be predicted if greater amounts of water were once in the atmosphere. In fact, this is exactly what is found. Serge Korff, a cosmic-ray authority, comments:

> There are two factors which would tend to increase the amount of tritium. One of these is that the intensity of cosmic radiation, and hence the rate of production of neutrons, might have been higher at some time in the geologic past. . . . The second possibility invoking action in the past assumes that at a time when the earth was warmer the atmosphere contained much more water vapor, and [the process of generating tritium from deuterium] might have been operating at a much higher rate than at present.[30]

PREDICTION 3: GREATER ATMOSPHERIC PRESSURE

Forty feet of precipitable water resting in a canopy above the ancient atmosphere would have increased the surface pressure considerably. This amount of water is equivalent to 1.18 atmospheres and would result in a surface atmospheric pressure under the canopy of 2.18 atmospheres.[31] Since air density and partial pressure of oxygen are both directly proportional to the atmospheric pressure, both of these atmospheric characteristics would have been multiplied by 2.18 times the present values. Thus, the density of air at the surface would be 0.00283 gm/cm³ (instead of today's value of 0.0013 gm/cm³), and the partial pressure of oxygen would be 348.73 mm of Hg (instead of today's value of 159.97 mm of Hg). It would be of great

29. *Handbook of Chemistry and Physics*, p. B-19.
30. Serge A. Korff, "Effects of the Cosmic Radiation on Terrestrial Isotope Distribution," *Transactions, American Geophysical Union* 35 (February 1954):105.
31. One atmosphere is equivalent to 34 feet of fresh water.

Scientific Evidence for the Vapor Canopy Model

interest to know if there were anything in the geologic record that could be more easily explained by these differing atmospheric parameters than by present theories.

The aerodynamics of the pteranodon. One of the marvels of natural history is the gigantic flying reptile called the pteranodon, whose remains are found in Cretaceous sediments. The wingspan of these flying reptiles has been estimated to be 6.95 meters. Table 5.2 gives the principal parameters of the pteranodon.[32]

TABLE 5.2

THE PRINCIPAL PARAMETERS OF PTERANODON INGENS

wing span	6.95 m
wing area	4.62 m²
weight	16.6 kgf or 163N
aspect ratio	10.5
frontal area (head & body)	0.1 m²

Many authors have expressed wonder at how the animal could ever have flown. Bellairs states, "Pteranodon had great difficulty in taking off from flat surfaces,"[33] while Romer comments, "How this animal could get itself into the air from level ground is difficult to understand."[34] The minimum flying speed necessary for these animals to sustain flight is easily calculated from the standard formulas,[35]

$$L = C_L(1/2)\rho v^2 S \quad (5.1)$$
$$D = C_D(1/2)\rho v^2 S \quad (5.2)$$

32. Bramwell and Whitfield, p. 556.
33. Angus de'A. Bellairs, *Reptiles*, p. 118.
34. A. S. Romer, *Vertebrate Palaeontology*, p. 146.
35. Bramwell and Whitfield, p. 555.

where S = the wing area, ρ = the density of the air, 0.0013 gm/cm^3; v^2 = the flying speed; C_L = the lift coefficient; and C_D = the drag coefficient. In order for the animal to sustain flight, the lift force, L, must be equal to or greater than the weight of the animal, Wt = mg. Solving for v^2,

$$v^2 = \frac{2mg}{C_L \rho S}. \quad (5.3)$$

Assuming a relatively high lift coefficient of 1 (as is commonly done),[36]

$$v^2 = \frac{(2)(16.6 \text{ kg})(9.8 \text{ m/sec}^2)}{(1)(1.3 \text{ kg/m}^3)(4.62 \text{ m}^2)}$$

$$v = 7.3 \text{ m/sec}$$
$$= 16.4 \text{ mph}.$$

This means that in order for the pteranodon to fly a wind of 16.4 mph must sweep across its wings, because it cannot run at all.[37]

A wind velocity of 16.4 mph is rated a "moderate breeze" by meteorologists.[38] It seems that this raises some problems for flight. The pteranodon apparently had to await a moderate breeze before it could take off from a standing position.

This clumsy arrangement would be somewhat lessened if the air density was greater. Under canopy conditions with ρ = 0.00283 gm/cm^3 v would equal 11.6 mph or a "gentle breeze."[39] Flight would have been more easily achieved for these flying reptiles with the greater atmospheric pressures created by the vapor canopy.

Of great interest, however, is the recent discovery of a pterosaur, a variation of the pteranodon, in some nonmarine

36. Ibid., p. 556.
37. Ibid., p. 569.
38. F. A. Berry, E. Bollay, and Norman R. Beers, eds., *Handbook of Meteorology*, p. 47.
39. Ibid. It is interesting to note that the average wind speed in the Dallas-Fort Worth area over the last ten years was 12.5 mph: David G. Lee, "Wind Power," *National Wildlife* 13 (August-September 1975):31.

rock in West Texas.[40] Its location in nonmarine rock is significant because that indicates it was not located near water surfaces. It had been thought that those animals fed largely on fish and were able to soar due to the thermal updrafts and turbulent updrafts created by water temperature and wave motion.[41] Furthermore, the topography in West Texas is flat and hence the updrafts for soaring created by hills and cliffs were not as prevalent. Under those circumstances, the pterosaur would have been largely dependent on wind velocity to sustain flight at all.

Most amazing was the apparent length of the wingspan. A humerus of 52 cm was found, which can be correlated to wingspan by the following equation:[42]

$$W = 29.7 H^{1.0116} \qquad (5.4)$$

where W = wingspan in cm, H is humerus length in cm. From (5.4), a humerus length of 52 cm yields a wingspan of 1616 cm (53 feet). From this we can make some relatively accurate estimates of its wing area and mass. "It can readily be shown that if one enlarges a flying creature without change of shape, then the mass increases in proportion to the cube of the wingspan, b, but the wing area only increases proportional to b^2."[43]

So the wing area of this Texas pterosaur was 24.9 m², and its mass was about 208 kg. We can see from Equation (5.3) that the minimum flight velocity would have been 25 mph or a "strong

40. Douglas A. Lawson, "Pterosaur from the Latest Cretaceous of West Texas: Discovery of the Largest Flying Creature," Science 187 (14 March 1975):947-48.
41. Bramwell and Whitfield, "Biomechanics of Pteranodon," pp. 565-71.
42. George G. Shor, Jr., "Letters, Could Pterosaurs Fly?" Science 188 (16 May 1975):677. Also, reported by Edwin H. Colbert as having a wingspan of 51 ft., E. H. Colbert, ed., "When Reptiles Ruled," Our Continent, A Natural History of North America, p. 95.
43. Bramwell and Whitfield, p. 559.

breeze."[44] However, under the increased atmospheric pressure of the canopy, a much more reasonable (but still high) value of 17 mph would have been required.

What about powered flight? "Pteranodon is large enough to cast doubt on its ability to fly under power. But it is difficult to see how such a creature could survive without this ability, and the wings are clearly designed to be flapped."[45] The pteranodon's minimum rate of sink was $v_s = 0.42$ m/sec.[46] This constitutes a loss of power by

$$\text{POWER LOSS} = mgv_s \qquad (5.5)$$
$$= (16.6 \text{ kg})(9.8 \text{ N/m}-\text{sec}^2)(0.42 \text{ m/sec})$$
$$= 68 \text{ watts.}$$

In order for flight to be sustained by power from the animal, the pteranodon must be able to deliver at least 68 watts of power. The maximum output power for birds today has been calculated at 98 watts.[47] Assuming an 80% efficiency in converting muscular power to thrust, the pteranodon had a useful power output of 78 watts compared with the minimum power for flight of 68 watts. Bramwell points out that this is "barely sufficient," particularly because the 98 watts output power figure is the upper maximum limit for birds today.

It would appear that the pteranodon must have had much more muscular tissue and a greater efficiency in converting muscular power to thrust than today's birds. The increased oxygen tension in the blood created by the larger partial pressure of O_2 under the canopy could conceivably have contributed to the animal's ability to deliver thrust and continue flight without a too-rapid buildup of oxygen debt.

44. Anyone who has developed the healthy habit of regular jogging will immediately recognize that a wind velocity of over 15 mph is sufficient to send the average jogger to his indoor treadmill.
45. Bramwell and Whitfield, p. 558.
46. Ibid.
47. Ibid., p. 559.
48. Ibid., p. 555. See pp. 555-60 for discussion of the equations and method on which the following discussion is based.

Scientific Evidence for the Vapor Canopy Model

Under the canopy the coefficient of drag would also increase. This has a direct bearing on the velocity of sink.[48]

$$\frac{v_s}{v} = C_D/C_L \tag{5.6}$$

Using the method outlined by Bramwell, and assuming that the wind profile drag is multiplied by 2.18 due to the increased atmospheric pressure (surface atmospheric pressure with 40 feet of precipitable water in the canopy), the minimum sink velocity would have been 0.59 m/sec. From Equation (5.5) we see that this equals a power loss of 96 watts. In other words, in order for one of these animals to have sustained powered flight under the canopy, its body would have had to have the capability of delivering 96 watts. In view of the fact that the maximum observed today is 98 watts, this creates an obvious problem. However, in all of the above calculations there are many variables and uncertainties. Furthermore, it is clear that even without the canopy, a greater muscular power and efficiency must be assumed for these flying reptiles. There is also the additional aid that increased oxygen tension would make in supplying energy to the muscles under the greater atmospheric pressure during the reign of the water heaven.

In conclusion, a note on the extinction of the pteranodon is appropriate. This gigantic creature was primarily a soaring reptile. It probably used powered flight only rarely and when necessary. Due to the aerodynamics of the wing sections, there is an upper and lower limit to the wind velocities under which a 16.6 kgf pteranodon could sustain flight. The lower limit appears to be around 16.4 mph, according to (5.3). The upper limit is around 31 mph.[49] Above 31 mph the sink velocity is so high, and the lift coefficient so low, that the animal could not maintain any kind of controlled flight. This raises some interesting speculations on how its extinction may have been related to the vapor canopy.

We assume that when Noah took two of every kind on the ark, pteranodons were among the animals preserved. Yet, for some reason, they were not able to survive the post-Flood environ-

---

49. Ibid., see table on p. 556 and note on p. 578.

ment and quickly became extinct. Bramwell's comments are worth quoting in full.

> If a specific reason for the extinction of Pteranodon is sought, then a change in climate could easily account for it. Pteranodon, with gliding speeds between 7 and 14 mtr/sec [16 and 31 mph] was superbly adapted to light wind soaring. If the average wind speed had risen by only 5 mtr/sec, this alone would make Pteranodon's mode of life impossible. Such a change in wind speed could be brought about by a cooling of the climate, giving greater differentiation of temperature between poles and equator, leading to faster overall wind speeds. The birds survived the Cretaceous extinction. It could be significant that they are faster flyers than Pteranodon, and would have been able to deal with stronger winds.[50]

An analysis of the biomechanics of these ancient reptiles indicates that their demise would have been occasioned by precisely the same kind of atmospheric phenomenon associated with the condensation of earth's vapor canopy. With the loss of the canopy, the greenhouse would disappear, and exaggerated pole-to-equator temperature differential would develop, leading to greatly increased wind velocities which may have been beyond the range of the pteranodon's ability to handle. Even if they survived these increased wind velocities, they would become extinct in the present world where the lower atmospheric pressure results in a reduced lift coefficient and an inability to fly.

Gigantism in the fossil record. Another of the marvels of the ancient world was the surprisingly large size of its faunal inhabitants. Giant lizards weighing over 40 tons were common. Why is it that these animals flourished at one time and are now absent? Why are there no giants (except for aquatic animals like whales) today? Since climatic conditions that are thought to have prevailed in ancient times do prevail today in certain areas of the earth, it is unlikely that gigantism can be explained in terms of abundant food supply and tropical climate. A number of discussions of why ancient climates may have been favorable to gigantism have been published. It is commonly argued that "spacing" was a factor.[51] The fewer animals per square mile of

---

50. Ibid., p. 578.
51. Edwin H. Colbert, *The Age of Reptiles,* pp. 144-45.

forage area means lesser effort in acquiring food. For a large animal that requires much food, this would enable him to survive more easily in that there would be less competition.

It has also been pointed out that the large size of dinosaurs would have been favorable for the maintaining of a constant body temperature in a cold-blooded organism. Large size means large heat capacity and resistance to minor weather variations. Hence, a cold-blooded animal could have survived more easily if it was larger because its body temperature was regulated by ambient temperature.[52]

Neither of these explanations account for the absence of giants today. It would be nice if their absence could be explained by some environmental condition that is not present today that may have been present then. One such environmental condition would have been an increased partial pressure of oxygen in the atmosphere.

The large size of these animals raises the theoretical question of how they were able to supply oxygen to their tissue mass. This question is also relevant to the gigantic insects and shells which used to live on the earth, as well as vertebrates. Insects, arachnids, and many other invertebrates, take in oxygen through the skin by diffusion. This raises the question of how large such an animal could become before it could not acquire sufficient oxygen to maintain its metabolism. "Further, if oxygen can make its way in only by diffusion from the surface, the bigger an animal the lower, under given conditions, will be the concentration of oxygen at its center. It is obvious that there must be some size at which the concentration becomes too low for activity, and that the animal cannot exceed this size."[53]

Thus, some invertebrates can exist only at certain size limits in order for the oxygen from the atmosphere to diffuse to the

52. See James R. Spotila et. al., "A Mathematical Model for Body Temperatures of Large Reptiles: Implications for Dinosaur Ecology," *The American Naturalist* 107 (May-June 1973):391-404; Warren P. Porter and David M. Gates, "Thermodynamic Equilibria of Animals with Environment," *Ecological Monographs* 39 (Summer 1969):227-44.
53. W. B. Yapp, *An Introduction to Animal Physiology*, p. 127.

center in sufficient concentration to sustain metabolic processes. Why are insects with 25-inch wingspans no longer found? Why are the giant shell creatures, spiders, and other invertebrates not in existence today? If these animals once lived in an atmosphere where the partial pressure of oxygen was greater than today, they would have been able to exist at larger sizes.

So for both the giant lizard and the invertebrate the theoretical consideration exists: the reason they no longer exist in these large sizes is because the partial pressure of oxygen in our atmosphere has dropped. If the earth had been surrounded by a vapor canopy, the atmospheric pressure would have been 2.18 atm (assuming 40 feet of precipitable water in the canopy) and partial pressure of oxygen would have been 348.73 mm of Hg instead of today's value of 159.97.

An increase in the partial pressure of oxygen does not increase the amount of oxygen carried by the hemoglobin in the blood of vertebrates. But it does increase the oxygen tension in the plasma. Presently, the oxygen tension in man in the alveolar sacs is about 100 mm of Hg. By the time it passes through the capillaries, it is reduced to about 45 mm of Hg. Since the oxygen tension in the interstitial fluids (body fluids between the capillaries and the cells) is only 40 mm of Hg, there is a net diffusion driving force of at least 5 mm of Hg of O_2 forcing oxygen into the cells of the body through the interstitial fluids.[54]

Could it be that, due to the greater oxygen requirements of the large vertebrates, they required more oxygen than the present diffusion driving force could supply? If the oxygen tension in the alveolar sacs was doubled due to increased atmospheric pressure, this would increase the oxygen diffusion force (it is probably not a linear increase) and hence enable the animal to deliver more oxygen to its biomass effectively.

So the great size of some animals in the past may be linked to this increased cardiovascular efficiency. The ratio between lung capacity and body mass would seem to be too small to

---

54. Arthur J. Vander, James H. Sherman, and Dorothy S. Luciano, *Human Physiology: The Mechanics of Body Function*, p. 315.

support such creatures as dinosaurs. This ratio would be even more improbable if the recent speculations about dinosaurs being warm blooded are true.[55] Warm-blooded animals require immensely greater quantities of oxygen to maintain their greatly increased metabolic rate. The lung capacity necessary to fully oxygenate a two-ton warm-blooded animal cannot be found in the fossils of dinosaurs that once roamed the earth.[56]

Due to the variables involved, there seems to be no way of meaningfully extrapolating back to ancient animals to check this. But a reduced oxygen tension in the atmosphere due to the condensation of the vapor canopy would result in one variable that could have some bearing on why giant animals do not live in today's atmosphere.

Presumably, Noah would have taken newly born dinosaurs on the ark. As they entered the post-Flood environment, and grew, they were unable to survive in a climate of reduced oxygen partial pressure, and they actually suffocated.

There is evidence that higher oxygen tension can be decidedly beneficial to biological systems. When a team of aquanauts were submerged in a diving bell for two weeks at 10 atmospheres, a striking healing occurred after one of them severely cut his hand. It was reported that the wound healed completely in 24 hours. It was theorized that the reason for this was that the higher oxygen tension created a greater diffusion driving force and imparted more oxygen at a greater rate into the wound. As a result, experiments in high-pressure surgery were begun, and hyperbaric surgery is now a common practice in certain situations. Also, it has been discovered that an effective treatment for some kinds of gangrene is to place the patient

55. Robert T. Bakker, "Dinosaur Renaissance," *Scientific American* 232 (April 1975):58-78; note also "Warm-Blooded Dinosaurs," a "Nova" television program of WGBH, 125 Western Avenue, Boston, Massachusetts 01234.
56. Kirby Anderson, M. S. evolution, Yale University. Research Associate with Probe Ministries, Dallas, Texas, personal communication, 22 August 1977.

in a high-pressure chamber for a period of time.[57] Thus, it would seem that a higher atmospheric pressure could have resulted in conditions that were favorable for the cure of some illnesses, and hence could have some bearing on longevity of life indicated in Genesis 5.

At the HBO (Hyperbaric Oxygen) Center in Lauderdale-by-the-Sea, Florida, Claude Kirk has been administering hyperbaric oxygen treatments for many years with startling results. Patients treated for short periods at 2.5 atm of pure oxygen and gradually decompressed showed remarkable relief from the effects of aging. Dr. Edgar End of Milwaukee, one of the nation's leading experts in hyperbaric oxygen treatment, said:

> Unquestionably, hyperbaric oxygenation can often reverse the side effects of aging. I've seen it work in scores of cases. It improves memory, increases energy and works remarkably well with men and women who were demonstrably senile. In addition, it is a highly effective treatment for strokes. I've had patients carried into the hyperbaric chamber after a verified stroke and walk out after the first treatment. It has been used successfully for gas gangrene, ostomyelitis, smoke inhalation and other problems.[58]

Although 2.5 atm of pure oxygen (1520 mm Hg of O_2) is considerably greater than the partial pressure of oxygen under a 40-foot vapor canopy (348.73 mm of Hg), the remarkable effects of this treatment do suggest an area for fruitful research. Could a relatively small increase in the partial pressure of oxygen when extended over an entire lifetime have similar or even greater effects than hyperbaric oxygen administered to senile patients in their seventies?

The great size of some of the dinosaurs may indicate longevity. It is well known that, within size and skeletal limitations, repiles continue to grow until death.[59] In this respect, reptiles

57. Don Wiggans, Ph. D., biochemistry, professor of biochemistry, University of Texas Health Science Center, Dallas, Texas, personal communication, December 1976.
58. Paul Martin, "Stay Young with Hyperbaric Oxygen," *Piedmont Airlines Inflight Magazine*, March-April 1977, p. 28.
59. J. T. Cunningham, *Reptiles, Amphibia, Fishes, and Lower Chordata*, p. 55.

Scientific Evidence for the Vapor Canopy Model

are different from mammals. Mammals have secondary centers of ossification in the growing ends of the bones. When these centers have replaced most of the surrounding cartilage, they fuse with the bone shaft so that no further increase can take place. Most reptiles do not possess these secondary centers, so their bones are free to grow throughout life.[60] So great size is sometimes an indication of old age in these animals. If the dinosaurs were enjoying longevity of life, this would correlate well with the biblical data that suggests that men did also (Gen. 5; 11).

PREDICTION 4: SHIELDING FROM COSMIC RADIATION

The earth is constantly being bombarded by radiation from the sun and from deep space. Thanks to the shielding effect of our present atmosphere, biology on this planet is effectively protected from the lethal effects of this cosmic assault. However, with a canopy surrounding the earth, an even greater degree of protection would have been afforded, and one might predict a reduced radiation level. This is thought to have a possible connection with longevity of life and carbon 14 production.

The Canopy and Longevity of Life. Nearly 75 years ago Isaac Vail proposed that the shielding effect of the water heaven reduced radiation levels and, as a result, the pre-Flood conditions simply "impelled long life.[61] More recently, V. L. Westberg argued that the life shortening of the post-Flood patriarchs (see Gen. 11) was caused by accumulated exposure from space radiation that had not been present prior to the Flood.[62] In 1961 Morris and Whitcomb suggested that the decrease in longevity was due to increased radiation levels. "Much of this decline, as well as other effects we have already discussed, can undoubtedly be attributed to the greatly in-

60. Angus de'A. Bellairs, *Reptiles: Life History, Evolution, and Structure*, p. 19.
61. Vail, p. 91; see also Howard W. Kellogg, *The Canopied Earth*, p. 16.
62. V. L. Westberg, *The Master Architect*, p. 13.

creased incidence of radiation upon the earth's surface and upon its inhabitants."[63]

Donald Patten made the ingenious observation that there seemed to be an exponential variable involved in the decline of longevity of the post-Flood patriarchs. Prior to the Flood, men lived an average of 912 years, but immediately after the flood longevity began to decline exponentially.[64] Patten attributed this exponential variable to the sudden increase of ultra-violet radiation and to the washdown of ozone with the canopy.

The exponential decay curve in Genesis 11. In order to test the plausibility of Patten's observation of an exponential variable in the declining longevity of the postdiluvian patriarchs, the age at death versus the number of the generation from Noah was plotted on semi-log paper. When this was done, a straight line described the best fit of the points; this suggests that an exponential variable is likely. A linear regression analysis was made using the data given in Genesis 11 to determine the equation of this line and the correlation coefficient. The data in Table 5.3 was used for this regression calculation.

In Table 5.3, it should be noted that Moses did not die at age 70. He lived to be 120 (Deut. 34:7). However, Moses says that *in his time,* 70 years had become the expected average lifespan, "As for the days of our life, they contain seventy years, or if due to strength, eighty years" (Psalm 90:10).[65]

63. Morris and Whitcomb, *The Genesis Flood,* p. 404.
64. Donald Wesley Patten, *The Biblical Flood and the Ice Epoch,* pp. 214-16.
65. It is generally agreed that Psalm 90 was written by Moses. The only serious objection that can be raised against this view is that Moses, Caleb, and Joshua are all said to have lived longer than seventy years. Yet Perowne has observed, "There is no evidence that the average duration of human life at that period was as extended as that of the few individuals who are named. On the contrary, if we may judge from the langauge of Caleb, who speaks of his strength at 85 as if it were quite beyond the common lot (Josh. 14:10), the instances mentioned must rather be regarded as exceptional instances of longevity." See J. J. Stewart Perowne, *The Book of Psalms,* 2:162.

TABLE 5.3

THE AGES AT DEATH OF THE POST-DILUVIAN PATRIARCHS

Patriarch	Age at Death	Number of Generation from Noah
Noah	950	0
Shem	600	1
Arpachshad	438	2
Shelah	433	3
Eber	464	4
Peleg	239	5
Reu	239	6
Serug	230	7
Nahor	148	8
Terah	205	9
Abraham	175	10
Isaac	180	11
Jacob	147	12
Moses	120 (but 70 the norm)	17

Based on the biblical genealogies,[66] Moses' generation falls in the seventeenth generation from Noah if Noah equals generation 0. A linear regression yields,

$$Y = 652e^{-0.136x} \qquad (5.7)$$

66. See 1 Chron. 2:4-11 where Amminadab is the seventeenth from Noah and lived around 1520 B.C., the period of the rise of Moses (Deut. 34:7). After Jacob the sequence goes: Judah, Perez (1 Chron. 2:4), Hezon, Ram, Amminadab. Amminadab's date is based on the dating of Robert Young, *Analytical Concordance to the Bible*, p. 32.

where Y = the age at death, and x = the number of generations from Noah, where at Noah's generation x = 0. In order to find out the statistical validity of this curve, a correlation coefficient must be determined. The correlation coefficient, r, measures the degree of fit of the given points to the least-squares straight line. When r = 1, the correlation is said to be exact. When r = 0, the variables are said to be uncorrelated with a linear equation. The correlation coefficient derived from Table 5.3 is r = 0.95. That means there is an extremely high correlation between the variables and the above equation. A glance at Figure 5.1 reveals that an exponential variable is likely.[67] The plot of the data in Genesis 11 is illustrated in Figure 5.1.

Equation (5.7) does not adequately explain the longevity of Noah. The first point on the graph on the Y axis is 950 years, but it should be closer to 652 years if an exponential variable is involved. It may be that the pre-Flood conditions protected Noah during the 600 years of his life before the condensation of the canopy (Gen. 7:6). Shem, similarly, lived out his early 98 years under canopy conditions (Gen. 11:10). The first child born in the new environment was Arpachshad, two years after the Flood (Gen. 11:10). If the linear regression is calculated from Arpachshad to Moses, leaving out Noah and Shem, the following equation results:

$$Y = 436e^{-0.119x} \qquad (5.8)$$

and a correlation coefficient of 0.94. In this equation, all of the data scatter around the straight line, and none are as far off as Noah.

---

67. Others have performed the regression analysis with similar results using the year after the Flood for the horizontal axis. For discussion see James E. Strickling, "A Quantitative Analysis of the Life Spans of the Genesis Patriarchs," *Creation Research Society Quarterly* 10 (December 1973): 149-54.

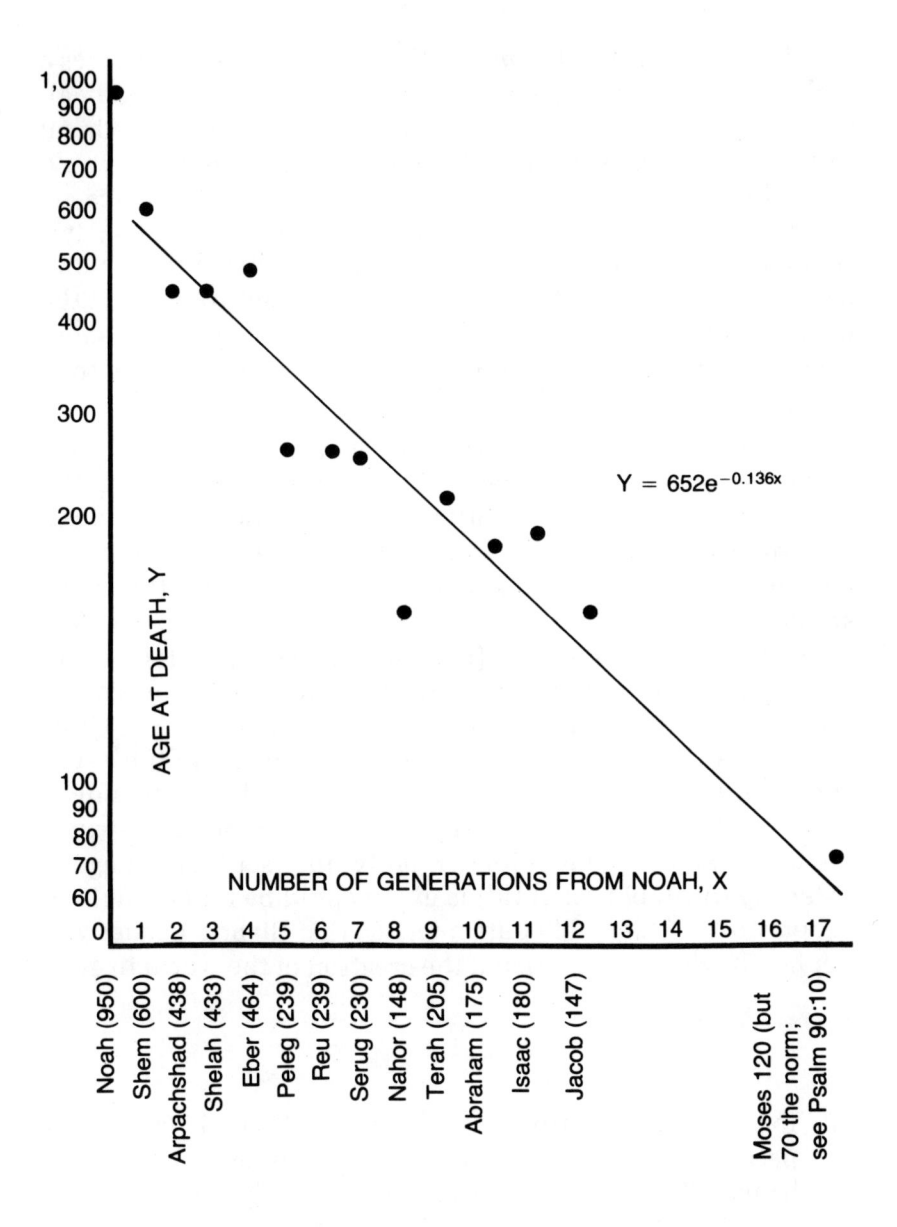

Scientific Evidence for the Vapor Canopy Model   161

$$Y = 652e^{-0.136x}$$

Fig. 5.1. — Semi-log Plot of Declining Longevity of Postdiluvian Patriarchs (Gen. 11).

This result has significant implications. First of all, it gives a high degree of credibility to the historical nature of the genealogy. The probablity that this account was a result of mythical influences is virtually zero. The odds that such a curve could result from anything but an actual historical circumstance are remote. There is nothing comparable in the Sumerian data. It is conceivable that scribes could have manufactured these numbers from exponential functions known in their time,[68] but the data in Table 5.3 are not *exactly* exponential. They scatter about such a function, thereby attesting to naturalness rather than artificiality.[69]

Second, this curve would tend to argue against the idea that there are gaps in the genealogy. If there were gaps in the genealogy, it would be difficult for an exponential decay curve to have resulted. In order to achieve that result, the gaps would have to be systematic and specific, not random. Furthermore, an absence of gaps seems to be attested to earlier (see Gen. 4:25-26), where a father-son (not a father-descendant) relationship is traced through the first three of the ten generations of the pre-Flood patriarchs in the genealogy of Genesis 5. Also, Jude informs us that Enoch was the seventh from Adam (Jude 14), and in counting the generations in Genesis 5, Enoch is indeed the seventh. So there are apparently no gaps in the first seven of the ten pre-Flood generations. Finally, the fact that the age at paternity (birth of first child) is given could be for chronological purposes.[70] This, of course, means that Bishop Ussher was not far off when he calculated the creation of the world in 4004

---

68. Exponential functions were used in the Old Babylonian period for computation of compound interest: O. Neugebauer, *The Exact Sciences in Antiquity*, p. 34.
69. See Charles Clough, "A Calm Appraisal of *The Genesis Flood*," pp. 99-100.
70. For full discussion of the exegetical basis for the gap view and the no-gap view of these genealogies, see H. David Clark, "The Genealogies of Genesis Five and Eleven."

B.C. I would be inclined, then, to date the Flood in the year 2346 B.C.[71]

I am well aware of the controversial nature of the above-proposed date of the Flood. It is not my intention to argue that the regression curve analysis proves a recent flood, only that it is another bit of evidence in favor of the no-gap interpretation of the geneaologies. Others have argued strongly for gaps in the geneaologies, and, if they are correct, this would remove considerable strain between the current accepted dating of archaeology and those of a strict interpretation of Genesis 5, 10, and 11.

However, it must also be remembered that the archaeological data is hardly sufficient to reject dogmatically the recent Flood date. Edwin Yamauchi, who is certainly no friend of a 2500 B.C. date for the Flood has nevertheless candidly admitted that there is a paucity of archaeological data upon which the ancient chronological schemes have been erected.[72] Yamauchi points out that probably less than 10% of what man has written or

71. This obviously creates immense problems in correlating the biblical dates with those attested by archaeology. It may be that the answer to this conflict resides in a greatly inflated time scale in the Egyptian historical material. Donovan Courville has argued that the Egyptian documents are inflated by some 800 years, and that a complete overhaul of ancient dating is necessary. See *The Exodus Problem and Its Ramifications* for a full discussion. All ancient dates are correlated with Egyptian dates for the time period in question (2500 B.C. to 1200 B.C.), hence an error there could drastically affect other dates as well. Note also Ronald D. Long, "The Bible, Radiocarbon Dating, and Ancient Egypt," *Creation Research Society Quarterly* 10 (June 1973):19-30; and Donovan A. Courville, "The Use and Abuse of Astronomy in Dating," *Creation Research Society Quarterly* 12 (March 1976):201-10, where he answers his critics who claim that astronomy has independently verified Assyrian and Egyptian dates.
72. Edwin M. Yamauchi, "Stones, Scripts, and Scholars," *Christianity Today* 8 (1969): 432-37.

made ever survives. Also only a fraction of the sites where these things can be found have even been discovered and recorded. Furthermore, less than 2% of all recorded sites have been touched by the excavator's spade, and only a tiny part of those areas that have been dug into have actually been excavated. Finally, only a small portion of the materials that have been excavated have been published, and often 50 years elapses between excavation and publication and general scrutiny by the community of scholars.

My point is simply this: in view of the extreme paucity of information presently available for scholarly analysis perhaps it is premature to reject dogmatically the strict interpretation of the Genesis geneaologies. Would it not be more prudent to hold tentatively to the no-gap interpretation (since it seems to be the most natural) and wait for the data to come in? Should such conclusive evidence be forthcoming that the Flood simply cannot be dated on archaeological grounds at 2500 B.C. then, and only then, would the strict interpretation need to be abandoned. In that event the gap view of the geneaologies gives the creationist scientist some breathing room to expand the date of the Flood back several thousand years and out of the range of serious conflict with archaeology.

A final and most significant implication of this decay curve is that it attests to some kind of environmental change that drastically affected the physiology of man and reduced his longevity from an average of 912 years prior to the Flood to 70 years 850 years after the Deluge. Such a decay curve is a common curve whenever a system in equilibrium is suddenly acted on in a way that results in pressure toward a new equilibrium. It can be seen in the discharge of a capacitor in the laboratory and in many other scientific experiments. It suggests that new factors were present in the post-Flood environment.

Could this curve be a result of new levels of ionizing radiation that scoured the earth as a result of the loss of its protective vapor shield? Those who answer that question in the affirmative argue from the extensive evidence that has established a definite link between radiation intensity and longevity of life in radiologists and in laboratory test animals.

Scientific Evidence for the Vapor Canopy Model 165

The radiation flux at the earth's surface. The earth is constantly being bombarded by cosmic radiation from the stars and from the sun. This radiation is of two basic kinds: electromagnetic and particle radiation. Particle radiation is composed of cosmic rays (streams of positively charged hydrogen nuclei), alpha rays (streams of positively charged helium nuclei), and beta rays (streams of negatively charged electrons).[73] Also, high energy neutron particles play an important part in the production of carbon 14 by upper atmospheric bombardment of nitrogen.

The second kind of radiation hitting the earth is electromagnetic. Table 5.4 presents the electromagnetic spectrum.[74]

TABLE 5.4

THE ELECTROMAGNETIC SPECTRUM

Band Name	Wavelength Angstroms (10^{-8}cm)	Microns (10^{-4}cm), μ
Cosmic Rays	0.0005A - 0.005A	
Gamma rays	0.005 - 1.4A	
X-rays[75]	0.1A - 100A	
Extreme UV[76]	100A - 1000A	0.01 - 0.1
Far UV	1000A - 2000A	0.1 - 0.2
Middle UV	2000A - 3150A	0.2 - 0.315
Near UV	3150A - 3800A	0.315 - 0.380
Visible	3800A - 7200A	0.38 - 0.72
Infra-red	longer than 7200A	0.72 -

73. For basic discussion see Isaac Asimov and Theodosius Dobzhansky, *The Genetic Effects of Radiation*, p. 22 ff.
74. Adapted from Albert Miller, *Meteorology*; Kinsell L. Coulson, *Solar and Terrestrial Radiation*, p. 143; and *Handbook of Chemistry and Physics*, p. E-206.
75. Note: there is an overlap between Gamma rays and X-rays.
76. UV = "Ultraviolet."

Thanks to our protective atmospheric blanket, very little of these harmful radiations ever reach the surface of the earth. In fact, our atmosphere is so effective in this regard that "essentially all of the incident solar radiation at wavelengths below 2950A is absorbed by the atmospheric gases, mainly the Hartley band of ozone."[77]

Careful measurements have computed the total exposure to the sex cells of men that come from these radiations and from man-made radiations. Table 5.5 records these data.[78]

The biological effects of electromagnetic radiation. It has long been observed that electromagnetic radiations have serious biological effects on human beings when absorbed in sufficient doses. In 1957, for example, Shields Warren reported:

> There is much evidence that overdoses of radiation lead to premature aging. Both animal experiments and observations of the life spans of radiologists indicate that doses of 1000 roentgens received over a long period of time may well shorten the life span about 10 percent. Data on the longevity of more than 82,000 physicians indicated that the average length of life of those not known to have had contact with radiation in the period 1930 through 1954 was 65.7 years, as against an average life span of 60.5 years for the radiologists.[79]

Radiation has an effect on both body tissue (somatic)[80] and sex cells (genetic). When X-rays or gamma rays hit a human sex cell, they ionize the cell and cause it to mutate.[81] These mutations are nearly always harmful and result in a general weakening of the species. The more seriously undesirable they are, the more likely they are to be removed by natural selection. The sum of these deleterious genes in the gene pool is called the genetic load. The size of the genetic load depends on two

77. Coulson, p. 143.
78. Asimov and Dobzhansky, p. 37.
79. Shields Warren, "Radiation and the Human Body," *The Scientific Monthly* (January 1957), p. 5.
80. For excellent introductory discussion see Norman A. Frigerio, *Your Body and Radiation.*
81. For general discussion of radiation and mutation rates in humans see H. J. Muller, "Radiation and Human Mutation," *Scientific American* 193 (November 1955):58 ff.

factors: the rate at which a deleterious gene is produced through mutation and the rate at which it is removed by natural selection. When the rate of removal equals the rate of production, a condition of genetic equilibrium is reached, and the level of occurrence of that gene remains stable over the generations.[82]

TABLE 5.5

RADIATION EXPOSURES IN THE UNITED STATES

	Millirems/yr.[83]
Natural Sources	
A. External to the body	
1. From cosmic radiation	50.0
2. From the earth	47.0
3. From building materials	3.0
B. Inside the body	
1. Inhalation of air	5.0
2. Elements found naturally in human tissues	21.0
Total, Natural Sources	126.0
Man-made Sources	
A. Medical procedures (X-rays, etc.)	61.0
B. Atomic energy industry, laboratories	0.2
C. Luminous watch dials, television tubes, radioactive industrial wastes, etc.	2.0
D. Radioactive fallout	4.0
Total, Man-made Sources	67.2
Overall Total	193.2

82. See Asimov and Dobzhansky, p. 17; also Bruce Wallace, *Genetic Load, Its Biological and Genetic Aspects*.
83. A millirem = 1/1000th of a rem. A rem is the "roetgen equivalent, man." The "rad" = the radiation absorbed dose. A rad of X-rays, gamma rays, or beta particles has a rem of 1, while a rad of alpha particles has a rem of 10 to 20. Also, 1 rad = 100 erg/gm or 6.24×10^9 electron volts/gm.

When earth's vapor canopy shield condensed, the penetration of solar radiation increased and undoubtedly had an effect in increasing the genetic load. Could this have had any possible effect on longevity? The answer seems to be "probably not directly." As will be discussed below, the levels of radiation necessary to have significantly burdened the gene pool with "weakening" genes are not present today in natural background radiation. However, there is a possibility of a significant indirect effect through the production of carbon 14. This is discussed below.

It might be theorized that when the canopy condensed, a "burst" of radiation flooded the gene pool with new mutations. However, the wavelengths that produce ionizing effects on the germ cells would never have penetrated the present atmosphere. Even if the protective ozone layer were disturbed (as it must have been) when the canopy precipitated, X-rays and gamma rays would never have penetrated to the surface, and it is these rays that cause genetic effects — not ultraviolet rays. Even if some X-rays did make it through and by chance mutated a sex cell of one of Noah's sons, it would have had to mutate specific gene loci, that is, a pair related to aging.[84] Then the problem is that this same loci would have to be mutated in all three of Noah's sons in order for the decrease in longevity to be explained. In view of the fact that nearly 10 million different combinations of chromosomes are possible in the sex cells of a single individual,[85] the probability that the same gene loci on all three individuals could be affected is small. Even though the genetic effects in experimental test animals have indicated a decrease in the longevity of their descendants after exposure to

---

84. "The existence of special genotypes for longevity is probable, although it is not known whether they provide a person with a generally over-all vitality of tissues and organs, or whether they act by way of single organs, such as the heart or some hormone-producing gland." Curt Stern, *Principles of Human Genetics*, p. 113.
85. Asimov and Dobzhansky, p. 8.

certain types of radiation,[86] because of the high levels of radiation employed in these tests, it is highly unlikely that this analogy is applicable to the post-Flood patriarchs.

From Table 5.5 it can be seen that less than 25% of the radiation the germ cells receive is from atmospheric sources. Furthermore, it is now known that less than 1% of all human mutations are caused by background radiation.[87] So, even if 100% of all background radiation were removed by the canopy (and only 25% of them could be removed), it would have little direct effect on the mutation of human sex cells, hence on the decreased longevity of Noah's descendants; nor could it have had any bearing on the longevity of the pre-Flood patriarchs.

It is generally acknowledged today that somatic mutations are a major cause of the aging process. Could the reduction in radiation levels prior to the Flood have had any bearing on a decreased rate of somatic mutation in human body tissue? Could a burst of radiation with the condensation of the canopy have any effect on radiation? The answer to both of these questions seems to be no.

Many studies have been performed on mice to determine the effects of X-rays and gamma radiation on longevity.[88] However, present evidence suggests a shortening of human life of 11% per 1,000 rads[89] for an entire lifetime. Since Table 5.5 indicates that the average dosage a man receives is only 12 rads in a lifetime (0.192 rad/yr × 67 yrs), we can see that present radiation levels have no effect on reduced longevity. Furthermore, these studies involve bombardment with X-rays and, even

86. W. L. Russell, "Shortening of Life in the Offspring of Male Mice Exposed to Neutron Radiation from an Atomic Bomb," *Proceedings of the National Academy of Science* 43 (1957):324-49.
87. Asimov and Dobzhansky, p. 36.
88. A. S. Iberall, "Quantitative Modeling of the Physiological Factors in Radiation Lethality," *Annals of the New York Academy of Sciences* 147 (October 1967):1-81.
89. Shields Warren, "Longevity and Causes of Death from Irradiation in Physicians," *Journal of the American Medical Association* 162 (September 29, 1956):466.

without a canopy, no X-rays reach the surface of the earth. Only visible and some ultraviolet and infrared radiation reaches the surface in any appreciable amount. Ultraviolet radiation will not penetrate deeply below the skin.[90] So while it is probable that somatic mutations have an effect on the aging process, it seems fairly well established that cosmic radiation contributes only in a minor way to somatic mutations. "It should not be inferred that radiations cause the mutations responsible for natural aging. The natural background radiations of our environment, caused by cosmic rays, etc., are very much too weak for that. The cause of these mutations is not yet known."[91]

Experiments have been conducted in which mice were placed hundreds of feet below the ground to shield them from all cosmic radiation. There was no indication of an increase in longevity in either the parents or their offspring.[92]

So it appears that canopy theorists have been in error when they appealed to the shielding effect of the canopy as a direct explanation for antediluvian longevity. Furthermore, it also seems incorrect to postulate that increased levels of radiation after the canopy precipitated had any direct bearing on the decrease of longevity. This is true because the levels of radiation experienced today are insufficient to have any effect and are of the wrong kind, that is, mostly ultraviolet instead of X-rays, and gamma rays.

Furthermore, even if there were a "burst" of radiation when the canopy precipitated, there would be no permanent effects on aging. This is because that burst would consist largely of ultraviolet light, which had been shielded out by the ozone in the upper levels of the canopy. Ultraviolet light has no effect on germ cells and hence could effect only the longevity of Shem,

90. Asimov and Dobzhansky, *The Genetic Effects*, p. 23.
91. Howard Curtis, "What Science Knows About Aging," *Think* (March-April, 1964), p. 17.
92. Dr. Johan Bjorksten, Director, Bjorksten Research Foundation, P.O. Box 775, Madison, Wisconsin, personal communication, 27 October 1976. Dr. Bjorksten is one of the leading researchers in the quest for the mechanisms of aging.

Ham, and Japheth. Shem may have died early due to skin cancer caused by this burst, but this gives no explanation for the continuing decrease in longevity observed in his descendants. This is so because the ozone shield once disturbed will gradually build itself up to present levels within thirty years, and present levels of ozone shield out the majority of ultraviolet radiation.[93]

However, it may be that increased radiation levels had an indirect connection with decreased longevity as will be discussed below.

The canopy and the cross-linkage theory of aging. The exponential variable discussed above in decreasing longevity requires explanation. At present it does not appear possible to explain it fully. This difficulty is increased by the fact that there is no certainty as to exactly what causes the aging process. Thus, before speculations on how the canopy may be related to aging can be advanced, science must first unravel the secrets involved in senescence.[94]

93. An intriguing explanation for the extinction of the dinosaurs involving a burst of cosmic ray flux due to exploding supernovae may have some relevance to the exponential function noted in Genesis 11. Terry and Tucker calculate that it is likely that the earth has been bombarded several times in the past with such a flux of 1000r of X-rays and gamma rays. Flux of this intensity would make it to the surface and cause vast mutation and loading of the gene pool and mass extinctions, also. See W. H. Tucker and K. D. Terry, "Biologic Effects of Supernovae," Science 159 (26 January 1968):421-23; and W. H. Tucker and K. D. Terry, "Cosmic Rays from Nearby Supernovae: Biological Effects," Science 168 (7 June 1968):1138-39.

94. For a review of some of the contemporary theories, see G. B. Price and T. Makinodan, "Aging: Alternation of DNA-Protein Information," Gerontologia 19 (1973):58-70; A. C. Upton, "Ionizing Radiation and the Aging Process," Journal of Gerontology 12 (1957):306-13; Johan Bjorksten, "The Crosslinkage Theory of Aging: Clinical Implications," Comprehensive Therapy 2 (February 1976):65-74.

At the present time, the cross-linkage theory of aging seems to be one that is gaining wide acceptance. The theory suggests that, beginning at birth, certain cross-linking agents begin to form bridges or links between large molecules in the body. In this way, the giant molecules of the body are rendered progressively more and more inactive. Over a lifetime, large aggregates of these cross-linked molecules accumulate, resulting in a greater and greater inability of these molecules to carry out biological functions at the molecular level. Imagine a large factory with thousands of workers in one huge room. Each day an evil person comes in and slips a set of handcuffs on a pair of workers so that it ties them together and makes it more difficult for them to work. As more handcuffs are added daily, the efficiency of the factory is gradually decreased. Eventually all work comes to a standstill. Cross-linked molecules are to the body molecules what handcuffs are to the factory worker.

When genetic matter is involved in these cross-links, mutations are often induced.[95]

> In a lifetime billions of crosslinkages will thus unavoidably be formed. Most of these can be reversed, but some of them cannot. These latter will accumulate over the years. The resultant aggregates are composed of proteins, nucleotides, polymeric fats, polysacharides, and any available large molecule at all which can react with any crosslinking agent at all, or which can be directly interlocked, will form parts in the resultant aggregates.[96]

When these aggregates of cross-linked molecules become dense enough, the body enzymes that aid in the dissolving of these aggregates can no longer penetrate, and cellular function is lost. It has been noted that the body produces more of these enzymes with increasing age. Thus, the quest for the fountain of youth is presently being focused on the discovery of enzymes of low enough molecular weight that can penetrate these aggregates and dissolve them. Bjorksten argues that it is self evident

95. Johan Bjorksten, "Aging, Primary Mechanism," *Gerontologia* 8 (1963):179-92.
96. Johan Bjorksten, "Some Therapeutic Implications of the Crosslinkage Theory of Aging," paper presented at the American Chemical Society, San Francisco, California, 2 September 1976, p. 8.

that the enzymes able to do this must exist, "Yet there must be in existence enzymes which can cope with these [cross-linked molecular aggregates], for otherwise, large fossil deposits of such crosslinked proteins would have been found."[97]

One such enzyme now being produced commercially under the name Microprotease MPB was isolated in 1973.[98] However, it has not yet been tested in human populations. In fact, no experimental work has yet been done to establish the potentially beneficial effect of this enzyme, although it has been used to dissolve cross-linked aggregates taken from autopsy victims.[99]

It appears, then, that in order to connect the canopy with longevity of life, it will be necessary to demonstrate that conditions under the canopy were such that the body might have naturally produced this enzyme, and that conditions after the canopy condensed hindered the natural bodily function of these enzymes in some way. Another possibility is that in the post-Flood world certain chemical changes in the environment, and notably in the atmosphere, may have introduced additional cross-linkage agents into the human body that were not present prior to the Flood.[100] One possibility is C-14.

After the Flood the C-14/C-12 ratio began increasing exponentially from zero (see discussion below) toward present

97. Ibid., p. 17.
98. R. U. Schenk and J. Bjorksten, "The Search for Microenzymes: The Enzyme of Bacillus Cereus," *Finska Kemists. Medd.* 82 (1973):26-46.
99. Bjorksten, "The Crosslinkage Theory of Aging," p. 72.
100. For the molecular biologist desiring to pursue the possible connections between canopy induced environmental conditions and the existence of various cross-linking agents, a discussion of known cross-linking agents is presented in Bjorksten, "Aging, Primary Mechanism," p. 183, and, "The Crosslinkage Theory of Aging," *Finska Kemists. Medd.* 80 (1971):23-38. They include aldehydes, sulfur, alkylating and acylating agents, quinones, antibodies, free radicals induced by ionizing radiation, and many metals and numerous other compounds.

levels. As C-14 is absorbed in living things, it is used in the manufacture of major body molecules (proteins, DNA). The trouble is that C-14 spontaneously decays into N-14 and emits ionizing radiation in the process. Since the effect of such radiation is inversely proportional to the distance between the C-14 atom and a DNA molecule, being right inside the molecule increases its possible effect in the disruption of various biochemical processes and even in the production of mutations.[101] Since the amount of C-14 in the atmosphere would be increasing in every generation, it would be predicted that each generation after the Flood would have a larger number of disfunctioning molecules and, possibly, a correspondingly reduced longevity.

If God, therefore, designed the prototype man able to live 900 years, and then the new C-14 levels were introduced, that could account for the exponentially decreasing longevity observed in Genesis 11. This sudden increase in C-14 production would have been directly attributable to the condensation of the vapor shield. Harold Armstrong assumed that "the rate of change or increase of the concentration of radioactive carbon is proportional to the rate of change or decrease of average lifetime."[102] With this assumption, he made an interesting attempt to establish a correction factor for the C-14 dating process based on the patriarchal genealogies. Granting certain assumptions, the correction factor brings many of the C-14 dates into closer harmony with the data from the genealogies. This would lend some credence to the idea that the decreased longevity was due to increased C-14 levels.

It may be significant that a change in dietary laws occurred right after the Flood (Gen. 9:3). Could this indicate that certain

101. Personal communication from Dr. A. E. Wilder Smith, F.R.I.C. (London), professor of pharmacology and consultant, Roggern, CH-3646 Einigen am Thunersee, Switzerland, September 12, 1979.
102. Harold Armstrong, "An Attempt to Correct for the Effects of the Flood in Determining Dates by Radioactive Carbon," *Creation Research Society Quarterly* 21 (January 1966):28.

Scientific Evidence for the Vapor Canopy Model 175

plants that had been available before the Flood were now extinct? These plants may have provided vitamins or enzymes that are needed by the body but cannot be supplied by today's food. Apparently, many cancer patients today use much more Vitamin E and C during their illnesses. Many biochemical pathways would cease to function if certain enzymes were not available. Since vitamins are co-enzymes, it is possible that the removal of one co-enzyme could shut down an entire biochemical pathway. The extinction of one plant that was the sole source for that co-enzyme, that is, the fruit of the tree of life, perhaps — (Gen. 3:24) would be sufficient to alter man's biochemistry and decrease his longevity.

The Canopy and Carbon 14 Production. Assuming the existence of a water vapor canopy, we would have to predict that the amount of C-14 at the surface of the earth before the Flood would be much less than it is today. As a consequence, dating calculations based on this method for pre-Flood dates would be much too high and give dates much older than actual. The radiocarbon dates depend on the ratio of radiocarbon (C-14) to "normal" carbon (C-12) in the organic, fossil remains of a plant or animal. Carbon 14 is a radioactive isotope of regular carbon and is formed when atmospheric nitrogen (N-14) is bombarded by cosmic radiation. So there is a certain amount of this material in the atmosphere at all times. As a result, all living systems ingest radiocarbon into their cellular material. As soon as they die, however, they immediately begin to stop ingesting C-14 from the atmosphere, and the C-14 already in their system begins to decay. Half of the original amount of C-14 in the biological system will decay every 5,770 years. This number is called the half life of C-14.

Carbon 12, or normal carbon, does not decay. Since all living organisms take in C-12 and C-14 as found in the atmosphere as long as the biological system is alive, the ratio of C-14/C-12 will remain the same in the biological system as it is in the air. But if the tissue dies and the equilibrium exchange between it and the environment ceases, then the amount of C-14 in the tissue will begin to dwindle by decay because it is no longer being replaced by stocks from the surrounding atmosphere. So if a particular sample has lost exactly half of its original C-14 content, then it is known that it is 5,770 years old.[103]

Now obviously this method assumes that the original amount of C-14 in the biological system is known. This original amount determination is based on the assumption that the C-14/C-12 ratio in the environment at the time of death equals that ratio today. Problems arise in knowing that original ratio. If the amount of radiocarbon in the earth's atmosphere at the time of the death of an animal was much less than the amount of radiocarbon today, it will appear that much more of the radiocarbon has decayed and hence that the animal is older than it really is.

If the earth was surrounded at one time by a water canopy, virtually no carbon 14 would be formed. This is because the canopy would sit on top of the present atmosphere and all the nitrogen under the canopy would have been shielded from the effects of cosmic radiation. At the top of the canopy, an ozone layer would be produced due to the disassociation of water vapor by cosmic rays. This would in turn act as an additional shield for the lower atmosphere. Very little of the lower atmosphere would diffuse up into the upper layers of the canopy due to the temperature inversion resulting from absorption of the terrestrial radiation in the canopy. This will be examined further in chapter 7. It would appear, then, that prior to the Flood, no carbon 14 was being produced, and samples dated by carbon 14 that are pre-Flood samples would appear to have infinite age.

Inasmuch as many of the carbon 14 dates are considerably older than biblical dates, the canopy shielding effect has commonly been evoked as a possible explanation.[104]

For example, if the original amount of C-14 in the atmosphere was only 2.5% of today's values, then the time necessary for the

103. For discussion of the method as explained by its discoverer, see Willard F. Libby, *Radiocarbon Dating*.
104. A. J. White, "Radio Carbon Dating," *Creation Research Society Quarterly* 9 (December 1972):157; R. H. Brown, "Radiocarbon Dating," *Creation Research Society Quarterly* 5 (September 1968):68.

Scientific Evidence for the Vapor Canopy Model   177

C-14 in the sample to decay to the 10% level is 29,749 years. So the sample is dated as if it started out with 100% of today's level, but it actually had only 2.5% of today's level, therefore leaving out of the calculation 29,749 years. It will appear to be 29,749 years too old. A sample dated, then, as being 35,000 years old is in fact only 5,251 years old.[105]

There is some evidence that the earth was at one time without radioactive carbon. Harold Armstrong observes:

> First of all, there appears to be practically no radioactive carbon in coal. So if we accept that much of the coal comes from vegetation which was buried at the time of the flood, and that the time back to the flood is not much more than the half life of radioactive carbon (for which, for the present purposes, the round figure of 5,500 will do), it must follow that there was practically no radioactive carbon in the atmosphere before the flood.[106]

Samples that were buried quite deeply, like coal, would characteristically be free from radioactive carbon. However, Flood deposits closer to the top could easily be contaminated, picking up a small amount of radiocarbon from the surroundings. So the indicated ages would be varied.

It should be mentioned that if the evidence of an exponentially decreasing magnetic field for the earth proves to be valid, then a reduction in carbon 14 levels could have been brought about by increased magnetic field intensity and not be connected with the vapor canopy at all.[107]

In 1966 Melvin Cook, a geochronologist and professor of metallurgy at the University of Utah, pointed out that there

105. This is based on the relation, $P = e^{-yt}$, where P = the fraction of C-14 left in the sample, y = the decay constant for C-14 = 1.24×10^{-4} yr., and t = time in years for original amount of C-14 to decay to P percent. Thus, $\ln(0.025) = (1.24 \times 16^{-4})t$; $t = 29{,}749$ years. Undoubtedly, this is one of the factors that explain why the C-14 dates are often much too old to fit into biblical chronology.
106. Armstrong, p. 28.
107. Thomas G. Barnes, "Decay of the Earth's Magnetic Moment and the Geochronological Implications," *Creation Research Society Quarterly* 8 (June 1971):24-29.

appears to be a discrepancy between the rate of carbon 14 production and the rate of carbon 14 decay.[108] If the earth is millions of years old, the rate of production and the rate of decay should be equal to each other, that is, equilibrium conditions should exist.[109] Cook estimated that the rate of carbon 14 decay was $R_d = 13.3$ atoms/gm. min. and the rate of production was $R_p = 18.4$ atoms/gm.min. Therefore, $R_d/R_p = 0.72$.[110]

Assuming that this present day ratio of R_d/R_p is correct, then the time in which the buildup of radiocarbon began can be computed from[111]

$$\frac{R_d}{R_p} = 1 - e^{-\frac{0.693T}{5730}}$$

where 5730 is the half life of carbon 14. Solving for T yields a value of $T = 10{,}525$ years ago, or 8555 B.C. (assuming 1970 as the reference point) for the time in which the buildup of carbon 14 began. This date corresponds poorly with the biblical date of the Flood, if we assume a no-gap chronology. When the canopy collapsed right after the Flood, the buildup of carbon 14 began. If the buildup began in 2346 B.C., today's R_d/R_p should equal 0.41 instead of 0.72, unless a sudden buildup occurred immediately after the Flood.

Since Cook published his analysis, new data have come in that apparently suggest that the R_d/R_p ratio is only *temporarily* out of equilibrium and has varied above and below unity due to

108. Melvin Cook, *Prehistory and Earth Models*, pp. 1-10.
109. According to Libby, equilibrium should be reached in 30,000 years, Libby, *Radiocarbon Dating*, p. 8.
110. Melvin Cook, "Radiological Dating and Some Pertinent Applications of Historical Interest, Do Radiological Clocks Need Repair?" *Creation Research Society Quarterly* 5 (September 1968):69.
111. Robert L. Whitelaw, "Time, Life and History in the Light of 15,000 Radiocarbon Dates," *Creation Research Society Quarterly* 7 (June 1970):64.

minute fluctuations in the earth's magnetic field.[112] However, these data are very equivocal and need further analysis before using them to deny the nonequilibrium radiocarbon model.

The Canopy and Rickets in Ancient Men. Although it may be difficult to connect the shielding effects of the canopy to longevity of C-14 calculations, there does seem to be some evidence that, at one time, the earth received lesser amounts of ultraviolet radiation. Absorption by water vapor effectively shields the earth from many of these rays today, but some of them still get through. The wavelengths of ultraviolet radiation most effective in the prevention and cure of rickets are in the 2700 to 3130 A range, with the maximum at 2800 A. Radiation in this range converts some of the sterols in the skin to vitamin D, which is necessary for the growth of healthy bones. Coulson observes, "It is interesting to speculate what would have happened to life on Earth if the Huggins band of ozone absorption were just slightly stronger, thereby preventing radiation in this range from reaching the surface."[113] With 40 feet of precipitable water in the atmosphere, *none* of this radiation would penetrate to the surface.

The presence of vitamin D in the system appears to increase the retention in the body of calcium that may be available in food. When the bones are without this vitamin, they become soft, and bow-legs, knock-knees, and many other deformities, especially of the spine and pelvis, may occur.[114] The source of vitamin D is either from sunlight's converting sterols in the skin to vitamin D or from food. Its primary source is green plants. Hence, if the earth was surrounded by a vapor canopy effectively shielding out all radiation-produced vitamin D, one would predict that men who went without proper vitamin D intake from foods would have rickets.

112. I. U. Olsson, ed., *Radiocarbon Variation and Absolute Chronology*; H. M. Michael and E. K. Ralph in *8th International Congress on Radiocarbon Dating* (1972), section 1, p. A-11.
113. Coulson, p. 146.
114. R. J. S. McDowall, *Handbook of Physiology*, pp. 281-83.

Is there any such evidence of bone disease in ancient men? For a long while it was believed that Neanderthal man, *Homo neanderthalensis*, was a so-called missing link. His stooped skeletal structure resulted in his being depicted as brutish, with heavy brown ridges and the crudest of habits. But it is now recognized that his skeletal features are possibly explained by bone disease, possibly arthritis or rickets. "Neanderthal man may have looked like he did, not because he was closely related to the great apes, but because he had rickets, an article in the British publication *Nature* suggests. The diet of Neanderthal man was definitely lacking in Vitamin D during the 35,000 years he spent on earth."[115]

Prior to the Flood, men apparently were vegetarians and, hence, due to the emphasis on eating green plants, the vitamin D deficiency never would have manifested itself. After the Flood — after the canopy collapsed — men became both vegetarians and meat eaters (Gen. 9:2-4). The eating of meat was now acceptable because, with the condensation of the water heaven and the penetration of ultraviolet radiation to the surface, another mechanism for generating the needed vitamin D was available apart from ingestion of green plants. So the above citation might be modified to read that either the diet of Neanderthal was lacking in vitamin D or ultraviolet radiation was shielded out.

It has been argued that the elimination of all ultraviolet light would have resulted in the complete cessation of photosynthesis.[116] This is not correct, for it is visible light that green plants use for photosynthesis.[117] Plants flourish in greenhouses under lighting provided by a tungsten bulb, which is rich in red

115. "Neanderthals Had Rickets," *Science Digest* 69 (February 1971):35.
116. John H. Fermor, "Paleoclimatology and Infrared Radiation Traps: Earth's Antediluvian Climate," in *A Symposium on Creation, VI*, ed. Donald Patten, p. 19. This is a helpful article suggesting a canopy model different from the one in this chapter.
117. James F. Ferry and Henry S. Ward, *Fundamentals of Plant Physiology*, p. 119.

light.[118] Many kinds of plants flourish with little light (10% illumination), and any increase in light intensity will retard photosynthesis.[119]

It is clear, however, that the absence of ultraviolet light would have negligible effect on the photosynthesis rates and, hence, on the amount of pre-Flood vegetation. "For equal intensities more photosynthesis appears to occur in the orange-short red and blue parts of the spectrum than in the green and yellow."[120] In fact, due to the presence of warmer climates, less surface wind, less erosion, and other factors, the CO_2 concentrations at the surface would probably be greater and photosynthesis would increase under the canopy, producing a luxuriant vegetation cover.[121]

Seen in this light, the widespread evidence of rickets in antediluvian man is evidence of the curse. Those who ingested sufficient vitamin D from green plants would have been rickets free. But since men did not immediately know of this connection, it is predictable that, for hundreds of years, millions of ancient men went without the necessary vitamin D requirements. While living in obedience to God in the protection of the Garden, God provided for all of man's vitamin needs; but when man chose to disobey, he paid not only spiritual but also physical consequences. Even when under the curse, however (Rom. 8:20), God still provided an adequate source of vitamin D in the greenhouse of the antediluvian earth.

It appears that all "fossil-men" are merely degenerate forms of Adam. The evidence of man's evolutionary development adduced from cultural and scientific advance is only illusionary. It simply represents the ability of one generation of men to pass on information inherited from a prior generation. This ability makes man different from the animals and enables him to build on what went on before. However, when first thrust out of the

118. Ibid.
119. Nicolai A. Maximov, *Plant Physiology*, p. 119.
120. "Photosynthesis," in *Van Nostrand's Scientific Encyclopedia*, p. 1776.
121. Ferry and Ward, pp. 129-33, have a discussion of the factors affecting the rate of photosynthesis.

Garden, he had to learn about disease, about germs, about the wheel, and many other things, then gradually build himself up. This is not evolution at all. Based on the canopy model, we would predict that men started out perfect and gradually degenerated physically; then as they began to discover things like penicillin and vitamin D, they gradually turned around this process of physical degeneration.

Conclusion. If the canopy is to be connected with ancient longevity there are two areas of possible connection: the lack of carbon 14 and the presence of a specific enzyme that would dissolve cross-linked molecules. The radiation shield of the canopy would eliminate carbon 14 production and therefore indirectly affect the formation of crosslinkage in cells. Also, the edenic climate of the ancient world would have made it conducive to the growth of many varieties of plants, one of which probably carried the specific enzyme for longevity. The plants carrying that enzyme apparently could not survive in the climate of the post-Flood world.

PREDICTION 5: A GLOBAL FLOOD

Without a doubt the collapse by condensation of such a vast vapor canopy would result in untold devastation and deluge all over the planet. For 40 feet of water to pour from the heavens over all the earth for a period of 40 days and nights (0.5 inches per hour) would unleash a fantastic flood catastrophe. The swollen rivers would wash sediment into the oceans. Sedimentation would be rapid as billions of tons of sediment were carried by the raging flood waters and redeposited. Volcanic activity and earthquakes would have led to the uplift of continents, tidal waves, and the formation of the mountain ranges. Such a worldwide catastrophe should have left clear evidence all over the rock record of its occurrence. Is there evidence, then, of a global flood?

To investigate this evidence fully, of course, would take us far beyond the scope of this book, which is designed to examine the pre-Flood vapor canopy. However, some comment seems appropriate. N. A. Rupke, of the State University of Groningen, the Netherlands, has presented a convincing case that the evidence of the geologic column suggests rapid catastrophic deposition, which one would predict on the basis of a global flood.[122] Several considerations suggest that the earth was at one time deluged by water.

Polystrate fossils. All over the world we find fossil beds in which a tree, for example, will protrude up through several layers of strata that were thought to be separated in time by several million years. The presence of these trees proves that the strata were laid down in the lifetime of the tree. That can only happen under the kinds of mechanisms resulting from rapid sedimentation. Such mechanisms would certainly be the product of a worldwide flood.[123]

Fossils. Surprisingly, one of the most obvious evidences of a flood is the presence of fossils themselves. Fossils are usually formed as a result of being buried by sedimentary rock, "To become fossilized a plant or animal must usually have hard parts, such as bone, shell or wood. It must be buried quickly to prevent decay and must be undisturbed throughout the long process."[124]

Fossils can be produced and preserved a number of different ways. In every case they must be formed rapidly, or the forces of erosion, bacterial decay, weathering, or other disintegrative processes will destroy them before the fossilization process is complete. Morris observes:

122. N. A. Rupke, "Prolegomena To a Study of Cataclysmal Sedimentation," in *Why Not Creation?*, ed. Walter E. Lammerts, pp. 141-79; for a full discussion of the geological evidence of a worldwide flood, see Morris and Whitcomb, *The Genesis Flood*, pp. 116-221. Note also Stuart E. Nevins, "Stratigraphic Evidence of the Flood," in *A Symposium on Creation*, III, ed. Donald W. Patten, pp. 33-65; Walter G. Peters, "Field Evidence for Rapid Sedimentation," *Creation Research Society Quarterly* 10 (September 1973):89-96.
123. Rupke, pp. 52-7.
124. F. H. T. Rhodes, H. S. Zim, and P. R. Shaffer, *Fossils*, p. 10.

It would be easy to give further illustration of fossil-bearing rocks from every "age" and from every part of the world, which must have been formed rapidly in order to have been formed at all. The very existence of fossils, especially in large numbers, is evidence of catastrophism on at least a local scale. Since fossil-bearing strata are ubiquitous, and in fact make up the entire "geologic column," there is therefore evidence of catastrophism everywhere.[125]

Absence of worldwide unconformities. The various strata of the geologic column are separated by "stratification planes" at the interface of the strata. These planes distinguish the material in the above strata from the material in the strata underneath the plane. These planes are evidence that there has been a time lapse in deposition or a slight change in one or more of the characteristics of the sediment-forming flow. Many factors affect such things as the transportation and deposition of sediment, flow velocity, flow direction, flow volume, flow depth, water temperature, and dissolved chemicals. If any one of these factors changes, then the sedimentary characteristics of the flow will change. Consequently, a stratification plane would form at any area of deposition and a new stratum would begin to form with slightly different characteristics.

If the process of deposition ceases for a long period of time, erosion sets in. This may be by water or, if the water flow stopped, by "weathering." If during this time period, the deposited sediment is uplifted or tilted by movements in the earth's crust, the period of erosion will cut off a portion of the beds that were lifted up, that is, the beds will be "truncated." When the surface of such a truncated bed is parallel to the stratification planes, it is called a "paraconformity"; if at an angle, it is called an "unconformity." When an unconformity exists between two sets of strata, it is obvious that there has been a period of erosion in between. In other words, the original deposition ceased, the bed was uplifted, years of erosion occurred, then, years later, new sedimentation processes occurred that buried the former strata and its eroded, truncated surface.

So major unconformities would indicate a time break, perhaps the end of one geological epoch and the beginning of

125. Henry Morris, ed., *Scientific Creationism*, p. 100.

another. However, there is no worldwide unconformity. A time break that is evident in one region is not apparent in another region at all. Thus, in one region there may be evidence of an unconformity that shows a time break between Paleozoic and Mesozoic strata, but in another region they seem to merge imperceptibly into each other. Now the fossil deposits that date the rock units all show evidence of rapid formation. If there are no time breaks between the various strata, then it seems rigidly necessary to conclude that the entire assemblage of rock units constituting the geological column shows evidence of rapid formation.

Morris summarizes the chain of reasoning under the following seven propositions:

1. Each stratum must have been formed rapidly, since it represents a constant set of hydraulic factors that cannot remain constant very long.
2. Each succeeding stratum in a formation must have followed rapidly after its preceding stratum, since its surface irregularities have not been truncated by erosion.
3. Therefore the entire formation must have been formed continuously and rapidly. This is further confirmed by the fact that its rock type required rapid formation, and its fossil contents required rapid and permanent burial.
4. Although the formation may be capped by unconformity, there is no worldwide unconformity, so that if it is traced out laterally far enough, it will eventually grade imperceptibly into another formation, which therefore succeeds it continuously and rapidly without a time break at that point.
5. The same reasoning will show that the strata of the second formation were also formed rapidly and continuously, and so on to a third formation somewhere succeeding that one.
6. Thus, stratum-by-stratum and formation-by-formation, one may proceed through the entire geologic column proving the whole column to have been formed rapidly and continuously.
7. The merging of one formation into the next is further indicated by the well-recognized fact that there is rarely

ever a clear physical boundary between formations. More commonly the rock types tend to merge and mingle with each other over a zone of considerable thickness.[126]

PREDICTION 6: VOLCANIC ASH MIXED WITH GLACIAL ICE

A sixth prediction from the model would be the mixture of volcanic material with the glacial ice in the polar and Antarctic regions. This grows naturally out of the model in that the suggested mechanism for precipitating the canopy was volcanic ash, according to Genesis 7:11 and Psalm 18:7-15. The ash, once hurled up into the canopy, would in turn wash down in the rainfall and would be buried in the glaciers and sediment formed as a result of the sudden temperature drops and great winds (Gen. 8:1).

Army cold regions geologist Anthony Gow took 7,100 feet of core samples from nine Antarctic glaciers. He found over 2,000 individual volcanic ash falls interbedded with the ice.[127] Gow suggests that these volcanic eruptions may have contributed to the cooling of the Antarctic atmosphere and brought about the Ice Age. He observes from the field data that between 30,000 to 16,000 years ago there was a "significant cooling" of the Antarctic atmosphere. The dating was based on C-14, which is based on certain assumptions that would be invalidated if a water vapor canopy did exist. So it is possible that these dates do coincide with the time of the Flood. The prediction of volcanic ash in glaciers has been confirmed by the field data.

A similar situation prevails throughout the Arctic regions of the North. The frozen muck of the Arctic tundras is literally strewn with volcanic material hundreds of feet deep, all evidencing a violent volcanic catastrophe.[128] This ash could

126. Ibid., pp. 115-16.
127. Anthony J. Gow, "Glaciological Investigations in Antarctica," *Antarctic Journal of the United States* 7, no. 4 (1972):100-101.
128. See Frank C. Hibben, *Lost Americans*, pp. 176-78. Extensive discussion of this point will be undertaken in chapter 12.

not have gotten into the muck unless the muck was soft and susceptible to turbulent mixing at the time of the volcanic activity. It is found dispersed among the fresh frozen remains of thousands of plants and animals. This again indicates a sudden cooling along with volcanic activity, precisely the prediction of the canopy model.

PREDICTION 7: A SUDDEN AND PERMANENT TEMPERATURE DROP IN THE POLAR REGIONS

With the loss of the vapor shield, the universally moderate climate that it produced would likewise be interrupted. In fact, particularly in the polar regions there would have been a sudden and permanent temperature drop over a period of 40 days. One might predict then, on the basis of the present model, that high in the northern latitudes, prior to the Flood, hundreds of thousands of lower latitude plant and animal types might have flourished and then suddenly disappeared. Furthermore, since such a canopy collapse would precipitate a rapid change in temperature, there should be evidence that many of those animals were frozen to death.

As later chapters will discuss, that is precisely the situation in the Arctic.[129] Abundant testimony exists to a catastrophic extinction of hundreds of thousands of animals, frozen in mid-motion and overcome by violent flood and wind, all over the tundra muck. In fact, the very presence of the frozen muck testifies to a sudden and permanent temperature drop. This muck is full of plant and animal remains to depths of several thousand feet. In numerous cases the remains are in a relatively fresh condition. Hippopotamuses, sabertooth tigers, elephants, and other low-latitude animals are found buried in the tundras, freshly preserved. Now if the muck were frozen at the time these animals lived, the animals could never have been thrust into the rock-hard frozen ground to be buried. At the time of

129. The Pleistocene extinctions and their connection with the collapse of earth's ancient vapor jacket are thoroughly discussed in chapters 10, 11, and 12. Documentation of the points made above is reserved for these chapters.

burial, therefore, the muck must have been in an unfrozen state. Today it thaws down only to about 18 inches every summer. Yet it could not have remained in such an unfrozen state or the animals buried in it would have immediately rotted. In fact, there is evidence that thousands of them were preserved; some are even edible today. This requires that the animals were frozen quickly after burial. Thus, the muck must have been soft at the time of burial (evidencing a warmer climate than today), and immediately after burial it must have frozen in order to preserve the fresh flesh of the animals (evidencing a sudden temperature change from warm to severely cold). Furthermore, the climate reversal must have been permanent or the animals would have completely rotted during following summers.

The prediction of the canopy model is, therefore, strikingly confirmed by the field evidence.

PREDICTION 8: FEWER METEORITES IN OLDER STRATA

The presence of a water heaven surrounding the ancient earth would have a marked effect on meteors falling to the surface of the earth. Because of the denser atmosphere created by the canopy, it is unlikely that as many meteors as today would get through to the surface, due to aerodynamic heating.[130] Under the present model, it is being assumed that the canopy surrounded the earth up until very recently. When the canopy condensed, the Ice Age began and meteors could now fall more freely to the surface of the earth. In short, one would predict that there would be evidence of fewer meteors in earlier strata. And, in fact, this is the case.

> In older geologic formations, no signs whatsoever of the presence of meteorites have been found, and we must ask ourselves whether this means that no meteorites fell in these early times — this would be a most significant finding — or whether they were not preserved, or whether we simply have not yet discovered them.[131]

130. For the calculation of the effects of aerodynamic heating, see chapter 6.
131. Fritz Heide, *Meteorites*, p. 119.

Indeed, this would be a "most significant finding" — one that precisely confirms the vapor canopy theory. The idea that the meteors are there but simply undiscovered is rejected by Heide himself:

> If we consider, moreover, that since the onset of modern coal mining, some fifty to fifty-five billion tons of coal have been mined, all of which have passed through the hands of people with a professional familiarity with stones, it is certainly remarkable that ancient meteoritic material has never been found or described up to now.[132]

Along a similar vein, Brian Mason concurs:

> The possible occurrence of meteorites in older geological formations has been a matter of considerable controversy. There seems to be no valid reason to suspect that meteorites have not fallen throughout geological time. Nevertheless, it has been remarked that no "fossil" meteorite has been discovered in the billions of tons of coal, limestone, etc., that have been mined and quarried . . . in the outcrop of a pre-Pleistocene formation.[133]

This is, of course, a probable prediction of the canopy model. A denser atmosphere would greatly increase the aerodynamic heating on an entering meteorite and melt it.

Another variety of meteorite — tektites, a glassy meteorite — reveals a similar pattern. None are found in pre-Pleistocene strata. According to Ralph Stair, "Neither tektites nor other meteorites have been found in any of the ancient geological formations."[134] Another author inadvertently puts his finger on the problem — the necessity for a formerly more dense atmosphere — when he says, "It is only the meteorites *that escape decomposition in passage through the atmosphere* that can possibly be recognized. . . . No meteorites have ever been found in the geologic column" (italics added).[135]

132. Ibid.
133. Brian Mason, *Meteorites*, p. 4.
134. Ralph Stair, "Tektites and the Lost Planet," *Scientific Monthly* 83 (July 1956):11.
135. Fred Whipple, *The New Astronomy*, p. 207; for further discussion see Peter A. Stevenson, "Meteoritic Evidence for a Young Earth," *Creation Research Society Quarterly* 12 (June 1975):23-25.

So the finding of "no meteorites" suggests that for some reason they were unable to "escape decomposition in passage through the atmosphere." The presence of a vapor canopy gives a satisfactory answer to why none seemed to have passed through.

PREDICTION 9: RESIDUAL AMOUNTS OF WATER IN THE STRATOSPHERE TODAY

The condensation of earth's vapor canopy would have undoubtedly left some water "up there." It is unreasonable to suppose that every molecule of water that existed above the pre-Flood troposphere would have precipitated down to the earth. A natural prediction growing out of the canopy hypothesis, then, would be the presence today of water vapor molecules in the stratosphere — remnants of the ancient water heaven.

It has been reported that just such water remnants do exist. Apparently, investigations carried out by rockets fired to great altitudes turned up evidence that water-cluster ions as large as $H^+(H_2O)_6$ are found at 85 kilometers in the D layer of the ionosphere.[136] One must ask how, under evolutionary models, did water vapor ions get from the surface of the planet to the upper reaches of the ionosphere? Webb observes, "A major problem for the atmospheric scientist concerns the abundance of water vapor in the upper stratosphere."[137] One satisfactory

136. E. E. Ferguson and F. E. Fehsenfeld, *Journal of Geophysical Research* 74 (May 1969):2217; A. D. Johanneson et al., "Detention of Water Cluster Ions at the High Latitude Summer Menopause," *Nature* 235 (1972): 212-17. The possible relevance of these articles to the vapor canopy was first suggested by Harold Armstrong, "Comments on Scientific News and Views," *Creation Research Society Quarterly* 6 (December 1969):139, and "Comments on Scientific News and Views," *Creation Research Society Quarterly* 9 (September 1972):134-35.
137. Willis L. Webb, *Structure of the Stratosphere and Mesophere*, pp. 129-30.

answer would be that these ions are simply remnants of a water heaven that God placed above the ancient "firmament."

PREDICTION 10: A CHANGED APPEARANCE OF THE HEAVENLY BODIES

With a canopy surrounding the earth containing an equivalent of 40 feet of precipitable water, a definite effect would have been produced on the visual appearance of the antediluvian heavens. The sun would have been somewhat dimmer and many fewer stars would have been visible. However, with the collapse of the canopy, the sun would have shone with new intensity, and many more stars would have come into view.

Is there any evidence of such a change? The only place one could go for such evidence would be human records. As briefly alluded to in chapter 4, there is extensive evidence in the cultural memories of the human race of a "new sun," who was victorious over a previously reigning sun. The appearance of many new stars should also have been recorded. It is striking that the first form of religious rebellion against God after the Flood centered on astrology and the Tower of Babel (Gen. 11). In chapter 9 we will fully analyze the appearance of the antediluvian heavens as compared to today's sky and the connection with ancient myths. We will show that there is an extensive array of evidence from the ancient myths that just such a change in visual appearance of the heavens as is predicted by the canopy model actually occurred.

Conclusion

Surely any model of prehistory that can correlate such seemingly unrelated things as the flight of the pteranodon, the ancient greenhouse, volcanic ash in tundra muck, and rickets in Neanderthal man is worthy of serious consideration. As mentioned in the introduction to this chapter, the efficiency of any theory is equal to the number of predictions correlated divided by the number of assumptions made. On the basis of the single assumption of an ancient water heaven, many unusual facts of the geological record are more easily explained and correlated with each other. It is in this that the "scientific evidence" for the existence of the ancient vapor canopy rests.

CHAPTER 6

Critique of Various Canopy Models

The major problem associated with *any kind* of canopy hypothesis is that there is no obvious mechanism for supporting more than a few inches of water in the present atmosphere. Some writers who have theorized on the canopy in the past have either ignored this problem, were unaware of it, or knew of it and tried inadequate solutions. Since water can only exist in four forms, four basic kinds of canopy theories have been proposed, each with its own peculiar ideas for support of the water heaven: the liquid, ice, cloud, and vapor canopy models[1] (that is, superheated, invisible steam, not droplets as in clouds).

THE LIQUID CANOPY MODEL

Stanley Udd has stressed the importance of a literal exegesis of Genesis 1, which seems to teach the existence of a literal liquid ocean above the ancient troposphere.[2] Because he views the statements of Genesis as true history and not borrowed myth, Udd is forced to search for some conceivable mechanism that would maintain the canopy in liquid form. He proposes a centrifugal force mechanism.

1. Actually, water could also exist as plasma, ionized gas. However, for a gas to exist in this state, the density must be incredibly small, and it would take a canopy of several hundred thousand miles depth to hold enough water.
2. Stanley V. Udd, "The Early Atmosphere" (Th.M. thesis, Grace Theological Seminary, 1974), and "The Canopy in Genesis 1:6-8," *Creation Research Society Quarterly* 12 (September 1975):90-93.

It seems quite probable, however, to suggest that a rotational motion supplied by creative fiat on the second day of creation could suspend a spherical plane of liquid water above the atmosphere. The exact mechanics of such a model cannot be supplied in this work. But it should be noted in defense of this proposal that equilibrium conditions between the forces of gravitational attraction and the inertia of matter are the mechanisms by which all celestial bodies are held in their courses.[3]

Thus, instead of a canopy Udd conceives of a thin "plate" in the plane of the equator like Saturn's rings. When the waters were raised up above the firmament, the centrifugal forces of the rotating earth arranged them into a ringlike plane surrounding the earth and in orbit.

Since there is nothing in the text of Genesis to say that the waters could not have arranged themselves in this fashion, there is no particular exegetical objection to this hypothesis. Indeed, this may be the way it happened.

However, several criticisms might be raised against this theory. First, at the distances necessary for this water to have been placed in orbit, the water would either turn to ice or would vaporize, hence it would not have remained in liquid form. The temperature of this "plate" would depend on how closely it approximated a "black body (an object that absorbs all the radiation falling upon it)." A perfect black body at the position of earth's orbit in space would attain a temperature of about 40° C.[4] If this is true, due to the zero vapor pressure of outer space, the water would vaporize. But in order to be completely faithful to the Genesis text Udd feels he *must* maintain that the water remained in its liquid state. "It is my opinion that the text suggests that the water remained in the liquid state."[5] Unless he wants to posit some kind of supernatural interference by God to insure its maintenance in liquid form, it would have turned to

3. Udd, "The Early Atmosphere," p. 62.
4. Clyde McKnight, Ph.D. atmospheric physics, department of meteorology, University of Nevada, personal communication, April 1977.
5. Stanley V. Udd, professor of Old Testament, Calvary Bible College, Kansas City, Missouri, personal communication, 12 March 1976.

ice or vapor. And if supernatural agencies were necessary, why not just leave it in a water shell as Genesis seems to describe, and assume that God simply maintained it in that form to begin with? Indeed, the liquid shell approach is the simplest and most straightforward implication of the Genesis text. If it were not for the fact that it is fraught with scientific difficulties, it should be accepted. Second, if it did not vaporize, the surface tension would break the plane into droplets and a cloud canopy would result.

There is, however, a severe objection to Udd's idea of liquid water in a ringed orbit. The kinetic energy would be such that when the water came down during the Flood (in 40 days), it would have heated the atmosphere to intolerable temperatures. The energy requirements demonstrating this point will be developed under the Ice Canopy Theory, but supernatural forces will again have to be called to the scene to prevent the collapse of the liquid water canopy from scalding the earth. Furthermore, there is no clear way to bring the canopy down in 40 days if it is in orbit.

It would seem that a model requiring so many supernatural "assists" is not as desirable as one that would not require any. Furthermore, there is nothing in the text of Genesis that requires that the water had to remain in liquid form — it would seem that it could have turned to ice, clouds, or vapor.

THE ICE CANOPY MODEL

The traditional approach followed by most writers on the canopy in the past has been to posit an ice canopy. It seems that Isaac Newton Vail was the first in modern times (early 1900s) to propose the canopy hypothesis. In his books *The Waters Above the Firmament* and *The Deluge and Its Cause* he argued that the ancient earth was surrounded by a vast ice canopy in the form of a circular cylinder, open at the poles. This thesis was expanded on more recently by Howard W. Kellogg in his books *The Canopied Earth* and *The Coming Kingdom and the Re-Canopied Earth* (1930s). In 1960, V. L. Westberg resurrected this idea, applied some of his engineering background to it, and produced the booklet *The Master Architect*, in which he proposed a spherical shell instead of a cylinder.

Vail and Kellogg developed this model at length, the latter simply following Vail's thesis but adding that the canopy would be restored during the Millennium. These writers have accepted the "gap theory" of Genesis 1:1-2, so they place most of the geological ages between these verses. Originally, as the nebular hypothesis early in this century taught, the earth was molten, and this heat threw the water of the planet into the skies. "When the earth was a molten mass of fire, there was no water upon it — all would be vaporized and sent to the skies."[6] For untold ages this water remained up there in rings. The water and other elements and compounds volatilized by the earth's heat sorted themselves into an orbit around the earth by molecular weight. Gradually the earth cooled, and the rings began to come down and the outer ones broadened.

> If all volatile elements were sent to the skies by the molten condition of the earth, they would there become assorted according to density and would arrange themselves much as we see Saturn's rings arranged. These seem to be arranged about the equator in harmony with the well-known laws of centrifugal force. As cooling progressed, it is probable that there would be a broadening of the inner ring into a belt-like form extending from the equator to the poles. Since gravity is constant and centrifugal force lessens as the poles are approached, the balance would soonest be overcome toward the poles, and the material above the poles would be deposited on the earth.[7]

It is said that during the period between Genesis 1:1 and 1:2, many such rings (canopies) cooled and crashed down to the earth. But when Genesis 1:2 begins, a great canopy of vapor or ice hangs above the earth.[8] Kellogg argues that this canopy was probably in ice form, not in vapor form: "If water is to be held above the earth by centrifugal force, it must be at a distance much beyond that of the clouds or even of the atmosphere, and at that distance the cold is excessive and the water would be

6. Howard W. Kellogg, *The Canopied Earth*, p. 3.
7. Ibid., p. 8.
8. Ibid., p. 11.

Critique of Various Canopy Models

congealed."[9] So these writers conceive of an ice canopy, which surrounded the ancient earth in the form of a kind of hollow cylinder or annular disc.

Theodore Schwarze seems to have adopted a similar idea: "In the 'canopy theory' . . . water . . . was shot out into or beyond the stratosphere where it solidified into hard ice, miles in thickness, forming an oblate spherical canopy around the earth."[10] Instead of a disc, Schwarze sees an entire sphere surrounding the earth.

V. L. Westberg suggests that when the water was originally lifted up above the firmament, it was in the form of ice crystals. These ice crystals "eventually interlocked,"[11] and a spherical ice shell resulted containing 450 feet of water. The bottom of this canopy was 350 miles from the surface of the planet.[12] How did it come down? God caused the sun to send out an exceptionally strong solar flare that melted a section of it, caused the rest of it to collapse when it lost its centrifugal force, and it "woofed down across the Antarctic continent." It remains today as the Antarctic ice cap.

MECHANICAL ENERGY REQUIREMENTS

One hardly knows where to begin in evaluating such unusual suggestions. Apart from the exegetically improbable gap-theory interpretation,[13] the scientific difficulties in such theories render them unlikely. Let us consider the mechanical energy requirements.

According to these theorists, the support mechanism was centrifugal force. Isaac Vail goes into some detail proving that

9. Ibid., p. 12.
10. C. Theodore Schwarze, *The Harmony of Science and the Bible*, p. 71; see also his *The Marvel of the Earth's Canopies*.
11. V. L. Westberg, *The Master Architect*, p. 9.
12. Ibid.
13. See Weston Fields, *Unformed and Unfilled*, pp. 1-146, for a thorough refutation of the gap theory.

centrifugal force will hold the ice canopy up.[14] It should be noted, however, that his calculations only apply to the situation at the equator as the centrifugal force mechanism will rapidly lose its effectiveness as the higher latitudes are reached. The total mechanical energy (ME) of this ice shell would simply be the sum of the kinetic energy of the shell (KE = $½I\omega^2$)[15] and the potential energy of the shell (PE = $mg_r h$). The equations and units used in the following discussion are:

a_r = acceleration in the radial direction = $r\omega^2 = v^2/r$ (6.1)

C_i = specific heat of ice at -252° to 0° C = 0.3 cal/gm[16]

C_w = specific heat of water = 1 cal/gm

F_c = centrifugal force = mv^2/r (6.2)

F_g = force of gravity = mg_r (6.3)

g_o = gravitational constant at the surface of the earth, 980 cm/sec²

g_r = gravitational constant at any altitude above the surface of the earth = $(R^2/r^2)(g_o)$ (6.4)

h = altitude of the bottom of the ice canopy = 350 miles or 5.633×10^7 cm; also used for Roche's limit = 9,108 miles or $14,657.9 \times 10^5$ cm

I = moment of inertia of a ring or thin-walled cylinder,[17] = mr^2 (6.5)

14. Isaac N. Vail, *The Waters Above the Firmament*, pp. 21-24.
15. George Shortley and Dudley Williams, *Elements of Physics*, 1:130.
16. Approximation from *Handbook of Chemistry and Physics*, p. D-158.
17. Shortley and Williams, 1:130.

Critique of Various Canopy Models

KE = kinetic energy of ice particle = $\frac{1}{2} I\omega^2$
(angular, for ice canopy); KE = $\frac{1}{2} mv^2$ (rectilinear, for particle entering from outer space), ergs (6.6)

L_f = latent heat of fusion of water = 80 cal/gm

L_v = latent heat of vaporization of water = 540 cal/gm

PE = potential energy = $mg_r h$, ergs (6.7)

Q_i = calories needed to warm m grams of ice from -252°C to 0° C = $mC_i(-T)$ = (0.3)(-252° C) = 75.6 cal/gm

Q_m = calories needed to melt m grams of ice
    = mL_f = (1)(80) = 80 cal/gm (6.8)

Q_t = total heat necessary to vaporize m grams of ice at -252° C into steam at 100° C = $Q_i + Q_m + Q_w + Q_v$ = 795 cal/gm (approximately) (6.9)

Q_v = calories needed to vaporize m grams of water at 100° C = mL_v

Q_w = calories needed to raise the temperature of water from 0° C to 100° C = $mC_w T$ = 100 cal/gm

r = radius from the center of the earth to the ice particle. For the ice canopy, r = 6.934×10^8 cm; for Roche's limit, r = $21,029.9 \times 10^5$ cm

R = radius of the earth = $6,371 \times 10^5$ cm

ω = angular velocity of the ice canopy.

In order to solve for KE (6.6), the value of ω at which the force of gravity and the centrifugal force equal each other must be determined. From (6.4), (6.1), (6.2), and (6.3), it is clear that this occurs when $\omega^2 = g_0(R^2/r^3)$. Relating this to (6.6) and (6.5), the KE of the ice canopy would be given by:

$$KE = \frac{mg_0R^2}{2r} = \frac{(6{,}371 \times 10^5)^2 (980)}{(2)(6.934 \times 10^8)} \qquad (6.10)$$

$$= 2.868 \times 10^{11} \text{ ergs/gm}$$

$$= 6{,}855 \text{ cal/gm.}$$

The potential energy of this ice canopy at 350 miles is given by (6.7),

$$PE = mg_rh = mg_0(R^2/r^2)h \qquad (6.11)$$

$$= m(980)\frac{(6{,}371 \times 10^5)^2(5.633 \times 10^7)}{(6.934 \times 10^8)^2}$$

$$= 4.66 \times 10^{10} \text{ erg/gm}$$

$$= 1{,}114 \text{ cal/gm.}$$

So the total amount of mechanical energy of Vail's ice cylinder (assuming it was as high as Westberg's ice shell) is 7,969 cal/gm, or 10 times the amount of energy necessary to turn ice at -252° C into steam at 100° C.

Westberg and Schwarze also seem to have overlooked the fact that a spherical shell would not remain a shell because of decreasing centrifugal force toward the poles. The polar ends of their shell would collapse. Assuming an ice shell stayed up, however, the same calculations using $I = \frac{2mr^2}{3}$ could be made which will obviously yield similar results.[18]

18. Dwight E. Gray, ed., *American Institute of Physics Handbook*, p. 240.

MECHANICS OF ICE ENTRY INTO EARTH'S ATMOSPHERE

What would happen to this ice as it came through the earth's atmosphere? The mechanism for bringing the ice down, according to Westberg, was that a section of the whirling ice shell was melted by a solar flare. Presumably it then flew apart, fragmented, and the ice chunks crashed to the earth below. Since the ice would have been in orbit, the orbiting particles could have been brought to the surface by assuming they were in an orbit of gradually decreasing radius (as many manmade satellites are today), and at the time of the Flood, the radius had decreased to the point where the particles were in contact with the denser parts of the earth's atmosphere and were slowed down sufficiently to cause a sudden fall towards the earth. In both of these cases, the mechanical energy of the ice would be immense as outlined above (6.10, 6.11). As these particles came through the atmosphere, they would undergo some melting by aerodynamic heating. Would any of the supercooled ice ever reach the earth?

Roche's limit and the Patten epic. Donald Patten in his book *The Biblical Flood and the Ice Epoch*[19] has posited another source for the ice of the Ice Age. He suggests that the earth was at one time visited by an invader planet from deep space. This invader planet was surrounded by either ice rings (like Saturn) or more probably had an icy satellite like Saturn's seventh moon, Hyperion (diameter 300 miles).[20] Temporarily disturbed by the earth's gravitational field, the visitor made two revolutions around the earth during an eight-month period.[21] During the first revolution, the icy satellite of the planet came within Roche's limit (that is, under 10,000 miles from the earth's core

19. For a negative review of this book see Joseph Hensen, et. al., "Book Review of *The Biblical Flood and the Ice Epoch*," *Creation Research Society Quarterly* 4 (March 1968):129-32.
20. Donald W. Patten, *The Biblical Flood and the Ice Epoch*, pp. 145, 126-27.
21. Ibid., p. 146.

or 6,000 miles from the earth's surface), and disintegrated into tiny fragments due to the gravitational stress of the earth overcoming the tensile stresses of the moon.[22] These tiny fragments were then ionized by cosmic radiation[23] and followed the magnetic field to the polar regions where ice at temperatures of -173° C (-279° F) penetrated the vapor canopy, precipitated it, and fell on the mammoths and other mammals, burying them in a storm of subzero hail and freezing them in their tracks.[24] Later, the invader departed from the earth, and subsequently became the planet known as Mercury.[25]

Roche's limit is the minimal distance between two planetary bodies at which the smaller will be disintegrated by the gravitational forces between them. At some critical distance, the gravitational forces producing tension on an invader moon would overcome the forces holding the moon together. This critical distance is known as Roche's limit.[26] Patten's application of this limit to a solid body has been challenged in view of the fact that it was originally derived for two binary stars, that is, liquid bodies.[27] However, Loren C. Steinhauer of M.I.T. has shown that Patten is correct in this instance and derived Roche's limit for the earth = 9,108 miles, (that is, 2.3 times the diameter of the earth = $2.3 \times 6,371 \text{ Km} = 1.465 \times 10^9 \text{ cm} = 9,108$ miles = 5,149 miles above the earth's surface).[28]

The manner of transport of the ice to the poles is described by Patten as follows:

22. Ibid., p. 148.
23. Ibid., pp. 134, 146.
24. Ibid., pp. 104-13, 146.
25. Ibid., p. 312.
26. Sir James Jeans, *Astronomy and Cosmogony*, pp. 217-24.
27. Philip H. Hoff, "Roche's Limit and the Patten Epic," *Creation Research Society Quarterly* 8 (June 1971):62-63.
28. Loren C. Steinhauer, Ph.D., "The Relevancy of Roche's Limit to the Flood-Ice Dump Theory," *Creation Research Society Quarterly* 8 (June 1971):63-65. Patten now prefers 2.7 earth diameters, or 7208 miles above the earth's surface, personal communication, 3 April 1977.

It is thought that the particles of ice, being electrically charged, were deflected, or shunted, or redirected by the magnetic field, as are charged particles during periods of sunspot activity. The particles apparently converged over the magnetic polar regions, and in converging, they bumped, experiencing intra-collisions, which reduced their velocity, causing them to decelerate, and proceeded to descent.[29]

So Patten seems to think that because they converged and "bumped," their velocity would have been slowed and they would have floated to earth. He has also suggested that the kinetic energy was lost as the particles bumped together hundreds of thousands of miles above the surface and lost heat.[30] However, as these particles entered the earth's gravitational field, they would gain kinetic energy as they accelerated. It is not clear how this "bumping" would significantly slow them down. Although Patten's epic does not relate directly to the canopy, except as a mechanism for precipitating it, the same physics involved in analyzing the effects of canopy ice particles coming through the atmosphere apply to the particles of this proposed fragmented icy satellite.

Aerodynamic heating on ice entering the earth's atmosphere. As the ice particle enters the earth's atmosphere from either the orbital path of the ice canopy or from 9,108 miles as in the Patten epic, aerodynamic heating will immediately begin to melt it. A certain fraction of the power generated by this heating will be expended in heating the ice, and the rest will be expended in heating the surrounding air or expended in a collision at the surface. Significant heating does not begin until the particle begins to penetrate the earth's atmosphere at about 75 miles up. Above that level, the density is so low that little heating occurs. The fraction of the power expended in surface heating of a body entering the earth's atmosphere with velocities of the order of satellite velocities depends on the $m/C_d A_c$ ratio, where m = the mass of the particle; C_d = the coefficient

---

29. Patten, p. 130.
30. Donald Patten, personal communication, 3 April 1977.

of drag, 1.5 assumed;[31] and A_c = the cross-sectional area of the particle or πr^2 (assuming spherical particles for purposes of discussion). From graphs in the *Handbook of Astronautical Engineering* we can estimate the amount of aerodynamic heating on the ice particle.[32]

Patten insists that the particles of his ice dump were gravel-sized like Saturn's rings, in which few of them were over a yard in diameter and most did not exceed an inch.[33] It would be interesting to see if such small pieces could make it through the atmosphere without melting. Large chunks might conceivably do so, but would one-inch-diameter pieces?

For a particle with a diameter of one foot, $A_c = 0.78$ ft² and m = 32.4 lb or 14,696.4 gm. From graphs in the *Handbook*, it can be discerned that the $m/C_d A_c$ ratio would be 27.7, and the total heat load on the particle would be about 5,850 BTU or 1,474,200 calories.[34] Since there are 14,696.4 gm in the particle, this amounts to about 100 cal/gm. In view of the fact that only 80 cal/gm, from (6.8), are needed to melt the particles, it is evident that the ice particles would have to have been larger than one foot in diameter if they were to reach the surface.

If this is true, then unless the particles were very large, none of them would have made it to the surface, and Patten's cascade of hail beginning the Ice Age is fiction. It might be argued that larger pieces did indeed begin the cascade but were melted and were only hail-sized when they hit, but Patten's epic requires tiny pieces. This raises some other problems of the dissipation of kinetic energy which we will look at shortly. It seems likely that such large chunks would be fractured and shattered by a combination of deceleration and thermal stresses. The deceler-

31. Dr. Edward Blick, professor of aeronautical engineering, University of Oklahoma, Norman, Oklahoma, personal communication, 17 February 1977.
32. Heinz Herman Koelle, ed., *Handbook of Astronautical Engineering*, Fig. 10-35, pp. 10-27.
33. Donald Patten, personal communication, 3 April 1977.
34. This value was determined by graphical analysis from Fig. 10-35 in the *Handbook of Astronautical Engineering*, pp. 10-27.

Critique of Various Canopy Models

ation force acting on the entering chunks depends largely on the angle of entrance, θ (see Fig. 6.1). Assuming an entry by gradual decay from orbit (such as might be experienced by fragmented particles of an ice canopy), the deceleration force would be 9.5 g (g = earth gravity) or 395 lb/ft² for the one-foot-diameter sphere.[35] The Army Cold Regions Laboratory[36] has determined that the compressive strength of -50° C ice is 80 kg/cm² or 163,584 lb/ft². For a sphere of ice entering the earth's atmosphere they estimate that the compressive strength would be about 200 kg/cm² or 409,622 lb/ft² as the maximum. So it can readily be seen that large chunks entering from orbital decay would not be shattered by deceleration forces.[37]

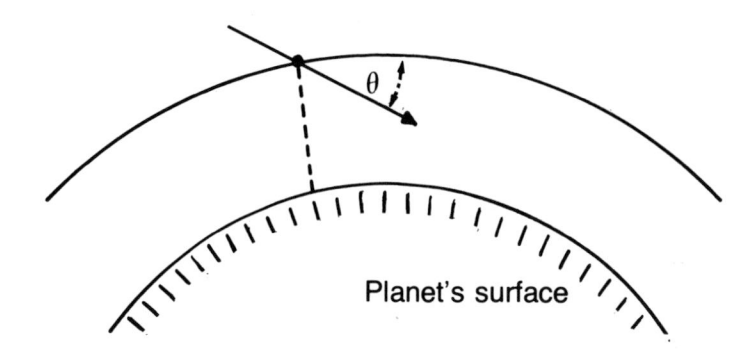

Fig. 6.1. — Coordinate System and Nomenclature Used in Equations of Motion.

35. F = (mg)(deceleration force) = (density)(volume) (32.2)(9.5) = (4/3)π(0.5)³(62.4 lb/ft³)(32.2)(9.5) = 9,994 poundals = 310 pounds-force. This force is applied across the cross-sectional area of the sphere. Thus, 310/π(0.5)² = 395 lb/ft². See *Handbook of Astronautical Engineering*, Table 10.3, pp. 10-13.
36. Army Cold Regions Laboratory, Hanover, New Hampshire, personal communication, 10 July 1977.
37. However, ice entry by orbital decay could never be accomplished in 40 days as the Bible requires. It would take several years.

What would be the shattering effects caused by deceleration forces on a particle entering at steep entry angles from deep space as Patten suggests? At a 90-degree entry (vertical), the deceleration is 324 g,[38] or 6,739 lb/ft². However, if the particle size were 10 feet, the deceleration force would be 270,000 lb/ft². With a radius of 20 feet the deceleration would be 539,000 lb/ft². Thus, any particle between 10 and 20 feet in radius or greater entering at 90 degrees would certainly shatter due to deceleration.

There is, however, an even more destructive force that would act on these ice particles — thermal stresses. As the ice enters the atmosphere from deep space, it would be warmed quickly from the temperatures of deep space (about -250° F) to much more moderate temperatures. A thermal gradient would be set up in the ice with the surface near 32° F and the interior near -250° F. According to the Army Cold Regions Laboratory, this would surely shatter the ice immediately. Calculations on this are quite complicated.

In the opinion of the scientists consulted at the Army Cold Regions Laboratory a combination of deceleration forces and thermal stresses would probably shatter the ice particles, and once shattered, they would all melt due to aerodynamic heating if their radii were small enough.

A more precise solution of the effects of aerodynamic heating is available to us and we will analyze two cases. First, the effects of aerodynamic heating on a particle entering at orbital velocities from a fragmented canopy will be discussed, that is, low-entry angles. Then, an approximation for the effects of ice entry at steep angles, 20° to 90°, will be made to "bracket" Patten's speculations on an ice dump from outer space.

Assuming a spherical ball of ice entering the earth's atmosphere with an initial velocity in the range of satellite orbital

---

38. *Handbook of Astronautical Engineering,* Table 10.3, pp. 10-13.

Critique of Various Canopy Models

velocities (25,950 ft/sec), the equation for the total heat absorbed during re-entry to the earth's surface is:[39]

$$Q = 15{,}900\ K_2 S (m/C_d A R)^{1/2} (\bar{Q}) \qquad (6.12)$$

where,

$K_2 = 0.5$ for spheres and hemispheres[40]

S = area wetted by boundary layer = $2\pi R^2$

m = body mass, slugs = $\rho(4/3)\pi R^3$

R = body radius in feet

$\bar{Q}$ = factor defined in NASA TR R-11[41]

C_d = drag coefficient (assume a value of 1.5).[42]

By converting from slugs to lbm for m, Equation (6.12) can be reduced to:

$$Q = 4055 (mR)^{1/2} \bar{Q}. \qquad (6.13)$$

The heat necessary to completely melt the ice particle is desired. This is given by,

$$Q = mC_i\ \Delta T + mL_f \qquad (6.14)$$

where $C_i = 0.3$ BTU/lbm·°F and $L_f = 144$ BTU/lb, from (6.8).

39. Dean R. Chapman, *Technical Report R-11, An Approximate Analytical Method for Studying Entry into Planetary Atmospheres*, NASA TR R-11, p. 11. Dr. Edward Blick suggested this general approach, personal communication, 17 February 1977.
40. Ibid.
41. Ibid.
42. Dr. Edward Blick, personal communication, 17 February 1977.

Now since m = $\rho(4/3)\pi R^3$ = $(62.4)(4/3)R^3$ = $261R^3$, by substituting Equation (6.13) into (6.14) and reducing, it follows that:

$$R = \frac{262\bar{Q}}{0.3 \Delta T + 144} \quad (6.15)$$

where R = the radius at which a particle will melt given a certain $\bar{Q}$ factor. If it is assumed that the ice temperature at the start of re-entry is -252°F and just before earth impact it is 33°F, then $\Delta T = 453°$ F and

$$R = 0.94 \bar{Q} \quad (6.16)$$

$\bar{Q}$ is a function of the initial re-entry speed, Lift/Drag ratio, and initial angle of entry, and has been tabulated by Chapman and Kapphahn.[43] Table 6.1 lists the various values of Q for different entry angles and the minimum ice radius, R, computed from Equation (6.16) assuming total melting of the particle.

TABLE 6.1

SPHERICAL RADIUS AT WHICH ALL THE ICE WILL MELT, L/D = 0

\multicolumn{3}{c}{Orbital Entry 25,950 ft/sec}	\multicolumn{3}{c}{Orbital Entry 38,925 ft/sec}
Entry Angle	$\bar{Q}$	R,ft.	Entry Angle	$\bar{Q}$	R,ft.
0	1.806	1.7	-4.2	3.030	2.85
-1	1.333	1.25	-8.0	1.400	1.32
-2	1.060	1.00	-10.0	1.223	1.15
-3	0.904	0.85	-20.0	0.846	0.80
-4	0.798	0.75	-25.0	0.757	0.72
-10	0.518	0.49	-30.0	0.695	0.65
-20	0.371	0.35	-40.0	0.611	0.57

43. Dean R. Chapman and Arline K. Kapphahn, *Tables of Z Functions for Atmosphere Entry Analyses*, NASA TR R-106.

Most of the ice coming in from an orbital entry would tend to enter at very shallow angles, less than -10°, so any particle of such a shattered canopy that was smaller than 0.5 ft. in radius would probably melt and never make it to the surface. Since a particle would have to be somewhat larger than this for the thermal and deceleration stresses to shatter it into something less than 0.5 ft. radius, it seems likely that such an ice canopy could indeed send some ice to the surface of the earth.

What about particles entering from deep space? Dr. Roger Simpson derived a simple approximation for calculating the effects of aerodynamic heating on particles entering from directly overhead, that is, entry angle of 90°.[44] In order to simplify a very complicated calculation and at the same time favor Patten's ice-dump theory, Simpson made the following assumptions:

1. The path of the ice particle is directly from overhead. When the ice comes in from this direction, the *least* amount of aerodynamic heating occurs since the particle is in the atmosphere for a lesser time than when it enters at a smaller angle.

2. From graphs in the *Handbook of Astronautical Engineering*, it was estimated that only about 10% of the heat generated by friction with the atmosphere is expended in heating the ice.[45]

3. It is assumed that the terminal velocity is reached very quickly after the particle begins accelerating from zero velocity at Roche's Limit, 9,108 miles. The terminal velocity is reached when the drag force on the particle exactly equals the gravitational force. This, of course, impossibly favors the Patten epic because it assumes that the particle is traveling at only about 500 mph instead of 17,000 mph, hence starting with a much smaller kinetic energy.

4. The coefficient of drag is unity.

44. Professor Roger L. Simpson, Ph.D., P.E., department of civil and mechanical engineering, school of engineering and applied science, Southern Methodist University, Dallas, Texas, personal communication, 1 November 1976.
45. *Handbook of Astronautical Engineering*, Fig. 10.33, pp. 10-24.

210   *The Waters Above: Earth's Pre-Flood Vapor Canopy*

5. The particles are spherical. This, too, of course, favors Patten because a rough particle of irregular shape will generate much more friction and will absorb much more heat.

With these assumptions, the following ratio between the final and initial radius of the ice particle would be:[46]

$$R_f/R_i = 0.166. \tag{6.17}$$

Table 6.2 tabulates the ratio between R_f and R_i for various values of R_i. These data correlate well with the data on Table 6.1 for orbital entry at steeper angles at higher velocity. In fact, the data on Table 6.1 for orbital entry at 38,925 ft/sec² can be applied to entry from deep space for the greater entry angles.

TABLE 6.2

RADIUS RATIOS FOR ICE ENTERING FROM ROCHE'S LIMIT

R_i, ft	R_f, ft
2500	415
1000	166
500	83
10	1.66
5	0.83
1	0.166
0.5	0.083

46. The full equation with an explanation of its parts is:

$$\frac{R_f}{R_i} = \exp\left[\frac{(4.24 \times 10^{-5})(r_i)}{h}\left(1 - \frac{r_o}{r_i}\right)\right],$$

where R_f = the final radius of the ice particle after being subjected to the effects of aerodynamic heating, ft; R_i = initial radius of the ice particle, ft; r_o = radius of the earth = 3,959 miles × 5,280 = 20,903,520 ft; r_i = distance from the center of the earth to Roche's Limit = 9,108 miles; and h = heat necessary to warm and melt a pound of ice from -252° F = 282 BTU/lbm.

Critique of Various Canopy Models

This seems to create a serious problem for Patten's epic. He requires that the ice particles entering from space be extremely small. This is necessary if they are to be influenced in any way by the earth's magnetic field and be shunted to the poles. Ionizing radiation can only ionize the ice molecules on the outer edge of the ice particle. Since these constitute only a very small fraction of the total number of molecules in the ice particle, in order for ionizing radiation to leave a charge significant enough for the particle to be moved by the earth's magnetic field, the particle would have to be extremely small, perhaps less than a millimeter in diameter. Particles that small will be completely vaporized by aerodynamic heating, and there would be none left for the ice dump.

Dissipation of kinetic energy. These theories can be viewed from another perspective. As the ice moves from either orbit or deep space to the surface, the kinetic energy will be dissipated by aerodynamic heating, atmospheric heating, and surface impact. Assuming that the ice made it to the surface, the kinetic energy of the particle would be dissipated at impact by melting of the ice, shockwaves, crater digging, and surface heating.

O'Keefe and Ahrens have calculated precisely what the energy partitioning would be on certain kinds of meteorites at impact velocities varying from 11,000 to 100,000 mph.[47] Depending on the material of the meteorite and the kind of surface, the fraction of kinetic energy of the meteoroid transformed into internal energy on impact varied from 0.7 to 0.91. The amount of kinetic energy resident in the planet's surface varied from 0.07 to 0.1. This kinetic energy was largely expended in the very hot ejecta from the surface. Most of the kinetic energy, therefore, "is converted into internal energy residing in the planetary surface material," that is, surface heat.[48] Also, for a

47. John D. O'Keefe and Thomas J. Ahrens, "Impact-Induced Energy Partitioning, Melting and Vaporization on Terrestrial Planets," Contribution Number 2907, Division of Geological and Planetary Sciences, California Institute of Technology, Pasadena, Calif. 91125, 1977.
48. Ibid., p. 18.

meteorite composed of iron, the amount of melt ranged from 5 times the meteoroid volume to over 275 times the meteoroid volume. In view of these calculations on iron, Ahrens concluded that all of the ice in Patten's epic would melt at impact, heat the surface, and be returned to the atmosphere by surface heating.[49] Since the particles under consideration are ice and not iron, it is likely that much of this kinetic energy would be utilized in vaporizing the ice into superheated steam, which would immediately return to the atmosphere and cause intensive heating. Less than 0.1% of the impact energy would be dissipated by seismic waves.[50]

Some simple calculations will reveal the impact of such an ice dump. Westberg postulates 450 feet of precipitable water in his ice canopy. This is equivalent to 7×10^{22} grams of ice. As computed above, the mechanical energy of such a canopy is 7,969 cal/gm (6.10, 6.11). Since there are 7×10^{22} grams in the canopy, the total mechanical energy of such a canopy would be 5.58×10^{26} calories. If 100% of this energy entered the earth's atmosphere by aerodynamic heating, the resultant atmospheric temperature increase (ΔT) would be given by:[51]

$$\Delta T = \frac{(ME) - Q_T}{m_a C_a} \quad (6.18)$$

So, $\Delta T = 5.2 \times 10^5$ degress C. Of course, in the case of the ice canopy, with extremely large chunks of ice it is possible that a small percentage of the kinetic energy will be expended in

49. Thomas Ahrens, Ph.D, Seismology Laboratory, California Institute of Technology, personal communication, 13 July 1977.
50. Ibid.
51. The parts of this equation are:
    ME = the mechanical energy of the canopy = 5.58×10^{23} kcal; Q_T = energy dissipated in warming, melting, and vaporizing the ice (from 6.9) = (795 kcal/kg)(7×10^{19} kg) = 5.565×10^{22} kcal; m_a = mass of the atmosphere today = 5.2×10^{18} kg; and C_a = specific heat of air = 0.172 kcal/kg·° C.

Critique of Various Canopy Models 213

surface heating rather than aerodynamic heating. However, even if 99% of the kinetic energy of the ice canopy were expended in surface heating and only 1% in aerodynamic heating, the net increase in atmospheric heating due to re-entry friction would be 6,239° C.

In the case of the Patten epic, a similar situation exists. Patten suggests that 12,000,000 mi^3 or 5×10^{22} gm of ice entered the atmosphere from Roche's Limit. Assuming these particles had reached near escape velocity (37,000 ft/sec = 1.12776×10^6 cm/sec), by the time they reached the areas of the earth's atmosphere where aerodynamic heating begins (75 miles), the total kinetic energy of this ice dump would have been 7.6×10^{26} cal.[52]

Again, as indicated above, these small particles would be completely melted by the earth's atmosphere, and the resultant temperature increase of the earth's atmosphere from this immense kinetic energy input would be 8×10^5 degrees C. If 99% of the energy was expended in surface heating and 1% in aerodynamic heating (which is ridiculous), still Patten's ice dump will heat the earth's atmosphere to 8,497° C.

What about a water canopy? The kinetic energy of such a canopy would be great. Assuming that its distribution of mass was approximately the same as Westberg's ice canopy, then the mechanical energy of the water canopy would be the same as the ice canopy, 7,969 cal/gm. The total energy depends on how much water Udd suggests was in the canopy. Assuming he sees the canopy as containing sufficient water to sustain a 40-day-and-night rainfall at 0.5 inch/hr, this means that the water canopy contains 6.216×10^{21} gm of water. Thus, the total mechanical energy of such a canopy would be 5×10^{25} cal. This energy expended in 40 days would heat the earth's atmosphere to 55,903° C. Even if he posits a 0.1 inch/hr "torrential

---

52. The equation would look like this:

$$KE = \frac{(5 \times 10^{22} \text{ gm})(1.12776 \times 10^6 \text{ cm/sec})^2}{2}$$

$$= 7.6 \times 10^{26} \text{ cal.}$$

downpour," the kinetic energy expended would raise the atmosphere temperature 11,000° C.

It must be granted that the above calculations on aerodynamic heating are only approximate. The real problem, however, in all these ice-canopy and ice-dump theories is that the tremendous amounts of kinetic energy involved must be accounted for.

If we were to argue in favor of the ice-dump theories, the possibility of dumping all that kinetic energy into the oceans would have to be considered. The oceans comprise 70.8% of the surface area of the earth, so 70.8% of the energy from the ice rings or from the ice dump could be absorbed by this mass with little effect on the ocean temperature. In fact, simple calculations reveal that the increase in ocean temperatures produced by dumping 70.8% of the thermal energy of Patten's ice dump would only be 0.37° C.[53] However, that still leaves 29.2% of the energy of Patten's ice dump (or 2.22×26 cal) to be expended in surface heating and thus be returned to the atmosphere.

In the case of the ice-ring canopy, or the ice-cylinder canopy, we might posit that the entire earth was covered with water before the ice began to fall. Then the kinetic energy of the ice rings or canopy could be absorbed by the oceans and never impact the ground and be returned to the atmosphere by surface heating.

However, this too has its problems. As this ice enters the atmosphere, it heats up the surrounding air by aerodynamic heating and a large portion of the kinetic energy of the ice rings would be expended in atmospheric heating. In fact, the impact velocity of a particle from an ice-ring canopy, or from an ice-cylinder canopy, or from an ice dump would be very small unless the initial radius of the particle was immense.

In fact, in the above approximations it was granted, for the sake of argument, that the ice particle would enter the atmosphere and impact the surface at high velocities. This assump-

53. $\Delta T = Q/C_W m$, where ΔT = change in ocean temperature; C_W = specific heat of water = 1 cal/gm; and m = mass of the oceans = 1.456×10^{27} gm (see "Ocean," in Van Nostrand's Scientific Encyclopedia, p. 1670). So $\Delta T = 0.37°$ C.

Critique of Various Canopy Models

tion was granted to ice-ring canopy theorists simply to avoid their problem of the dissipation of kinetic energy in the atmosphere itself. However, over 99% of the kinetic energy of the ice particles would never reach the surface but would be expended in aerodynamic heating of the atmosphere. This is easily seen from the relation[54]

$$V_f = 172(R)^{1/2} \text{mph},$$

where, V_f = the terminal velocity at impact and R = the initial radius of the ice particle in miles. So in the case of an ice-ring canopy containing 40 feet of water the KE of the ice particles would be about 8,000 cal/gm. The terminal velocity for 0.5 ft radius particles (anything smaller will melt completely and nearly all the energy will be expended in heating up the atmosphere) would be 75 cm/sec. This corresponds to a KE = 6.69×10^{-5} cal/gm, which means that 99.999% of the initial kinetic energy of the particles in the ice ring was expended in atmospheric heating.[55] If this were expended in the required 40 days of the Flood, it would heat the atmosphere to 56,000° C.

It may be safely concluded, then, that the ice ring, ice cylinder, and water canopy theories are physical impossibilities. Their collapse would result in a literal scalding of the earth as all of their kinetic energy was expended in 40 days.

The Cloud Canopy Model

Donald Patten has suggested that the canopy was a permanent cloud cover, "The permanent cloud cover of the earth, in the model which follows (to the best of our judgment and understanding), may have been 3,000 to 5,000 feet thick, and

54. Derived from Chapman, *An Approximate Analytical Method for Studying Entry into Planetary Atmospheres*, by Professor Edward Blick, personal communication, 17 February 1977.
55. Using the same method as in (6.11) where mph × 44.704 = cm/sec, and erg/gm × 2.39×10^{-8} = cal/gm.

ranged between 5,000 and 10,000 feet above sea level."[56] He suggests that, due to this immense canopy, a universal greenhouse effect would have resulted.[57] Curiously, Patten objects to the idea of a canopy many miles thick on the basis that sunlight could not penetrate such a thick canopy.[58] Yet, as we will demonstrate, little sunlight could penetrate a cloud canopy either.

Several objections might be raised against Patten's idea. First, the cloud canopy that he proposes will contain only a few inches of rain — far too little to sustain a 40-day global rainfall. Patten suggests that the source of the rain was "low-latitude slop-over of the ice dump."[59] However, as argued in chapter 2, it seems that Moses intends to inform us that the source of the rain was not from extraterrestrial sources, but was from "the waters above" (Gen. 1:6).[60]

But there is a more basic objection to the idea of a cloud-cover canopy: it will have exactly the opposite effect that Patten predicts. Instead of creating a universal greenhouse, a cloud cover 3,000 feet thick would plunge the surface temperature below freezing.

A simple approximation for determining the surface temperature of the earth as a function of the optical depth of the atmosphere and the extent of the cloud cover has been developed by Eddington,[61]

$$T^4 = \frac{(1 - A)S(2 + 3\lambda/2)}{8\sigma} \qquad (6.19)$$

---

56. Donald Patten, "The Pre-flood Greenhouse Effect," in *A Symposium on Creation, II*, p. 12.
57. Ibid., pp. 13-19.
58. Ibid., p. 24.
59. Ibid., p. 25.
60. See pp. 63-65. The source of the *Flood* was not the canopy, except incidentally, but was the "fountains of the deep."
61. Discussed by R. M. Goody in *Atmospheric Radiation I, Theoretical Basis*, p. 332.

where A = the albedo of the earth; S = the solar constant[62] = 1.92 cal/cm² min; σ = the Stephan-Boltzman constant[63] = 8.128 × 10⁻¹¹ cal/cm²·°K⁴·min; and λ = the optical depth. The optical depth is calculated from the mass absorption coefficient of the absorbing gas. In the gray atmosphere model outlined by Goody, the optical depth is assumed to be unity for the infrared absorption spectrum under consideration.[64] The albedo of the earth today is 0.36.[65] Plugging this value into the above relation yields a mean surface temperature for the earth today of 285° K = 54° F which is reasonable.

However, with a cloud canopy surrounding the earth, the albedo of the earth would jump to 0.8, a common value for thick clouds such as those which Patten is suggesting.[66] Substituting 0.8 into Goody's approximation yields a mean surface temperature of -75° F, hardly a tropical greenhouse. If the albedo was increased to only 0.5, T = 23° F.

A final objection to the cloud canopy idea is simply that it would block out all starlight, and yet the text of Genesis seems to imply that stars were visible prior to the Flood (see Gen. 1:14-18).

The Water Vapor Canopy Model

The final possibility as to the form of the water heaven is that it consisted of water vapor, or superheated invisible steam. Indeed, this is the view popularized by Morris and Whitcomb in *The Genesis Flood*, and is the one most often assumed in creationist literature today. However, there is an apparent difficulty with the vapor canopy hypothesis that has resulted in its abandonment as a viable scientific model by many competent

62. *Handbook of Chemistry and Physics*, p. F-176.
63. Seymour Hess, *Introduction to Theoretical Meteorology*, p. 353.
64. See Andrew P. Ingersol, "The Runaway Greenhouse: A History of Water on Venus," *Journal of the Atmospheric Sciences* 26 (November 1969): 1192-93 for discussion.
65. *Handbook of Chemistry and Physics*, p. F-176.
66. Horace Robert Byers, *General Meteorology*, p. 33.

scientists.[67] The major problem seems to be that there is simply no apparent mechanism by which the atmosphere, as it is *presently* constructed, could hold anywhere near the 40 feet of water required to sustain a 40-day global rainfall.

It is easy to demonstrate that for a saturated atmosphere with a sea-level temperature of 28° C and in saturation-adiabatic equilibrium the total precipitable water that this atmosphere could hold is only 10.54 cm, or about four inches.[68]

Some have suggested that the vapor canopy containing many feet of water was maintained up above the atmosphere because it was lighter than air and "floated." Rimmer argued that since water vapor is lighter than the surrounding air, "it ascends quickly and naturally."[69] Morris and Whitcomb suggested a similar idea:

> It is known, however, that the region above about 80 miles is very hot, over 100°F and possibly rising to 3000°F, and is in fact called the thermosphere for this reason. High temperature, of course, is the chief requisite for retaining a large quantity of water vapor. Furthermore, it is known that water vapor is substantially lighter than air and most of the other gases making up the atmosphere.[70]

However, temperature alone is not sufficient to hold the water vapor. In that region today, the number density (number of molecules/cm^3) is so small that there is no absorption of solar energy and conduction to the surface of a body placed there. But Morris and Whitcomb are correct that with a dense canopy of water vapor, extremely high temperatures would be present — but due to a different physics than that which produces the hot thermosphere today.

Furthermore, this "lighter than air" mechanism violates a basic law of physics — Dalton's Law of Partial Pressures. Ac-

67. Robert Whitelaw, Robert Newman, Bernard Ramm, for example.
68. Byers, p. 113.
69. Harry Rimmer, *Modern Science and the Genesis Record*, 1:74.
70. Henry M. Morris and John C. Whitcomb, *The Genesis Flood*, pp. 240-41, 256.

cording to Dalton's Law, whenever a gas is introduced into an empty container, the molecules distribute themselves randomly and uniformly throughout the container (diffusive equilibrium). Also, this random distribution goes on, regardless of the presence of the other gases.[71] There is no known way to prevent these molecules of water vapor and air from diffusing equally throughout the "empty container" (the atmosphere). If that were not true, one might ask why the present atmosphere is not layered according to molecular weight. If it were, all of the CO_2 would be at the bottom and all life would become extinct.

If a massive amount of water vapor was placed above the atmosphere and was distributed in hydrostatic equilibrium throughout the gravity field, it would immediately begin to diffuse toward the surface. If the pre-Flood troposphere is imagined to consist of layers, the molecules of water vapor will gradually diffuse into these layers.

From Figure 6.2 we observe that as the molecules diffuse down from the canopy, they gradually "fill up" each level. Each level can only contain so many molecules of water vapor before they will gradually condense and precipitate out as rain. The maximum number of molecules that can be maintained in a layer depends on the saturation vapor pressure, which is a function of temperature only. Once a greater number of molecules enters the layer than the saturation vapor pressure can contain, the layer becomes supersaturated and it "rains out." The saturation vapor pressure at L_5 is determined solely by the surface temperature. So the surface temperature determines how many molecules from the canopy can diffuse down before rainfall begins. At 82° F the saturation vapor pressure is only 37 millibars, or 15 inches of water. That means that the total amount of weight of precipitable water that can be maintained above that layer is only 15 inches.[72] If the weight of water vapor exceeds that amount, then the saturation vapor pressure in L_5 will be exceeded, and it will rain. As a result of this process, the entire canopy would condense out rapidly.

71. Shortley and Williams, Elements of College Physics, 1:348, 384.
72. Byers, p. 106.

CANOPY (WATER VAPOR)

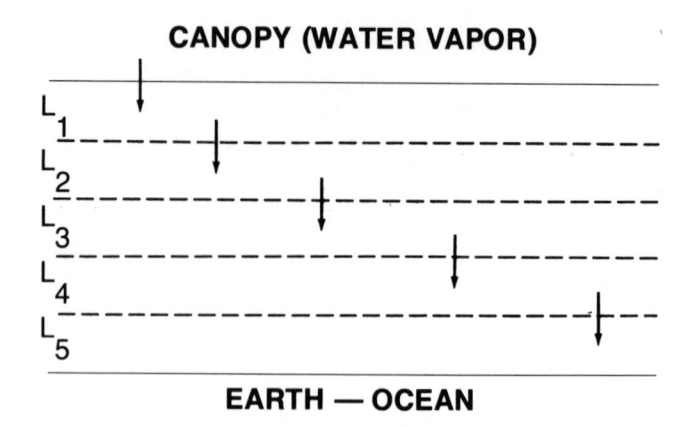

```
L₁ ─────────↓──────────────────────
L₂ ────────────↓───────────────────
L₃ ───────────────↓────────────────
L₄ ──────────────────↓─────────────
L₅ ────────────────────────↓───────
```

EARTH — OCEAN

Fig. 6.2 — The Diffusion of Water Vapor from the Canopy to the Surface of the Earth.

In the present atmosphere, turbulent mixing due to convective updrafts and pole to equator temperature differences causes the atmosphere to remain in a constant state of flux. The water vapor just above the canopy as conceived by the above authors would be disrupted and mixed with the atmosphere and immediately diffused down to the surface where it would quickly saturate L_5 and condense as rain.

As pointed out above, the present atmosphere could contain a maximum of four inches. This is based on the present vertical temperature profile, which falls off rapidly at higher altitudes. With massive amounts of water vapor in the air, however, the infrared trapping (greenhouse effect) might be great enough to keep the temperatures at upper altitudes much higher. No matter how hot it got, however, as long as turbulent mixing and molecular diffusion occur, the maximum amount of water that the atmosphere could hold would be 15 inches if the surface temperature was 82° F.

So unless some kind of support mechanism for this large amount of water can be found, the theory must be abandoned. It is to this support mechanism that our attention must now be directed.

CHAPTER 7

What the Pre-Flood Atmosphere Was Like

In spite of the difficulties involved in supporting a water vapor canopy described in chapter 6, there are some possible solutions to this problem. In fact, these possibilities are based on well-established physics. However, at this point we must face a fundamental question. According to the text of Genesis (as argued in chapters 1 and 2), a literal liquid ocean was lifted up above the atmosphere — not ice, not clouds, and not water vapor. If the text says that, then what justification is there for positing *any* kind of canopy other than the one Moses specifically intended to tell us about, that is, a liquid one?

THE SIGNIFICANCE OF THE "WATERS ABOVE" FOR MODERN SCIENCE

We must recall the discussion outlined in chapter 1 on the significance of a scriptural text for modern science. Assuming that present-day scientific laws prevailed from the Fall to the Flood, it is scientifically impossible to account for the canopy if it remained in a liquid form. So unless we want to appeal to a 2,000-year miracle (Fall to Flood), we must reject the liquid ocean canopy. If, of course, the Bible gave any indication that the miraculous reigned during that era, we might be justified in appealing to some sort of miraculous support mechanism and some more miracles to remove the kinetic energy (see chapter 6). The significance of the "waters above" for science, then, is that they must have been maintained in a way that is scientifically possible as far as known scientific law today. As we will demonstrate in the following discussion, only if the water was maintained in a vapor form would it be possible to contain it above the atmosphere and, at the same time, solve the related scientific problems. For this reason, we propose that when God lifted up the deep from the surface of the earth and arched it over the ancient atmosphere, He instantly turned those waters into vapor form (superheated transparent steam) and established them in a pressure-temperature distribution that would not require miracles to maintain. The only basis for assuming this switch is that there is no indication in the Bible that these waters were maintained miraculously, we assume that God maintained them according to the laws of nature that are known today and that He Himself had established.

We readily admit that Genesis *does not* teach the existence of a pre-Flood vapor canopy. Moses simply says that God placed a canopy of liquid water above the ancient atmosphere. However, if scientific laws today existed then, it is *necessary* that God turned that water into vapor, even though Moses does not tell us that He did this. In a similar vein when Micah speaks of "showers on vegetation" (Mic. 5:7), it is necessary to assume that photosynthesis was going on even though Micah did not intend to teach us this specifically.

The exegetical basis for the vapor canopy theory, then, rests on its significance for modern science. It is the only way of accounting for these upper waters according to the laws of nature as perceived today. However, in view of the fact that Genesis does not specifically teach that such a vapor canopy existed, it cannot be stated that this theory is the teaching of the Bible. Should some presently unknown physics be discovered in the future by which a *liquid* ocean could be maintained, the vapor canopy theory will be readily abandoned.

What follows, then, is a theory — a theory based on the significance of the words of Moses for modern science — but a theory that is not explicitly taught in Genesis. Should the physical assumptions on which the following theory is based be one day disproved by scientific advance, the veracity of the words of Moses will not be affected in any way. It will simply mean that our model of the ancient atmosphere was deficient.

As mentioned above, the major problem associated with the vapor canopy hypothesis is that the atmosphere, as it is pre-

sently constructed, will not hold anywhere near the 40 feet of water required to sustain a 40-day global rainfall. However, the ancient atmosphere would have been characterized by several unique phenomena that would have rendered it extremely stable. It will be necessary to explicate the factors generating this stable atmospheric configuration before explaining the proposed solution to the difficulty of maintaining the water vapor above the ancient atmosphere.

The Temperature Structure of the Ancient Atmosphere

In order to deal with the potential problems raised in the last chapter concerning the support of some 40 feet of precipitable water in the atmosphere, it is first necessary to discuss the temperature structure of such an atmosphere. Indeed, the calculation of the vertical temperature profile is the central problem of the vapor canopy model. This will be more fully appreciated as the discussion unfolds.

ATMOSPHERIC RADIATIVE HEAT TRANSFER

For many years numerous ingenious partial solutions to the problem of the vertical temperature structure of theoretical model atmospheres have been developed.[1] This is a "state of the art" kind of problem for which, to this date, no complete solutions have been found. With the advent of high speed computers and the new generation of memory chips, we are getting closer to the day when a general solution may be possible and practical.

Two basic methods have been employed. First, the so-called "time-stepping" technique developed by Manabe and others

1. For a comprehensive review see V. Ramanathan and J. A. Coakley, Jr., "Climate Modeling through Radiative-Convective Models," "*Reviews of Geophysics and Space Physics*" 16 (November 1978):465-89.

was published in a now classic series of papers in the 1960s.[2] One of the problems of the time-stepping method, in spite of its apparent accuracy, is that it may take upward of 100 iterations and much computer time to solve.

Second, in recent years matrix approaches have been developed where the equations of radiative transfer are developed for each level of the atmosphere, then solved simultaneously. James Coakley reports an efficient numerical approach that required only four iterations.[3]

The general procedure for all methods is as follows. First, a heuristic temperature-altitude profile is assumed. Then the hydrostatic equation must be introduced:

2. Syukuro Manabe and Fritz Möller, "On the Radiative Equilibrium and Heat Balance of the Atmosphere, " *Monthly Weather Review* 89 (December 1961):503-32; Syukuro Manabe and Robert F. Strickler, "Thermal Equilibrium of the Atmosphere with a Convective Adjustment," *Journal of the Atmospheric Sciences* 21 (July 1964):361-84; Syukuro Manabe and Richard T. Wetherald, "Thermal Equilibrium of the Atmosphere with a Given Distribution of Relative Humidity," *Journal of the Atmospheric Sciences* 24 (May 1967):241-59.
3. James A. Coakley, Jr., "An Efficient Numerical Approach to Radiative-Convective Equilibrium," *Journal of the Atmospheric Sciences* 34 (September 1977):1402-7. Coakley's model draws heavily on the following articles, which are a good introduction to the present methods of calculating vertical temperature profiles in theoretical model atmospheres: V. Ramanathan, "Radiative Transfer within the Earth's Troposphere and Stratosphere: A Simplified Radiative-Convective Model," *Journal of the Atmospheric Sciences* 33 (July 1976):1330-46; C. D. Rogers and C. D. Walshaw, "The Computation of Infra-red Cooling Rates in Planetary Atmospheres," *The Quarterly Journal of the Royal Meteorological Society* 92 (1966):67-92; Robert D. Cess, "Radiative Transfer Due to Atmospheric Water Vapor: Global Considerations of the Earth's Energy Balance," *Journal of Quantitative Spectroscopy and Radiative Transfer* 14 (1974):861-71.

$$\frac{dP}{dz} = -\rho z \tag{7.1}$$

where P = pressure; z = altitude; and ρ = density.

Then we calculate the density and pressure of all the absorbing gases at each altitude. Fortunately, planetary atmospheric models are presently available for this purpose.[4] Then, knowing the density and pressure at each altitude, it is possible to compute the optical depth of each atmospheric gas in each spectral interval (wavelength interval) at each altitude. By "optical depth" we mean the mass of absorbing medium per unit area normal to the radiation (gm/cm^2).

From this, the absorption can be calculated for each spectral interval. After a layer absorbs energy, it changes temperature. This absorption comes from the radiation emitted by layers above and below and from the sun. Because the layers now have different temperatures from the initial assumed profile, they all now radiate at different levels to the adjacent layers. This radiation will, in turn, be absorbed and a new temperature profile will result, which is slightly different from the initial assumed profile. Once the new profile is established, new optical depths are calculated and a new profile is calculated once again. This process is repeated over and over again ("iterated") until the last profile is within a certain predetermined amount of the next to last, and at that point the calculations are stopped and radiative equilibrium is achieved.

The process of radiative transfer in the atmosphere is immensely complicated. The interested reader should refer to the classic textbooks on the subject.[5] The process described above

4. David E. Pitts, *A Computer Program for Calculating Model Planetary Atmospheres*, NASA Technical Note, NASA TN D-4292, p. 60.
5. R. M. Goody, *Atmospheric Radiation I, Theoretical Basis* 436 pp.; K. Ya. Kondratyev, *Radiation in the Atmosphere*, 912 pp.; The most practical recent work at the engineering level is G. W. Paltridge and C. M. R. Platt, *Radiative Processes in Meteorology and Climatology*, 300 pp.

requires sophisticated modeling on the computer, but some simplified approximations are possible.[6]

THE CANOPY TEMPERATURE PROFILE

As mentioned above, the ultimate solution of the vapor canopy problem requires an extensive computer simulation. However, it is possible to demonstrate the plausibility of the vapor canopy theory with some rather crude approximations.

In 1913 a classic paper was published by R. Emden in which he detailed the first attempt to describe the temperature structure of the earth's atmosphere with a simple analytical formulation.[7] Goody develops Emden's argument in the idiom of the modern transfer equation[8] and Paltridge and Platt give what is perhaps the most lucid presentation of the Emden model.[9]

Beginning with the basic transfer equation, Emden showed that the temperature structure of the atmosphere could be described by the following equations:

$$B_\nu(T \text{ at} \tau_\nu) = B_\nu(\tau_\nu) = F_\nu(1 + 1.5\tau_\nu)/2\pi \qquad (7.2)$$

$$B_\nu(T_g) = F_\nu(2 + 1.5\tau_\nu)/2\pi \qquad (7.3)$$

where $B_\nu(\tau_\nu)$ is the Plank function at the wavenumber ν; τ_ν is the optical depth; F_ν is the net infrared flux (positive in the upward direction) equal to the net solar energy absorbed at the ground (or in the major radiating surface of the planet such as a cloud layer) of the wavenumber ν; and T_g is the Plank temperature at the ground.

6. A more sophisticated model is presently being pursued by the author in conjunction with Dr. Klaus Potsch, a theoretical physicist at the Technical University of Vienna.
7. R. Emden, "Strahlungsgleichgewicht und Atmosphärische Strahlung," *Sitz. K. Bayer. Akad. Wissensch.*, München, 1913.
8. Goody, p. 332.
9. Paltridge and Platt, pp. 245-52.

The optical depth, τ_ν, is given by

$$\tau_\nu = \int k_\nu \rho \, dz$$

where k_ν is the mass absorption coefficient for radiation of wavenumber ν; ρ is the density; and z is the altitude. In the canopy model, 40 feet of precipitable water or 1,219 cm are being assumed. Thus $\int_0^\infty \rho \, dz = 1{,}219$ cm. The problem is to find a value of k_ν for each absorbing gas in the atmosphere: ozone, carbon dioxide, and water vapor. In the following model, the solar spectrum has been divided into 35 spectral intervals and Table 7.1 gives the values of k_ν in each interval. To find the optical depth for each spectral interval, the values of k_ν from Table 7.1 are multiplied by 1,219.

To find F_ν the net solar radiation absorbed at the ground must be determined. As solar radiation insulates the earth, it intersects the plane πr^2 (r = the radius of the earth). So the total solar input into the earth-atmosphere system is:

$$\text{INPUT} = \pi r^2 (1 - A_\nu) SC_\nu \tag{7.4}$$

where A_ν is the spectral albedo, that is, the reflectivity of a cloud or ground surface to each wavelength of impinging radiation (see Table 7.1); SC_ν is the value of the solar constant at the wavenumber ν. In order for the system to be in radiative equilibrium this amount must be equal to the amount radiated upward by the major radiating surface of the planet. Since the earth is a sphere, it will radiate at:

$$\text{OUTPUT} = 4\pi r^2 F_\nu \tag{7.5}$$

Setting (7.4) and (7.5) equal to each other yields:

$$F_\nu = \frac{(1 - A_\nu) SC_\nu}{4} \tag{7.6}$$

TABLE 7.1

CONSTANTS USED IN RADIATIVE HEAT TRANSFER CALCULATIONS[10]

Wavenumber $\nu,(m^{-1})$	Mass Absorption Coefficient $k_\nu,(m^{+2}kg^{-1})$ O_3 CO_2 H_2O	Integrated Plank $SC_\nu,(Jm^{-1}sec^{-1})$	Spectral Albedo cloud	surface
0 6.000E+4	0.00 0.00 0.000	10.727	0.000	0.00
6.000E+3 2.500E+4	0.00 0.00 50.000	751.519	0.010	0.05
2.500E+4 3.500E+4	0.00 0.00 10.000	1309.710	0.010	0.05
3.500E+4 4.500E+4	0.00 0.00 1.000	2290.220	0.022	0.03
4.500E+4 5.500E+4	0.00 0.00 0.300	3527.020	0.035	0.03
5.500E+4 6.200E+4	0.00 0.11 0.100	3336.900	0.035	0.03
6.200E+4 7.200E+4	0.00 44.00 0.010	6188.400	0.032	0.03
7.200E+4 1.000E+5	0.00 0.00 0.010	28007.600	0.025	0.03
1.000E+5 1.050E+5	0.10 0.00 0.010	6907.420	0.015	0.03
1.050E+5 1.290E+5	0.00 0.00 0.010	42487.900	0.050	0.05
1.290E+5 1.350E+5	0.00 0.00 0.200	13225.400	0.050	0.05
1.350E+5 1.470E+5	0.00 0.00 4.800	29832.500	0.050	0.05
1.470E+5 1.560E+5	0.00 0.00 30.000	25468.800	0.025	0.05
1.560E+5 1.640E+5	0.00 0.00 3.000	24965.400	0.023	0.05
1.640E+5 1.800E+5	0.00 0.00 20.000	56800.700	0.017	0.05
1.800E+5 1.960E+5	0.00 0.00 1.400	66412.500	0.100	0.05
1.960E+5 2.200E+5	0.00 0.00 0.000	118715.100	0.100	0.05
2.200E+5 2.460E+5	0.00 1.00 0.000	155961.100	0.100	0.05
2.460E+5 3.060E+5	0.00 0.00 0.000	476257.000	0.100	0.05
3.060E+5 3.530E+5	0.00 0.00 1.000	492799.000	0.170	0.05
3.530E+5 4.040E+5	0.00 0.00 2.300	657712.000	0.150	0.05
4.040E+5 4.400E+5	0.00 0.00 0.500	541746.000	0.200	0.05
4.400E+5 5.240E+5	0.00 0.00 0.000	1508190.000	0.400	0.15
5.240E+5 5.540E+5	0.00 0.00 8.800	618437.000	0.500	0.15
5.540E+5 7.040E+5	0.00 0.00 0.000	3655900.000	0.600	0.15
7.040E+5 7.500E+5	0.00 0.00 3.000	1285390.000	0.600	0.15
7.500E+5 8.770E+5	0.00 0.00 0.000	3854280.000	0.800	0.15
8.770E+5 8.980E+5	0.00 0.00 0.200	672065.000	0.600	0.15
8.980E+5 1.060E+6	0.00 0.00 0.000	5388830.000	0.800	0.15
1.060E+6 1.105E+6	0.00 0.00 0.100	1533300.000	0.600	0.35
1.105E+6 1.200E+6	0.00 0.00 0.000	3240990.000	0.800	0.25
1.200E+6 1.255E+6	0.00 0.00 0.010	1861830.000	0.690	0.25
1.255E+6 1.360E+6	0.00 0.00 0.000	3485380.000	0.800	0.25
1.360E+6 1.390E+6	0.00 0.00 0.004	973100.000	0.750	0.23
1.390E+6 4.800E+6	0.50 0.00 0.000	31525800.000	0.800	0.06

Substituting (7.6) into (7.2) and (7.3) yields:

$$B_\nu(T_g) = \frac{SC_\nu(1-A_\nu)(2+1.5\tau_\nu)}{8\pi} \quad (7.7)$$

$$B_\nu(T_\tau) = \frac{SC_\nu(1-A_\nu)(1+1.5\tau_\nu)}{8\pi} \quad (7.8)$$

When the function $B_\nu(T)$ is integrated over all angles and wavenumbers, the flux density $\sigma T^4/\pi$ results. Integrating the right hand side of (7.7) and (7.8) yields an expression for the temperature at the ground, T_g, and the temperature of every level of the atmosphere T_τ as a function of the optical depth.

$$T_g^4 = \frac{(1-A_\nu)(2+1.5\tau_\nu)}{8\sigma} \int_{\nu_1}^{\nu_2} SC_\nu d\nu \quad (7.9)$$

$$T_\tau^4 = \frac{(1-A_\nu)(1+1.5\tau_\nu)}{8\sigma} \int_{\nu_1}^{\nu_2} SC_\nu d\nu \quad (7.10)$$

where σ is the Stephan-Boltzman constant = 5.6697×10^{-8} J m^{-2} K^{-4} sec^{-1}.

The function SC_ν, the solar flux at the wavenumber ν, is described by the Plank function:[11]

$$SC_\nu(T) = \frac{2hc^2\nu^3}{EXP(ch\nu/kT)-1} \quad (7.11)$$

---

10. This data was collected by Dr. Potsch, personal communication, September 1979. The integrated Plank function was calculated on a TRS-80 Level II microcomputer by the author. Dr. Potsch gathered this information from Kondratyev, Paltridge and Platt, and Walter M. Elsasser and Margaret F. Culbertson, "Atmospheric Radiation Tables," *Meteorological Monographs* 4 (August 1960):43.
11. Paltridge and Platt, p. 43.

where h = the Plank constant, 6.6256×10^{-34} J sec; c is the velocity of light, 2.9979×10^8 m sec^{-1}; v is the wavenumber (1/wavelength), m^{-1}; k is the Boltzman constant 1.3805×10^{-23} J K^{-1}; and T is the temperature of the sun, 5,762° K.

Equation (7.11) was integrated over 35 wavenumber intervals using a Gaussian quadrature to yield the spectral solar radiance in units of W m^{-2} emitted from the surface of the sun.[12] The results are tabulated in Table 7.1.

In a recent analysis of the canopy temperature profile employing the Emden approximation, Morton neglected the integration of (7.11) over all wavenumbers and ignored the critical dependence of the albedo and the mass absorption coefficient on the wavenumber. As a result, the reported canopy temperatures are much too high, and his discussion is invalid.[13]

Morton modeled the canopy as a gray atmosphere, that is, the absorption coefficient being independent of the wavenumber. Although this approach may be useful for the present earth, it can only lead to serious errors when an atmosphere as dense as the canopy is considered.

Morton also errs in assuming that 1 cm of precipitable water is equal to one optical depth. Since most of the terrestrial radiation is in the 8 to 13.5 μ range where the absorption coefficient is 0.01 m^{2}k^{-1}, the total optical depth is considerably less than 1,219, which he employed.

In order to determine the temperature variation with height, a relationship between optical depth and altitude is needed. For an approximation Goody assumed:[14]

$$\tau_v = \tau_v^* \, \text{EXP}\,(-z/H) \tag{7.12}$$

12. These values must then be multiplied by a "distance factor," DI, to give the value of the spectral solar irradiance impinging on the top of the earth's atmosphere: DI = (solar constant)/σT^4 or (1,353 J m^{-1} sec^{-1})/(5.6697 × 10^{-8} J m^{-2}K^{-4} sec^{-1}) (5,762)^4 = 2.16493E-05, where 1,353 Jm^{-1} sec^{-1} is the value of the solar constant at the top of the earth's atmosphere.
13. Glen Morton, "Can the Canopy Hold Water," Creation Research Society Quarterly 16 (December 1979):164-70.
14. Goody, p. 333.

where z is altitude and H = RT/MG; R is the gas constant, 8.3143 J mol⁻¹ K⁻¹; T is the temperature at altitude z,°K; M is the molecular weight of water vapor, 18.0153, or air, 28.9644; G is the acceleration of gravity, 9.806 m sec⁻²; and τ_v is the total optical depth at the bottom of the atmosphere or canopy for the spectral interval v.

We may now proceed to define the temperature structure of the ancient atmosphere using (7.9) and (7.10). First, we will assume no clouds and see what kind of vertical temperature profile and lapse rate will result. Then, the saturation vapor pressure will be calculated for each altitude, using the following:[15]

$$e_s = (6.0278 \times 10^{-3}) \, 10^{(aT/b+T)} \text{ mb} \quad (7.13)$$

If the atmospheric pressure in the canopy ever exceeds the saturation vapor pressure, e_s, at that altitude, there is a probability of cloud formation and a radically different temperature structure from the one described in Table 7.2.

We begin by writing (7.9) and (7.10) in the following manner, substituting F, total net flux, for σT^4:

$$F_g = \frac{(1-A_v)(2+1.5\tau_v)}{8} \int_{v_1}^{v_2} SC \, dv \quad (7.14)$$

$$F_\tau = \frac{(1-A_v)(1+1.5\tau_v)}{8} \int_{v_1}^{v_2} SC_v dv$$

where F_g is the total flux contribution in each spectral interval at the ground and F_τ is the same at each level or optical depth in the atmosphere. This flux is the total due to water vapor, ozone, and carbon dioxide absorption.

$$F_g = F_{H_2O} + F_{O_3} + F_{CO_2} \quad (7.14)$$

So the term $(1-A_v)(2+1.5\tau_v)/8$ must be multiplied by the integrated intensities of SC_v over the selected 35 spectral intervals. The sum of these products for each absorbing gas is then added

15. Berry, Bollay, and Beers, *Handbook of Meteorology*, p. 343; a = 7.5, b = 237.3, and T is temperature in degrees C.

together to give F_g. F_g in turn is related to the ground temperature, T_g, and F_τ + o the temperature at each level, T_τ, by:

$$T_g = (F_g/\sigma)^{1/4} \tag{7.15}$$
$$T_\tau = (F_\tau/\sigma)^{1/4} \tag{7.16}$$

A final point of interest will be the lapse rate of temperature between various levels, z, of the canopy atmosphere. This is significant because if the lapse rate of temperature follows a certain value, we will get vertical lifting and turbulence. The lifting of vapor to high altitudes by vertical convection has the effect of cooling the parcel. Cooling, in turn, may result in condensation and cloud formation. As a parcel of vapor is accelerated upward, it is cooled according to Poisson's equation:[16]

$$T/T_0 = (P/P_0)^{(R/mC_p)} \tag{7.17}$$

where T and P are the final temperature and pressure; T_0 and P_0 are the initial temperature and pressure; R is the universal gas constant; m is the molecular weight of water vapor; and C_p is the specific heat capacity of water vapor at a constant pressure, 1.850 J gm^{-1} K^{-1}. Thus $R/mC_p = 0.249$.

Rising parcels of vapor cooling in this manner, cool at the so-called dry adiabatic lapse rate or,[17]

$$LR_d = \frac{dT}{dz} = -G/C_p \tag{7.18}$$

For air, $C_p = 1{,}005$ J kg^{-1}K^{-1} and the dry adiabatic lapse rate is 9.75° C/km and for the vapor canopy $LR_d = 5.3°$ C/km.

Once the temperature has been calculated for each value of z, altitude, then the temperature lapse rate is given by:

$$\gamma = \frac{T(z-1) - T(z)}{z} \tag{7.19}$$

assuming a linear temperature change between each level.

16. Horace Robert Byers, *General Meteorology*, p. 79.
17. Ibid., pp. 83-84.

The stability criteria for an unsaturated parcel of vapor are:[18]

$LR_d > \gamma$: Stable
$LR_d = \gamma$: Neutral
$LR_d < \gamma$: Unstable

Thus, unsaturated parcels in layers whose temperature lapse rates exceed 5.3° C/km will be unstable and experience lifting, cooling, and possible condensation and resultant cloud formation. Byers comments, "It is not difficult to show that ... adiabatic expansional cooling is the most effective process" of cooling a parcel in the atmosphere.[19]

Finally, the pressure at each altitude, assuming (7.19), is given by:[20]

$$P(z) = P(z-1) \frac{T(z)}{T(z-1)}^{\frac{GM}{R\gamma}}$$

The altitude of the base of the canopy was calculated using:

$$z = -H \ln(P/P_0) \qquad (7.21)$$

where P_0 is the pressure at the surface of the earth, or 2.18 atm, and P is the pressure at the canopy base, or 1.18 atm. Equation (7.21) assumes that the temperature at the base of the canopy is equal to the temperature at the surface of the planet due to a negligible optical depth of the present atmosphere (less than 3) in comparison to the optical depth of the canopy.

With these assumptions the temperature profile of a cloudless canopy atmosphere with 10 times the present amount of ozone (due to high altitude photo dissociation of H_2O), three times the present amount of CO_2, and 1,219 cm of precipitable water was calculated.[21] Also, as a test of the model, the surface temperature of the present earth was calculated both with a 100% cloud cover and without it, that is, with a completely cloudless sky.

18. Seymour L. Hess, *Introduction to Theoretical Meteorology*, p. 99.
19. Byers, p. 91.
20. Hess, p. 83.
21. According to Byers, p. 40, present ozone levels are on the order of 0.03 kg m $^{-2}$, and CO_2 = 25 kg m $^{-2}$.

The results of these initial calculations were quite revealing. For the present atmosphere with 3 cm of precipitable water, the computed surface temperature for a cloudless sky was 36° C (97° F), which is reasonable for the earth in the absence of the reflective capabilities of its usual 50% cloud cover. For an earth with a 100% cloud cover the model yields a surface temperature of −37° C (−35° F), which is quite reasonable. No attempt was made to model the more realistic case of a 50% cloud cover. The model seems to give good results when applied to the present atmosphere, and this in turn gives a degree of confidence about its application to the canopy.

When the numbers for the vapor canopy were inserted, a surface temperature of 314° C (597° F) resulted. The vertical temperature structure is given in Table 7.2.[22] A surface temperature for a cloudless sky of 597° F is much lower and more reasonable than the 2,142° F surface temperature reported by Morton in his gray model.[23]

A study of Table 7.2 reveals some interesting things. First, note that at 35 km the canopy vapor pressure (atmospheric pressure) exceeds the saturation vapor pressure. This means that cloud formation in the upper regions of the canopy is probable (see Fig. 7.1). Note also that the temperature lapse rate is everywhere above 5.3° C/km, which means that great convection cells would develop through such a canopy. The lapse rate from the canopy base to the ground is negligible and considerably less than the 9.75° C/km required for convective instability. So beginning at the canopy base, convection cells will develop, causing the rising, cooling, and condensation of vapor parcels and resulting cloud formation in at least the lower regions of the canopy. This data seems to invalidate Morton's conclusion, "Thus Dillow's model has a serious flaw in that clouds could not form under a very thick canopy."[24] In fact, clouds will most probably form. Morton should have calculated vertical temperature structures instead of just base temperatures.

22. These calculations were performed on a TRS-80 Level II microcomputer requiring 48 K RAM.
23. Morton, p. 167.
24. Ibid., p. 168.

Tablets from the library at Tell-Mardikh, ancient city of Ebla. Among these tablets are creation and flood stories similar to those in the book of Genesis. The accounts are much more similar to the biblical accounts written by Moses (c. 1450 B.C.) than to the Babylonian accounts (c. 1700 B.C.), yet the tablets are dated at 2300 B.C. Because the creation account on them is far more advanced than the Babylonian version, we must question the old critical assumption of the unilinear evolution of religion. Also, this find argues against the notion that Genesis is merely borrowed from Babylonia. Photo courtesy of Religious News Service.

Model of the ziggurat in Babylon. It is likely that the biblical Tower of Babel took this shape. That tower was dedicated to the worship of Marduk, the god who was involved with the constellations of the zodiac in Babylonian mythology. The presence of such idol centers after the Flood suggests a radical change in the appearance of the heavens because of the sudden emergance of many new stars as the vapor canopy precipitated. Photo courtesy of the Oriental Institute, the University of Chicago.

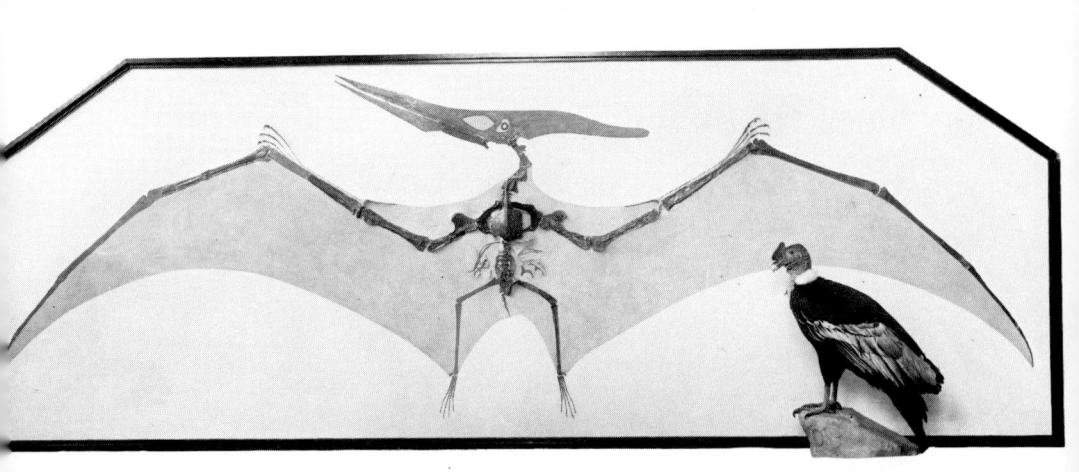

Pteranodon (Giant Pterodactyl)—large Mesozoic flying reptile. Top: A complete Cretaceous fossil skeleton and restored body outline. This specimen has a wingspread of about 20 ft. Bottom: A drawing showing the probable life appearance of the pteranodon. Calculations indicate that in order for the animal to fly in the present atmosphere, a moderate breeze of 16.4 mph would have to be present continually. The need for this unlikely situation would be eliminated with the presence of Earth's ancient water heaven and the resultant increase of surface pressure and air density. Under the canopy, only a gentle breeze of 11.6 mph would be required. Photos courtesy of the American Museum of Natural History.

On March 4, 1979 this remarkable photograph was taken of the planet Jupiter by the Voyager 1 spacecraft. The first evidence that Jupiter may have a ring around it was based on this photo. A line has been drawn around Jupiter to show the position of the extremely thin, faint ring. The ring thickness is estimated to be 19 miles or less. Jupiter is surrounded by a kind of canopy of ammonia clouds floating in a dense methane atmosphere. Photo courtesy of the National Aeronautics and Space Administration.

This mosaic photograph of Jupiter was assembled from six violet images taken by the Voyager 1 spacecraft on February 27, 1979 at a distance of 4 million miles from the planet. The great red spot is located below the center of the photo. Note the turbulance associated with the equatorial jet (clocked at 260 mph) and the more northerly atmospheric current, as seen at the top of the photo. These atmospheric currents represent, among other things, attempts by the atmospheric system to balance the heat budget between the equator and the poles. Such upper atmospheric jet streams undoubtedly characterized the earth's ancient vapor canopy and served the same function as the jet streams on Jupiter. Photo courtesy of the National Aeronautics and Space Administration.

This four-photo mosaic of Io, one of the planet Jupiter's moons, was made from photographs taken by the Voyager 1 spacecraft on March 4, 1979 at a range of 234,087 miles. Of great interest is the absence of any obvious impact features that are identifiable in this hemisphere, which suggests to scientists that Io's surface is quite young. Some of the features are thought to be of volcanic origin. This evidence is somewhat surprising in view of prevailing theories that the planets and moons originated simultaneously billions of years ago. Perhaps the solar system is not so old after all. Photo courtesy of the National Aeronautics and Space Administration.

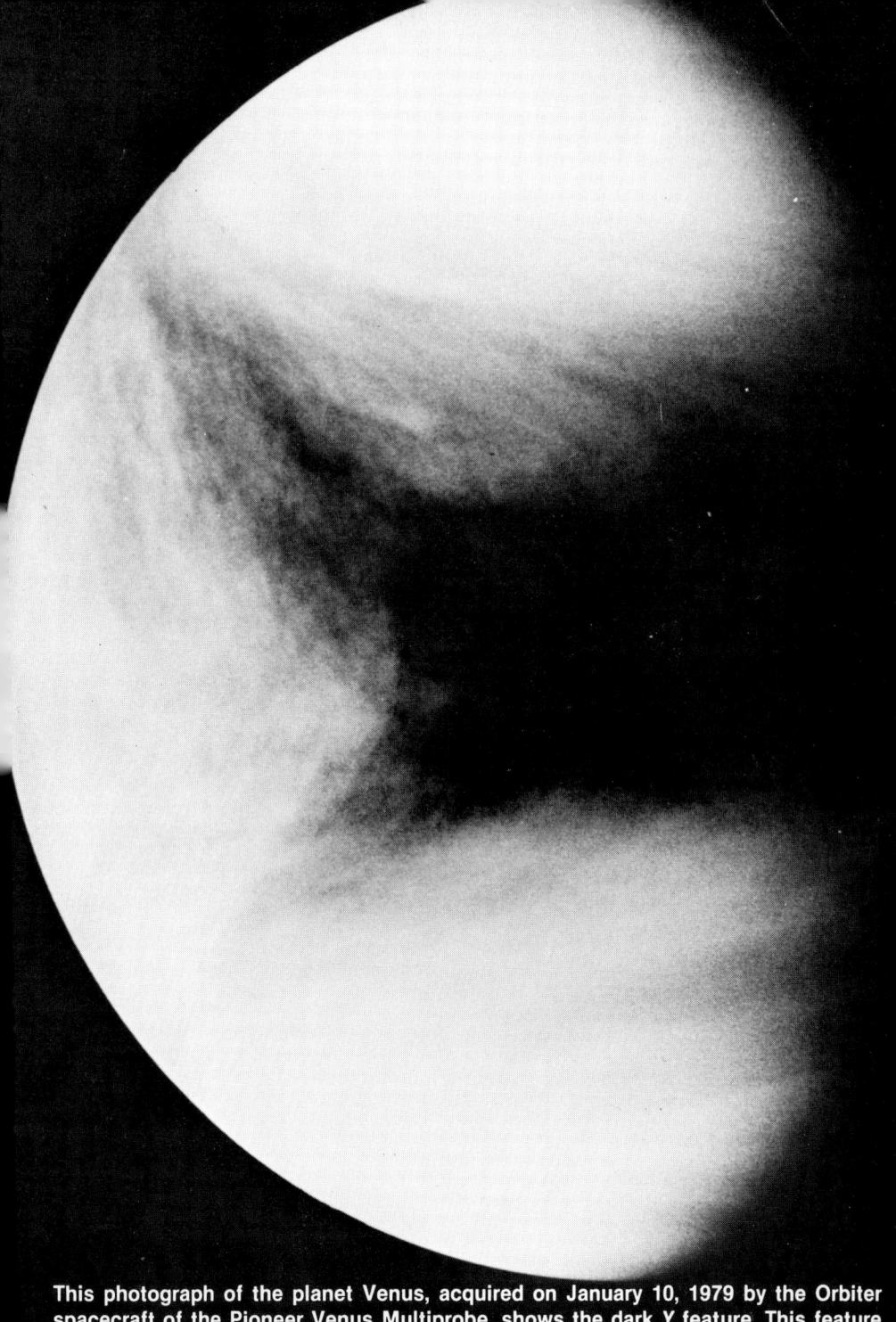

This photograph of the planet Venus, acquired on January 10, 1979 by the Orbiter spacecraft of the Pioneer Venus Multiprobe, shows the dark Y feature. This feature reflects atmospheric motions associated with jet streams, by which the heat budget is balanced. The photo was taken from an altitude of 29,700 miles. The Multiprobe, which split into four probes and a bus, entered Venus's atmosphere on December 9, 1978 and sent back extensive data before the searing atmosphere destroyed the probes on the surface. The surface temperature of Venus has been measured at 890° F. Photo courtesy of the National Aeronautics and Space Administration.

This photograph of the planet Venus was taken by the Orbiter spacecraft of the Pioneer Venus Multiprobe on January 14, 1979 from an altitude of 40,000 miles. The cloud canopy on Venus consists possibly of hydrochloric acid, water vapor, and other substances. It floats in an atmosphere that is largely carbon dioxide (more then 80%). The base of the Venus canopy is about 20 miles from the planet's surface. Notice the swirls in the clouds. These swirls are likely indicators of global circulation whereby the heat budget between the equator and the poles is balanced. Because of this atmospheric circulation, the temperatures at the poles of Venus are the same as those at the equator. A similar situation may have existed on the ancient earth under the vapor canopy. Photo courtesy of the National Aeronautics and Space Administration.

Fossil tree trunk in the upright position, South Joggins, Nova Scotia. This tree trunk, penetrating up through several layers of strata, argues for rapid sedimentation, such as would be caused by a global rainfall and ensuing flood. Many illustrations of this kind of "polystrata" fossil can be found. See Harold G. Coffin, "Research on the Classic Joggins Petrified Trees, *Creation Research Society Quarterly* **6 (June 1969): 35-44. Photo courtesy of Outdoor Pictures.**

Ice wall on the bank of the Beresovka River where the Beresovka mammoth was found in 1901. Photo courtesy of the Smithsonian Institution.

The position of the body of the Beresovka mammoth (head and forelegs) on the cliff. Photo courtesy of the Smithsonian Institution.

Side view of the Beresovka mammoth after partial excavation. Unchewed bean pods were found in the mouth of the animal, and the seeds of flowers were discovered in the stomach. Note that the head and back of the animal had been devoured by carnivores before the scientists arrived. The mammoth obviously experienced a sudden death and was frozen solid shortly thereafter. Photo courtesy of the Smithsonian Institution

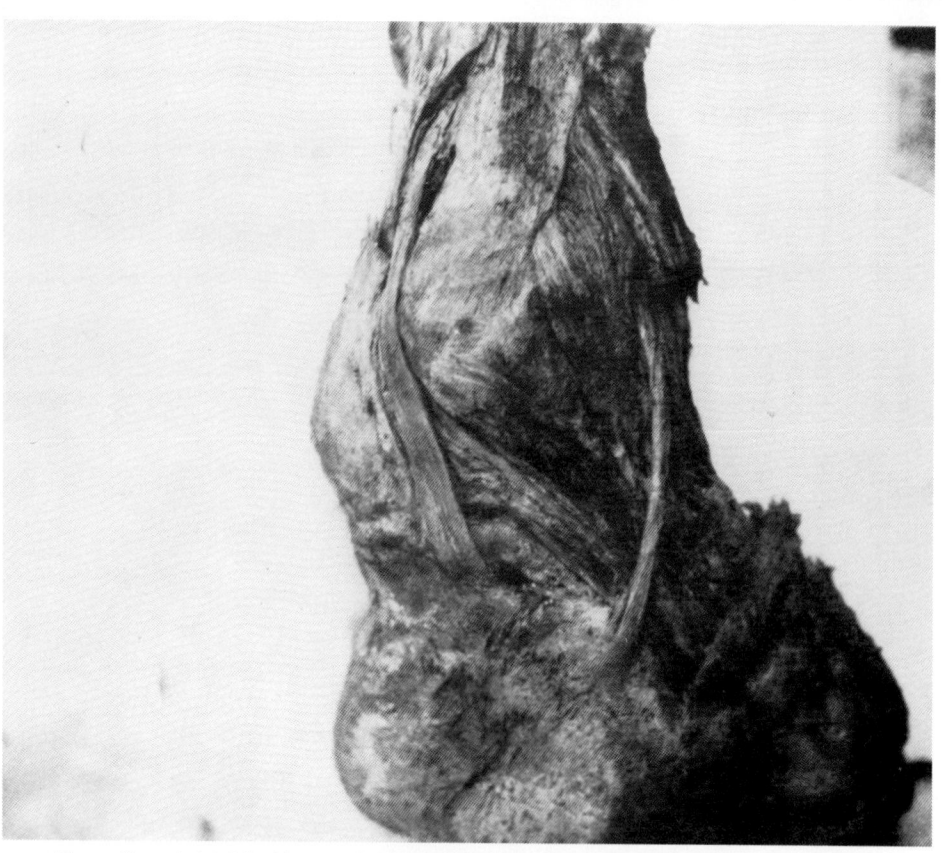

Top: the right hindfoot of the Beresovka mammoth; bottom: its left forefoot. The animal was so well preserved that the dogs of the expedition gladly devoured its flesh when pieces were thrown to them. Photo courtesy of the Smithsonian Institution.

The Beresovka mammoth stuffed and on display in a museum in Leningrad. The trunk and head are made of artificial materials, but the rest of the skin is the actual skin of the mammoth. It has been reconstructed according to the position in which it was found. Photo courtesy of the Smithsonian Institution.

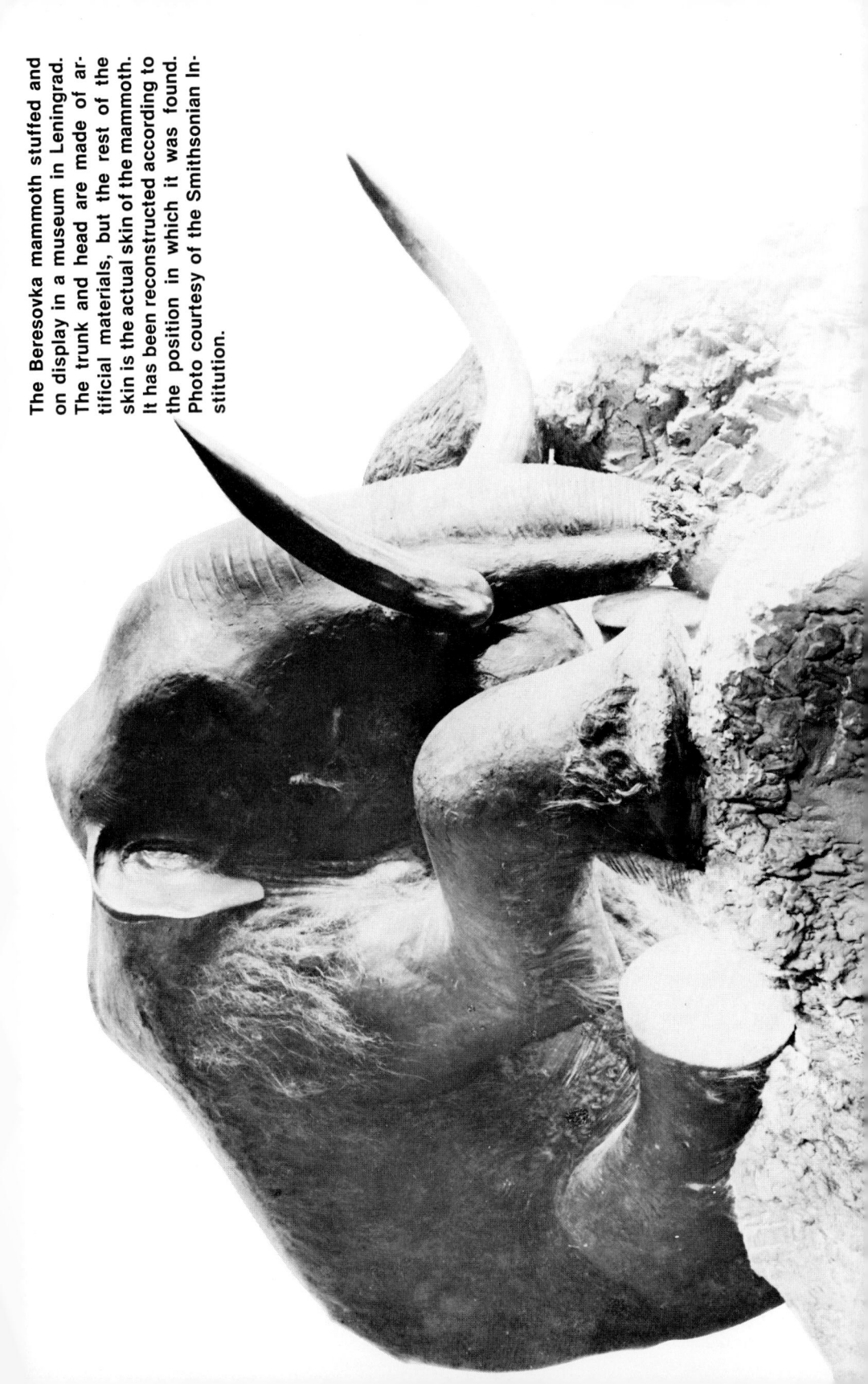

A piece of the Beresovka mammoth's skin. The French scientist and dermatologist H. Neuville demonstrated that the skin was similar to that of a present-day African elephant—it lacked the oil producing gland that would have rendered the animal impervious to the cold. He proved that mammoths were not cold-weather animals, contrary to what was popularly believed about them. Photo courtesy of the Smithsonian Institution.

Soviet scientist S.F. Zhelnin looking at a completely preserved body of a baby mammoth upturned by a bulldozer from the permafrost ground in the Frunze Gold Fields, Susumansky District, Magadan Region, Siberia in June 1977. The mammoth was found in a block of ice and was immediately rushed to research laboratories in Leningrad. Christened "Dima" by her discoverers, her blood and tissues have been carefully studied by the Soviet scientists. In April 1978 they sent a slab of quick-frozen mammoth steak from Dima to the National Academy of Sciences in the United States. Photo courtesy of Tass, from Sovfoto.

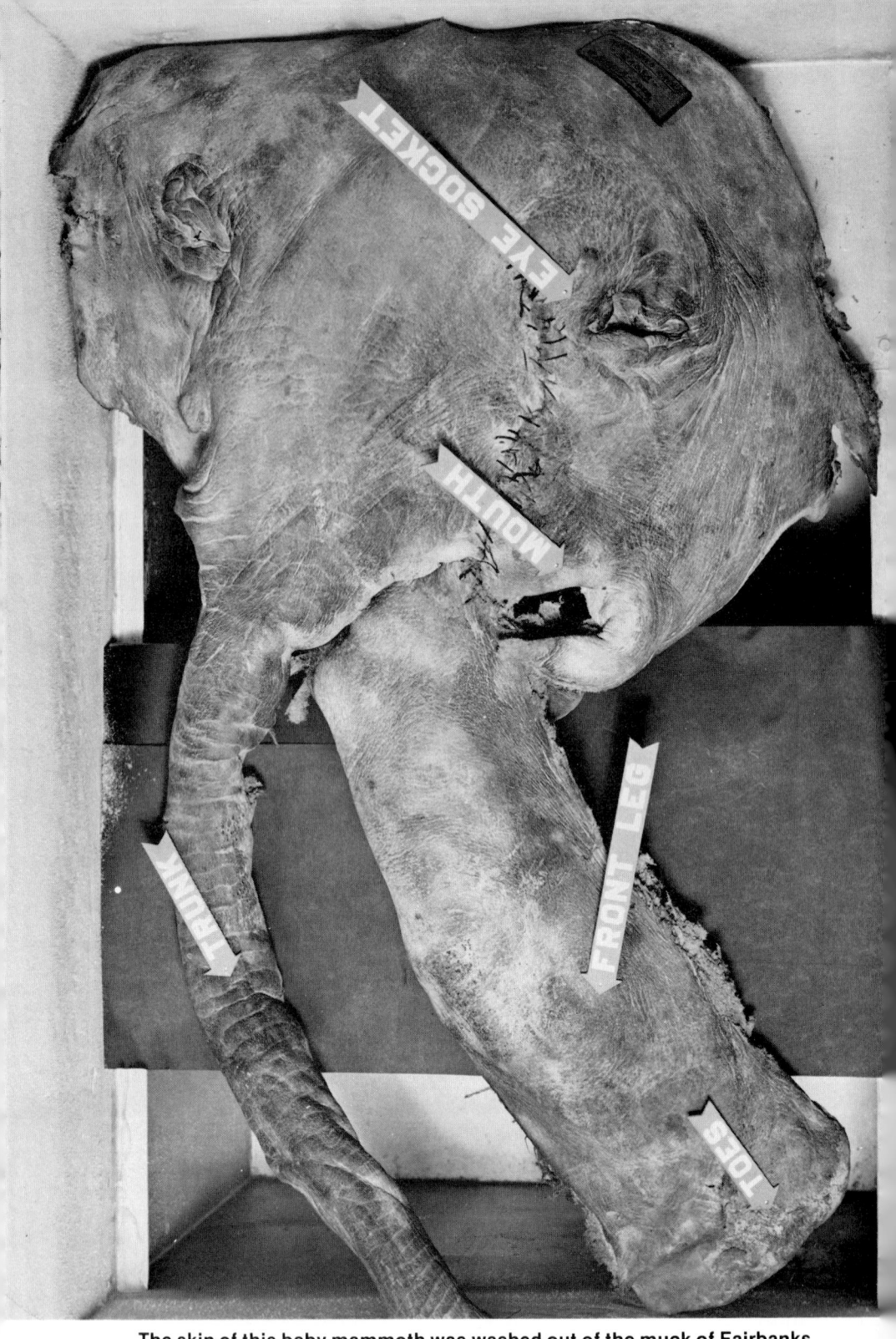

The skin of this baby mammoth was washed out of the muck of Fairbanks Creek in Alaska on August 28, 1948, by the Fairbanks Exploration Company. Photo courtesy of the American Museum of Natural History.

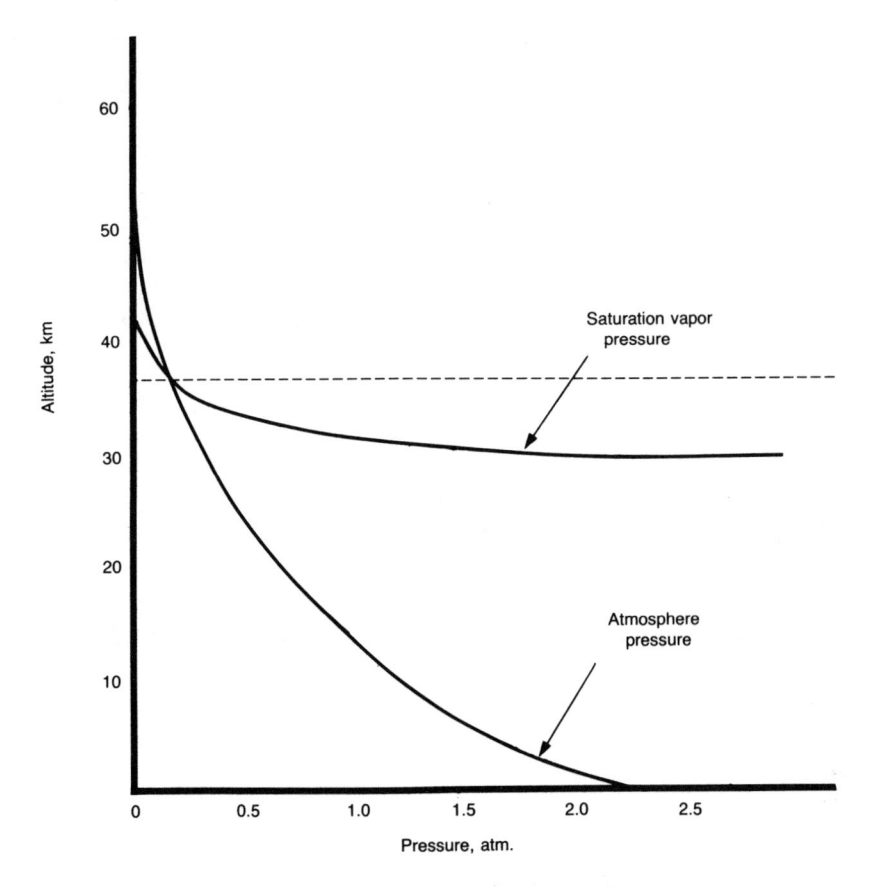

Fig. 7.1 — Theoretical canopy atmosphere with no clouds, 1,219 cm of precipitable water, 10 times today's value of O_3, and three times today's value of CO_2.

Once the convection cells began to redistribute the heat of the canopy, a radiative-convective equilibrium profile will be established with a canopy base temperature that is considerably less than 597° F. Furthermore, since the poles receive on the average 40% less radiation than the equator, the polar temperature of such a canopy would be about 244° C (471° F). This will aid in the redistribution of heat in the canopy due to heat transport via canopy "jet streams" (such as are presently observed on Venus[25]) to the poles in an attempt to balance the heat budget.

Let us now pursue the implications of these results. First, the presence of a cloud layer at the top of the canopy has the effect of reducing the solar input into the system. Paltridge and Platt observe, "High clouds above most of the atmosphere's water vapor tend to decrease solar absorption by reflecting energy back to space before it encounters an appreciable optical mass of water vapor."[26] Although this cloud layer was certainly not continuous, and perhaps not thick due to the lower density in the region, it is reasonable to assume that it had the effect of reducing the solar input by 35%.

In the lower regions of the canopy where the convective cells would have produced a cloud formation, a 100% cloud layer would have been established, which would raise the albedo of the earth considerably above that of the clear sky model calculated in Table 7.2. Assuming this reduction in solar constant and the cloud spectral albedos in Table 7.1, and the method described in (7.2) to (7.16), a new canopy temperature is calculated, T_O. However, because the canopy is undergoing convection and the heat is being redistributed, T_O, the canopy base temperature, must be inserted in (7.22) to determine the true base temperature, the radiative-convective base temperature.

What then is the radiative equilibrium temperature? The average temperature through the convective layers of the canopy is given by:[27]

$$T_{cv} = \frac{MGT_O}{MG + \gamma R} \qquad (7.22)$$

where T_O is the radiative equilibrium temperature of the canopy base, 472° K; $R = 8,314$ J kmol^{-1}; $G = 9.806$ m sec^{-2}; and $M = 18.0153$ kmol.

25. Bruce Murray et al., "Venus: Atmospheric Motion and Structure from Mariner 10 Pictures," *Science* 183(29 March 1974): 1310-14.
26. Paltridge and Platt, p. 19.
27. Derivation by Clyde McKnight, Ph. D. in atmospheric science, personal communication, 1 May 1977.

TABLE 7.2

CANOPY TEMPERATURE PROFILE ASSUMING 1,219 CM OF PRECIPITABLE WATER, NO CLOUDS, 10 TIMES TODAY'S VALUE OF OZONE AND THREE TIMES TODAY'S VALUE OF CARBON DIOXIDE (CALCULATED POLAR TEMPERATURE = 244° C)

Altitude (km)	Temperature (° C)	Atmospheric Pressure (atm)	Saturation Vapor Pressure (atm)	Temperature Lapse Rate (° C/km)
0	314.22	2.18	113.01	
10.6	314.22	1.18	113.01	
11.6	295.96	1.11	87.64	
12.6	287.45	1.05	77.36	8.51
13.6	278.96	0.98	68.04	8.49
14.6	270.35	0.93	59.47	8.60
15.6	261.63	0.87	51.65	8.72
16.6	252.79	0.81	44.53	8.85
17.6	243.81	0.76	38.10	8.98
18.6	234.69	0.71	32.32	9.12
19.6	225.43	0.67	27.16	9.26
20.6	216.01	0.63	22.60	9.42
21.6	206.44	0.58	18.59	9.58
22.6	196.69	0.54	15.11	9.74
23.6	186.77	0.50	12.12	9.92
24.6	176.67	0.46	9.57	10.11
25.6	166.36	0.43	7.43	10.30
26.6	155.86	0.40	5.67	10.50
27.6	145.15	0.37	4.23	10.71
28.6	134.23	0.34	3.09	10.92
29.6	123.09	0.31	2.20	11.14
30.6	111.74	0.28	1.52	11.35
31.6	100.18	0.26	1.02	11.55
32.6	88.45	0.24	0.66	11.74
33.6	76.57	0.22	0.41	11.88
34.6	64.60	0.19	0.24	11.97
35.6	52.62	0.18	0.14	11.97
36.6	40.77	0.16	0.08	11.85
37.6	29.20	0.14	0.04	11.57
38.6	18.13	0.13	0.02	11.07
39.6	7.79	0.11	0.01	10.34
40.6	− 1.58	0.10	—	9.37
50.6	−40.49	0.02	—	1.24
56.6	−44.60	0.01	—	0.42

The problem is the determination of γ, the temperature lapse rate throughout the convective layer. According to Paltridge and Platt[28] and Byers, a layer undergoing lifting and convection will eventually redistribute the temperature in such a way that the temperature lapse rate through the convective layer is equal to the dry adiabatic lapse rate. So we may set γ = to LR_d = 0.0053° C/m, and T_{cv}= 378° K (105° C or 221° F).

This technique is standard in operational models for making the so-called "convective adjustment" to the radiative equilibrium profile to determine the radiative-convective equilibrium profile. Ramanathan and Coakley explain:

> The effects of convection are included implicitly by assuming that convection maintains a critical temperature lapse rate within the convective region .... For an atmosphere in which the condensation processes are unimportant the critical lapse rate is the adiabatic lapse rate.... Whenever the radiative equilibrium lapse rate is greater than the critical lapse rate, the lapse rate is set equal to the critical lapse rate. This lapse rate adjustment has come to be known as the convective adjustment.[29]

So as the parcel rises and before it produces condensation, the lapse rate is the dry adiabatic lapse rate. After condensation the critical lapse rate is the saturation adiabatic lapse rate.

Parcels cooling at the rate of 5.3° C/km will saturate and condense within one to two km and so clouds will form. Once saturation and condensation occur, the release of latent heat through the condensation process will warm the rising parcel and it will rise at the saturation adiabatic rate which is much slower — about 2° C/km.[30] It should be pointed out that the presence of clouds does not necessarily mean rain. In fact,

28. Paltridge and Platt, p. 248.
29. Ramanathan and Coakley, p. 467.
30. See Hess, p. 94. Don Mansfield of Vienna reduced equation (7.3) of Hess to LR_s = 6.13E-8 (PT/e_s), where P, TC°K, and e_s are the pressure, temperature, and saturation vapor pressure of the layer.

What the Pre-Flood Atmosphere Was Like

according to Byers, "The vast majority of clouds do not produce rain."[31]

At some point, the lifting condensation level will be reached (LCL). The altitude for the LCL could be precisely calculated, but the present model is inadequate. However, it is sufficient to say for the present discussion that at some point it will occur, when the parcel temperature has decreased below the boiling point. Once cloud formation begins, the temperature profile described in Table 7.1 would change radically. The maximum temperature of the cloud base would be 100° C. Assuming that the cloud forming convection cell near the canopy base had a vertical temperature lapse rate equal to the saturation adiabatic lapse rate, then the cloud temperature would decrease with altitude at 2° C/km. Eventually a point would be reached where the cloud top temperature would be equal to the environmental temperature. At that point, the top of the convection cell would be reached, and pure vapor would exist above the cloud layer until near the very top of the canopy where the fine mist formation would occur. With the present model it is not possible to calculate the thickness of the cloud layer, but if it was 10 km thick, then the temperature of the cloud top would be 80° C.

Under these conditions, the altitude of the base of the canopy would be given by:[32]

$$Z_C = \frac{R(T_C - T_S)\ln\left[\dfrac{P_C}{P_S}\right]}{MG\ln\left[\dfrac{T_C}{T_S}\right]} \quad (7.23)$$

where T_C = temperature of the canopy base, 373° K; T_S = surface temperature, 293° K (see 7.24); M = molecular weight of dry air, 28.96; P_C = hydrostatic pressure at the canopy base, 1.18 atm; and P_S = surface pressure, 2.18 atm. So Z_C = 6 km.

What about the temperature profile of the canopy above the cloud layer? This too could be precisely calculated, but the

---

31. Byers, p. 356.
32. Hess, p. 83. This assumes a linear temperature lapse rate.

present model is not adequate. It is clear, however, that it will tend toward an isothermal distribution due to two factors: the cloud layer at the top and the ozone formation at the top. These two conditions will put a kind of "lid" on the upwelling radiation from the cloud layer below and tend to level the vertical lapse rate. This "leveling" effect would not happen at the surface of the earth under the clouds because of the lack of absorbing gas at the surface.

THE CALCULATION OF SURFACE TEMPERATURE

We now come to the crucial issue: Under the canopy conditions outlined above, would the surface temperature of the earth be habitable for life? It has seemed inconceivable to some that with a hot canopy above, the surface could enjoy a climate acceptable for human habitation. R. H. Brown, for example, observes, "How can a ball within a shell be maintained under equilibrium conditions, and without a heat pump that requires independent energy input, at a lower temperature than the shell as long as there is radiation interchange on any basis whatsoever, between the ball and the shell."[33]

In a similar vein Robert Whitelaw has objected, "In such a pressure-cooker world under a scalding 270° F sky, life of course would be impossible."[34]

The answer to this concern is that due to the presence of the cloud layer near the canopy base, the characteristics of the radiation field would have been entirely changed, and a massive temperature inversion would have resulted.

Although the Emden model used above is useful, it has several serious drawbacks. Paltridge and Platt summarize one of them, "The model predicts only negative lapse rates in the stratosphere when it is known that positive lapse rates [temper-

33. Robert Henry Brown, Geoscience Research Institute, personal communication, 22 March 1979.
34. Robert Whitelaw, "The Canopy Theory and the Rift-Drift-Shift Theory," private research paper, personal communication, 29 February 1976.

ature inversions] exist at low latitudes."[35] In fact, according to Byers, temperature inversions are extremely common, "One of the most important characteristics of air masses is the development within them of temperature inversions. Their occurrence is so widespread that it is the rule rather than the exception to find them somewhere in the atmosphere."[36]

In order to solve for the temperature at the surface, the calculation must be divided into two components, from the canopy top to the cloud layer, and from the base of the cloud layer to the surface. Paltridge and Platt explain,

> With respect to their effects on the atmospheric cooling rates above and below them, they (clouds) can be regarded as black objects radiating at cloud temperature. The radiation is thus "decoupled" above and below the cloud and the equations of radiative-cooling can be integrated separately with appropriate boundary values of the plank function B(T).[37]

The cloud, then, radiates toward the earth at cloud temperature, at the black body temperature $\sigma T_c^4 = B(T)$. If there were clouds, as the preceeding discussion has established, the highest temperature at which they could radiate would be the boiling point, or 100° C. We have argued that due to adiabatic expansional cooling, the vapor parcels were reduced to that temperature by 14 or 15 km. So a cloud radiating at 100° C (373° K) becomes our upper boundary condition. How then can such a temperature be reduced to 20° C (68° F) at the earth's surface?

In the discussion to follow we will assume a gray model atmosphere under the canopy, (that is, the mass absorption coefficient is independent of wavelength) in contrast to the more accurate non-gray model described for the canopy itself. We begin by dividing the earth's atmosphere between the canopy base and the surface into three layers (see Fig. 7.2).

---

35. Paltridge and Platt, p. 249.
36. Byers, p. 275.
37. Paltridge and Platt, p. 207.

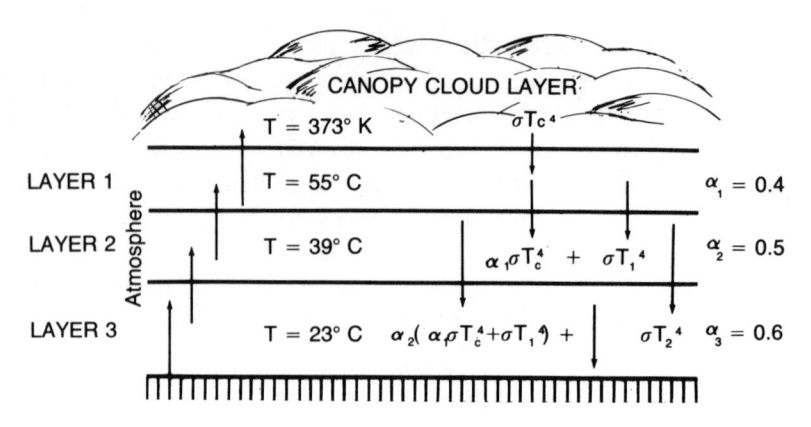

242   The Waters Above: Earth's Pre-Flood Vapor Canopy

```
                    CANOPY CLOUD LAYER
              T = 373° K          σTc⁴
LAYER 1 ─────────────────────────────────────── α₁ = 0.4
             T = 55° C
LAYER 2 ─────────────────────────────────────── α₂ = 0.5
             T = 39° C        α₁σT_c⁴ + σT₁⁴
LAYER 3 ─────────────────────────────────────── α₃ = 0.6
             T = 23° C  α₂(α₁σT_c⁴+σT₁⁴) +    σT₂⁴
```

Fig. 7.2 — Model of the Pre-Flood Atmosphere.

Each layer has a certain transmissivity (the percentage of radiation transmitted through it to the adjacent layers or 1-absorbitivity). Considering first of all the downward Plank radiation from the canopy cloud layer, we begin a radiation balance scheme for each layer in which the total radiation in and out of each layer equal each other, that is, each layer is in radiative equilibrium. Thus B(T) enters layer 1 from the canopy radiating at σT_c^4, canopy base temperature, 373° K. A portion of σT_c^4 is transmitted through layer 1 to layer 2. That transmitted portion is $\alpha_1 \sigma T_c^4$, where α_1 is the transmissivity of layer 1. Layer 1 will also radiate into layer 2 at σT_1^4. So the total amount of radiation out of layer 1 into layer 2 is $\alpha_1 T_c^4 + T_1^4$ (dropping the σ, which will cancel out later on).

By the same reasoning the amount of radiation entering layer 3 from layer 2 is given by $\alpha_2 (\alpha_1 T_c^4 + T_1^4) + T_2^4$, and so on. This process is continued downward to the surface, and then upward from the surface back into the canopy. Then the fluxes into each layer are set equal to the total flux out and, after rearranging, three simultaneous equations result:

$$\begin{aligned}
\text{LAYER 1} &- A(1)T_1^4 + B(1)T_2^4 + C(1)T_3^4 = D(1)T_c^4 \\
\text{LAYER 2} &- A(2)T_1^4 + B(2)T_2^4 + C(2)T_3^4 = D(2)T_c^4 \quad (7.24) \\
\text{LAYER 3} &- A(3)T_1^4 + B(3)T_2^4 + C(3)T_3^4 = D(3)T_c^4
\end{aligned}$$

The layer coefficients, A, B, C, and D, are all functions of the layer transmissivities α_1, α_2, α_3. If we assign a value to the

What the Pre-Flood Atmosphere Was Like

layer transmissivities, since T_C is known (373° K), we have three simultaneous equations with three unknowns that can be easily solved by Gaussian elimination with partial pivoting.

The values assigned to α_1, α_2, and α_3 are somewhat arbitrary: $\alpha_1 = 0.4$, $\alpha_2 = 0.5$, and $\alpha_3 = 0.6$, corresponding to a decrease in the density of water vapor from the canopy base to the surface. With this configuration of absorbing gas under the canopy a surface temperature $T_3 = 293°$ K or 68° F results. The proposed temperature structure is described in Figure 7.3.

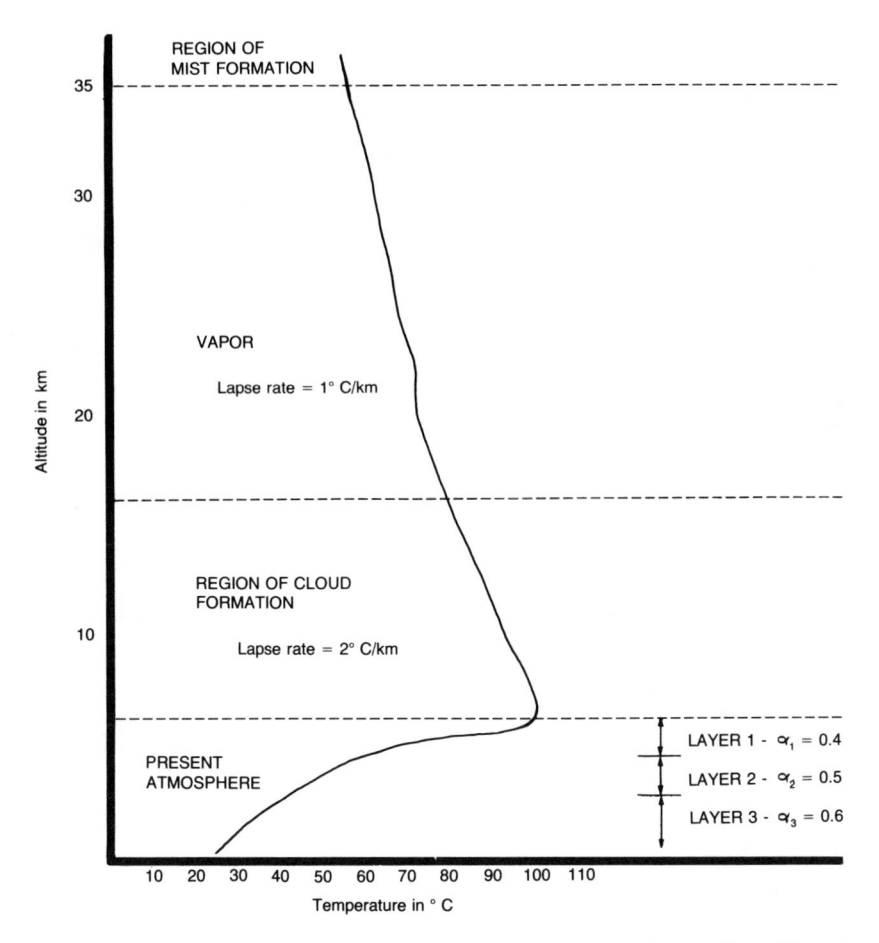

Fig. 7.3 — Proposed Temperature Structure of the Pre-Flood Atmosphere and Vapor Canopy.

In (7.24) a gray model atmosphere was assumed. A more sophisticated model, of course, would be non-gray and would therefore introduce another factor, which would lead to a temperature inversion: radiative cooling at the surface. The water vapor under the canopy cloud layer absorbs with varying intensity in different spectral intervals (see Table 7.1). However, radiation from the earth is most intense in the 8 to 13.5μ (1.29E6 m^{-1} to 1.05E6 m^{-1}) "window." This happens to be the region in which water vapor absorbs the least intensely of all of the infra-red bands. The mass absorption coefficient in this spectral interval is only 0.01 m^{2}kg^{-1}. Therefore the greatest radiation passes right through this window and is not trapped to heat up the earth below.

As a result, the surface of the earth radiates more than the atmospheric layers immediately above it trap and absorb. If the density of the absorbing gas increases with height, such a situation will produce a temperature inversion with heating above and none or little below. The heating above occurs because even though the absorption bands are weak, eventually, if the atmosphere is thick enough, it will absorb the upwelling terrestrial radiation even in the window region. This is exactly the same process that produces the well-known temperature inversion at the tropopause: "The combined effect of three absorbers could produce the inversion at the tropopause. One of the important effects here is the heating resulting from O_3 absorption of radiation coming from the ground through the water vapor window."[38]

In the canopy configuration the increasing depth of water vapor with increasing altitude would have the same effect as the O_3. If the ozone layer resided at the surface in the present atmosphere, the heat would never escape through the window and the surface temperature of the earth would be much hotter. In a similar vein if the dense water vapor canopy continued right on down to the earth's surface, the window would be closed there and a humid hothouse would have been the result. Hess summarizes this phenomenon as follows:

---

38. Manabe and Strickler, p. 372.

What the Pre-Flood Atmosphere Was Like 245

From roughly 5 to 8μ, there is a strong absorption band of H_2O. Beyond 8μ, the absorption becomes smaller up to about 13.5μ ... This relatively transparent window in the atmospheric absorption spectrum falls in the wavelength regions where the earth's surface radiates most strongly.[39]

We therefore conclude that Morton errs once again when he says, "For a canopy of any appreciable thickness the optical depth for even the most weakly absorbing part of the window is still enough to completely block the direct escape from the surface of radiation of those wavelengths."[40]

The canopy does not block the direct escape of radiation "from the surface." It is true that radiation passing from the surface up through the window will eventually be trapped in the canopy, but it will not be trapped at the surface and heat the surface.

NIGHTTIME VISIBILITY

With a partial cloud layer at the top and a total cloud cover around 6 km, an apparent difficulty arises with the biblical indications that the stars were visible in the pre-Flood heavens (Gen. 1:14-19). In fact, some have objected that at nighttime clouds would form due to atmospheric cooling and in the daytime they would burn away due to solar heating. Morton explains, "During the day clouds would be absorbing direct solar radiation. This would cause their temperature to rise. If the temperature rise were of a sufficient magnitude, the clouds would dissipate during the day. During the night, on the other hand, the cooling atmosphere would favor the formation of the clouds."[41]

Actually precisely the opposite effect would occur. The cloud layer at the canopy base is formed by the convection cells generated by solar heating. During the night, without solar

39. Hess, p. 135.
40. Morton, p. 168.
41. Glen Morton, senior geophysicist with the Atlantic Richfield Company, Dallas, Texas, personal communication, letter, 14 July 1979.

heating, the lapse rates through the convecting cells would drop below the critical adiabatic lapse rate and convection would cease; as a result, the entire cloud layer would dissipate except for the very fine, low density, intermittent mist/cloud at the top. So Adam and his family would normally have seen a clear night sky.

CONCLUSION

The numerical expositions above lead us to a canopy atmosphere such as depicted in Figure 7.3. Having approximated the temperature profile of such a canopy, it is now possible to see how many feet of precipitable water could have been maintained in the ancient atmosphere.

THE STABILITY OF THE PRE-FLOOD ATMOSPHERE

The geological record indicates that the topography of the ancient earth may have been considerably different from today's. One characteristic in particular that would have lent stability to the ancient atmosphere is the apparent lack of major mountain ranges. (See E.H. Colbert, "Evolutionary Growth Rates in the Dinosaurs." *Scientific Monthly* 69 (August 1949): 71.) It is generally believed that most mountain building is a comparatively recent phenomenon connected with the Pleistocene. The biblical statements indicate that major mountain building activity did take place during the Flood and immediately after it (Gen. 7:11; Psalm 104:8). In the model to follow it will be assumed that during the pre-Flood era, there were *no* mountains. Certainly, there may have been rolling hills, but no major mountains. Therefore the lower edge of the canopy (about 30,000 feet) would never be in danger of intersecting the landscape. Furthermore, the convective updrafts produced by the wind's blowing against the sides of steep mountains would have been severely limited. This would reduce eddy diffusion.

The only way a vapor canopy could have been maintained above the ancient atmosphere would have been to eliminate convective turbulence and reduce eddy diffusion, which

What the Pre-Flood Atmosphere Was Like

would have caused the canopy to mix quickly with the lower atmosphere and diffuse downward to the surface in a matter of hours. Is there any known physics that would have resulted in such a stability, and would it occur as a result of the existence of the vapor canopy? In fact, there are two such physical mechanisms that would severely reduce eddy diffusion and convective turbulence and provide a stable regime in which the atmosphere could conceivably contain enormous amounts of water above what it is able to sustain today. These physical mechanisms are a temperature inversion and Taylor stability.

THE CANOPY PRODUCED TEMPERATURE INVERSION

When God divided the waters, our present theory requires that He must have immediately turned the liquid water into vapor form. Assuming that natural laws observed today were operating prior to the Flood, immediately this water vapor would have distributed itself in hydrostatic equilibrium in the gravity field. What do we mean by "hydrostatic equilibrium"?

If we were to imagine a column of air with a cross-sectional area of 1 cm^2 extending to the top of the atmosphere, the pressure at the bottom of that column (that is, sea level) is equal to the weight of the air above it. Due to the force of gravity, any water vapor placed above the atmosphere will immediately be acted on by gravity and pulled toward the surface of the earth. The water vapor would continue its gravity-induced descent until the molecules of the air below became so bunched together that they began to "push up" against the downward pressure of the weight of the molecules above. When the upward force equals the downward force at every level, the system is said to be in hydrostatic equilibrium. Any amount of water placed above the atmosphere will quickly distribute itself into this equilibrium configuration due to the forces of gravity. It is for this reason that it is impossible to posit vast amounts of water vapor above the atmosphere "floating" and maintained by great temperatures. As long as the water vapor molecules are in contact with the gravity field, they will quickly sort themselves into this equilibrium distribution. Once this equilibrium situation has been achieved, the vertical variation of pressure with altitude is given by the hydrostatic equation (7.1).[42]

We encounter a problem, however, with water vapor. The weight of all the water vapor above determines the pressure of the water vapor at the bottom level of the canopy, just as in the case of any other gas. Unless the temperature is sufficiently high, that weight will result in a vapor pressure that exceeds the saturation vapor pressure of water vapor in the bottom increment, and it will condense out as rain. The saturation vapor pressure of water vapor is a function of temperature only and can be found by reference to the engineering steam tables.[43]

Thus, in order to keep the water vapor in vapor form it is necessary to assume a temperature distribution throughout the canopy high enough to keep the saturation vapor pressure of each increment of the canopy greater than the hydrostatic pressure of the weight of the water vapor above that layer. If a canopy model of 40 feet of precipitable water is assumed, that means that the weight of water vapor above the bottom layer of the canopy is 40 ft × 0.4335 lb/ft^2 = 17.34 lb/in^2. From the steam tables, it can be seen that if this represents the saturation vapor pressure, the corresponding temperature must be 220° F (104.4°C) at the bottom of the canopy. Any temperature above the boiling point (100°C) also will be sufficient.

The preceding discussion of the vertical temperature structure establishes that the canopy would indeed be hot enough to support 40 feet of water. It also shows that a massive temperature inversion would have resulted. In such a configuration, eddy diffusion of vapor to the surface would have been eliminated, and the atmosphere would have been able to maintain tremendous amounts of water above it.

The stabilizing influence of such temperature inversions are well known among meteorologists, and discussions of the physics involved can be found in any basic meteorology text.[44]

42. See Byers, pp. 82-83, for a discussion of hydrostatic relationships.
43. *1967 Steam Tables*, pp. 2-9.
44. Hess, pp. 95-100; Byers, pp. 93-98; and Louis J. Battan, *Weather*, pp. 24-30.

What the Pre-Flood Atmosphere Was Like

For a simple conceptual model of the physics involved, consider Figure 7.4. Imagine a parcel of air, A, that is suddenly jostled and moved downward into the troposphere. As it moves downward, it moves from a region of 100° C heat to 60° C heat. As soon as it enters the lower region, it is now hotter than the surrounding 60° C air. As a result, it is less dense and hence lighter than the surrounding air. This produces a buoyant force that drives the parcel back up into the canopy. In a similar way, if some cooler parcel was jostled from below and driven up into the hotter canopy, it arrives at a cooler temperature than the surrounding water vapor and is, therefore, heavier and more dense. As a result, it will immediately sink back into the troposphere.

CANOPY, 100° C

TROPOSPHERE, 60° C

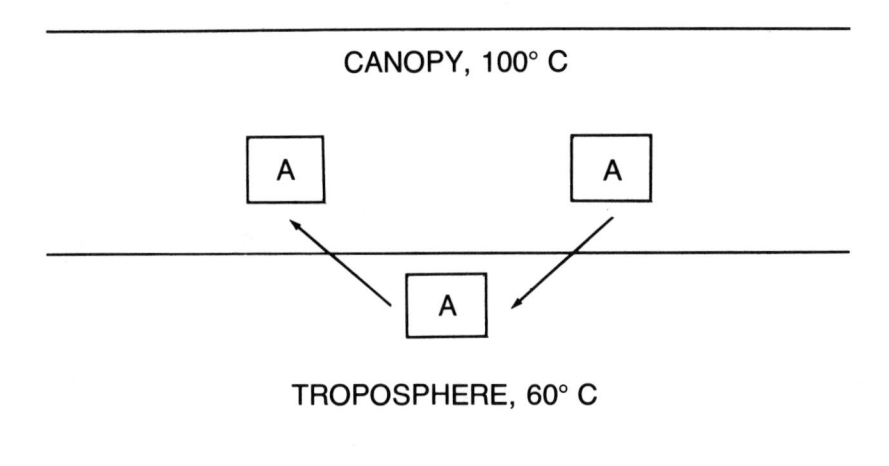

Fig. 7.4 — Movement of a Parcel of Air into a Temperature Inversion.

These stabilizing tendencies are further enforced by the expansion and contraction of the moving parcel. When our imaginary parcel moves from the canopy to the lower troposphere, it not only moves from a region of greater temperature to one of lower temperature, but it also moves from a region of lesser pressure to one of greater pressure. Pressure increases as the parcel moves downward because it is going deeper into the atmosphere and more atmosphere is above it. It is just like going deeper under water. As pressure on the parcel increases, the parcel is compressed, and a compression results in higher temperature inside the parcel. Thus, the parcel becomes even hotter than 60° C and is even more forcibly restrained from penetration into the troposphere.

It is clear that the canopy temperature inversion would result in an extremely stable regime at the interface of the canopy and the lower troposphere, significantly reducing any convective turbulence, and thus enabling much water to be maintained above the ancient atmosphere. In today's atmosphere, little water could be maintained, simply because there is no such global temperature inversion.

TAYLOR STABILITY

In the field of fluid mechanics, great attention has been given to the situations under which layers of fluids surrounding a rotating cylinder will remain in a laminar flow. When the fluid remains in laminar flow, it is said to be "stable." If mixing occurs between the layers of the fluid, so-called "Taylor instability" has developed, and Taylor vortices are observed (stable circular flows of fluid, see Fig. 7.5). Taylor noted that when water in a tank was made to rotate steadily as a solid body, some interesting things occurred when ink was introduced into the system. The fluid would draw the ink into thin sheets, and these sheets always remained parallel to the axis of rotation. Taylor noted, "The accuracy with which they remained parallel to the axis of rotation is quite extraordinary."[45] Since this is precisely the situation under the vapor canopy, a discussion of this phenomenon is pertinent.

The pre-Flood atmosphere can be visualized as the "ink." It is layered between two concentric cylinders — the earth and the canopy bottom. Under certain conditions, the atmosphere will stay parallel to the axis of rotation. In other words, there would be no turbulent mixing at the interface of the canopy and the lower atmosphere. This would, of course, contribute significantly to the maintenance of the vapor canopy.

45. Cited by S. Chandrasekhar, *Hydrodynamic and Hydromagnetic Stability*, p. 2.

What the Pre-Flood Atmosphere Was Like   251

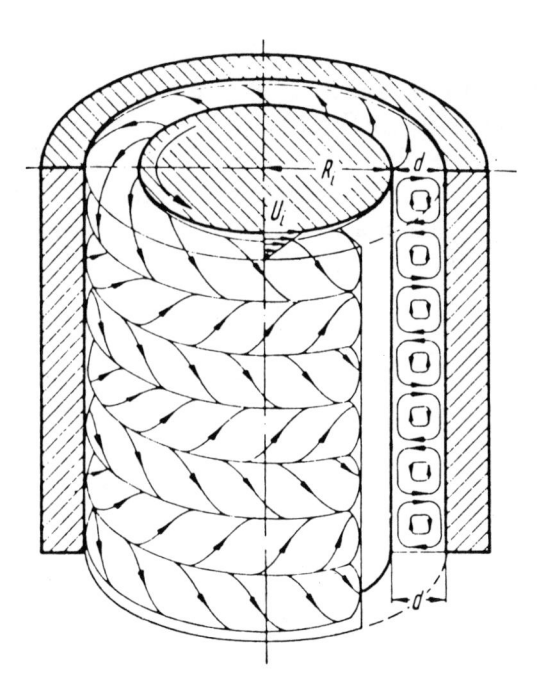

Fig. 7.5 — Taylor Vortices Between Two Concentric, Rotating Cylinders. Inner cylinder rotating, outer cylinder at rest; d = width of annular gap.[46]

Taylor defined a Taylor number to correlate certain parameters of the two rotating cylinders involved into a dimensionless ratio that could be used to determine when such a system would become unstable and the laminar flow disrupted. The Taylor number is defined as:[47]

$$K = \frac{4\Omega^2 R_1^4 (1-\mu)(1-\mu/\eta^2)}{v^2 (1-\eta^2)^2} \tag{7.25}$$

where Ω = the angular velocity of the inner cylinder, or in the canopy model of the earth; R_1 = the radius of the earth; μ = the ratio of the angular velocity of the outer cylinder (the inner rim

46. Hermann Schlichting, *Boundary-Layer Theory*, p. 501.
47. Chandrasekhar, p. 6.

of the canopy) to Ω; η = the ratio of the radius of the inner cylinder, R_1, to the radius of the outer cylinder, R_2; and v = kinematic viscosity, or the coefficient of viscosity divided by the density of the fluid contained between the two rotating cylinders (the ancient atmosphere). Figure 7.6 illustrates the application of this equation for the Taylor number to the ancient atmosphere.

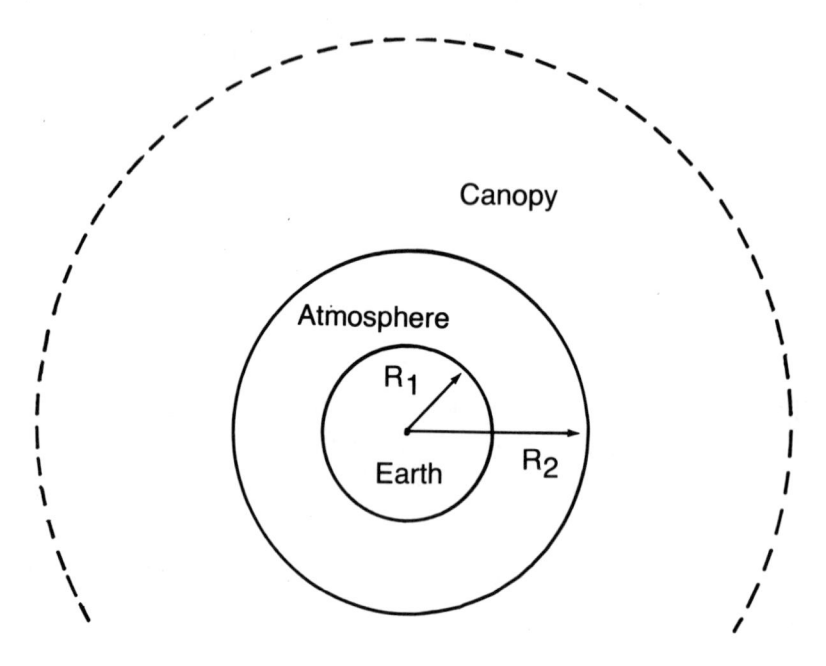

Fig. 7.6 — Model of the Taylor Stability of the Ancient Atmosphere (not according to scale).

So the two cylinders are the inner rim of the canopy and the surface of the earth. The fluid that is to be analyzed is the pre-Flood atmosphere contained between these two rotating plates. Modeling the outer rim as a solid plate is a common modeling technique in aerodynamics, even though no such plate actually exists. However, if the molecules of the fluid at the outer rim are everywhere parallel to the inner cylinder, then the effect is the same as if a literal solid plate existed. Due to the

What the Pre-Flood Atmosphere Was Like

temperature inversion and the greenhouse effect, the bottom of the canopy would be very stable and would eliminate vertical and horizontal winds.

The kinematic viscosity is inversely proportional to the density, hence it is directly proportional to the temperature of the ancient atmosphere. This can be seen from the equation of state of an ideal gas.[48]

$$\rho = P(m/R)(1/T) \qquad (7.26)$$

As long as the Taylor number remains below a certain critical Taylor number, K, the fluid contained between the rotating cylinders will remain in laminar flow, and there will be no convective turbulence. It would be of great interest to know what the critical Taylor number of the pre-Flood atmosphere was. Unfortunately, while Taylor numbers have been defined for cylinders,[49] they have not been defined for spheres. However, "The Taylor number for a sphere in a fluid will have the same type of dependency as for a cylinder in a fluid. It will be highly dependent on the viscosity, density, and 'atmospheric thickness.'"[50]

So even though the earth's atmosphere is not a cylinder but a sphere, the similar factors defined in the equation for the Taylor number of a cylinder apply to a sphere.

John Burkhalter, an atmospheric physicist with Auburn University, did his doctoral work on supercritical Taylor vortex flow.[51] He has suggested that when God created the earth's atmosphere, He would probably have started it out in an equilibrium state, which is called Couette flow.

48. Byers, p. 71.
49. See J. E. Burkhalter and E. L. Koschmieder, "Steady Supercritical Taylor Vortices after Sudden Starts," *Physics of Fluids* 17 (November 1974): 1929-1935; J. E. Burkhalter and E. L. Koschmieder, "Steady Supercritical Taylor Vortex Flow," *Journal of Fluid Mechanics* 58 (1973):547-60.
50. John Burkhalter, Ph. D., personal communication, 26 February 1976.
51. J. E. Burkhalter, "Experimental Investigation of Supercritical Taylor Vortex Flow."

Now let us make the assumption that the earth and atmosphere were created in a perfect state (which I believe to be true). The initial flow field for the atmosphere in this perfect state would have been Couette flow for a sphere immersed in a uniform fluid. It is possible that this situation could have been maintained with the pressure gradient forces being slightly larger than the inertial forces. If the atmosphere were thicker than it is today, as one would logically conclude, then the critical Taylor number would have been fairly large.[52]

Assuming that the atmosphere was created in an equilibrium state, then the angular velocity of the inner rim of the canopy would be equal to the angular velocity of the surface of the earth, and from (7.25) the term $(1-\mu)$ would equal zero. So whatever was the critical Taylor number of the pre-Flood atmosphere, it was clearly far above zero, and, as Burkhalter suggests, far above even today's values. As a result, it would appear that the atmosphere of the pre-Flood world (that is, the "fluid" between the plates) may have been in a very stable condition and lacked any turbulent mixing.

It is known that the Taylor number of today's atmosphere is above the critical value due to the fact that jet streams are apparent in the upper atmosphere. What would have caused the Taylor number of zero of the pre-Flood world to rise above the critical value and induce Taylor instability and a global rain?

A major factor would be a significant cooling. From (7.26) and (7.25) it is clear that the Taylor number varies inversely with temperature. So a drop in temperature would raise the Taylor number. As will be discussed in a later chapter, the activity of numerous volcanoes may have thrown a cooling volcanic cloud cover above the canopy and drastically reduced its temperature, precipitating extensive rainfall. As the rain fell, ν would decrease (as density decreased), and therefore the Taylor number would be forced upward even more. A third factor may have caused a gradual *decrease* of the critical Taylor number downward, that is, the loss of water vapor and dissociated hydrogen off the top of the canopy into outer space. Burkhalter continues:

52. Burkhalter, personal communication, 26 February 1976.

What the Pre-Flood Atmosphere Was Like 255

> As the earth continued to rotate in its infant stages (perhaps over a period of hundreds of years), it could have gradually lost some of its atmosphere to outer space as theorized for many other planets and moons. During this period, Couette flow would have been maintained as long as the Taylor number was below the critical value. As the atmosphere became thinner, the critical Taylor number decreased until at sometime in history, the atmosphere became inertially unstable. At this time, catastrophic phenomena would have taken place.[53]

So the Taylor number of the pre-Flood atmosphere was increasing, and the critical Taylor number was decreasing. At some point a global instability would have set in.

> The Couette flow would suddenly (hours, days, or weeks) have formed into toroidal shaped rings around the earth. Initially there would have been (perhaps) many rings which would have caused very large vertical air currents and consequent cooling, etc., of the vapor state atmosphere. Considerable condensation (rain) would have occurred, accompanied by strong winds. After some period of time, a specific pattern would have resulted in which the toroidal rings would have remained as long as the Taylor number was above the critical, as it apparently is today, and specific well-defined wind patterns would have resulted. It is a well-known and established fact that the cells or toroidal rings do exist on the earth today. There are three in the northern hemisphere and three in the southern hemisphere. As a matter of interest, the North East Trade Winds form a part of one of these cells.[54]

Burkhalter concludes, "In conclusion, it is highly possible that the vapor state in the pre-Flood era could have existed and the logical sequence of events described above could have occurred."[55]

53. Ibid.
54. Ibid.
55. Ibid. However, it may be questionable that these cells as they are constructed today are Taylor vortices as Burkhalter suggests. A similar cell pattern has been produced in laboratory atmospheric simulations based on thermal differences between the poles and the equator by Rossby and Fultz. Furthermore, computer simulated climate models have predicted a similar flow pattern without any reference to concentric cylinders and a moving fluid in between; see Battan, pp. 44-51. Also, there is no "outer cylinder" today because the canopy has condensed.

In order to understand the physical forces involved in Taylor stability better, it is helpful to visualize the atmosphere as located between two concentric cylinders, each with a width equal to the distance between the equator and approximately 30 degrees north and south latitude. These cylinders are rotating at exactly the same velocity. Furthermore, as described above, the earth is under the influence of a universal temperature inversion. The canopy creates a universal greenhouse effect. Toward the top of the canopy there would have been much movement of water vapor from the equator toward the poles in order to balance the heat budget. Since the area of the canopy located over the equator receives much more solar radiation than the area over the poles, a movement from the high pressure over the equator to the low pressure over the poles would ensue. This transport of heat by atmospheric movement might keep the temperature of the canopy over the equator and the poles nearly the same (precisely the same situation that prevails on Venus[56]).

Therefore, in the lower regions of the canopy, just above the atmosphere, there could well have been little atmospheric movement. The temperature of the bottom of the canopy radiating earthward from the poles would then be close to that radiating earthward at the equator. As a result, there would be a pole-to-equator temperature equilibrium, hence only minor air transport in the lower atmosphere or in the lower area of the canopy (the outer "rim" of the two concentric cylinders). The Taylor number would therefore have been near zero as mentioned above.

The only forces acting on a parcel of air in the lower atmosphere would be the centrifugal force throwing air out and gravity-produced pressure gradient forces pulling the air parcel in. At what point would an instability set in? An instability (hence turbulent mixing) would occur when a random disturbance was amplified instead of being dissipated. "The task of the stability theory consists in determining whether the disturbance is amplified or whether it decays for a given mean mo-

---

56. Richard M. Goody and James C. G. Walker, *Atmospheres* (Englewood Cliffs, N.J.: Prentice-Hall, 1972), p. 65.

tion; the flow is considered unstable or stable depending on whether the former or the latter is the case."[57]

Under what conditions would a disturbance be amplified? This would occur when a parcel of air below a disturbance was continuously or repeatedly "bounced" upward into the disturbance, carrying a larger amount of angular momentum than the layer into which it was bounced could dissipate. If the horizontal velocity of flow of the parcel of air was greater below than above, then when that parcel was raised to the upper level it carried with it a greater amount of angular momentum than the surrounding air. In order for angular momentum to be conserved, the energy associated with the momentum increase must be dissipated by viscous transport to the surrounding air (fluid). If the disturbance was able to dissipate the additional energy at a greater rate than energy was being added to the disturbance, then the disturbance would not be amplified, but would be "damped," and the atmosphere would remain in a stable state. Its ability to dissipate energy would be dependent on the viscosity of the surrounding air which is related to density and temperature.

However, if the angular momentum of the particles continuously moving into the area of the disturbance was such that a larger amount of energy was transferred than the disturbance could dissipate, then the disturbance would continue to grow in intensity, and a large-scale instability would result. It is obvious that the key to creating a global instability is to introduce a velocity profile where the velocity of the layers differs significantly so that *continuous* transport of momentum between the layers will result in instability. Momentum is a function of the mass, velocity, and distance of the parcel from the axis of rotation. A change in temperature will change the density and hence the mass of the parcel, and the viscosity of the layer which must dissipate its energy. Therefore, either a change of temperature or a change in the velocity or a change in radius of the "outer rim" could result in a change in stability.

Now the Taylor number is a dimensionless ratio that relates all the factors such as mass, velocity, viscosity, and radius.

57. Schlichting, p. 440.

Different masses and different velocities can exist in various layers of the atmosphere and the atmosphere still remain stable and laminar provided the ratio of the masses, velocities, and radii is not such that the Taylor number that defines that ratio exceeds a certain critical value.

Burkhalter describes laboratory experiments in which he observed the introduction of a serious disturbance into the fluid located between two concentric rotating cylinders in which the Taylor number was subcritical. He observed that, no matter how the fluid was stirred up, it would quickly return to laminar flow, and no turbulent vertical mixing would occur. The same situation may have existed in the pre-Flood earth. Local and severe disturbances or variations in weather may have occurred, but they would have had no effect in generating a global instability and coincident convective turbulence and eddy diffusion. It seems likely then that, under these assumed antediluvian conditions, no local disturbances would be amplified but would be damped, and the atmosphere would remain stable without any vortices or vertical motions.

The Maintenance of the Vapor Canopy

It will now become clear how many feet of water vapor may have been maintained, perhaps indefinitely, above the ancient troposphere. There is one possible mechanism that might have contained this water vapor. Due to the stabilizing influences of the global temperature inversion and of Taylor stability, the atmosphere below the bottom of the canopy would have been in an extremely stable, laminar state so that little convective turbulence or mixing would have occurred between the canopy and the ancient troposphere. Only molecular diffusion needs to be considered, and eddy diffusion would be zero.

In order to calculate how long it would take for the canopy to diffuse down to the surface of the earth, it will arbitrarily be assumed that in the 1 km layer under the canopy the air is *completely* stable. This is a reasonable assumption based on observation of present-day temperature inversions. Furthermore, since the temperature inversion extends all the way to the surface, it is likely that eddy diffusion would be insignificant most of the way down. Thus, assuming only a 1 km totally stable layer is conservative. There is absolutely no eddy diffusion or convective turbulence due to the temperature inversion and Taylor stability. However, as one gets closer to the surface, it is possible that eddy diffusion might begin to play a more prominent role. This is due to the fact that the albedos of various parts of the earth's surface vary from 0.1 for forests, 0.2 for oceans, and 0.45 for sandy areas.[58] As a result, differing amounts of radiation will be absorbed at the surface in these different areas, and different temperatures will result. In order to balance these slight temperature variations, gentle breezes and winds might prevail as they do today. There would be no major wind systems, however. So once the vapor had diffused down through the first 1 km layer, it might diffuse more rapidly the rest of the way down to the surface, due to the mixing and gentle breezes there.

The calculation of molecular diffusion involves computer iterative techniques. In order to secure a reliable approximation, Dr. Larry Vardiman, a meteorologist with the Bureau of Reclamation, was consulted.

Vardiman starts out assuming a temperature profile similar to Figure 7.3, which was calculated above. He also assumes 34 feet of precipitable water in the canopy and a surface pressure of 2,026.5 millibars and surface temperature of 300° K or 27° C. The temperature at the interface between the atmosphere (air) and the canopy is set at 400° K or 127° C. This is sufficient to sustain over 40 feet of precipitable water in vapor form in the canopy. The pressure at the bottom of the canopy would be 1013 mb (34 ft of H_2O = 1 atm. = 1013 mb). Due to the temperature inversion, there is no wind or vertical mixing in the 1 km below the canopy, and hence the primary mode of diffusion downward will be molecular diffusion. This process is described by Fick's law:[59]

$$\frac{dM}{dt} = \frac{-DAd\rho}{dz} \qquad (7.27)$$

58. Byers, p. 33.
59. For discussion of Fick's law see J. P. Holman, *Heat Transfer*, pp. 426-32.

where $\frac{dM}{dt}$ = the flux of water vapor through a boundary in units of gm/cm². sec; D = the diffusivity of water vapor through air in units of cm²/sec; A = an area through which water vapor is being diffused, assumed to be 1 cm²; and $\frac{d\rho}{dz}$ = the density gradient of water vapor in the vertical direction z in units of gm/cm³/cm.

Basically this equation says that the rate of diffusion of water vapor through a unit area is proportional to the negative gradient of vapor density. So the largest rate of diffusion of water vapor downward will occur immediately below the interface at time zero. As vapor diffuses downward, the gradient below the interface will decrease, reducing the rate of diffusion. So Vardiman assumes that the initial conditions involved a layer of water vapor and a layer of air separated by an impenetrable membrane. As soon as the membrane is removed, vapor diffusion downward begins at time zero.

The equation for D is:

$$D = D_0(T/273° K)^{1.81} \quad (1000 \text{ mb}/P) \qquad (7.28)$$

where D = diffusivity at pressure and temperature of interest; D_0 = diffusivity of water vapor into air at T_0, P_0 = 0.241 cm²/sec; $T_0 = 0°C = 273°K$; P_0 = 1000 mb; and P = pressure of interest.

Because of the pressure and temperature dependence of the diffusivity, a finite difference scheme was developed to integrate equations (7.27) and (7.28). Seventy 100-meter-thick layers were modeled from the surface to the air-water interface, as shown in Figure 7.7. Layers are denoted by the dotted lines with j running from 1 to 70. Seventy-one levels were modeled as denoted by the solid lines with i running from 1 to 71. A diffusivity was calculated at each layer.

Temperature, pressure, and diffusivity were assumed to remain constant with time.

Vapor was assumed to diffuse downward, but air was not assumed to diffuse upward. Neither was the upward diffusion of water vapor back into the canopy considered. If air and water vapor had been allowed to diffuse upward, it would have slowed the net diffusion of water vapor downward. So the present calculation will be conservative by overestimating the rate of diffusion downward.

What the Pre-Flood Atmosphere Was Like

P(mb)	T(°K)	H(km)		Level (i)	Layer (j)
1013	400.0	7.0	_____	1	
			- - - - -		1
1022	398.6	6.9	_____	2	
			- - - - -		2
1031	397.1	6.8	_____	3	
			- - - - -		3
1040	395.7	6.7	_____	4	
			- - - - -		4
1049	394.3	6.6	_____	5	
			. . .		
1982	302.8	0.2	_____	69	
			- - - - -		69
2004	301.4	0.1	_____	70	
			- - - - -		70
2026	300.0	0.0	_____	71	

Fig. 7.7 — Finite Difference Model with 70 Layers, Each 100 Meters Thick.

The vapor density at level one ($i = 1$) is computed from the ideal gas law (Equation 7.26) assuming vapor saturation at 400° K.

Because of the assumption of no water vapor in the air below the canopy, no diffusion will occur below the first layer under the interface during the first time step. That is, no diffusion will occur between levels 1 and 2. At the second time step, diffusion occurs between levels 1 and 2 and between levels 2 and 3. At the end of 70 time steps, diffusion occurs through all 70 layers, although the rate at the lowest levels is extremely small. This "marching" of water vapor downward one layer at a time for the first 70 time steps is an artificiality of the initial assumptions, but does not affect the simulation after about five time steps from the time a layer has vapor in it.

Figure 7.8 shows the rate of diffusion through layer 1 for the first 250 years in terms of an equivalent depth of liquid water. Since the rate of diffusion will always be greatest in layer 1, and since all water vapor must be diffused through this layer, this graph provides an estimate of the maximum rate of diffusion.

It can be seen from Figure 7.8 that the maximum rate of diffusion at the end of the first year is 0.77 cm/yr and decreases rapidly to 0.1 cm/yr in about 120 years. If the curve in Figure 7.8 is extrapolated to 1,656 years, and the diffusion integrated over the entire 1,656 years (from Adam to the Flood), the total water diffused through layer 1 is just over 1 meter of liquid water. This is less than 10% of the total 34 feet of water initially assumed to be in the canopy, which has diffused through the first layer 100 meters under the canopy in 1,656 years. At this rate, it would take 12,190 years for the 40 feet of H_2O (1,219 cm) to diffuse through the first 100-meter layer. So it is evident that the canopy will take an extremely long time to diffuse to the surface.

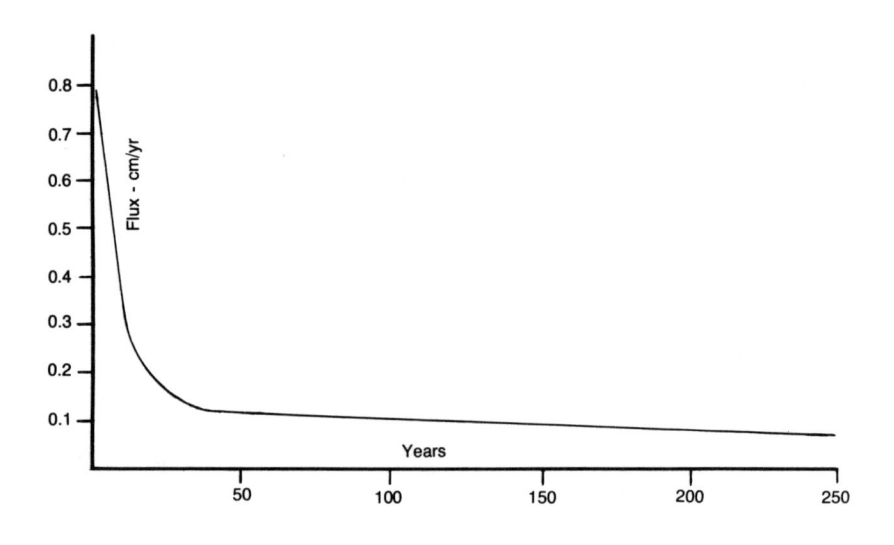

Fig. 7.8 — Plot of the Flux of Water Vapor through the Nearest 100 m Layer beneath the Canopy as a Function of Time.

The calculations show that the vapor initially diffuses downward rapidly then begins to slow as the gradient decreases. By 250 years only 1 millibar of vapor (about 1 cm of liquid water) has reached the 5.75 kilometer level (about 1 km below the canopy). This is less than 0.1% of the total vapor pressure at the base of the initial canopy. At a rate of 1 cm/250 yrs, it would take 304,750 years for the canopy to diffuse through the 1 km level.[60]

Vardiman concludes, "These results, based strictly on molecular diffusion, show that with the assumed initial distribution of water vapor, air, and temperature, the vapor canopy is highly stable with time and could have easily remained in the upper atmosphere from its creation to the flood 1,656 years later."[61]

It appears likely, then, assuming completely stable air for 1 km under the canopy, that the canopy could be maintained for a very long period of time. In 250 years, only 1 cm would have diffused down to the areas of the troposphere where eddy diffusion might begin to play a part.

A Decaying Canopy — Theological Implications

We are led, in the model above, to suggest a "decaying" canopy. It should be noted, however, that this presents no problem with the certain flood that such an initial condition would one day render necessary. The fact that the canopy was in a decaying condition and that one day a flood would result necessarily implies that the judgment of the Flood was divinely foreordained. So the rebellion and sin of man, which necessitated that Flood, was also included in the eternal plan (see Eph. 1:11).

60. These extrapolations are incorrectly based on linear extrapolation instead of exponential. Thus, it would actually take longer.
61. Larry Vardiman, Ph. D., meteorologist with the Bureau of Reclamation, Denver, Colorado, personal communication, 13 January 1977.

It may appear that a conflict is then set up between God's eternal plan and human free will and responsibility. If the sin of man, which necessitated a coming flood, was included in the plan, how can man be held accountable? This is precisely the problem Paul addresses in Romans 9:14-19 regarding the hardening of Pharaoh's heart. If God hardened his heart (9:18), then how can God hold Pharaoh responsible (9:19)? Paul never completely answers this difficulty; he only says, "On the contrary, who are you, O man, who answers back to God?" (9:20).

The classic illustration of such foreknowledge of the sinful acts of men is found in Acts 2:22-23. Here we are told that Jesus was "delivered up by the predetermined plan and foreknowledge of God," and that "godless men" put Him to death. His death was predetermined, and therefore the means of its accomplishment, that is, the sinful acts of sinful men, was also included in the eternal plan. Yet God still held these sinful men responsible for what they had done. In a similar way the fact of a decaying canopy and its necessary implications of a certain future judgmental flood in no way violates human responsibility.

These are mysteries of God's providence that He has not yet seen fit to explain to us fully. The point here is that in view of the parallel examples in Scripture this offers no valid objection to the canopy model presented in this chapter.

Furthermore, it should be pointed out that the sun and the entire universe are in a decaying situation. So someday all of life will become extinct apart from a supernatural intervention. It is possible that prior to the Fall a different set of natural laws prevailed. It could be, for example, that the Second Law of Thermodynamics, the law of decay, which requires the canopy to diffuse to the surface, was not operative until the entire creation was subjected to vanity with the fall of Adam (see Rom. 8:20-21). So had man not sinned, the canopy would have been maintained indefinitely; but with his sin a certain future judgment became inherently necessary.

Conclusion

The canopy problems introduced in this chapter have been discussed at an elementary level. Full solution to the vertical temperature structure awaits a computer-simulated global climate model which will incorporate the equations of radiative heat transfer as well as atmospheric dynamics. It appears, however, that the canopy model discussed in this chapter is based on sound physical principles.

A number of secondary difficulties appear as well. It is to these concerns that our attention must now be directed.

Chapter 8

Some Problems with the Vapor Canopy Theory

The central problem in the vapor canopy model has been that there is no obvious support mechanism for maintaining many feet of water in the atmosphere. The possibilities described in the preceding chapter are plausible answers to this difficulty. However, any model as complex as what is here being described has vast implications that need to be explored. What follows is a summary of some of the more obvious major considerations that need to be quantified before the vapor canopy model is worthy of general consensus.

THE PRECIPITATION OF THE CANOPY

Based on the biblical statements concerning the breaking up of the fountains of the deep (Gen. 7:11), it seems reasonable to suppose that a major factor involved in disrupting the pre-Flood atmosphere was volcanic activity. The Hebrew word translated "burst open" is *baga*, and is used of breaking forth of water masses (Prov. 3:20) and sometimes of faulting of the earth (Zech. 14:4). Although its use is general, it seems reasonable to posit that in the Genesis account the word refers to the bursting of subterranean waters and accompanying faulting and, perhaps, volcanic activity. Also, throughout the tundra muck, one finds numerous deposits of volcanic ash that parallel the finds in Antarctica. Presumably, the volcanic dust particles were expelled into the canopy (note the ease at which this could have been accomplished if the canopy base was only 6.0 km) during the months prior to the Flood and before the "fountains of the deep" (Gen. 7:11) erupted. On the day of the Deluge, this volcanic activity expanded to a global scale, and the "windows of heaven were opened."

Could volcanic activity provide sufficient condensation nuclei to precipitate a canopy containing 6.219×10^{21} cm³ of precipitable water?[1] The size of an "average" raindrop varies from 0.05 cm to 0.5 cm. Assuming an average radius of 0.275 cm, the volume of a raindrop would be $V = 4\pi r^3/3$ or 0.087 cm³. The total number of particles needed then would be the volume of the canopy divided by the volume of the average raindrop, or 7.15×10^{22} particles.[2] According to Humphreys, the volcano Katmai (1912) ejected 173.4×10^{22} particles into the atmosphere, which took several years to fall back to the earth.[3] So we can see that even one volcano would supply more than the needed condensation nuclei to precipitate the entire canopy. The problem is not in the number of nuclei but in getting them distributed sufficiently around the earth and cooling the canopy sufficiently to reach the saturation point. Over the areas of a volcanic eruption, rainfall would be immense — perhaps four inches per hour or more. When several thousands of these volcanoes began to erupt all over the earth, the atmosphere would become severely disrupted, cooling would result, and rapid dispersal of these nuclei through the canopy might be possible.[4] It would appear, then, that perhaps a year of pre-Flood atmospheric instability probably built up due to these eruptions, and these local instabilities precipitated into a global instability on the day of the Deluge.

1. This is the volume of water in a vapor canopy containing 40 feet of precipitable water.
2. Horace Robert Byers, *General Meteorology*, p. 343. Note discussion in Richard M. Goody and James C. G. Walker, *Atmospheres*, pp. 115-17.
3. W. J. Humphreys, *Physics of the Air*, p. 599.
4. A computer model developed by Barrie Hunt, a meteorologist at the Australian Numerical Meteorology Research Centre estimates that it would take 150 days for the dust from a volcano the size of Krakatoa (27 million tons) to spread from its original equatorial origin over the earth's surface; see "What Happens if the Sun Turns Off?" *Design News*, 5 May 1977, p. 15.

Some Problems with the Vapor Canopy Theory

THE HEAT LOAD

A major problem arises in the canopy theory when we undertake a careful analysis of the total heat load on the atmosphere generated by a vapor canopy. A number of physical factors contribute to this total heat load, H_t.[5]

THE TOTAL HEAT LOAD OF THE CANOPY

Latent heat of condensation. Every time a gram of water vapor condensed out of the canopy, 600 calories/gm of heat were released into the canopy. Since the weight of the canopy has been estimated to be 6.219×10^{21} gm, that means that for the entire canopy to precipitate a latent heat, $H_l = (6.219 \times 10^{21} \text{gm})(600 \text{ cal/gm}) = 3.73 \times 10^{24}$ calories would be released into the atmosphere. If this amount of heat were all absorbed by the earth's atmosphere, the resulting temperature increase is given by:

$$\Delta T = \frac{Q}{mC_p} \tag{8.1}$$

where ΔT = the temperature change, °C; Q = the latent heat released, H_l; m = the mass of the atmosphere, 5.2×10^{18} kg;[6] and C_p = the specific heat at a constant pressure of air, 0.442 kcal/kg·°C.[7] Solving for ΔT yields a temperature increase of 1,623° C. This, of course, is impossible.

Heat lost in temperature change from 100° C to 25° C. If the canopy existed at temperatures of 100° C, then considerable heat must have been given off in cooling it down to present atmospheric temperature levels. That heat of cooling, $H_{tc} = C_p \Delta T \, m$, where C_p = the specific heat at a constant

---

5. The following analysis was suggested by Henry Voss, Ph.D. in electrical engineering, research associate at the University of Illinois, personal communication, October 1976.
6. *Handbook of Chemistry and Physics*, p. F-199.
7. Byers, p. 451. C_p = 1850J/kg·° K = 0.442 cal/gm·°k.

pressure - 0.442 kcal/kgm·° C; and m = the mass of canopy, 6.219 × 10²¹gm. Thus, H_{tc} = 2.06 × 10²³ cal.

Heat lost by atmospheric expansion. As the atmosphere expanded during the decompression that would go on during the 40 days of rainfall, the surface pressure would drop from 2.18 atm to 1 atm. This constitutes work done by the atmosphere, hence a reduction in the heat load due to the use of calories in doing this work. The work in joules done during this atmospheric expansion is given by:[8]

$$W = \int p \, dv.$$

This would amount to H_a = 1.68 × 10²³cal.[9]

$$H = 8,000m$$

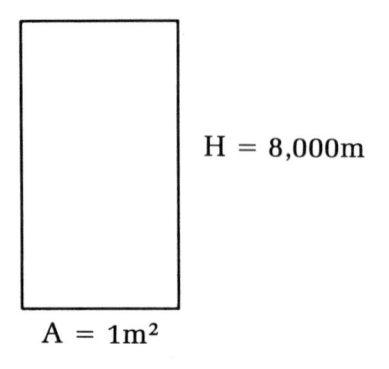

$$A = 1m^2$$

From the equation of state, PV = nRT, and P = nRT/V, therefore,

$$W = \int (nRT/V) dV = nRT \int_{\underline{HA}}^{HA} (dV)/V.$$
$$\phantom{W = \int (nRT/V) dV = nRT \int_{HA}^{HA} (dV)/V.}2.18$$

8. Ibid., p. 75 for a discussion on this.
9. Assume a cylinder running from the bottom of the atmosphere all the way to the top of 1 m² cross-sectional area. The scale height of this cylinder, H, is 8,000 m (the height of a theoretical atmosphere of homogenous density); see Seymour L. Hess, *Introduction to Theoretical Meteorology*, p. 81. So the volume of the cylinder is V = HA.

Some Problems with the Vapor Canopy Theory

This would express the work done during an isothermal expansion (that is, T constant) in the cylinder as that atmosphere expanded from its volume under the canopy (HA/2.18) to its volume today (HA).

Since nRT = PV, P = 2.18, and V = HA, then nRT = 2.18HA. Integrating these figures yields,

$$W = 2.18HA[\ln(HA) - \ln(HA/2.18)]$$

$$= 2.18HA[\ln(2.18A)].$$

Since A = 1 m²,

$$W = (2.18 \text{ atm})(8{,}000 \text{ m})(\ln 2.18)$$

$$= 13{,}591.43 \text{ m}^3 \cdot \text{atm}$$

$$= (13{,}591.43 \text{ m}^3)(1.0136 \times 10^5 \text{ N/m}^2)$$

$$= 1.378 \times 10^9 \text{ N} \cdot \text{m, or ``Joules''}$$

$$= 3.293 \times 10^8 \text{ cal, for the atmospheric expansion in the column of 1 m}^2 \text{ cross-sectional area.}$$

The reduction in heat load for the entire atmosphere = (calories/m² of cylinder)(area of earth, m²), or $(3.293 \times 10^8 \text{ cal/m}^2)(4)(\pi)(6{,}371.2 \times 10^3)^2 = H_a = 1.68 \times 10^{23}$ cal.

Heat given to the atmosphere by friction. As the raindrops from the canopy fell to earth, heat was generated due to the friction between the raindrops and the air. This heat was approximately equal to the potential energy of the canopy, $H_p = mgZ_{ave}$ or 8.88×10^{22} cal.[10]

10. In this equation m = the weight of the canopy, 6.219×10^{18} kg; g is the acceleration of gravity, 9.8 m/sec²; and Z_{ave} is the "average" height of the canopy, roughly 20,000 ft or 6 km (from 7.23). This yields $H_p = 3.72 \times 10^{23}$ joules or 8.88×10^{22} calories.

Total heat load. The total heat load on the atmosphere created by the vapor canopy was then,

$$H_t = H_l + H_{tc} - H_a + H_p \tag{8.2}$$
$$= 3.86 \times 10^{24} \text{ cal.}$$

If all of this was absorbed by the lower atmosphere, it would be sufficient to raise the atmospheric temperature 2,100° C.

POSSIBLE MEANS OF REDUCING THE HEAT LOAD

The problem of reducing the heat load is *not* unique to the vapor canopy hypothesis. Anyone who believes in a global rainfall and a global flood has precisely the same difficulty in accounting for the heat load. If there were only a few inches of water in the vapor canopy and most of the water for the rainfall did come from volcanic activity, as suggested by some, the same difficulties arise.

In order for rain to fall, it must condense out of the volcanic vapors thrust up into the atmosphere, and if the rain is to fall globally for 40 days through recycled volcanic steam that rises and condenses, all the latent heat of the steam must likewise be released. Assuming that the global average rainfall rate produced by this volcanic steam was 0.5 inches/hour (or even 0.1 in/hr or less), we still have 3.358×10^{24} cal latent heat. Furthermore, all of that steam must be cooled from at least 100° C to 30° C (which adds another 2.172×10^{23} cal of heat).

Finally, without a canopy, there is no removal of heat due to atmospheric expansion as would have occurred under the canopy hypothesis. So the canopy model is not only not unique among Flood models in having a heat load problem, but it actually has less of a problem than those that reject the vapor canopy idea.

Heat loss by radiation. It may appear that the latent heat could be lost into outer space during the 40 days of rain. Seymour Hess summarized the difficulty:

> You suggest precipitation rates of 5 cm per hour or 5 gm/cm²/hr. With latent heat of about 600 cal/gm, there is released 50 cal/cm²/min which must be radiated away. This is 25 times greater than the mean rate at which sunlight falls on the earth. From another point of view, this is the temperature at

which a black body radiates if its temperature is 885° K. I conclude that there is no feasible way to get rid of so much latent heat in a few hours.[11]

So it appears that heat loss by radiation during the 40 days of rain would be insignificant compared to the total heat load.

Heat loss by droplet formation. Some of the latent heat would be removed prior to the Flood because not all of the canopy would be in vapor form. Perhaps several feet of precipitable water could have been stored in clouds near the interface region between the canopy and the troposphere. Through this interface region it is likely that there would be a rapid temperature drop because of decreasing vapor density, and thus small droplet formation is a good possibility.

Heat loss by pre-Flood cooling. In order for the temperature not to increase due to the precipitation of the canopy, most of the heat load ($H_t = 3.86 \times 10^{24}$ cal) must be radiated away prior to the Flood.

So we must direct our attention to mechanisms that could have cooled the canopy and reduced it to cloud droplets and mists prior to the Flood. We have several possibilities.

First, it is plausible to believe that prior to the Flood the entire canopy became a cloud. Although the Scriptures do not mention this, they do speak of rain of a global extent beginning suddenly. This can only occur out of clouds, so the earth must have become shrouded with clouds before the "windows of heaven" were opened. How could this have happened?

A most likely mechanism is that of volcanic activity. The Scriptures seem to mention volcanic activity as part of the Flood itself (Psalms 18:7-15; 104:8; Gen. 7:11), and it is not at all unreasonable to posit that the precipitating mechanism of the Flood was extensive volcanism in the year preceding the Deluge.

Let us assume then that about a year prior to the Flood 30 or 40 volcanoes began to erupt. These volcanoes would throw

11. Dr. Seymour L. Hess, department of meteorology, Florida State University, personal communication, 3 November 1975.

many cubic miles of dust into the canopy and would generate considerable cooling. However, due to the extremely stable nature of the temperature inversion and Taylor stability, they would have little effect on generating a global instability, hence global rainfall, unless the canopy first cooled considerably, so that precipitation could occur on a universal basis. The very fact that there was rain requires us to believe that prior to the Flood, the canopy must have cooled. So only local disturbances would have developed around the area of the eruptions, with the majority of the dust of large particle size falling right back to earth through the bottom of the canopy, with little global effect.[12] The violent updrafts over the volcanic areas would immediately be damped when they penetrated the inversion. Battan notes that updrafts of 50 m/sec are immediately dampened when they encounter strong temperature inversions today.[13]

Although the larger particles would have fallen back to earth quickly, the smaller particles would have been distributed throughout the atmosphere and carried by convection to the top, then they would fall very slowly, taking several years to descend. After the eruption of Krakatoa (1883), it was estimated that it took three years for the dust to settle from the atmosphere.[14]

Because of the presence of the cloud cover of volcanic dust particles at the top of the canopy, up to 30 times more infrared could have been radiated than solar radiation was absorbed.[15] All of the visible light would have been reflected or scattered, and only the ultraviolet and infrared part of the solar spectrum would be absorbed, which constitutes a very small percentage of the solar constant. As a result, no direct beam visible radiation would come to the cloud layer at the base of the canopy, be

12. In the higher regions of the canopy this dust would create a massive cloud. In the lower region, miles below, the area would remain dust free.
13. Louis J. Battan, *Weather*(Englewood Cliffs, N.J.: Prentice-Hall, 1974), p. 25.
14. Humphreys, p. 599.
15. Ibid., p. 596.

Some Problems with the Vapor Canopy Theory

partially absorbed, reflected, and re-radiated as infrared and be "trapped" below. Consequently, the canopy would immediately begin to cool as long as the visible radiation (0.4μ – 0.8μ) was scattered and reflected by the cloud cover at the top of the canopy.[16] Under these conditions, the radiation balance at the top of the canopy would be given by:

$$Q\uparrow = \text{(radiation absorbed)} - \text{(radiation radiated)} \quad (8.3)$$
$$= \pi r^2 (\text{S.C.})(1-A) - 4\pi r^2 \sigma T^4$$

where $Q\uparrow$ = the new upward flux from the top of the canopy, cal/min; S.C. = the solar constant, 1.92 cal/cm²min; A = the albedo of the top of the canopy after dust distribution, 0.5; r = the radius of the earth, $6,371 \times 10^5$ cm; and T = the radiative temperature of the canopy, °K.

The cooling of the canopy takes place in three phases: t_1 = cooling period from 100 °C to condensation point;[17] t_2 = the period during which the latent heat of condensation is being released and radiated into space; and t_3 = the period during which the canopy cools from 100° C to present atmospheric temperature, 25° C.

16. Barrie Hunt's computer model indicates 20 volcanoes the size of Krakatoa would be sufficient to begin a new ice age: "What Happens if the Sun Turns Off?" *Design News*, 5 May 1977, p. 15.
17. Condensation into mists does not necessarily result in rain. In order for rain to occur, the temperature must drop below the boiling point, which it will not do as long as the process of condensation and removal of latent heat is going on. Also, the temperature must drop sufficiently below the boiling point for saturation to occur. Furthermore, condensation nuclei are needed, and they would not be available in the lower regions of the canopy for some time after the volcanic eruptions because the volcanoes would have thrown the dust at least 50 miles into a canopy whose base was only at 3 or 4 miles altitude.

It will be assumed that t_1 is negligible, although it could be calculated using the method outlined for t_3 below.[18]

During t_2 the entire canopy was condensing into fine mist droplets and all the latent heat of the canopy was radiated away into space according to 8.3. During this period the radiating temperature of the canopy would have been a constant 100° C and no rain could have occurred because the canopy temperature was at the boiling point (373° K). Thus, period t_2 = 478 days, or about 16 months.

In order to calculate t_3, an "average" radiating temperature must be determined. With accuracy sufficient for the present approximation, the following may be used:

$$T_{ave} = \left[\frac{T_i^4 \; T_f^4}{2}\right]^{1/4}$$

where T_i = the initial temperature, 373 °K; and T_f = the final temperature, 298 °K. Therefore, T_{ave} = 342 °K.

Assuming that A = 0.8 during the Flood, the value of Q ↑ during the period t_3 = 5.18 × 10^{18} cal/min or 7.46 × 10^{21} cal/day. The time period t_3 occurs during the Flood after the rains begin. The following amount of heat must be removed during this time:

$$H_{t_3} = H_{tc} + H_p - H_a$$
$$= 2.06 \times 10^{23} \text{ cal} + 8.88 \times 10^{22} - 1.68 \times 10^{23}$$
$$= 1.27 \times 10^{23} \text{ cal}$$

Therefore, t_3 = (1.27 × 10^{21} cal)/(7.46 × 10^{21} cal/day)
       = 17 days.

It appears that the entire heat load of the canopy could therefore be removed during the 16 months prior to the Flood and during the Flood itself. Even though the above solutions are

18. The value of t_1 depends upon the calculated temperature profile of the canopy. In chapter 7 we argued that the temperature of the canopy base was 100°C. It could have been slightly lower.

only approximate, there is a final means of heat load removal that would be able to solve much of the problem by itself.

So for about a year before the Flood the earth was shrouded in clouds, sunlight was blocked, and canopy temperatures as well as surface temperatures began to decline. Although this might seem to be a rather lengthy time, it may not necessarily be so; in fact, it could be an indicator of the grace of God. The inhabitants of the antediluvian earth were given a year's warning that something was amiss and that Noah's proclamations of doom were correct. The fact that there is no biblical mention of this one-year phenomenon is not necessarily significant. The biblical account does not mention clouds either, but they surely must have formed in order for it to have rained.

As the canopy cooled over this year-long period, it was reduced to small droplets, mists, and clouds. As a result, the majority of the latent heat was all given up prior to the Flood. Perhaps 15 months prior to the Flood marked the onset of the volcanic activity.

What held these small mist and cloud droplets up during that time? Due to the constant volcanic activity, the tropopause would have been severely disrupted, and the canopy would have been mixed with the lower atmosphere, thus distributing air throughout the canopy while at the same time lowering its base to one or two miles. The presence of this air would provide an atmosphere for these newly formed cloud droplets in which to "float." This, in turn, would delay their arrival as rain at the earth's surface.

Heat loss by mass transport. Although the above means certainly would have reduced the heat load, mass transport of water droplets from the vapor canopy into the oceans would have eliminated it. Simple calculations will show that the entire heat load of the canopy could be dumped into the oceans with virtually no effect on oceanic temperatures.[19]

19. $\Delta T = Q/C_W m$, where Q = the total heat load of the canopy = 3.86×10^{24} cal; C_W = the specific heat of water = 1 cal/gm; and m = the mass of the present oceans = 1.456×10^{27} gm (see "Ocean," in *Van Nostrand's Scientific Encyclopedia*, p. 1670). Therefore, $\Delta T = 0.003$.

What we propose here is that the canopy had cooled drastically due to some of the above considerations. Then as it began to rain, raindrops ranging in temperature from 40° C to 50° C fell into the oceans, carrying all the remaining heat of the canopy with them. So in some sections of the planet a very warm rain would have fallen in the earlier phases of the Flood. This would have been no threat to Noah because this hot rain would not necessarily have been universal. In fact, it would have predominated over the ocean areas where volcanic and orogenic activity causing cooling updrafts would have been minimal. The areas of the canopy over regions of volcanic activity and storm fronts would have been so cool that subfreezing hail and snow would result. The volcanic deposits across the far north and Antarctica suggest that these regions were areas of drastic cooling.

Oxygen Toxicity and Nitrogen Narcosis

A common objection to the canopy hypothesis is that the increased atmospheric pressures under the canopy would lead to oxygen toxicity, and animal life would be impossible.[20]

However, under the model we are presenting this would be no problem. The partial pressure of oxygen under the canopy would be 2.18 times the partial pressure today, or 2.18 × 159.97 mm of Hg = 348.73 mm of Hg. Oxygen toxicity only becomes a problem when the partial pressure of oxygen reaches 380 mm of Hg.[21] So assuming that the oxygen level of the pre-Flood atmosphere was the same as today, 20%, no toxicity would occur under a surface atmospheric pressure of 2.18 atm. In fact, up to

20. Robert E. Kofahl, "Critique of Canopy and Other Models," *Creation Research Society Quarterly* 13 (March 1977):202-6. Kofahl argues that a 1,000 ft. canopy would be impossible on this basis.
21. Vernon B. Mountcastle, ed., *Medical Physiology*, 1:1565. *The McGraw-Hill Encyclopedia of Science and Technology* (1971), 4:284, gives a value of 0.65 atm or 494 mm of Hg of O_2.

51 feet of water could be placed in the water heaven before this would become a problem.

Other factors, however, might make it possible to contain even more than 51 feet of water in such a canopy. Not only would the vapor canopy increase the partial pressure of O_2, but it would also increase the partial pressure of CO_2. This has the effect of requiring higher oxygen tension to saturate the blood.[22] Furthermore, there are fish today that endure enormous oxygen tensions in their blood and have no difficulty with oxygen toxicity. The lining cells of the swim bladder of these deep-swimming fish amazingly enable the fish to sustain 100 atmospheres, 15,790 mm Hg of O_2 with no oxygen poisoning.[23] Perhaps the animals of the pre-Flood world were similarly equipped.

There are other possible ways to contain more than 51 feet in the water heaven with no ill effects to humans. It is possible that, when God set up the water heaven, 50% or more of the present atmosphere was diffused throughout the canopy with the canopy still several miles above the surface of the earth. This would have the effect of reducing the oxygen concentration at the surface of the earth by 50%, so that the partial pressure of oxygen would be 50% × 159.97 × 2.18 = 174.37 mm of Hg of O_2 at the surface under the canopy. Since a partial pressure of 380 mm of Hg can be tolerated, one could increase the amount of precipitable water in the canopy to (380/174)(51 ft) = 111 feet. This would increase the pressure at the canopy base to 0.105 atm (due to the oxygen in the canopy) plus 3.265 atm due to the water vapor = 3.37 atm. As a result, the base of the canopy would be at four kilometers instead of six kilometers (see Equation 7.23).

A related problem involves the decompression that Noah and his family went through during the 40 days of rain when the pressure at the surface dropped from 2.18 atmospheres to 1 atmosphere. However, this again is not a problem, for rule-of-thumb estimates for surfacing from deep-sea chambers suggest

22. Karl F. Lagler, John E. Bardach, and Robert R. Miller, *Ichthyology*, pp. 239-61.
23. Ibid.

five days of ascent for every 1,000 feet of depth under the water.[24] Since the canopy involved only 40 feet of water, the decompression could be accomplished in less than one day.[25]

CLIMATE UNDER THE CANOPY

It is quite likely that under canopy conditions there would have been no rain on the surface of the earth. In fact, in the opinion of the meteorologists consulted, the earth would have been watered by "mists."[26] This is a striking parallel to where Moses stated that prior to the Flood there was no rain and that the earth was watered by "mists" (Gen. 2:5).

Under these conditions, however, an apparent problem arises: how were the river systems replenished without rain? Robert Whitelaw has summarized the difficulty:

> First of all, if there were such a tranquil pre-flood world, without atmospheric turbulence either in latitude or altitude and if for 2,000 years the entire earth was daily watered by mist alone, where did all the mist-water come from? We may not have it condensed out of the canopy far above. Nor may we invoke the present hydrologic cycle to bring it from the sea, for had there been winds to carry it there would soon be clouds, rain and rainbows. But if the mist was merely ground moisture which daily evaporated and nightly condensed, how did none of it escape into a stream and thence to the sea? And if it did, how was it ever replaced? And if it did not, how could there be any rivers such as Pison, Gihon, Hiddekel and Euphrates, plus

---

24. Mountcastle, 1:1587. Also many thanks to John R. Meyer, Ph. D., assistant professor of physiology and biophysics, University of Louisville Health Sciences Center, Louisville, Kentucky, personal communication, September 1976, for his help in quantifying this matter.
25. This value is extrapolated from decompression curves in Mountcastle, 1:1588.
26. Larry Vardiman, Ph. D. in meteorology, Bureau of Reclamation, Denver, Colorado, personal communication, May 1976; Henry Voss, Ph. D. in electrical engineering, University of Illinois Aeronomy Laboratory, personal communication, 26 February 1977.

Some Problems with the Vapor Canopy Theory

surely others not named? They could not spring from glaciers or snowfields since without rain or snow these sources would soon vanish; and if from underground springs, what replaced the ground water?[27]

The answer to Whitelaw's objection is that he errs in assuming that the canopy requires no winds. All the canopy would prohibit is major atmospheric circulation systems (global circulation), but local winds and gentle breezes would be common, due to the differences in albedo between various ground covers and the water surfaces and the different heat capacity of ocean and land. Because the ocean has a greater heat capacity than the land, its temperature does not vary much during the day. The land, however, becomes much warmer.

Battan summarizes:

> Along coast lines, it is common to experience sea breezes on summer afternoons. They occur because the sun's rays increase the temperature of the land and the air just above it more than they raise the temperature of the air over the water. As a result, a low-altitude pressure gradient develops from water to land. Cool air from over the sea (or lake) moves over the land and bathes the coast with sea breezes. Over the land, air rises, moves out to sea aloft, and sinks over the sea in a form of a convection cell.[28]

As a result, there would have been a continuous gentle movement of breezes from water to land areas all over the world, carrying mist which would settle on the land at night when the land cooled and the air over it became saturated.

Furthermore, such a movement of mist might be adequate to replenish the river systems of the ancient world. The average global rainfall today is 0.27 cm/day.[29] This figure is an average over the entire land and sea areas. So a rather small amount of rainfall on a global basis accounts for all the river systems and lakes in our world today. This rainfall occurs over very small geographical areas and accumulates in underground springs and natural reservoirs. However, under the canopy, the mist from the seas would be spread over a broader geographical area.

27. Robert L. Whitelaw, "The Canopy Theory and the Rift-Drift-Shift Theory," personal communication, 16 February 1976.
28. Battan, p. 34.
29. Ibid., p. 81.

The precise manner in which this mist was developed in sufficient quantities to supply the river systems remains to be worked out. It is certainly possible that the Pishon, Gihon, Tigris, and Euphrates (Gen. 2:10-14) were supplied by underground springs. It is also possible that the hydrologic system of the ancient world was considerably different and did not have major river systems but only small creeks and streams and large inland lakes. It is also possible that much of the antediluvian hydrological cycle was subterranean rather than atmospheric.

An attempt to quantify the mechanics of such a hydrological cycle was being attempted by D. Russell Humphreys (Ph. D. in physics, research engineer at the General Electric Company High Voltage Laboratory) in 1978.[30] Arguing from a number of biblical passages that might suggest a vast reservoir of subterranean water in the antediluvian world,[31] Humphreys proposes that the release of these waters under high pressure would result in a mist literally going up from the earth (see Gen. 2:5). In view of the fact that the storage capacity of the earth for such waters is massive, he suggests that the earth could be watered almost indefinitely by such geysers.

As the water was released in this manner, it would suddenly expand and cool, thus not adding significantly to the heat budget of the pre-Flood troposphere, yet at the same time resulting in a heavy dew regime. It is also possible that the source of the water for the major river systems was likewise large reservoirs of water at great depth. Statements in Scripture such as, "With blessings of heaven above, blessings of the deep that lies beneath" (Gen. 49:25), do seem to imply the existence of such subterranean water. The word translated "deep" here is t^ehôm, the same word used for the primeval ocean in the Creation account (Gen. 1:2). Certainly the phrase "the fountains of the great deep" (Gen. 7:11) indicates such a reservoir in view of

30. D. Russell Humphreys, "Is the Earth's Core Water? Part One: The Biblical Evidence," *Creation Research Society Quarterly* 15 (December 1978): 141-47.
31. See Gen. 1:1-2; 2:5-6; 7:11; 49:25; Exod. 20:4; Deut. 5:8; Job 38: 6-11; Psalms 24:1-2; 135:6; Prov. 8:24-28; Ezek. 31:14-16; 2 Pet. 3:5-6.

Some Problems with the Vapor Canopy Theory   283

the fact that it was the eruption of these fountains that resulted in the majority of the flood water. The Scriptures do say the earth was watered by a mist, and it must be assumed that the mist was sufficient.

The Dynamics of the Canopy

As mentioned in chapter 7, due to the fact that the canopy exhibits an environmental lapse rate greater than the critical lapse rate, great convection cells would have developed. At the same time, because there was much less radiation received at the poles than at the equator, there would have been a large movement of water vapor poleward to carry the heat to the poles and so balance the heat budget.

It may seem unlikely that such a mechanism could indeed result in an equal temperature at the bottom of the canopy at the poles and the bottom of the canopy at the equator. Certainly today, even with the tremendous velocities of the jet stream, no such temperature equilibrium is achieved. Why should it have been achievable in the canopy?

The answer to this objection is that precisely the same situation prevails on the planet Venus. The temperatures at the poles and at the equator are the same even though the radiation received is different. At present there are no completely satisfactory theories to account for this. Goody comments, "The temperature is the same at the equator as at the poles. Our theory still predicts that σT^4 is equal to the absorbed flux of solar radiation; although this is small at the poles and large at the equator, no variation to T_e is, in fact, observed."[32]

Since the only parallel situation known reveals a pole to pole greenhouse, there is no obvious reason for denying that the same situation existed when earth was surrounded by its ancient water heaven.

Some other parallels from Venus are instructive. No less than four temperature inversions have been observed at different

32. Goody and Walker, p. 65. T_e = effective temperature, see Equation (7.6) where $Te^4 = F_v/\sigma$

altitudes.[33] Also, at least two major systems of jetlike spiral streaks in each hemisphere have been noted. They merge into a bright polar ring at 50° latitude. There is no evidence of instability on a global scale in these features or evidence of structures similar to large-scale cyclonic eddies.[34] It is theorized that these jet streams convey sufficient heat to the poles to keep them at the same temperature as at the equator.

So there does not seem to be any a priori difficulty in the canopy hypothesis based on concerns from atmospheric dynamics and balancing the heat budget.

Infrared Cooling

Some have expressed concern over the viability of the vapor canopy model in that infrared cooling at the top of the canopy could result in condensation of the canopy as rain at the top.[35]

Infrared cooling occurs as a result of the differences between the radiation spectrum of the re-radiated radiation from the earth and that of the sun. At the top of the canopy, little solar radiation is absorbed because the sun does not radiate principally in the wavelengths where water vapor absorbs. The bulk of solar radiation is in the near ultraviolet to near infrared ($0.2\mu - 0.9\mu$). However, the canopy only radiates in the infrared and mostly beyond 0.9μ. So at the top of the canopy little radiation is being absorbed, and much is being radiated; as a result, a net cooling would result. Several factors offset this difficulty.

First, at the top of the canopy the temperature does not need to be as high in order to maintain the vapor in the vapor phase.

33. H. T. Tyler et al., "Venus: Mass, Gravity Field, Atmosphere, and Ionosphere as Measured by the Mariner 10 Dual-Frequency Radio System," *Science* 183 (29 March 1974):1299.
34. Bruce Murray et al., "Venus: Atmospheric Motion and Structure from Mariner 10 Pictures," *Science* 183 (29 March 1974):1311.
35. Fred M. Snell, Ph. D. in atmospheric physics, department of biophysical sciences, State University of New York at Buffalo, personal communication, December 1976.

This is because the amount of precipitable water above an "upper" level of the canopy is considerably less than that above a "lower" level.

Second, due to photodissociation of water vapor and the subsequent formation of ozone, an immense ozone layer would rest at the top of the canopy. Ozone will not condense out as rain when temperature drops, and as a result will "trap" the infrared radiation from below in a kind of "greenhouse" at the top of the canopy, keeping the area there much hotter.

Third, we must remember that the effects of the convection cells, created by the super-critical environmental temperature lapse rate of the canopy, will cause the cooler vapor to sink into the hotter areas, and an isothermal canopy would tend to result. These convection cells would keep the top of the canopy nearly as hot as the bottom.

Conclusion

Although much remains to be done, we can see that the model presented in the preceding two chapters is based on well-established physical principles. There are several unsolved problems, but it is no longer possible to dismiss the canopy theory as unsound scientifically. Before moving on to the effects of the canopy's condensation, we will undertake a brief examination of its optical transparency.

Chapter 9

Radiation and the Vapor Canopy

A frequent objection raised against the vapor canopy hypothesis is that such a quantity of precipitable water in the atmosphere would result in the total eclipse of all starlight. Often this objection is based on the incorrect assumption that the canopy has many miles of precipitable water.[1] Others have argued against the notion of a vapor canopy on the grounds that it is not helpful from a scientific standpoint in that water vapor will block out visible light just as effectively as a liquid water canopy.[2]

The latter objection is based on the faulty assumption that the interaction of light with water is independent of the phase in which it exists. In actual fact, however, the phase in which the water exists (liquid or vapor) has a significant effect on how it will attenuate visible radiation. Furthermore, more light will be blocked out by water in vapor form than water in liquid form. So one would hardly opt for vapor canopy idea solely on the grounds that it solves the scientific problem of visibility through the canopy.

Since the Genesis account seems to indicate that men were able to see the stars, it would seem necessary that the thickness of the canopy could not be such that it would cause the extinction of visible star radiation (Gen. 1:16). It has been suggested

1. Donald W. Patten, "The Pre-flood Greenhouse Effect," in *A Symposium on Creation II*, p. 24. Also, see Robert E. Kofahl, "Critique of Canopy and other Models," *Creation Research Society Quarterly* 13 (March 77):202-05, where a 1,000-foot canopy is assumed.
2. Stanley Udd, "The Early Atmosphere," p. 65.

that the stars did not become visible until after the Flood in order to avoid this difficulty; they were only *created* (but not visible) on the fourth day. However, because the ancients were clearly able to calculate time in years, the sun and the moon must have been visible (Gen. 5). Since Moses makes no distinction between the apparent visibility of the various luminaries (Gen. 1:14-17), and since the sun and the moon are declared to be visible, it seems more natural to assume that he intended to teach that the stars also were visible to Adam. It is only the physical problems involved of starlight penetrating such a vast vapor blanket that would cause some to entertain this unlikely interpretation. Hence the question remains: What would be the effect of the proposed 40 feet of precipitable water distributed throughout many miles of a thermal vapor blanket on the visual appearance of the antediluvian heavens?

THE MAGNITUDE OF STARLIGHT

Astronomers traditionally posit six magnitudes of starlight on the basis of the visibility of stars to the naked eye. This classification was made on the basis of visual observations of ancient Greek astronomers. A magnitude of "1" was the magnitude of the *brightest star* visible to ancient stargazers, and a magnitude of "6" was the dimmest. With the advent of modern telescopes greater precision has been introduced into this scheme. It was found that the ancient classification fell into a nearly perfect mathematical ratio of intensities between magnitudes of about 2.5:1. This ratio between magnitudes has been officially standardized at $(100)^{0.2}$: 1, or about 2.512:1.[3] A 100-watt bulb held 6.25 miles away has the same visual intensity on the human eye as a star of the first magnitude.[4] The sun has a visual magnitude of -26.72.[5] (The negative sign is used to extend this system to describe the magnitudes of celestial objects

3. W. Kruse and W. Dieckuoss, *The Stars*, p. 61.
4. Shea L. Valley, ed., *Handbook of Geophysics and Space Environments*, pp. 21-29.
5. Cecilia Payne-Gaposchkin, *Introduction to Astronomy*, p. 268.

having much brighter intensities than 1.) Sirius, the brightest star, has a magnitude of -1.6, instead of 1, under this standardized system.[6] Our modern telescopes have now pulled in stars whose magnitude is +24.[7] This system gives us the relative intensities of starlight as it appears to the human eye. So a star of the first magnitude is 2.512 times as bright in appearance as a star of the second magnitude, and 100 times, exactly, as bright as a star of the sixth magnitude. A simple equation for the relationships between star magnitudes is:[8]

$$\frac{I_2}{I_1} = 10^{0.4 \, \Delta m} \qquad \Delta m = m_1 - m_2, \qquad (9.1)$$

where m_1 and m_2 are the visual magnitude numbers, and the I_1 and I_2 refer to the relative intensity of the starlight at those magnitudes usually expressed in lumens per unit area. Table 9.1 describes the relative intensities among the six magnitudes of visible stars.

TABLE 9.1

RELATIVE INTENSITIES OF VISIBLE STARS

VISUAL MAGNITUDE	RELATIVE INTENSITY	NUMBER OF STARS OF THAT MAGNITUDE[9]
1	1.00	20
2	0.40	65
3	0.16	200
4	0.063	500
5	0.025	1,400
6	0.010	5,000
		Total 7,185

6. Kruse and Dieckuoss, p. 76.
7. Valley, pp. 21-29.
8. Ibid.

A star of magnitude 3 is only 0.16 times as bright in appearance to the human eye as a star of magnitude 1, and so on.

In order to get a practical grasp as to what these numbers mean, consider the following comparisons. The full moon has a magnitude of -12,[10] and the sun, having a visual magnitude of -26.72, is therefore 772,680 times brighter than the moon. A common value for the illuminance of a 0 magnitude star is 2.54×10^{-10} lm/cm² (incident intensity at the top of the earth's atmosphere).[11] This is equivalent to 2.36×10^{-7} lm/ft² (that is, foot candles). The sun, on the other hand, has an incident intensity at the top of the atmosphere of about 12,000 candles.[12] So the sun is 5×10^{10} times brighter than a zero magnitude star.[13] A 100-watt incandescent lamp at a distance of one foot gives about 150 footcandles.[14] Table 9.2 gives some comparisons of various intensities of various light sources. (There may be some discrepancies among the figures given here, for they are from various compilations, in which somewhat different conditions may have been assumed. But the figures will serve to indicate the orders of magnitude involved.)

9. William Tyler Olcott and Edmund W. Putnam, *Field Book of the Skies*, p. 498.
10. Kruse and Dieckuoss, p. 62.
11. Dale Pleticha, Ph. D., Cornell University, astrophysics department, personal communication, 23 February 1976; see J. Thewlis, gen. ed., *Encyclopaedic Dictionary of Physics*, 7:2, gives a value of 2.4×10^{-10} lm/cm² for incident intensity of a 0 magnitude star.
12. George Shortley and Dudley Williams, *Elements of Physics*, 2:505.
13. Computing from (9.1), an exact value of 4.875×10^{10} times brighter is computed.
14. Shortley and Williams, 2:504.

TABLE 9.2

LUMINANCES AND VISUAL MAGNITUDES OF STANDARD LIGHT SOURCES[15]

LIGHT SOURCE	VISUAL MAGNITUDE	APPROXIMATE AVERAGE LUMINANCE (Cd/cm^2)[16]
Sun	-26.72	160,000.00
Moon	-12.00	0.25
Flashbulb	-24.01	16,000.00
Candle Flame	-13.50	1.00
Fluorescent Lamp	-13.28	0.82
Sirius (brightest star)	-1.6	9.12 × 10^{-7}

Also, the total light of all the stars in the heavens is equal to that of 1,092 stars of visual magnitude 1.0.[17]

A final point needs to be emphasized. The eye has different levels of sensitivity to different wavelengths, (such as colors) of the visible electromagnetic spectrum. The visible spectrum ranges from about 4,000 Angstroms to 7,000 Angstroms. The 7,000 A end of the spectrum approaches infrared radiation (heat), and the 4,000 A end of the spectrum approaches ultraviolet (the kind of light that produces a suntan). An

15. Luminance refers to strength of light received. For astronomical sources this refers to light received at the earth; for the other sources, at a typical distance.
16. *Handbook of Chemistry and Physics*, p. E-205. Note that these values are only approximate, so the ratio of the luminances will not always equal the ratio of the visual magnitudes.
17. Olcott and Putnam, p. 496.

Angstrom unit, indicated by A, is 10^{-8}cm. The eye is nearly 100 times as sensitive to yellow-green light (5,500 A) as it is to either infrared or ultraviolet.[18] For this reason, one's judgment of brightness depends primarily on yellow-green, even though the stars radiate all wavelengths.[19] The average wavelength of light from the stars perceived by the human eye is 5,280 A.[20]

THE ATTENUATION OF STARLIGHT

As starlight penetrates the atmosphere, its intensity is reduced (attenuated) by absorption and scattering. The importance of absorption on visible radiation is relatively insignifinant and can be neglected.[21] Scattering, however, is very important and is of two basic kinds: Rayleigh and very small particle (aerosols). Both of these scattering phenomena obey Beer's Law:[22]

$$I = I_0 e^{-KL(\sec \theta)}, \qquad (9.2)$$

where I_0 is the "incident" intensity of the starlight at the top of the earth's atmosphere; I is the resultant intensity after being scattered by a medium whose path length is L; and θ is the angle from the vertical (zenith) at which the light ray enters the atmosphere. The term, KL, is called the "optical depth" of the

STAR I_0 ⟶ | L | ⟶ I EARTH
ATMOSPHERE

Fig. 9.1 — Rayleigh Scattering and Beer's Law.

18. Shortley and Williams, 2:493.
19. Payne-Gaposchkin, p. 262.
20. Ibid., p. 278.
21. Valley, p. 7-6.
22. Horace Robert Byers, *General Meteorology*, p. 32. Strictly, this relation holds only for the assumption of a flat earth. However, it is a sufficiently good approximation to the true situation.

medium. The equation for the coefficient of Rayleigh scattering, K, for a gas, is given by[23]

$$K = \frac{32\pi^3 (n-1)^2}{3 N\lambda^4}, \tag{9.3}$$

where N = the number of molecules/cm³; λ = the wavelength in centimeters, and n = the refractive index. Since the term (n-1) is directly proportional to the number density,[24] N, K is directly proportional to the number density of the attenuating medium. The Rayleigh coefficient is inversely proportional to the fourth power of the wavelength. It is this strong wavelength dependence of K that causes our sky to appear blue and our sunsets red. When λ is large, KL is small and there is less scattering. So at the 7,000 A (red) end of the spectrum there is less scattering than there is at the 4,000 A (blue) end. Hence blue light is scattered to a much greater extent by the air molecules and we have a blue sky. As the optical path of the light ray increases, blue light is scattered so much that very little remains in direct sunlight compared with the red wavelengths. This is why the sun appears red close to the horizon. "The ratio for blue light at 4,250 A to that for red light at 6,500 A under the same conditions would be $(650/425)^4 = 5.48$. Thus, the scattering of blue light is 5.48 times the scattering for red light."[25]

> Sunlight, which is basically white, often reaches the earth with a reddish tinge. This is especially noticeable at sunset when the light passes through its longest path of atmosphere, and is explained by the fact that the blue light has been scattered by the atmosphere and only the reddish portions reach us directly. . . . On the earth, scattering is the process mainly responsible for reducing the visibility or distance from which objects can barely be seen. Under hazy or dusty conditions the light from a distant object may be completely attenuated by scattering before reaching the eye. Direct absorption by the haze particles is of some importance, but scattering is the main effect.[26]

23. Ibid., p. 28.
24. Ibid., p. 29.
25. Ibid., p. 28.
26. Ibid.

Because K is directly proportional to the density of the attenuating medium, it follows that the denser the medium, the larger KL will be, hence the greater the scattering. This holds true for gases. However, when water is in the liquid phase, its molecules are more highly ordered and interact less frequently with a penetrating beam of light; so it is actually easier for light to penetrate water in the liquid phase. This will be demonstrated in the following discussion.

In order to calculate the optical depth of the pre-Flood atmosphere, which is assumed to contain the gases of the present atmosphere plus 40 feet of water in vapor form, the optical depth of the water vapor must be added to the optical depth of today's atmosphere. The optical depth for Rayleigh scattering (the Rayleigh optical depth or optical depth of a Rayleigh atmosphere) has already been worked out for the standard atmosphere at all wavelengths. The KL_p (for $\lambda = 5{,}280$ A) of the present atmosphere with aerosols present is 0.346.[27] For an approximation for the pre-Flood troposphere this value will be used even though the aerosol levels of the pre-Flood atmosphere were probably considerably lower.

Above the pre-Flood troposphere was the vapor canopy. It is now necessary to derive an expression for the KL of the vapor canopy. It will be helpful if this can be done as a function of the amount of precipitable water in the canopy and independent of any particular temperature, pressure, or density distribution. John R. Baumgardner suggested the following derivation.[28]

To find the optical depth KL, the expression for the Rayleigh scattering coefficient (9.3) is integrated over the optical path through the canopy. Thus,

---

27. Extrapolated from tables in *Handbook of Geophysics and Space Environments*, pp. 7-21-27.
28. John R. Baumgardner, M.S., is presently completing his Ph.D. in geophysics, and has several years experience as an optical physicist in laser physics with the air force; personal communication, May 1976.

Radiation and the Vapor Canopy

$$KL = \int_{\text{optical path}} \frac{32\pi^3(n-1)^2}{3N\lambda^4} dx, \qquad (9.4)$$

where n is the local index of refraction of water vapor, λ is the wavelength in cm (5,280 × 10⁻⁸), and N is the local number density in particles/cm³. It is desired to derive an expression for KL in terms of ω, the centimeters of precipitable water in the canopy.

Let us change the variable of integration from distance x through the vapor to distance ω through an equivalent depth of liquid water. The conversion factor would be

$$\frac{dx}{d\omega} = \frac{\text{density of liquid}}{\text{density of vapor}}$$

$$= \frac{1 \text{ gm/cm}^3}{\left[\dfrac{18.0153 \text{gm/mole}}{2.24 \times 10^4 \text{cm}^3/\text{mole}}\right] \left[\dfrac{N}{N_{STP}}\right]}$$

$$= 1.243 \times 10^3 \left[\frac{N}{N_{STP}}\right]$$

where N_{STP} is the number density of a gas at standard temperature and pressure (STP). Furthermore, the term (n-1) is proportional to the number density N, and at STP for water vapor it has the value 2.54 × 10⁻⁴.[29] Therefore, we may write (9.4) as

$$KL = \frac{32\pi^3}{3\lambda^4} \int_{\text{optical path}} \frac{[(2.54 \times 10^{-4}(N/N_{STP})]^2 [1.243 \times 10^3 (N_{STP}/N)]}{N} d\omega$$

and observe that the number density dependence cancels inside the integral. With N_{STP} = Avogadro's number/molar volume = 2.69 × 10¹⁹ particles/cm³ (that is, 6.0238 × 10²³/2.24 × 10⁴), we obtain:

---

29. *Handbook of Chemistry and Physics*, p. E-223, where n varies from 1.000249-1.000259.

$$KL = \frac{32\pi^3(2.54 \times 10^{-4})(1.243 \times 10^3)}{3.4(2.69 \times 10^{19})}\omega$$

or $KL = 1.269 \times 10^{-4}\omega$. (9.5)

If the canopy contains 40 feet of precipitable water, $\omega = 1{,}219$ cm, and the optical depth of the canopy $KL_C = 0.155$.

It seems reasonable to posit that when God lifted the water above the firmament, it was pure water with no aerosols present. If this is so, the canopy would be pure water vapor with no particulate matter. However, because of the ionization of the water vapor and some meteorite dust, probably some aerosols accumulated in the canopy. True aerosols are particles with a radius of about 3×10^{-4} cm; those larger than that will settle out.[30] Meteoritic dust is generally that size or larger. So it would either settle out of the canopy or, in most cases, burn up as it hit it and never get through. However, meteoritic dust and small ions (particles with a radius less than 2×10^{-6} cm) would be found in the canopy and would have some effect on Rayleigh scattering.

In the present atmosphere, the KL_p of a pure Rayleigh atmosphere is increased by 0.23 to account for the presence of aerosols. So although the computed value for a Rayleigh atmosphere is 0.116, a value of 0.346 or 0.35 is used.[31] Since there was no industrial pollution, lower winds, and high humidity, it will be assumed that the aerosol level of the canopy was less than 50% of today's aerosol level. So 50% of $0.23 = 0.115$ and will be added to the computed canopy KL_C for a generous approximation.

The total optical depth for the canopy including aerosols would then be $0.155 + 0.115 = 0.27$, yielding a KL for the pre-Flood atmosphere of:

30. Byers, pp. 342-43.
31. Extrapolated from tables in *Handbook of Geophysics and Space Environment*, p. 7-21-27.

$$KL_t = KL_p \times KL_c$$

$$= 0.346 + 0.27$$

$$= 0.616. \tag{9.6}$$

For purposes of comparison, we may now calculate the attenuation that would occur if the canopy had remained in liquid form. The expression for the Rayleigh coefficient for water in its liquid phase is given by[32]

$$K = \frac{24\pi^3 N(n^2-1)/(n^2+1)V^2}{\lambda^4},$$

where N is the number density of liquid water at STP = Avogadro's number divided by the gram molecular weight of water or $6.0225 \times 10^{23}/18.0153 = 3.43 \times 10^{22}$ particles/cm³. V is the volume of a water molecule and is given by $4/3\pi r^3$, where r is the radius of a water vapor molecule or 1.442×10^{-8}cm.[33] Solving for V, we get 1.258×10^{-23}cm³. The term n refers to the index of refraction of liquid water at STP = 1.33348.[34] For a wavelength of $5,280 \times 10^{-8}$cm, $K = 3.97 \times 10^{-5}$. Since L = 40 feet or 1,219 cm, KL_c for a liquid water canopy would be 0.0484. So it is apparent that water in the liquid form will attenuate less radiation of this wavelength (5,280 A) than water in the vapor phase. The KL of a vapor canopy is $0.155/0.0484 = 3.2$ times as great as the KL of a liquid canopy.

Starlight (5,280 A) will not be eclipsed by Rayleigh scattering until KL approaches 4.605.[35] So before starlight would be eclipsed by the *vapor* canopy, over 1,071 feet of water would

32. Byers, p. 28.
33. Leonard B. Loeb, *The Kinetic Theory of Gases*, p. 643.
34. *Handbook of Chemistry and Physics*, p. E-222.
35. See discussion on pp. 300-301.

have to be placed above the pre-Flood troposphere (for visibility from directly overhead).[36]

VISIBILITY IN THE PRE-FLOOD HEAVENS

What did Adam and Noah see when they looked up into the night sky or gazed at the daylight sun under canopy conditions? Some rather interesting phenomena may have marked the antediluvian heavens. From Equation (9.2), we see that the attenuation of the starlight will vary with the zenith angle. For the simple case of light coming in directly from above (zenith = 0), $KL = 0.616$ [from (9.6)]. So the pre-Flood intensity I_{pf} is related to the intensity I_0 incident of the top of the canopy by

$$I_{pf}/I_0 = e^{-0.616}$$

or

$$I_{pf} = 0.54 I_0.$$

In other words, the light of wavelength 5,280 A when it hit the eye of Adam was only 54% as bright as when it entered the top of the pre-Flood canopy.

Since the optical depth of today's atmosphere is about 0.35, the present day intensity I_p is

$$I_p = 0.70\ I_0.$$

Therefore,
$$I_{pf} = 0.77\ I_p.$$

36. Canopy optical depth resulting in total extinction = (total extinction optical depth) − (optical depth of present atmosphere + estimated increase in optical depth of canopy due to presence of aerosols) = 4.605 − (0.346 + 0.115) = 4.144. From (9.5), $\omega = KL/1.269 \times 10^{-4} = 4.144/1.269 \times 10^{-4}$ = 32,656 cm = 1,071 ft. This applies for a zenith angle of 0.

Radiation and the Vapor Canopy

From this, the following adjustments in star magnitudes relative to today would have existed on the pre-Flood earth as shown in Table 9.3. The dimmest stars visible to man are those of the sixth magnitude where their relative intensity is 0.010. Hence, on the adjusted intensity scale, which gives the pre-Flood starlight intensity relative to today, any stars which are less than 0.01 will not be visible. This means that only 6th magnitude starlight will be eclipsed on the pre-Flood earth. All of the rest of the stars would be visible.

TABLE 9.3

PRE-FLOOD ADJUSTED INTENSITIES RELATIVE TO TODAY

MAGNITUDE	RELATIVE INTENSITY	ADJUSTED INTENSITIES FOR PRE-FLOOD RELATIVE TO TODAY, $I_{pf} = (0.77) I_p$	NUMBER OF STARS VISIBLE TODAY
1	1.00	0.770	20
2	0.40	0.306	65
3	0.16	0.123	200
4	0.063	0.049	500
5	0.025	0.019	1,400
6	0.010	0.008	5,000

Due to the skylight of the moon, only stars of magnitudes 1-4 are regularly visible today.[37] Hence in Table 9.1, the 7,185 potentially visible stars are actually visible only under the most ideal conditions of no moon backlight. Therefore stars of relative intensity 0.025 and dimmer are not normally visible today. A look at the adjusted intensity scale reveals that 0.025 falls between the 4th and 5th magnitudes on the pre-Flood earth also. Hence the pre-Flood sky would often have looked approximately like today's when the full moon was out. When the

37. Dr. Frank Clark, professor of astronomy, physics department at the University of Kentucky, personal communication, February 1976.

moon is dark today, about 2,500 stars are visible at any one place and time.[38] (People living in the northern hemisphere cannot see some of the stars visible to the people living in the southern hemisphere, and we can view only a fraction of the sky at one time. Also, the optical depth is greater near the horizon, causing dimmer stars not to be visible there.) Assuming the same percentage applied to the antediluvian heavens, 34%, this means that on a clear night with no moon, Adam potentially could see 34% of all stars of magnitudes 1-5 or 34% × 2,185 = 743 stars. At any one time, however, only those of the 743 that were high enough in the sky would actually be visible. Adam did not see the 1,700 6th-magnitude stars (34% × 5,000) that are visible today.

In the above discussion, it was assumed that the zenith angle was zero, that is, only starlight coming in directly from above was considered. Now we must examine the effects of various zenith angles.

It is obvious from (9.2) that as the zenith angle increases, the optical depth KL (sec θ) will increase. Now since a hundredfold increase in scattering will reduce a first magnitude star to sixth magnitude, that is, to the verge of visibility, it follows that an increased optical depth which satisfies the relation

$$e^{-KL(\sec \theta)} = 0.01$$

will yield the value of KL for extinction of all starlight by the earth's atmosphere. This relation is satisfied when KL (sec θ) = 4.605. Now at what zenith angle, θ, will this occur? Since the pre-Flood KL was calculated to be 0.616 and the present KL = .35, an increase in optical depth of 4.605 − 0.266 = 4.339 is needed.[39] So sec $\theta_{ext} = \frac{4.339}{0.616} = 7.043$, and $\theta_{ext} = 82°$, where θ_{ext} = the extinction zenith angle. This means that all stars at a greater distance than 82° from the perpendicular will not be visible (all stars 8° above the horizon and lower). As the zenith angle varies, more and more stars will come into view as the vertical is approached. Table 9.4 presents the angles at which

38. Olcott and Putnam, p. 498.
39. The value 0.266 is the difference between KL_c and KL_p = 0.616 − 0.35 = 0.266.

Radiation and the Vapor Canopy

stars of various magnitudes will come into view. The starlight of each magnitude will be eclipsed when the optical path is such that it will reduce the starlight of that particular magnitude to the intensity of the sixth magnitude.

As mentioned above, an increase of the optical depth to 4.605 will reduce a first magnitude star to sixth magnitude, that is, to the verge of visibility. What increase in optical depth would be necessary to reduce a second, third, fourth, and fifth magnitude star to a sixth magnitude? This may be calculated from Equation (9.1).

$$\frac{I_2}{I_1} = 10^{-0.4(m_2 - m_1)}$$

The intensity ratio I_6/I_m between a sixth magnitude star and one of another magnitude, m, is given by $10^{-0.4(6-m)}$. Since that ratio represents the increase in optical depth necessary to extinguish the starlight of that magnitude, it follows that the value of $e^{-KL\sec\theta}$ that equals that ratio is the value for extinction. So by taking the natural log of I_6/I_m (the natural log of $10^{-0.4(6-m)}$) the value of $KL \sec \theta$ for extinction can be determined and from this the value of θ. As discussed above, relative to today 0.266 must be subtracted from the optical depth value to determine the actual optical depth increase over today's values for total eclipse.

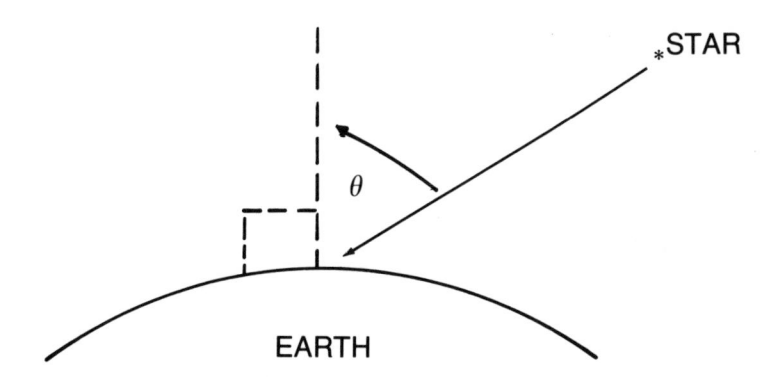

Fig. 9.2 — The Effect of a Greater Zenith Angle, θ, on the Optical Path of a Light Ray.

302   The Waters Above: Earth's Pre-Flood Vapor Canopy

TABLE 9.4

ANGLES ABOVE THE HORIZON (90−θ) AT WHICH STARS OF VARIOUS MAGNITUDES WOULD BECOME VISIBLE UNDER THE CANOPY COMPARED WITH TODAY

MAGNITUDE	6−m	$10^{-0.4}$ (Δm)	OPTICAL DEPTH INCREASE FOR TOTAL ECLIPSE ln (I_6/I_m) −0.266	θ_{ext} (CANOPY)	θ_{ext} (TODAY)	ANGLE ABOVE HORIZON UNDER CANOPY (90−θ_{ext})
1	5	0.010	4.339	82	86	8
2	4	0.025	3.422	80	85	10
3	3	0.063	2.499	76	83	14
4	2	0.158	1.579	67	80	23
5	1	0.398	0.655	20	68	70

The angle (90 − θ) is the angle above the horizon at which stars of the magnitudes 1, 2, 3, 4, 5 respectively will first come into view. In Figure 9.3 the angles are degrees above the horizon and the magnitude numbers are the magnitudes of stars that will be visible at those angles.

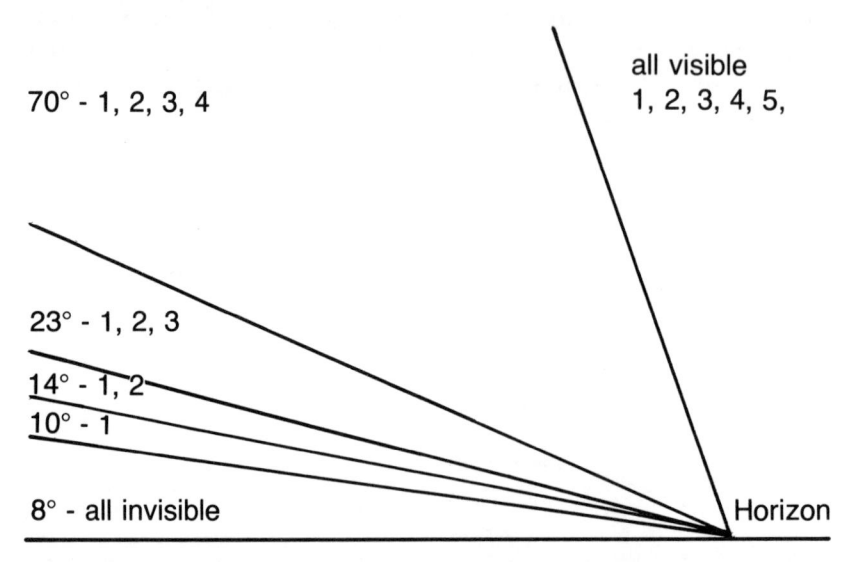

70° - 1, 2, 3, 4

all visible
1, 2, 3, 4, 5,

23° - 1, 2, 3
14° - 1, 2
10° - 1

8° - all invisible   Horizon

Fig. 9.3 — Angles above the Horizon at Which Stars of Various Magnitudes Would Come into View Under the Canopy.

It is evident that even though each magnitude of star is distributed uniformly throughout the heavens, only a fraction of the total sky is visible for each magnitude. The area of the sky for each magnitude varies with the zenith angle. The equation for the area of the sky as a function of the angle θ is,

$$A = 4\pi r^2 \sin^2(\theta/2), \tag{9.7}$$

where θ is the zenith angle.

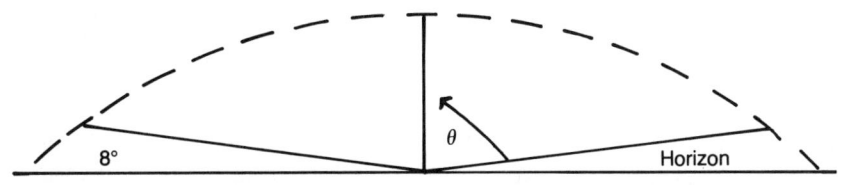

Fig. 9.4 — Section of the Pre-Flood Sky in Which Stars Were Visible.

For first magnitude stars in the pre-Flood heavens $\theta = 82$. Hence the ratio of the area of the sky visible today, A_p, to that visible under the canopy, A_c, is,

$$\frac{A_p}{A_c} = \frac{\sin^2(82/2)}{\sin^2(86/2)} = \frac{0.43}{0.47} = 0.91.$$

This means that 91% of today's sky was available for first magnitude stars before the Flood.

From equation (9.7) it is evident that the fraction of the heavens that were visible for each magnitude relative to today's heavens is A_c/A_p. So although 743 stars were potentially visible to Adam,[40] only a percentage of that number was visible at any one time.

When Adam looked up into the antediluvian heavens, assuming 40 feet of precipitable water in the vapor canopy, he saw about 255 stars on a clear night when the moon was dark (see Table 9.5). If the moon was full, the fifth magnitude stars would have been obscured, and he would have seen only 209 stars.[41] So when the canopy condensed and Noah left the ark, he

---

40. See discussion on pp. 299-300.
41. The number of stars visible under the canopy (255) at one time, minus 5th magnitude stars potentially visible under the canopy (46), = 255 - 46 = 209; see Table 9.5.

would have seen 2,500-255 = 2,245 new stars (assuming clear night and no moon).[42] It is interesting to note that the 27th of a lunar month would be nearly the dark of the moon (see Gen. 8:14).

What about the sun? Because of the total cloud cover the sun would rarely be seen. It would appear only as a bright spot in the cloud cover or sometimes as a reddish disc on the horizon at sunrise or sunset. The sun would have been somewhat redder in color due to the Rayleigh scattering of the blue light (much more of the red light relative to blue would "get through"). The sight of a suddenly distinct and bright yellow orb for a sun on the post-Flood earth must have been quite a striking comparison for Shem, Ham, and Japheth to relate to their descendants. Even today at sunset, a bright red sun is often observed. This would have been quite pronounced under the canopy.

TABLE 9.5

THE NUMBER OF STARS OF EACH MAGNITUDE VISIBLE IN THE PRE-FLOOD HEAVENS

MAGNITUDE	NUMBER OF STARS OF MAGNITUDE n	NUMBER OF STARS POTENTIALLY VISIBLE TO ADAM (34%)[43]	NUMBER OF STARS VISIBLE UNDER THE CANOPY = (A_c/A_p) × (NUMBER OF STARS ACTUALLY VISIBLE TODAY)[44]
1	20	7	$(\sin^2 41/\sin^2 43)(7)$ = 6
2	65	22	$(\sin^2 40/\sin^2 42.5)(22)$ = 20
3	200	68	$(\sin^2 38/\sin^2 41.5)(68)$ = 59
4	500	170	$(\sin^2 33.5/\sin^2 40)(170)$ = 125
5	1,400	476	$(\sin^2 10/\sin^2 34)(476)$ = 46
	2,185	743	Total 255

42. See discussion on pp. 299-300.
43. This, of course, is the same as the number potentially visible today for magnitudes 1-5. Today, however, the 6th magnitude stars are also visible and so 34% × 5,000 = 1,700 for a total of about 2,500 stars visible today.
44. Values of A_C and A_p are calculated for extinction zenith angles, θ_{ext} in Table 9.4 and from Equation (9.7).

Astrology, Sun-Worship, and the Collapse of the Canopy

Surely the condensation of the ancient vapor canopy would have left a marked impression on the minds of Noah and his sons and their wives as they described the appearance of the pre-Flood heavens in comparison to the heavens after the Deluge. The sight of an additional 2,245 stars and of a bright yellow ball in contrast to the reddish disc of the pre-Flood sky must have provided fertile soil for the subsequent development of some pagan ideas. In particular, the pagan religions ascribed to the stars and the sun a personal nature, hence would have seen in these accounts, passed on down from the sons of Noah, a reference to a battle among the gods.

Sun Worship in the Ancient Near East

A common thread in most of the myths of the ancient Near East is that of the worship of the sun. In many of these myths the worship of the sun was preceded by the worship of the sky god, the water heaven, or an inferior sun. Often in the myths the present sun has replaced a former sun.

The entirety of Egypt's religion revolved around the worship of Ammon-Re, the sun god. In Greece the former sun Hyperion was replaced after the banishment of the water heaven by the present sun Helios. Helios supposedly was drowned in the ocean and then raised as the luminous sun.[45]

A similar theme is echoed in Indian religion; the sun that reigned during the rule of the water heaven was Ahura-Mazda. With the banishment of Varuna (the water heaven), a new sun, Mithras, took over after conquering the darkness.[46] Again, the theme of a new sun could reflect the physical fact of the change in the appearance and intensity of the old sun, due to the attenuation of sunlight under the canopy.

45. Felix Guirand, *Greek Mythology*, p. 84.
46. See the discussion in John Ferguson, *The Religions of the Roman Empire*, p. 47, and "The Brahmanic Charma, India," in *New Larousse Encyclopedia of Mythology*, p. 326.

In Mesopotamia, Marduk, the original sun god, was taken over by Shamash, the new sun god.[47]

It is curious that in most of the myths it is the sky god (Ouranos of the Greeks) who is original, and the sun god comes along later as the central deity. As Ferguson has observed, "The sun gives light and life. But it is the sky-god, not the sun-god, who predominates in early religion."[48] In Egypt Ammon-Re began to absorb the other gods by the fifth dynasty. In Persia Ahura-Mazda (the old sun) is viewed as the sky god and is supreme over the sun.[49]

In this connection Velikovsky has noted a peculiar theme in many ancient myths — the sun ages.[50] It is quite common to find a reference in the myths to a new sun in the sky at the beginning of every new age. The Mayas, for example, numbered their ages by giving them the names of the consecutive suns. Interestingly enough, the first sun was the "Water Sun." It was followed by several eras, each marked by a new sun (Earthquake Sun, Hurricane Sun, and Fire Sun) to which various catastrophes were attributed.[51]

Ixtililxochitl (c. 1568-1648), a student of the traditions of the Indians of South America, described the world ages by the names of suns. Again, the "Water Sun" was the first age, which was ended by the Deluge.[52] Other successive ages followed.

The idea of a series of sun ages is found in Mexican writings. Symbols of the successive suns are painted on the pre-Columbian literary documents of Mexico.[53]

The Buddhist sacred book *Visuddhi-Magga* has a chapter on "World Cycles."[54] Three destructions of the world are dis-

47. Ferguson, p. 44.
48. Ibid.
49. Ibid.
50. Immanuel Velikovsky, *Worlds in Collision*, pp. 50-52.
51. Brasseur, *Sources de l'histoire primitive du Mexique*, p. 25, cited by Velikovsky, p. 50.
52. Alexander, *Latin American Mythology*, p. 91, cited by Velikovsky, pp. 50-51.
53. Humboldt, *Researches*, II, 16, cited by Velikovsky, p. 51.
54. Warren, *Buddhism in Translations*, p. 322, cited by Velikovsky, p. 51.

cussed — one by water, one by fire, and one by wind. Apparently, after the Deluge, a "second sun" appeared. In the future more suns will appear. The seventh sun's arrival will result in the whole world's bursting into flames.[55]

The aborigines of Sarawak, Brunel, and Sabo (north of Borneo) even today, believe that the sky was originally low, that six suns perished, and at present the world is illuminated by the seventh sun.[56]

Why is it that in so many of the ancient traditions the word "sun" is substituted for the word "epoch"? Velikovsky asks, "Did the reason for the substitution of the word 'sun' for 'epoch' by the peoples of both hemispheres lie in the changed appearance of the luminary . . . ?"[57]

Velikovsky, of course, cites these legends to substantiate a different thesis than that of the collapse of a pre-Flood vapor canopy. However, just such a "banishment" of the "water heaven" would precipitate the described visual phenomena. This would explain the sudden burst of sun worship found all over the ancient Near East at about the time (on biblical reckoning) that Noah got out of the ark. Within 150 years of that time, the entire human race was immersed in idolatry once again (see the Tower of Babel), so it is not surprising that the pattern described by Paul in Romans (1:18-32) would have led to the worship of the sun. Given the "personal" nature of the sun, it would have been natural for men to have viewed "him" as a victor in a celestial battle.

THE WORSHIP OF THE STARS

It is interesting to note that the ancient Near East was involved not only in sun worship, but also in star worship, or astrology. This form of idolatry has frequently been associated with the ziggurats, or "temple towers," constructed in and around the ancient city of Babylon. The next historical event mentioned in Genesis after the Flood and the condensation of the canopy was the insurrection at Babel (ancient Babylon).

55. Ibid., p. 51.
56. Roland B. Dixon, *Oceanic Mythology*, 9:178.
57. Velikovsky, p. 52.

Although the essence of that rebellion was clearly the pride of man and his desire to be independent of the Creator, its association with a ziggurat (Tower of Babel) suggests that astrology may have been the particular form of idolatry that was judged.

There seems to be general agreement that the actual remains of the biblical Tower of Babel have been uncovered. The tower was located in a temple complex known as E-sag-ila, "The house whose head is raised up." Alongside many shrines of the gods, the ancient Tower of Babel pointed toward the heavens. It was called E-temen-an-ki, "The house of the foundation of heaven and earth."[58] This house had seven stories, and the top story was the residence of the god Marduk. Cassuto says, "There can be no doubt that the Biblical story refers specifically to the city of Babylon and the ziggurat Etemenanki therein."[59] This 90-foot tower, the house of Marduk, was a center for astrological worship. The Babylonians conceptualized the gods as stars and constellations.[60] The erection of the Tower of Babel is specifically referred to in the *Enuma Elish*:

> They raised up the head of Esagila on high level with the Apsu
> After they had built the lofty stagetower of the Apsu.
> They established an abode for Marduk, Enlil, and Ea.[61]

The above reports the building of the temple tower made in celestial Babylon. Marduk then builds on earth below one for himself that is patterned after the heavenly model.

> A likeness of what he made in heaven
> Let him make on earth.[62]

58. U. Cassuto, *A Commentary on the Book of Genesis*, 2:227.
59. Ibid., p. 229.
60. Gerhard F. Hasel, "The Polemic Nature of the Genesis Cosmology," *The Evangelical Quarterly* 46 (April-June 1974):81-103.
61. *Enuma Elish*, Tablet VI, line 62, trans. by Alexander Heidel, *The Babylonian Genesis*, p. 48.
62. Ibid., Tablet VI, line 112, p. 50.

The stars had great significance to the astrologically minded Babylonians. Their connection with the Zodiac and with Marduk was well known.

He created stations for the great gods;
The stars their likenesses, the signs of the zodiac he set up.[63]

Here Marduk's creation of the pathways of the gods (the stations or points of the zodiac) is described. It was Marduk who established the zodiac. The "likenesses" of the gods are the constellations, the signs of the zodiac. From this we may conclude that in the temple of Marduk, E-temen-an-ki (the biblical Tower of Babel), the zodiac and star worship had a prominent place.

The primary purpose of the tower seems to have been to provide a house for the god. By using the stairway the deity could descend to the lower level of men. By housing Marduk there in Babylon, communication between heaven and earth was assured,[64] that is, between the gods (stars) and men. In fact, at Larsor, the tower there is even named "House of the link between heaven and earth."[65] Although it is debatable that the purpose of the Tower of Babel was related to observation of heavenly bodies,[66] there is some evidence that this may have been a secondary function.[67]

It is clear, then, that the biblical Tower of Babel served as a center for astrology and star worship. It was in that tower that post-Flood man's prideful rejection of the true God was epitomized in his unity around the worship of the stars instead of the fear of the Lord.

Why was it that within 150 years of the Flood, the worship of the stars had already become virtually a one-world religion? Saggs suggests, "There is the theoretical consideration that the idea can only have arisen in a milieu where celestial bodies were regarded as divinities affecting the life of mankind."[68]

63. Ibid., Tablet V, lines 1-2, p. 44.
64. André Parrot, *The Tower of Babel*, p. 64.
65. Ibid.
66. Ibid., p. 58.
67. H. W. F. Saggs, *The Greatness that Was Babylon*, p. 338.
68. Ibid., p. 460.

Much of the religion of the ancient Near East was devoted to getting the stars, the moon, and the sun on the side of the worshiper by means of magic. The people concluded that the stars affect conditions on earth. Why did they draw this conclusion? Could it be that after the greatest flood and cataclysmic destruction that mankind ever knew, over 2,000 new stars appeared in the heavens? Like the victorious sun, the stars (that is, the present gods) were victorious over the forces of chaos and restored order to a shattered planet. Surely they must control the destinies of men.

Whether or not this explains the origin of astrology is, of course, debatable. What is clear, however, is that the first recorded event after the Flood in the Bible is the rebellion at the Tower of Babel. We find no mention of astrology or sun worship prior to the Flood. Yet suddenly men are worshiping the stars. Why? The changed appearance of the postdiluvian heavens supplies a satisfactory answer.

The apostle Paul clearly explained how the true story related by the sons of Noah became perverted into the worship of idols, the stars, "For even though they knew God, they did not honor Him as God, or give thanks" (Rom. 1:21). In other words, mankind after the Flood knew all about the true God. From Noah's sons men learned that the Deluge had been an act of judgment. "But they became futile in their speculations, and their foolish heart was darkened. Professing to be wise, they became fools, and exchanged the glory of the incorruptible God for an image in the form of corruptible man, and of birds and four-footed animals and crawling creatures" (Rom. 1:21-23).

Instead of seeing the Deluge as an evident warning that God deals with justice in the affairs of men, professing themselves to be wise, they concluded that the post-Flood appearance of the stars (victorious gods) demonstrated that the stars rule the earth. So they worshiped "images" such as Orion, the Great Bear, Pegasus, Aquarius, Virgo, Leo, and other constellations which were in the likeness of their gods.

Chapter 10

The Riddle of the Frozen Giants

The opening remarks of Aleksandr Solzhenitsyn in his now-famous *Gulag Archipelago* remind all students of natural history of one of the most perplexing mysteries of the northern tundras: the existence of thousands of frozen animal remains:

> In 1949 some friends and I came upon a noteworthy news item in *Nature*, a magazine of the Academy of Science. It reported in tiny type that in the course of excavations on the Kolyma River a subterranean ice lens had been discovered which was actually a frozen stream — and in it were found frozen specimens of pre-historic fauna some tens of thousands of years old. Whether fish or salamander, these were preserved in so fresh a state, the scientific correspondent reported, that those present immediately broke open the ice encasing the specimens and devoured them with relish on the spot.[1]

No inquiry in the whole range of natural history, perhaps, is more fascinating than the study of frozen remains. Of particular interest are the mammoth carcasses found in Siberia and Alaska. Both children and scientists have their imaginations stirred when they read how in the barren, inhospitable wastes of northern Siberia, where neither tree nor shrub will grow, where the land for hundreds of miles is covered with a damp moss barely sprinkled for two months with a few flowers, and for the rest of the year locked in ice and snow, where only the hardiest of polar animals can now survive — the white fox, the polar bear — there are found below the ground vast quantities of bones of elephants and other beasts whose appetites needed corresponding supplies of food. Our interest rises to the highest pitch when we observe that this vast cemetery not only teems

1. Aleksandr I. Solzhenitsyn, *The Gulag Archipelago*, 1:ix.

with fresh bones and beautiful tusks of ivory, but with the carcasses and mummies of these great animals so well preserved in the perpetually frozen soil that bears and wolves, and even men in some cases, can feed on them. As recently as February 1976 it was reported that Russian fox trappers frequently use mammoth meat as bait in their fox traps.[2] This has long been talked about by other writers.[3] Lydekker has observed, "In many instances, as is well known, entire carcasses of the mammoth have been found thus buried, with the hair, skin and flesh as fresh as in frozen New Zealand sheep in the hold of a steamer. And sleigh dogs, as well as Yakuts themselves, have often made a hearty meal on mammoth flesh thousands of years old."[4]

As we will point out in the discussion to follow, phenomena such as this suggest a catastrophe of continental proportions, which precipitated a sudden "deep freeze" and coincided with the mysterious Pleistocene extinctions. Although a continental catastrophe seems to be called for, the mechanisms necessary to generate the associated atmospheric and meteorological phenomena have been unimaginable, hence more uniformitarian concepts have been embraced. How can the climate suddenly change at a rate rapid enough to deep freeze many animals, bury others, and permanently change the climate of an entire continent from a moderate to a severe regime? As we will suggest, the condensation of the vapor canopy may supply the needed mechanism that could be the answer to the riddle of the Pleistocene extinctions.

The Worldwide Mammoth Cemeteries

The outstanding source of information on the elephant remnants is found in a monumental book by Sir Henry Hoyle

2. Bob Gooding, reported on Channel 8 News, Dallas, Texas, 9 February 1976.
3. I. P. Tolmachoff, "The Carcasses of the Mammoth and Rhinoceros Found in the Frozen Ground of Siberia," *Transactions of the American Philosophical Society* 23 (1929):vii.
4. Richard Lydekker, "Mammoth Ivory," *Smithsonian Reports*, 1899, p. 363.

The Riddle of the Frozen Giants

Howorth, *The Mammoth and the Flood*. This practically unobtainable book, published in 1887, gathers much of the extant geological literature, coupled with firsthand observations, into a solid factual case for a global deluge. Howorth was hostile to biblical Christianity[5] and was not motivated by a desire to "prove the Flood," but was forced to believe in the Deluge by the geological evidence. Unfortunately, many modern writers on the mammoth question have neglected Howorth's classic work, and, as a result, propose theories that Howorth himself refuted by judicious appeals to factual geological evidence almost a century ago.[6]

The most valuable treatment of the question from a noncatastrophic point of view is that of Tolmachoff, who quotes extensively from Howorth.[7] Most of the firsthand literature on the mammoth question, unfortunately, is in Russian, hence still not generally available.

The mammoth is a close relative of today's Indian elephant. Some were the same size, about 10 feet at the shoulder,[8] with an

---

5. See Henry H. Howorth, *The Mammoth and the Flood*, p. ix, where he speaks negatively of biblical revelation. On p. xv he explains why he has adopted his views of Deluge geology. "In taking up this position, I am not arguing against the government of the Universe by law, but merely protesting against measuring the possibilities and limits of the universal law by our experience of it."
6. For example, William R. Farrand, "Frozen Mammoths and Modern Geology," *Science* 133 (March 1961):729-35, suggests many gradualistic theories and nowhere refers to Howorth's work which long ago refuted them.
7. Tolmachoff says of Howorth, "Especially important in this direction was Howorth's book, *The Mammoth and the Flood*, in which an amazing amount of literary data has been brought together by that author." Tolmachoff observes that, after checking Howorth's citations with the original source material, he concluded that Howorth was a reliable source. See Tolmachoff, "The Carcasses of the Mammoth."
8. Bjorn Kurten, *Pleistocene Mammals of Europe*, p. 137.

8½ cm (3.3 in.) thick layer of fat under the skin.[9] The imperial mammoth stood 14 feet high at the shoulder.[10]

The unusual thing about these animals is that their remains are found all over the northern tundras in both Siberia and Alaska, mostly north of the Arctic Circle. In this region, the tropical Indian elephant would perish quickly. Frozen carcasses of mammoths have been reported for centuries in China long before mammoth bones were discovered in Europe.[11] The first mention of the mammoth is found in Chinese ceremonial books of the fourth century. B.C.[12] On four occasions scientific expeditions were actually able to get to the site before the carcass was rotted or devoured by wild animals:[13] the Adams mammoth (1806) in the delta of the Lena River, the Herz mammoth from the Beresovka River (1901),[14] Stenbock-Fermor's mammoth from the Great Lyakhov Island (1906), and Vollosovich's mammoth from the Sanga-Yurakh River (1907).

Howorth documents numerous finds of mammoth carcasses where the soft parts were freshly preserved.[15] These finds span the entire length of Siberia and are mostly within the Arctic Circle.[16] He also cites the presence of a rhinoceros carcass which has been stuffed and is now in the Zoological Museum in Leningrad.[17]

It will be helpful to group these discoveries by geographical areas — Siberia, Europe, and North America.

9. Ibid., p. 138.
10. Carl O. Dunbar and Karl M. Waage, *Historical Geology*, p. 477.
11. Tolmachoff, p. viii.
12. Ibid., p. 11.
13. Farrand, p. 731.
14. O. F. Herz, "Frozen Mammoths in Siberia," *Annual Report of Smithsonian Institution*, 1903, pp. 611-25.
15. Howorth, pp. 80-89.
16. For a good map of the 39 Siberian carcasses known to Tolmachoff in 1927, see Tolmachoff, p. 20. Most of the animals are buried in sediments north of the Arctic Circle.
17. Howorth, p. 82.

The Riddle of the Frozen Giants

THE MAMMOTH IN SIBERIA

For centuries reports of mammoth bones and flesh have come from northern Siberia. Numerous finds have actually been examined by scientists, most of them from the New Siberian Islands and within 100 miles of the Arctic Ocean seashore.[18]

Long ago the mammoth carcasses of Siberia caught the attention of Baron G. Cuvier, who wrote:

> In the northern regions, it has left the carcasses of large quadrupeds which became enveloped in the ice, and have thus been preserved even to our own times, with their skin, their hair and their flesh. If they had not been frozen as soon as killed, they would have decomposed by putrefaction. And on the other hand, this eternal frost could not have previously occupied the places in which they have been seized by it for they could not have lived in such temperatures.[19]

In other words, how did these giants become trapped in the hard permafrost? The ground must have been soft for them to have plunged into it, which suggests a warm temperature; but if a warm temperature prevailed, then how could their flesh have been preserved from putrefaction? This is the central problem of the remains and it has never been satisfactorily answered. The canopy condensation may provide that solution. Most of the Siberian mammoths are found in sediments dating prior to 10,500 years ago (assuming the validity of present-day dating methods).[20]

In 1712-1715 a Chinese ambassador traversed Siberia on his way to the Volga, to try to induce the Torguts, a tribe of Kalmuts who had settled there under Russian protection, to return to their old homes on the Chinese frontiers. In commenting on the natives and the mammoths at Yeniseysk, the Chinese envoy, Tu Li Shin, said, "The flesh of the animal is of a very refrigerating quality, and is eaten as a remedy in fevers. The foreign name of this animal is Ma-men-tu-va [that is, mammoth]; we call it

---

18. Bassett Digby, *The Mammoth and Mammoth Hunting Grounds in Northeast Siberia*, p. 96.
19. Baron G. Cuvier, *Essay on the Theory of the Earth*, p. 14.
20. Farrand, p. 733.

Keeshoo."[21] In 1706 in a letter from an ambassador of the Czar to the emperor of China, the ambassador observed, "In the Spring when the ice of the river breaks, it is driven in such vast quantities, and with such force by the high swollen water, that it frequently carries very high banks before it and breaks off the tops of hills, which falling down, discover these animals whole, or teeth only, almost frozen to earth, which thaw by degrees."[22]

The soil of the Island of Maloi is nearly completely composed of fossil mammoth bones, according to a government land surveyor sent there in 1775; its banks expose new bones with every storm.[23] On one of these New Siberian Islands bones of a rhinoceros and a musk ox, as well as ivory, often as fresh and white as that from Africa, have been found. "So numerous are the mammoth remains in the soil of the Liachof [Lyakhov] Islands that Sannikof describes the whole soil of the islands appearing to consist of them."[24] Hunters say that when the sea recedes after the easterly winds, a fresh supply of mammoth bones is always washed up on the shore. The Hydrographic Expedition of the Arctic Ocean under Captain B. A. Vilkitzk found the frozen carcass of a mammoth in the Haffner Fiord on the Taymyr Peninsula at latitude 76° 30' north and longitude 116° 15' east.[25] This area today has one of the most severe weather climates on earth. It is inconceivable that an elephant could ever survive there.

In 1787 near the delta of the Alazeya River, which flows into the Arctic Ocean, a mammoth was found with body, skin, and hair in complete preservation. It was located in an upright position in an ice fissure.[26]

In 1972 Boris Rusanov and Pyotr Lazarev heard of yet another

21. Stauton's narrative, published in 1723-26 at Peking and translated into English by Sir George Stauton in 1821, pp. 70-71, cited by Howorth, p. 77.
22. Cited by Henry Fairfield Osborn, *Proboscidea*, 2:1124.
23. Howorth, p. 51.
24. Ibid., p. 54.
25. Tolmachoff, p. 39.
26. Ibid., p. 7.

The Riddle of the Frozen Giants

mammoth find on the banks of the Shandrin River.[27] When hosed out, it proved to be complete except for its tusks, which had been cut off by some hunter. This mammoth apparently was quite old as evidenced by the absence of its back molars. What was of particular interest, however, was that the internal organs were tolerably intact, although semidecomposed in a solid frozen block weighing 550 pounds, comprising the stomach, intestines, and other internal organs. Seeds and grasses from the intestines indicated that the mammoth died in autumn.

A recent interesting mammoth find was made in a remote mountainous province of northeastern Siberia.[28] A perfectly preserved baby mammoth, christened "Dima" by her excavators, was found by a member of a team of free-lance gold prospectors along the sides of the little Kirgilyakh stream, a tributary of the Kolyma River, which flows into the Arctic Ocean. In June 1977 a prospector's bulldozer uncovered a polygonal block of muddy ice containing a curious dark mass, which when thawed out by steam spray turned out to be a mammoth carcass.

Dima had chestnut-colored hair, measured 45 inches long and 41 inches high, and had tiny ears and a 22-inch trunk with the two distinctive "fingers" at its end that appear in many Stone Age cave paintings. She had died at the age of six months. This mammoth has now been stuffed and is on display at the Zoological Institute at the University of Leningrad. The German magazine *Bunte* reported concerning Dima, "All of its internal organs, yes, even its blood have been preserved completely and unchanged since those far off times. That is why Professor Zaitsev of the University of Leningrad considers this find to be, so far, the most important one, whose examination will give us new information."[29]

27. John Massey Stewart, "Frozen Mammoths from Siberia Bring the Ice Ages to Vivid Life," *Smithsonian* 8 (December 1977):61-68.
28. Ibid.
29. *Bunte*, October 20, 1977, p. 138, cited by Hans Krause, *The Mammoth in Ice and Snow?*, p. 7.

Not only have mammoth remains been found in Siberia, but the remains of frozen rhinoceroses as well. A rhinoceros *tichorhinus* was found in a cave at latitude 68° 30' north.[30] The rhino, of course, is a tropical animal today.

As mentioned earlier, Howorth documents numerous finds of well-preserved mammoth carcasses.[31] Concerning these he writes,

> This completes the list of so-called mummies of the great pachyderms whose discovery has been described. As they occur in such very remote and inhospitable districts, seldom visited except by the indigenous polar peoples, it is probable that these examples form only a tithe of those which have occurred during the last two centuries, but which have not been recorded.[32]

In other words, the extremely improbable coincidence of finding so many carcasses suggests that there are thousands of carcasses left to be found. If we were to jump into an acre of hay and regularly find needles, we would normally conclude that there must be millions of needles in the haystack in order for any one of them to have a probability of being found.

The Beresovka mammoth. One of the most intriguing finds was that of the Beresovka mammoth on the Beresovka River in 1901. At this site, a perfectly preserved whole carcass was excavated 60 miles within the Arctic Circle and 2,000 miles north of the present range of living elephants.[33] The expedition that excavated the mammoth was led by Dr. Otto F. Herz, a zoologist on the staff of the Russian Academy of Science's museum, M. E. V. Pfizenmayer, a zoological preparator of the Academy's museum, and M. D. P. Sevastianov, a geological expert of Yurievsk University. It was found frozen into a cliff of the River Beresovka, a right tributary of the Kolyma River, 200 miles northeast of Srednekolymsk and 1,000 miles west of the Bering Strait. The mammoth was located in the midst of a

30. Tolmachoff, pp. 29-30.
31. Howorth, pp. 80-89.
32. Ibid., p. 89.
33. Dunbar and Waage, p. 34.

The Riddle of the Frozen Giants

landslide, so was not found in the location where it died.[34] By the time the scientists got there, the head had been exposed for over two years, and much of it had been eaten by wolves and other local carnivores. It originally was exposed during spring thaws when floods began to thaw the cliff into which it was frozen. So some of it had time to rot and refreeze during the two summers before it was examined by the scientists.

One striking thing about the mammoth was that well-preserved food fragments were found in the mouth and between the teeth.[35] This can only mean that the animal met with a sudden death and did not even have time to swallow its last meal. The excavators built a house over the mammoth and began to thaw it out. The stench was so bad from the rotten parts that initially the work was unbearable.[36]

Further indication of a sudden death was found in blood that was collected in great masses due to a hemorrhage. It was found to be in such a good state of preservation that it could be examined as easily as the blood of recent animals. It was even possible to establish the relationship of the blood to the Indian elephant.[37] Much decayed food was found in the stomach, and its walls were badly decayed.[38] The decay on the wall of the stomach appears to be due to the mammoth's back having been torn open by wild animals; the vital organs had been eaten. So it had lain exposed almost to the stomach for two summers before the scientists arrived.

One afternoon, the left shoulder was severed from the body, and under it the scientists made a startling discovery:

> The flesh under the shoulder, fibrous and marbled with fat, is dark red and looks as fresh as well-frozen beef or horsemeat. It looked so appetising that we wondered for some time whether we would not taste it. But no one would venture to take it into his mouth, and horseflesh was given the preference. The dogs ate whatever mammoth meat we threw to them.[39]

34. Tolmachoff, p. 87.
35. Digby, p. 117.
36. Ibid., p. 119.
37. Tolmachoff, p. 35.
38. Digby, p. 128.
39. Ibid., p. 129.

Apparently, though some parts of this mammoth had rotted away during its exposure to the sun, other parts, not so exposed, remained as fresh in appearance as when the animal had originally died, and the meat, in Herz's own words, looked fresh enough to eat. Pfizenmayer adds, "As soon as it thawed, however, it entirely changed its appearance. It became flabby and grey, and gave off a repulsive ammoniacal stench that pervaded everything."[40]

The flesh and fat of the right leg were also well preserved.[41] Bits of frozen blood were found, which, when heated, turned into dirty, dark red spots; this condition frequently indicates a sudden death. Another interesting and unexpected feature was an erect male genital.[42] This condition is normally explained by a death due to suffocation, such as drowning.[43]

As the stomach was cut open, the most amazing discovery of all was made. The scientists found 24 pounds of vegetation in it. Although much of the vegetation was decayed, some was apparently in an excellent preserved state.[44] Many of those plants still grow in Siberia today — however, in the summer only. Others are found only far to the south, proving that the climate must have been much warmer when the mammoth lived. For example, common buttercups were found in the stomach.[45] In fact, the remains were so well preserved that it was actually possible to distinguish between species. This suggests that the stomach temperature was lowered in a relatively short time.

The animal was thought by Herz to have fallen into a crevasse from which it was unable to extricate itself. As it fell, it pulled in a landslide of soil and ice after it and buried itself. This thesis is partially substantiated by the fact that the pelvis was frac-

---

40. E. W. Pfizenmayer, *Siberian Man and Mammoth*, p. 103.
41. Digby, p. 131.
42. Ibid., p. 132.
43. Tolmachoff, p. 35.
44. Osborn, 2:1127.
45. Detailed documentation and discussion of the stomach contents will be presented below.

tured as was the right foreleg.[46] However, there is ambiguous geological evidence for such a crevasse, and it seems unlikely that such a means of death would have resulted in such well-preserved stomach remains, which require very low temperatures. It would seem that Sanderson's observation that the broken hip shows that some very strong force must have been exerted on it either before or after death is equally likely.[47]

The animal is presently exhibited in the Zoological Museum of the Academy in Leningrad as a stuffed animal, with the skeleton exhibited separately nearby.[48] The frozen skin has been cleaned, softened, and prepared, and the animal has been actually stuffed like a modern quadruped, and placed in the attitude in which it originally died. The skin of the head and ears is artificial, and a model of the base of the proboscis has also been added.[49]

The lessons of the animal are striking. At first glance, it appears that a large animal was peacefully grazing on buttercup flowers and was suddenly overtaken by a deep freeze in the middle of summer. The plant remains in the stomach of the Beresovka mammoth indicate that the animal died in late July or early August. Furthermore, the animal froze quickly enough to leave these stomach contents in a well-preserved state and for at least some of the meat on the carcass to be edible.

Fresh meat. A specific characteristic of the mammoth reports coming out of the Siberian wastes, as well as the Alaskan tundras, are the accounts of fresh meat being eaten by humans. This is often ridiculed by historical geologists, but solely on the ground that no scientist was actually there and ate the meat.[50]

46. Digby, p. 123.
47. Ivan T. Sanderson, "Riddle of the Frozen Giants," *Saturday Evening Post,* 16 January 1960, p. 82.
48. Tolmachoff, p. 34.
49. A. S. W., "The New Mammoth at St. Petersburg," *Nature* 68 (30 July 1903):297-98.
50. Although Herz himself seems to testify to meat fresh enough for dogs to eat on the Beresovka mammoth, as discussed above.

The persistence of these traditions, however, is striking and will now be considered.

The ancient Manchu Dictionary reports that mammoth steak was considered to be very "wholesome" in ancient China.[51] The Chinese emperor Kanghi (1662-1722) wrote a treatise on physics and natural history, which was translated by Jesuit Father Cibot. He writes of the mammoth, calling it "Fyn Shu":

> The cold is excessive and almost continual on the coasts of the Northern Sea beyond the Tai Tuung Kiang. It is there that is found the animal Fyn Shu, whose appearance is that of a rat, but which is as big as an elephant.... Its flesh is very cold and excellent for cooling the blood.... Its flesh is very good for those who have been overheated.[52]

Pfizenmayer cites the *Mirror of the Manchu Speech* (1771 edition) in which the statement is made, "The ice-rat, or mountain-stream rat, lives on the ground under the thick ice of the northern regions. *Its flesh is edible.* Its hair is several feet long and is used to make a woven material which keeps out damp."[53]

Already mentioned is the 1712 account of a Chinese ambassador who reported that the flesh of the mammoth was commonly eaten as a remedy in fevers.[54] In 1809 Hedenstrom, a Russian government official, found a mammoth in the New Siberian Islands. When he brought the bones home in order to fashion a perfume out of them, he noticed that fat began to flow out of them as they thawed out by the fire. "He was surprised that the marrow in spite of its age did not emit a putrid scent."[55] In other words, it had not decayed and was fresh, like the reports of fresh meat. In 1857 the natives of the Island Mostakh dug up a carcass:

---

51. Cited by H. H. Howorth, "The Mammoth in Siberia," *The Geological Magazine,* September 1880, p. 411.
52. Cited by Howorth, *The Mammoth and the Flood,* p. 78, and Pfizenmayer, p. 4.
53. Pfizenmayer, p. 4.
54. Howorth, *The Mammoth and the Flood,* p. 77.
55. Tolmachoff, p. 26.

The Riddle of the Frozen Giants 323

The skin according to natives was about two inches thick, and so well preserved that it could be used to make dog harnesses. The fat was a little yellowish on the surface, but snow white deeper. It was used by natives to lubricate small local boats known as nyetca. The flesh, pink on the surface, was bright red deeper. The natives did not try to eat it themselves.[56]

In 1877 a mammoth was found in Southern Siberia and a report was made about a peasant: "The man obstinately affirmed he truly had eaten the supposed skin, but added: 'seasoned with butter, what is not possible to eat.'"[57] In other words, seasoning can make the unedible edible.

Dr. Leopold von Schrenck, chief of the Imperial Academy of Sciences at Petrograd (1869), visited the Samoyede country and published the following account: "The mammoth, in the conception of the Samoyedes, is a gigantic beast which lives in the depths of the earth, where it digs for itself dark pathways, and feeds on earth. They account for its corpse being found so fresh and well preserved on the ground that the animal is still a living one."[58]

Pfizenmayer reports that the natives asked him whether or not he had eaten the Beresovka.[59] That suggests that eating mammoth flesh was known to them. The natives were familiar with fresh mammoth steak, even if a scientist was not present every time they sat down to enjoy a meal. Pfizenmayer, who was on the site at the excavation of the Beresovka mammoth, says of the latter, "The fat here and on the elastic cushions of muscle and tissue on the soles was very well preserved, and in colour and consistency, differed in no way from that of a newly killed animal."[60]

Charles Hapgood cites a personal talk with Joseph Barnes, a former correspondent of the *New York Herald Tribune*, in which Barnes remarked on the delicious flavor of some mam-

---

56. Ibid., p. 31.
57. Ibid., p. 30.
58. *Bulletin of the St. Petersburg Academy* (vol. III, p. 335), cited by Howorth, *The Mammoth and the Flood*, p. 76.
59. Pfizenmayer, p. 126.
60. Ibid., p. 163.

moth meat served to him at a dinner at the Academy of Sciences in Moscow in the 1930s.[61]

After surveying the evidence for fresh remains, Howorth summarizes and makes the following points:

> Not only does the frozen ground preserve the flesh deposited in it, but it is quite clear that no flesh could remain intact in this way unless it were permanently frozen, and it follows inevitably that the bodies of mammoths, etc., which are now found intact in the Siberian tundra must have been frozen immediately after death, and have remained frozen since they were first entombed. If they had been subject to alternate congelation and melting with the intermittent seasons they would assuredly have long since decayed. We are not dealing here with animal substances deposited in bogs, and changed into such organic compounds as adipocere, but of flesh so unchanged that it has all the character of the animals which have recently died when examined under the microscope, while it is readily eaten by the wild animals that live on the tundra. The flesh is as fresh as of recently taken out of Esquimaux cache or a Yakut subterranean meat-safe.[62]

THE MAMMOTH IN EUROPE

Siberia is not the only place in which the remains of the giant pachyderms are found. In fact, in Europe the evidence of vast mammoth cemeteries is equally impressive. However, in these deposits only rarely are soft parts found preserved. This is, of course, to be expected in that the present mean temperature is above freezing, and they would simply rot. It should be noted, however, that the discovery of a complete skeleton proves the same kind of catastrophic burial as the finding of a frozen carcass:

> It is equally clear that the finding of a skeleton intact, and with its bones all in position, is, under such conditions, equivalent to the finding of a carcass, and shows that such a skeleton was, when buried, clothed with flesh, just as the bodies in North Siberia are now, and that this is only the absence of the necessary cold which has interfered with its complete preservation.[63]

Howorth gives extensive documentation of skeletons of mammoths found all over Europe buried in such a way as to

61. Charles H. Hapgood, *The Path of the Pole*, p. 261.
62. Howorth, *The Mammoth and the Flood*, pp. 93-94.
63. Ibid., p. 155.

The Riddle of the Frozen Giants 325

indicate that they were overwhelmed by flood waters.[64] Amazingly, in the same strata as the mammoth, are found cave bear, rhinoceros, hyena, horse, deer, oxen, bison, red-deer, reindeer, antelope, ass, badger, lynx, fox, wolf, ibex, marmot, leopard, and several kinds of birds. He says, "To enumerate every known find would be to map out almost every square mile of country."[65] He documents mammoth finds all over Europe — from the Urals to Poland, from the White Sea to the Black, Germany, France, Hungary, the Alps, from the Bering Strait as far west as the Pyrenees and the latitude of Rome in Italy. The rhinoceros and the hippopotamus (today living only in Africa and India) are found, along with mammoth remains, all over the Mediterranean area.[66] This would seem to suggest that the mammoth was a warm-weather animal and was not adapted to cold, as is often assumed.

A recent article summarized many mammoth finds in southern Sweden. The finds were all from drift gravel. Although the article argues that the animals were buried in outwash from melted glaciers and transported, their presence in drift could just as well indicate their burial in flood sediments. Fragments of the fossils were left unaffected by disintegration.[67]

How did these vast accumulations of mammoth skeletons originate? Such immense fossil graveyards covering an entire continent would suggest a continent-wide flood catastrophe.

THE MAMMOTH IN NORTH AMERICA

Almost everywhere we turn on the North American continent, a similar story meets us. A total of 217 individual mammoth carcasses have been found in peat bogs of New York State

64. Ibid., p. 157 ff.
65. Ibid., p. 102.
66. Ibid., p. 108.
67. B. E. Berglund, S. Hakansson, and E. Lagerlund, "Radiocarbon-dated Mammoth (Mammuthus Primigenius Blumenbach) Finds in South Sweden," *Boreas* 5 (March 1976):177-91.

alone.[68] Once again it is the great Howorth to whom we must turn for the most extensive documentation on the mammoth in North America. He gives nearly 40 pages of documentation of finds all over Alaska and North America that precisely match the kinds of deposits found in Europe and Siberia.[69] Along with the mammoth remains, bison are found north of Eschscholtz Bay (66° latitude), whereas today they do not go farther north than 62°.[70] Of special interest are the remains of horses found above 66° latitude, which today never venture farther north than 49° in North America.[71] He concludes, "The remains of the mammoth and its companions are found in Alaska, and as far north as Point Barrow, under the same wintry conditions that they occur in Asia."[72] Point Barrow is located at 73° north latitude and is on the northernmost tip of Alaska. The discovery of mammoth remains in this locality is astounding.

Numerous other animals have been found in the vast cemeteries of the Alaskan muck, mixed in with the remains of the mammoths. Flint reports that bears, wolves, fox, badger, wolverine, saber-toothed tiger, a jaguar, lynx, wooly mammoth, mastodon, two horses, camel, saiga antelope, four bisons, caribous, moose, a ground sloth, and several rodents have all been discovered. He says, "The number of individuals is so great that the assemblage as a whole must represent *a rather long time*. The large cats and the ground sloth may seem surprising, but their significance *must remain unexplained* until their stratigraphic position is better known" (italics added).[73]

The above quotation is interesting in that it reveals the reasoning process of one who is a priori committed to long time spans. Instead of concluding that all of these animals lived together at the same time, as the evidence seems to suggest, he is forced, due to his evolutionary assumptions, to stretch out

68. Dunbar and Waage, p. 478.
69. Howorth, *The Mammoth and the Flood*, pp. 257-93.
70. Ibid., p. 264.
71. Ibid., p. 264.
72. Ibid., p. 266.
73. Richard Foster Flint, *Glacial and Pleistocene Geology*, p. 471.

The Riddle of the Frozen Giants 327

their accumulation over a long period. Normally we would conclude that such a vast array of animals buried in the muck would suggest a common catastrophe of continental proportions that suddenly overtook them. Since that cannot be allowed, a gradual accumulation of fossils over a long time period must be assumed. However, when it comes to explaining a tropical saber-toothed tiger's surviving in the Arctic tundra, we are told that must remain unexplained until their stratigraphic position is better known. It is perfectly explainable if we want to believe that the climate was once warm enough to sustain these animals and that they lived with the mammoths, then all were overwhelmed at once by a catastrophe. The reason the stratigraphic position is not "better known" is that what it seems to be cannot be because the continent-wide catastrophe that Howorth so fully documents cannot have occurred; it violates the metaphysics of uniformity.

In 1908 the remains of a mammoth carcass were removed from a bluff at Elephant Point overlooking Eschscholtz Bay, Alaska (66° north latitude), just below the Arctic Circle.[74] Pieces of soft flesh and tendons still clinging to the skeleton were found. A study of the area convinced Quackenbush, the leader of the expedition, that the animal could not have been caught in a bog.[75] Underneath the mammoth they found some grass stalks that were still particularly green. Near the head, "a small, thin sheet of chewed grass cut out of the frozen sandy silt close to the lower jaw was as brilliantly green as on the day it grew."[76] Here again, it appears, as in the case of the Beresovka mammoth, that the animal must have been in the process of chewing its last meal and did not even have time to swallow the food before it was suddenly killed. The fact that the grass was green suggests that the death came suddenly, for vegetation turns rather quickly after being severed from its roots unless the process is

74. L. S. Quackenbush, "Notes on Alaskan Mammoth Expeditions of 1907 and 1908," *Bulletin of the American Museum of Natural History*, 1909, p. 107.
75. Ibid., p. 109.
76. Ibid., p. 110.

arrested by freezing. Apparently this grass never thawed out but was protected in the bluff for thousands of years, while the mammoth itself was exposed and rotted or was eaten by carnivores.

Another interesting find on a neighboring hill in the same stratum was a tree growing up throughout the stratum:

> The forked trunk of a tree six inches in diameter was found imbedded vertically in the bluff close to the end of one of the glaciers suggesting that it had grown on the bank of the stream. . . . The tree stump was traced by digging down into the frozen silt and its spreading roots followed for three or four feet; bark surrounded the stem below the line of frost, and from all appearances, the tree had grown in situ.[77]

Such a find is certain proof of rapid deposition of sediments. This would suggest that this mammoth was overcome by a rapid burial. Furthermore, the existence of such a tree suggests a more moderate climate than exists there today.

Even the infants of the mammoth population did not escape the fate of the herds. On August 28, 1948, a baby mammoth was washed out of the muck by the Fairbanks Exploration Company.[78] The skin covering the face and trunk and the right foreleg with some flesh still on it were present, along with some of the bones. It is now on display at the American Museum of Natural History. In the same muck, a large lionlike cat, a camel, and a horse were found.[79] These animals could never survive the present climate. This is another find in which the mammoths and animal types of moderate temperatures are found together, suggesting again that the mammoths may have been warm-weather animals and not adapted to cold any more than the horse, the lion, or the tiger is today.

THE NUMBER OF THE FROZEN REMAINS

William Farrand has attempted to dismiss the evidence of the frozen carcasses. In particular he reacted to a statement made by

77. Ibid., p. 112.
78. Harold E. Anthony, "Nature's Deep Freeze," *Natural History* 58 (September 1949):299.
79. Ibid., p. 300.

The Riddle of the Frozen Giants

Ivan Sanderson that "absolutely countless numbers" were killed and frozen into this "horrific indecency."[80] He would, no doubt, be even more upset by anthropologist Charles Hapgood's observation, "The arctic wasteland is a burial ground for hundreds of thousands of mammoths, a hairy species of elephant, now extinct, that seem to have died about 10,000 years ago and been quickly deep-frozen, some in mid-summer. Frozen mammoth bodies have been found so perfectly preserved that their flesh is almost as delicious today as fresh beefsteak."[81]

Farrand is aware of only 39 mammoth carcasses that have been examined by scientists. Several more have been found since he wrote (1961). Based on the amount of ivory taken out of Siberia, he estimated that the total population of the mammoth herds was about 50,000.[82] Then he made a seeming non-sequitur:

> The ratio of frozen specimens (around 39) to the probable total population (more than 50,000) is of the order of magnitude expected among terrestrial mammals on the basis of chance burial. Furthermore, the occurrence of nearly whole carcasses is extremely rare (only four or five have been found), in spite of the numerous expeditions for fossil ivory and other exploration in northern Siberia.[83]

Certainly, precisely the opposite conclusion could and, perhaps, should be drawn. Mammoth carcasses are continually being exposed in river banks. During the spring thaws the streams begin to swell and creek beds expand, washing away many feet of sediment. As this happens, more and more animals are exposed, tumble out of fossil formations and thaw in the spring sun. An exposure like this will decompose these animals

80. Sanderson, p. 82.
81. Charles Hapgood, "The Mystery of the Frozen Mammoths," Coronet, 48 (September 1960): 75.
82. Farrand, p. 733; Tolmachoff, p. 14, considers this figure much too small. Furthermore, the total mammoth population is obviously thousands of times larger than the number of tusks men have counted in the past 200 years. The tusks indicate herds of millions of mammoths.
83. Farrand, p. 733.

rather quickly and, more often than not, before they are ever seen by the scarce human population. In fact, it is much more likely that such an animal would fall out of a bluff and decompose long before human eyes came on the bones than it is that a trapper would ever see the fleshly parts immediately after exposure in a creek bank.[84] The very odor of the tundra in the New Siberian Islands has suggested to many that the soil must be full of rotten meat, yet 99% of these remains have never been "seen" by human eyes.[85] Therefore, in an area as vast as Siberia and Alaska, the discovery of 39 carcasses is an astounding coincidence that would normally suggest that there must be thousands more.

Statistical statements such as these greatly raise the ire of those within the community of evolutionary geologists. At the time Farrand made his statistical comment (1961) no serious work had yet been done to establish an objective mathematical base for statistical analysis of fossil remains. One of the first published studies on this subject was in 1967.[86] So it appears that Farrand has simply made subjective personal statements without any serious consideration of the true probabilities involved.

Furthermore, the carcasses Farrand refers to are the ones scientists were *actually able to examine*. Apparently, Farrand

84. Digby, pp. 16-17, describes a gradual thawing and refreezing over a period of 50 years before an animal is finally revealed. This explains why some parts are so rotten.
85. Tolmachoff, p. 41.
86. See John Clark and Kenneth K. Kietzke, "Paleoecology of the Lower Nodular Zone, Brute Formation in the Big Badlands of South Dakota," *Fieldiana: Geology Memoirs* 5 (1967):114-40. A survey of the factors affecting population statistics in this article reveals two things: (1) there is insufficient data to make an accurate statement about the actual number of frozen carcasses; and (2) if anything, the available data would suggest a large number of frozen remains must still be buried. The factors described by these authors suggest a strong bias favoring finding a small fossil and against finding a large one, such as a mammoth.

would have us believe that only those carcasses studied by the scientists can be accepted as legitimate finds. What of the numerous reports for the past 2,000 years going all the way back to ancient China? As mentioned earlier, finding a mammoth in the millions of square miles of frozen muck is like finding a needle in a haystack, but can the finding of 39 of them be explainable by coincidence? Would that not indicate the presence of thousands of other finds? This seems to be a plausible conclusion for several reasons.

First, the human population is small in the Arctic regions. So few humans live in this severe climate that it is highly unlikely that an explorer would stumble on a mammoth carcass by chance.

Second, the region abounds in vast ivory tombs. All over these tundras "countless thousands" of ivory tusks are found. Osborn commented:

> The ivory industry of Siberia, dating back to very ancient times, furnishes a very good idea of the immense former number of mammoths, as discovered (or still buried) in the frozen ground of Siberia, estimated by Middendorf (1885) at 20,000 during the past two centuries and by Nordenskiold (1882) at a very much higher figure. The highest estimate is 46,750 animals discovered during the last two and a half centuries; a corresponding estimate is that 250 specimens were discovered annually.[87]

Pliny traces mammoth ivory as far back as Alexander the Great (c. 330 B.C.). The ancient Chinese used it. Arab traders in the ninth and tenth centuries established trade routes from Siberia to Persia and prospered in the ivory trade. Most of the ivory dug out of European deposits is worthless because it has lost the greater part of the animal matter. A factor frequently overlooked in the discussions of the Siberian mammoth remains is that the ivory brought back is frequently well preserved and not denuded of animal material:

> The mammoth ivory of the Siberian tundras, which, in the best preserved specimens, retains the whole of the original animal matter, and, except when stained by earthly infiltrations is suitable for the purpose of the turner as the best product of the African elephant. . . . the burial, or at least the

---

87. Osborn, 2:1162.

freezing, must have taken place comparatively quickly as exposure in their ordinary condition would speedily deteriorate the quality of the ivory.[88]

Not only does the existence of 39 carcasses indicate a sudden deep freeze, but so does the presence of nearly 50,000 tusks. Mammoth ivory must be frozen quickly or it will lose its animal matter, but the mammoth ivory commonly has well-preserved animal matter (pulp) in it. If it is not kept from this rotting pulp, it will become stained and unsuitable for carving. The ivory of the African elephant today must similarly be kept from contact with rotting flesh or it quickly loses its value.

> In a country where the ivory of at least 250 animals is collected yearly, the greatest part of it out of frozen ground, *the number would be increased hundreds of thousands of times if it were possible to register all the cases in which soft parts were found along with the bones.* The abundance of the remnants of these animals is shown by the fact that near the cliffs in which carcasses are found, one usually perceives a putrid smell, although no rotten remnants may have been seen [italics added].[89]

Hence we are confronted with the equivalent of well over 50,000 carcasses, not just 39. Perhaps Sanderson's reference to "countless numbers" is not far off after all.

Third, there is often a significant delay in the receipt of a report. Digby says, "Usually, when the news does leak through, so long a period has elapsed that the chances are that the carcass has been rotted away by the summer sunshine, or torn to bits by wolves and foxes."[90] The problem of destruction by carnivores is especially severe. Pfizenmayer stresses that in every find in which he was involved extensive damage had been done to the animal by other animals before the scientists were able to get there.[91] So when a mammoth carcass is first spotted, it may take several years for the report to pass on from the natives to the scientific authorities. During that time the carcass has frequently been destroyed.

88. Lydekker, p. 363.
89. Tolmachoff, p. 41.
90. Digby, p. 97.
91. Pfizenmayer, pp. 7, 103.

The Riddle of the Frozen Giants 333

Fourth, for various reasons the natives are hesitant to report the numerous carcasses they do see. This is partially due to bad experiences they have had with previous scientific expeditions as well as to various superstitions they entertain about the evil that will befall someone who touches the flesh of a mammoth. Tolmachoff comments:

> It is quite certain that only a small part of such discoveries used to be reported. Superstition, dread of troubles connected with the arrival of an expedition and with participation in its work (which for the local population, often was compulsory), the meager chance of getting a premium, etc., usually led the discoverer to content himself only with picking up the tusks of a mammoth, leaving the carcass undisturbed if he had found one.[92]

Fifth, the difficulties involved in even getting to the reported find are enormous. The expedition organized to excavate the Beresovka mammoth in 1901 traveled a thousand miles on sleds and horses.[93] Furthermore, it is only during the summer that the discoveries can be examined, yet at that time travel is almost impossible. Again Tolmachoff, who is committed to a noncatastrophic interpretation of the data, observes:

> During the summer, the most favorable time for the discovery of frozen carcasses, all journeys of any length are practically stopped except the travel by boat on rivers and lakes or along the seashore.... All this suggests that the chance of discovering a good specimen of a frozen mammoth or rhinoceros is still present, and could be increased by a rational organization of scientific expeditions to the Northern Siberia.[94]

Sixth, the discovery of a piece of flesh has the same significance as the discovery of a complete carcass. Where there is now only a piece of flesh left due to years of thawing and refreezing, there must have been at one time a complete carcass frozen in the muck. Tolmachoff admits: "The preservation of a complete carcass, or of a few ligaments on bones, or of a piece of hide, is exactly the same phenomenon, dependent on the same

92. Tolmachoff, p. 41.
93. For detailed descriptions of the incredible hardship imposed on travelers looking for mammoths, see Pfizenmayer, pp. 9-81.
94. Tolmachoff, p. 41.

special conditions, which has to be explained in the same way. For this reason, discoveries of a more or less complete carcass of a mammoth, or of isolated and small remnants of soft parts have been treated alike."[95] Since it is evident that there must be thousands of fleshy remnants, and since a fleshy remnant must be explained in the same way as a complete carcass, it is not at all unlikely that the tundra graveyards contain thousands of complete carcasses still frozen; in fact, that seems almost certain.

Finally, the only frozen remains that are likely to be reported at all by natives are those in which there is a financial benefit. That narrows the field to mammoth ivory. Hence thousands of other remains may never have been reported if they were observed. As Tolmachoff says, "Carcasses of other animals, as of the musk ox, horse, ox, etc., must be very common in the frozen ground of Siberia, but local people usually do not pay attention to them."[96]

These factors establish that indeed there probably are "countless thousands" and even hundreds of thousands of frozen remains yet to be discovered. Pfizenmayer, the leader of the Beresovka expedition, observed, "As huge numbers of them must have lived in the Arctic regions during the thousands of years of the Diluvial Age, we can be sure that the number of buried bodies that have come to light even since Siberia came under Russian rule — i.e., since the beginning of the seventeenth century — *must be far larger than we are aware of*" (italics added).[97]

This conclusion is precisely the opposite of that drawn by William Farrand.

95. Ibid.
96. Ibid., p. 19. This may explain why, to date, no frozen human remains have been reported. Stewart comments, "One day, perhaps, a perfectly preserved human being several millennia old may appear; there is no basic reason why not." See "Frozen Mammoths from Siberia," p. 68.
97. Pfizenmayer, p. 102.

The Climate of Siberia and Alaska During the Mammoth Age

Of crucial importance to an adequate theory explaining the cause of the mammoth extinctions is the related question of the kind of climatic regime that prevailed in their lifetimes. Needless to say, one's philosophical attitude toward the possibility of a catastrophic extinction or a gradual extinction plays a part in how the data are interpreted. Those skeptical of catastrophe explanations tend to level the distinctions between the climate of ancient and modern Siberia. Those who want to see a catastrophe explanation tend to emphasize the difference. The problem seems to boil down to this: if the mammoths lived in a moderate climate, then some continental climatic upheaval must have occurred in the association with their burial. On the other hand, if a climate similar to today's existed then, then more gradual and presently observed processes might account for their frozen remains. If the climate were at that time warm, then the mammoths must have frozen soon after their burial, or they would have decayed and no soft parts would be found in the tundras. So a warm climate would suggest a sudden catastrophe in which the mammoths were buried and permanently frozen by a climatic reversal from warm to severely cold. Because the physical mechanism necessary to produce such a phenomenon is unknown to meteorology, and certainly unobserved today, the tendency in much of the literature on the mammoth question has been to stress the similarity of ancient and modern temperatures.

In the following discussion we want to show that the mammoth was decidedly *not* adapted to cold weather and would have perished immediately if the temperature then compared with that of today. Furthermore, in the condensation of earth's ancient vapor canopy we find the physical mechanism for the continental climatic upheaval required by the catastrophe interpretation of the data. The question then is: Was the Siberian mammoth adapted to a cold climate such as now prevails?

THE MAMMOTH'S ADAPTATION TO COLD

In view of the fact that soft parts of mammoth carcasses have been found as far north as the Taymyr Peninsula in central northern Siberia,[98] the question of how a mammoth could survive in such a climate is crucial. This area, well within the Arctic Circle, today has one of the most severe climates on earth. In fact, the Arctic tundras where these carcasses are found are practically abandoned by most fauna. One sees an occasional musk ox, a solitary bear, but "for most of the year, the tundra stands as an ultimate wilderness, empty and austere."[99] Nordenskjold reported the present-day climate of Siberia as follows:[100]

January	-56° F	July	+60° F
February	-52° F	August	+53° F
March	-40° F	September	+36° F
April	+ 7° F	October	+ 7° F
May	+32° F	November	-36° F
June	+56° F	December	-49° F

The lowest temperature ever reported on the tundras is -93.6° F at Verkhoyansk below the southern edge of the Siberian tundra, 1,500 miles from the North Pole.[101] These dry, windswept plains, with piercing blizzards and biting cold, hardly make an ideal environment for an elephant. How could they have survived this incredible climate? It is easy, we are told, because the evidence suggests that the mammoth was uniquely adapted to this environment, so there is no need to posit warmer conditions than now. This evidence of the mammoth's adaptation to cold is fivefold.

98. Tolmachoff, p. 41.
99. Lincoln Barnett, "The Arctic Barrens," in *The World We Live In*, p. 201.
100. N. A. E. Nordenskjold, *The Voyage of the Vega Around Asia and Europe*, cited by Charles Hapgood, *The Path of the Pole*, p. 255.
101. "The Arctic Barrens," p. 203.

The Riddle of the Frozen Giants

The fat layer. It is well known that scientists found a 9 cm layer of fat under the thick hide of the Beresovka mammoth.[102] This has often been interpreted as proof that the mammoth was well protected against cold because fat is a poor conductor of heat. However, for an animal the size of an elephant, 9 cm (3.54 in.) is hardly an unusual amount of fat and would offer relatively little protection. Furthermore, a fat layer is now known to indicate a large food supply and not adaptation to cold. Hapgood cites a personal communication with Dr. Charles P. Lyman, professor of zoology at Harvard, in which Lyman stated:

> It is true that many animals become obese before the winter sets in but for the most part it seems likely that they become obese because they have an ample food supply in the fall, rather than that they are stimulated by cold to lay down a supply of fat. Cold will ordinarily increase the metabolic rate of any animal which means that it burns up more fuel in order to maintain its ordinary weight, to say nothing of adding weight in the form of fat. The amount of muscular activity in the daily life of either type of elephant is certainly just as important as the stimulus to cold as far as laying down a supply of fat is concerned.[103]

Hapgood concludes:

> The best opinion of physiologists is opposed to the view that the storage of fat by animals is a measure of self-protection against cold. The consensus is, on the contrary, that large fat accumulation testifies to ample food supply, obtainable without much effort, as indeed is the case with human beings. Physiologists agree that resistance to cold is mainly a question of the metabolic rate, rather than of insulation by fat.[104]

If anything, a large layer of fat implies a warm climate conducive to the production of a large and easily obtainable food supply rather than a cold climate.

It should also be noted that some tropical animals today have fat layers under their skins. The rhinoceros, for example, has about two inches.[105] The fat layer of this animal is hardly related to cold climate.

102. Herz, p. 621.
103. Hapgood, p. 254.
104. Ibid., p. 253.
105. B. J. Bridge, *African Wild Life* 8 (March 1954):37, cited by Hans Krause, *The Mammoth in Ice or Snow?*, p. 92.

Also, reindeer and caribou bulls have little or no fat in winter.[106] It would appear that the presence or absence of a fat layer has little to do with adaptation to cold. In 1950 biologists P. F. Scholander, V. Walters, R. Hock, and L. Irving tested the body insulation of some Arctic animals at Point Barrow, the northernmost tip of Alaska on the Arctic Ocean. During the winter of that year they tested the fur of the shrew, grizzly bear, polar bear, marten, weasel, white fox, red fox, eskimo dog, dall sheep, wolf, seal, ground sloth, beaver, lemming, hare, reindeer, and caribou. They concluded:

> Except for a thermally insignificant localized fat pad on the rump of the reindeer and caribou, none of the mammals (except the seals) has any significant layer of subcutaneous fat or blubber. *Subcutaneous fat is a heavy and poor insulator compared to fur and does not seem to play any role at all in the insulation of terrestrial arctic animals* [italics added].[107]

So the fat layer of the mammoth afforded him no help in adapting to a cold climate.

The wooly coat. The mammoth was well endowed with a fur coat and a wooly overcoat 25 cm. long.[108] This is generally taken as proof that the mammoth was well adapted to cold.[109] However, the presence of fur or hair is not necessarily an indication of protection against cold. Consider, for example, the hairy mountain Malaysian elephant that inhabits a tropical region today.[110] The Sumatran elephant from Burma, *R. lasiotis*, has a thick hair covering on its belly and legs, a hairy tail, and bristles at the end of its ears.[111] In fact, thick fur means nothing, as many animals of the equatorial jungles, such as tigers, have thick fur.

106. See Krause, p. 92, for a discussion of this.
107. P. F. Scholander et al., "Body Insulation of Some Arctic and Tropical Mammals and Birds," *Biological Bulletin* 99 (1950):226, cited by Krause, p. 93.
108. Herz, p. 614.
109. Karl W. Butzer, *Environment and Archaeology*, p. 245; Farrand, p. 730; Digby, p. 120.
110. Digby, p. 35.
111. Howorth, *The Mammoth and the Flood*, p. 46.

The Riddle of the Frozen Giants

All of this, however, is somewhat beside the point. An important fact, first reported in 1919 by the French zoologist and dermatologist H. Neuville, has been too often neglected in contemporary studies of the mammoth. Neuville performed a comparative microscopic study of sections of the skin of a mammoth and that of an Indian elephant and demonstrated that they were identical in thickness and structure. Furthermore, both animals lack sebaceous (oil producing) glands in the skin. The absence of these glands makes it impossible that the animal could have survived in a cold-weather climate. After a study of some well-preserved pieces of mammoth skin supplied to the Laboratory of Comparative Anatomy at the Paris Museum and the skin of the Stenbok-Fermor mammoth, Neuville concluded, "On the mammoth as well as on the elephant, the hair occurs without its accustomed annex, the sebaceous gland."[112] After pointing out that the skin of the mammoth and that of the tropical African and Indian elephants are exactly alike, he observed:

> We have, therefore, two animals very nearly related zoologically — the mammoth and the elephant — one of which lived in severe climates while the other is now confined to certain parts of the Torrid Zone. The mammoth, it is said, was protected from the cold by its fur and by the thickness of its dermis. But the dermis, as I have said, and as the illustrations prove, is identical in the two instances: it would therefore be hard to attribute a specially adaptive function to the skin of the mammoth.[113]

He continued:

> The very peculiar fur of the mammoth thus furnished only a precarious protection against cold, a protection analogous to that enjoyed at present by few mammals of the tropical zone. Its dermis was, it is true, very thick, but no more so than that of existing elephants. It appears to me impossible to find, in the anatomical examination of the skin and pelage, any argument in favor of adaptation to cold.[114]

112. H. Neuville, "On the Extinction of the Mammoth," *Annual Report Smithsonian Institute*, 1919, p. 331.
113. Ibid., p. 331.
114. Ibid., p. 332.

This lack of sebaceous glands has been confirmed by more recent studies.[115]

It is commonly known that the presence of grease produced by sebaceous glands renders wool resistant to cold. Mammals deprived of sebaceous glands are very rare. The two-toed sloth of Central and South America and the golden moles of Africa are examples, and it is well known that sloths are particularly sensitive to cold and damp.[116] Today's elephants also lack these glands.[117]

The necessity of the presence of oil-producing glands in the skin to render the pelage resistant to cold was graphically illustrated recently in West Virginia. The local population was being overrun by blackbirds, which were destroying crops and generally making life unbearable. Several methods of extermination were tried, all of which were unsuccessful. Finally, it was decided that at the next cold night, planes would be sent aloft carrying detergent to spray the entire blackbird population. The purpose of the detergent was to break down the oil in the feathers of the animals to destroy their protection against the cold. A similar procedure was employed against a plague of blackbirds in Alabama (January 1977).

Oil in the hair impedes the penetration of moisture, and this protects the skin from frozen ice. So it appears impossible that the mammoths were in any way adapted to cold.

Digby reacted to Neuville's analysis: "That theory, cuticle glands or no cuticle glands, is untenable unless you adduce ground for the species not moving out of North Siberia when North Siberia became no longer congenial to it."[118] Digby's preoccupation with gradualism has led him to overlook the obvious point: the reason the mammoths did not leave the area when the climate changed is *because they did not have time to*

115. M. L. Ryder, "Hair of the Mammoth," Nature 249 (10 May, 1974):190, although Ryder does not seem to be aware of the consequences of this for adaptation to an Arctic climate.
116. Neuville, p. 332.
117. Ryder, p. 190.
118. Digby, p. 70.

The Riddle of the Frozen Giants

leave; the change must have been sudden and catastrophic. It appears that Digby is willing to throw out the clear testimony of a microscopic examination of the skin because he is already committed to a metaphysics that does not allow a continental climatic upheaval.

Tolmachoff also disagrees with Neuville on the grounds that the animal skins used by mankind as protection against cold are dead skins, not only deprived of any glands and secretions, but carefully cleaned from any grease and moisture. In fact, Arctic natives do everything possible to keep their dressing furs dry and not oiled.[119] Tolmachoff seems confused here. Dead skins *do* provide protection against cold, and they obviously have no oil-producing glands in them. But if those same skins were the skins of a live animal, the lack of oil glands would render them defenseless from freezing, and the skin would die; and, of course, so would the animal. The skin itself must be kept alive by this protection in order for the animal to be kept alive. The reason the dead skins give protection to man is because they form a kind of heat trap between human skin and the skin of the fur. This gives excellent insulation and prevents damage to the man, regardless of what happens to the fur (within limits). A dead skin does not need protection against cold, but a live skin does.

A recent inquiry to the British Wool Industry Research Association confirmed Neuville's thesis: "It seems reasonable, therefore, to assume that the wool wax is responsible not only for conferring protection against the weather, but also for the maintenance of the fleece in an orderly and hence more efficacious state."[120] So it appears that the hair of the mammoth, deprived of oil, would offer poor protection against the dampness of an Arctic blizzard.

Not only does the skin of the mammoth lack sebaceous glands, but it also lacks erector muscles. Without these muscles the ability of any fur coat to protect the skin against cold is

119. I. P. Tolmachoff, "Note on the Extinction of the Mammoth in Siberia," *American Journal of Science*, 14 (July 1927):67.
120. Hapgood, p. 253.

greatly reduced. When an animal such as a wolf, for example, feels cold, it raises its fur by means of these erector muscles. This has the effect of creating more air pockets, hence better insulation for it. This is similar to our putting on a thicker sweater. However, mammoth skin lacked these erector muscles,[121] yet all known Arctic animals today have them.[122]

The fat-rumped tail. When the Beresovka mammoth was excavated, a short broad tail that effectively covered the anus was discovered on the carcasses. This anal flap covering has been taken as proof of the animal's adaptation to cold.[123] However, the fat-rumped sheep, which lives in the center of Africa in the tropics, has the same fatty tail.[124]

Furthermore, tropical elephants today have precisely the same kind of anal covering that the mammoths had.[125] In fact, when scientists at the National Museum of Natural History in Stuttgart (West Germany) measured the anal flap of a large African bull elephant shot in Tanzania, its width turned out to be 18 cm,[126] exactly as wide as that of the Beresovka mammoth.[127] If an elephant living today in a hot tropical region has an anal flap as large as that of the wooly mammoth, how then can the hairy mammoth's anal flap prove adaptation to the Arctic cold?

Caribou and moose. It is often argued that there is no problem assuming that the mammoth lived in a cold climate because the caribou and the moose survive the Arctic winter today. Harold Anthony, curator of the Museum of Natural History, observes,

121. Ryder, p. 191.
122. See Krause, p. 52, where he cites personal communications with scientists at the National Museum of Natural History in Stuttgart, 22 February 1977.
123. Tolmachoff, "Note on the Extinction of the Mammoth in Siberia," p. 68.
124. Neuville, p. 333.
125. Sylvia K. Sikes, *The Natural History of the African Elephant,* cited by Krause, p. 88.
126. Krause, p. 88.
127. Pfizenmayer, p. 236.

"Both caribou and moose survive the present Alaskan winter despite the heavy snow and the low temperature. It seems hardly necessary to have a milder climate in order for the mammoth to exist, and a milder climate would lessen the likelihood of a carcass being frozen and held intact for thousands of years."[128]

But the caribou and moose do have sebaceous glands and erector muscles in their skin, which gives them a pelage that provides a defense against the blizzards of the Arctic.

Food remains. One of the most surprising results of the Beresovka excavation (1901) was the discovery of the remains of numerous plants of various species in the stomach of the carcass. Many of these plants are found growing in the tundra in the same area today during the summer. From this it has been concluded that the climate then was the same as now. Digby, for example, maintains, "All of these latter plants, traces of which were found in the teeth and stomach of the Beresovka mammoth, grow in the region today indicating that the climate was neither cooler nor warmer than it is now."[129]

We will undertake a full discussion of the significance of these plant remains in the next chapter. At this point, however, we need to point out that the above reasoning seriously distorts the evidence. First, although it is true that many of these plants found in the stomach of the mammoth still sprinkle the Siberian landscape, these same plants are found far to the south. For example, the same species of wheatgrasses found in the stomach of the mammoth are also found in the Great Plains of North America.[130] The common buttercup found in the stomach ranges all the way from the tundra in the north to Cape Horn, flourishing also in Florida.[131] The *Alopecurus alpinus sin* (foxtail grass), according to the Russian expert who did the

128. Anthony, p. 301.
129. Digby, p. 143; see also Tolmachoff, "The Carcasses of the Mammoths," p. 47.
130. A. A. Case, botanist associated with College of Veterinary Medicine, Columbia, Missouri, personal communication, 6 January 1976.
131. Ibid.

original study on the mammoth remains, "is closely related to varieties found south of the tundra and not to those presently there."[132] Sukachev says in regard to the *Agropyron cristatûm* (L) Bess:

> Remains of this plant are very numerous in the contents of the stomach. They are so well preserved that there is no doubt as to the exact species. The finding of these plants is of very great interest. Not only are they scarcely known anywhere in the arctic region, they are even so far as I have been able to discover, very rare also in the Yakutsk district. . . . It is a plant of the plains. . . . The general range of this plant includes southern Europe.[133]

Botanist Case, after examining Sukachev's list, observed, "The plants named in the letter from Jody Dillow are mostly arboreal plants that existed before the last ice age, and they range from Alaska to Hudson Bay, and South to the Gulf of Mexico or even into Mexico."[134]

The existence in the stomach of the mammoth of a plant that still grows today does not prove that the climate then was the same as now. It only proves that there is a comparable climate during the summer to that in Florida, the Mediterranean, or even Mexico, since these same plants are found in these regions today. Even Farrand is forced to admit that the flora associated with the "Beresovka and Mamontova mammoths indicates a climate slightly warmer than the present."[135] Reid positively asserts that the plants found with the mammoths are not characteristic of a cold environment.[136]

It is particularly interesting to note that "the fact that most of these undigested remains of the Beresovka mammoth's last meal have seeds attached to them shows that the beast died in

132. V. N. Sukachev, "Examination of Plant Remnants Found within the Food of the Mammoth Discovered on the Beresovka River Territory of Yakutsk." (Petrograd, 1914, in Russian), trans. from the French by Mrs. Norman Hapgood, cited by Charles Hapgood, *Path of the Pole*, p. 266.
133. Ibid. Southern Europe is the Mediterranean area.
134. Case, personal communication.
135. Farrand, p. 733.
136. *Geological Magazine* 8 (1881):505, cited by Neuville, p. 327.

The Riddle of the Frozen Giants

autumn."[137] Sukachev agrees: "The discovery of the ripe fruits of sedges, grasses, and other plants suggests that the mammoth died during the second half of July or the beginning of August."[138]

This agrees (within 80 days) with the biblical indications that the Flood began on the seventeenth day of the "second month" (Gen. 7:11). It is generally agreed that the "second month" refers to Heshvan (October-November) in the Jewish calendar.[139] So according to the Bible, the Flood began on about October 22.[140]

A consideration of the evidence for the mammoth's special adaptation for cold leads to the conclusion that, in fact, it was not well adapted at all. Furthermore, there seems to be convincing evidence supporting the thesis that the climate of ancient northern Siberia must have been much warmer than today.

EVIDENCE OF A WARM CLIMATE

Several factors suggest that a moderate rather than the present severe climate prevailed in northern Siberia.

The mammoth was not adapted to cold. As pointed out above, the mammoth of Siberia was no more adapted to cold than the tropical Indian elephant.

Moderate fauna and flora. Along with the mammoth remains throughout Alaska and Siberia we find numerous examples of

137. Digby, p. 143.
138. Sukachev, "Examination of Plant Remnants," cited by Hapgood, p. 268.
139. U. Cassuto, *A Commentary on the Book of Genesis,* 2:83; C. F. Keil and F. Delitzsch, *The Pentateuch,* 1:145.
140. Filby has observed that the date for the beginning of the Flood may be what is behind the worldwide legends of "the day of the dead," which occurs in November. Frederick A. Filby, *The Flood Reconsidered,* pp. 106-7.
141. Digby, p. 151; Tolmachoff, "The Carcasses of the Mammoth," p. 71.

plants and animals that could not have survived if the ancient climate was as severe as today's. What good does it do to argue that the mammoth was adapted to cold when it is impossible to use this argument in the case of several of the other animals? For example, Baron Toll, the Arctic explorer, found remains of a saber-toothed tiger and a 90-foot plum tree with green leaves and ripe fruit on its branches over 600 miles north of the Arctic Circle in the New Siberian Islands.[141] Today the only vegetation that grows there is a 1-inch-high willow. In fact, no such hardwood trees grow today anywhere within 2,000 miles of those islands:

> Therefore the climate must have been very much different when they got buried; and, please note, they could not have been buried in frozen muck which is rock-hard, nor could they have retained their foliage if they were washed far north by currents from warmer climes. They must have grown thereabouts, and the climate must have been not only warm enough but have had a long enough growing period of summer sunlight for them to have leafed and fruited.[142]

Toll comments on the scarcity of food and the presence of pine needles and poplar leaves frozen in the muck.[143] These observations indicate both a warm climate then and an insufficient food supply today to accomodate vast mammoth herds. Along with the fruit tree, the remains of a wooly rhinoceros, a mammoth, and a horse were found by Toll. The warm-weather hippopotamus has also been found in the tundra's frozen muck.[144] The region in which the Beresovka mammoth was uncovered is a veritable graveyard of moderate-climate types of animals. Mixed in the same landslide in which the Beresovka mammoth was found were the remains of a bison and a wild horse. Pfizenmayer observed, "There is hardly one place on the banks of rivers and lakes in the district of Yakutsk in which prehistoric remains of animals have been found that has not yielded skeletal fragments of the prehistoric wild horse."[145] In

142. "Much About Muck," *Pursuit* 2 (October 1969):68.
143. Cited by Digby, p. 150.
144. Butzer, p. 325.
145. Pfizenmayer, p. 176.

The Riddle of the Frozen Giants

fact, the remains of an entire frozen horse carcass have been reported.[146]

Nordenskjold speaks of mammoth remains being found in an area of the tundra that is completely frozen today and mixed with driftwood originating from the mammoth period. The Russian natives of Siberia call the wood "Noah's wood." The trees that produced this wood no longer survive in the area.[147] Sannikof found on the island of Kotelnoi the skulls and bones of horses, buffaloes, oxen, and sheep in such abundance that these animals must formerly have lived there in large herds. At present, however, the icy wilderness produces nothing that could afford nourishment, nor would they be able to endure the climate. Sannikof concludes that a milder climate must formerly have prevailed here, and that these animals may, therefore, have been contemporary with the mammoth, whose remains are found in every part of the island. Another circumstance whence he implies a change of climate, is the frequent occurrence here, as well as in the New Siberian Islands, of large trees partially fossilized.[148]

The story is the same in Alaska. Everywhere mammoth remains are mixed with those of moderate-climate types. A lion has been uncovered in the frozen Alaska tundra;[149] this animal frequents only tropical regions today. At Elephant Point, right on the Arctic Circle, the remains of a mammoth, a bison, and a horse were found; more horses were found farther north.[150] Quackenbush reports the existence of a beaver dam near the mammoth find at Elephant Point.[151] Moffitt found a beaver dam in silts on Old Glory Creek near Deering. Beaver-gnawed wood has been reported in the Kougarok region, buried in ice.[152] The

---

146. Ibid., p. 177.
147. Howorth, *The Mammoth and the Flood*, p. 67.
148. Cited by Howorth, *The Mammoth and the Flood*, p. 66.
149. Sanderson, p. 39.
150. Quackenbush, pp. 115, 121.
151. Ibid., p. 111.
152. Stephen Taber, "Perennially Frozen Ground in Alaska: Its Origin and History," *Geological Society of America Bulletin* 54 (1943):1486-88.

northern range of the American beaver coincides with the limits of the forest line, but these beaver dams and beaver-gnawed pieces of wood are found in frozen silts beyond the present forest line. These facts led some of the scientists associated with the *U. S. Geological Survey* to conclude that the Pleistocene climate was somewhat milder than that of present time, as proved by the fact that "large trees have been found associated with horse and mammoth remains in deposits of muck in regions which are now treeless."[153] As pointed out above, the wild horse today is never known to venture above latitude 49° north, whereas these deposits are located north of latitude 66°.[154]

Dr. Jack A. Wolfe in a recent *U. S. Geological Survey Report* told that Alaska once teemed with tropical plants. He found evidence of mangroves, palm trees, Burmese laquer trees, and groups of trees that now produce nutmeg and Macassar oil.[155]

In view of these facts it seems pointless to hear the endless refrain that the mammoth was adapted to the cold when the horse, hippopotamus, lion, saber-toothed tiger, and rhinoceros were not.

Food supply. In order to supply food for the vast mammoth herds the climate surely must have been warmer than today's winter in the tundra. Howorth summarizes this difficulty:

> Is it possible that these great animals could have lived under the conditions now prevailing on the tundras? I think I may say without hesitation that no inquirer, no student of this question, who has either himself been in Siberia, or who knows what the conditions of a Northern Siberian climate are, has ever answered this question affirmatively. Pallas, Meddendorf, Baer, Brandt, Schmidt, Schrenk, etc., are all agreed that the vast herds of mammoths and the associated animals could not live in Northern Siberia under its present conditions.[156]

153. A. J. Collier, F. L. Hess, P. S. Smith, and A. H. Brooks, "The Gold Placers of Part of Seward Peninsula, Alaska," *U. S. Geological Survey Bulletin* 328 (1908):90.
154. Howorth, *The Mammoth and the Flood*, p. 264.
155. Reported in the *Dallas Times Herald*, 24 April 1978.
156. Howorth, *The Mammoth and the Flood*, p. 57.

Even during the brief summer from July 13 to August 5 there are constant north winds and frosts at night. Wrangel says, "The vegetation of summer is scarcely more than a struggle for existence."[157] Most of today's tundra in northern Siberia is barren wilderness, and little will grow on it during the winter. It is constantly swept by terrible icy winds and is covered with moss and sprinkled with a few humble flowers. "On such feeding ground it is physically impossible, as has been well said, that elephants and rhinoceroses could exist."[158] Today's elephants exist primarily on foliage and small branches of trees (which grow shoulder high in the jungles and in the beds of African rivers), and they would probably starve in a pasture today where the grass is short. This is true today even in the summer. But in the winter, which in northern Siberia lasts for ten months every year, and during which the ground is covered with deep snow and is swept by the terrible north wind, only a few hardy animals such as the raven, snowy owl, polar fox, and polar bear (carnivores, not vegetarians) are able to survive. Recent geological literature seems to concur with the thesis that the mammoth "could not have found sufficient food in winter in 77° north latitude if the climate was as severe as it is today."[159] Even Lyell (the founder of modern-day geology) was constrained to admit, when faced with these facts, "that it would be impossible for herds of mammoths and rhinoceroses to subsist at present throughout the year."[160]

Incredibly, Digby still clings to the notion that vast herds could have lived there throughout the winter. The answer is, he says, that they simply stayed in the proximity of a few clusters of trees. "The mammoths kept to the neighborhood of trees for shelter from the piercing winter winds and blinding blizzards, and for proximity to their winter supply."[161] However, we can hardly imagine hundreds of thousands of mammoths, rhinoceroses, and other animals huddling together in the

157. Ibid., p. 58.
158. Ibid., p. 59.
159. Taber, pp. 1486-88.
160. Cited by Howorth, *The Mammoth and the Flood*, p. 60.
161. Digby, p. 138.

meager protection of a few trees that might, by chance, survive the Arctic winter.

Most of the animal remains are found well above today's tree line and many in the New Siberian Islands, which are totally treeless.[162] Permafrost keeps the ground permanently frozen for hundreds of feet. Every summer the top few feet thaw, permitting the growth of Arctic vegetation, but that thaw "does not penetrate deep enough to encourage the roots of trees, save for a few stunted specialized forms."[163] So the southern limit of the permafrost line marks the upper limit of the world's forests.[164] Consequently, the mammoths that are found buried in the permafrost could not have been surviving off trees that do not grow in the permafrost, unless the permafrost did not then exist, in which case the climate must have been much warmer.

Furthermore, the amount of vegetation required to feed such herds is astronomical. A modern elephant in captivity eats 500 pounds of hay per day.[165] In the wild, they apparently require at least two tons a week and 30 gallons of water a day.[166] The average rainfall of much of the area in which the mammoths are found is less than ten inches annually.[167] This is the annual rainfall of the Sahara Desert. Even though evaporation is negligible, how can hundreds of thousands of mammoths requiring 30 gallons of water a day survive in a desert by sucking snow?

The presence of these vast herds requires a copious food supply, which in turn requires a much more moderate, humid climate than presently prevails in the tundras.

162. *Hammond World Atlas,* p. 5.
163. "The Arctic Barrens," p. 199.
164. Ibid., p. 201.
165. E. Lendell Cockrum, *Introduction to Mammology,* p. 389; see "Much About Muck," pp. 68-69; "Elephant," in *Van Nostrand's Scientific Encyclopedia,* p. 939, where it is noted that the African elephant has been known to consumer 1,000 pounds of twigs, fruit, or leaves a day.
166. Filby, p. 21.
167. *Hammond World Atlas,* p. 56.

The Riddle of the Frozen Giants 351

Similarity to the Indian elephant. A histological examination of mammoth bone,[168] a comparative anatomical examination of mammoth skin and that of a modern elephant,[169] and a serological examination of the blood of the Beresovka mammoth[170] all establish that the mammoth and the Indian elephant are extremely closely related. Since the Indian elephant cannot survive in subzero temperatures, one would presume that an intimate relative with exactly the same skin and bone could not endure it either. These similarities suggest that the mammoth, therefore, lived in a moderate climate as does its Indian cousin.

The frozen muck. Perhaps the most direct proof that the climate of northern Siberia must have been warm during the mammoth age is found in the muck in which the mammoths are buried. Muck is frozen soil bound together by water. When this frozen soil melts, it results in an appalling, and often stinking, sort of soup composed of goo with silt, sand, pebbles, and boulders, often with masses of preserved, semidecayed or fully decayed vegetable and animal matter. A glance at a world map will show that it lies only in low-level plains or tablelands. Yet according to Russian scientists, who have major land areas covered with the substance, in some places they have drilled down 4,000 feet and still did not reach solid rock.[171] This requires that the lands now blanketed with the material must, at one time, have been much higher above sea level, so that the muck could have been deposited on them or that the ancient sea level was once 4,000 feet lower. In view of the fact that the muck is bound by water with vegetable and animal remains scattered uniformly throughout its depth, could it be evidence of catastrophic sedimentation? The burial of these animal remains required rapid sedimentation such as is not going on today. Here one finds evidence of a deluge followed by a permanent

168. H. C. Ezra and S. F. Cook, "Histology of Mammoth Bone," *Science* 129 (February 1952):465-66.
169. Neuville, pp. 329-31.
170. Pfizenmayer, p. 114, and J. K. Charlesworth, *The Quaternary Era*, 2:794.
171. "Much About Muck," pp. 68-69.

climate change that gradually froze the muck down to a depth of 4,000 feet. It would appear that if today's climate prevailed then there is no conceivable way the mammoths could have been buried. Today the permafrost extends down for over 1,000 feet, and it is obvious that a frozen or unfrozen carcass could not be driven into frozen earth. The very existence of the millions of bones and soft parts buried in the muck means that, at one time, the permafrost did not exist and, therefore, that the climate was much warmer. Howorth summarizes:

> Now, by no physical process known to us can we understand how soft flesh could thus be buried in ground while it is frozen as hard as flint without disintegrating it. We cannot push an elephant's body into a mass of solid ice or hard frozen gravel and clay without entirely destroying the fine articulations and pounding the whole mass into a jelly, or would we fail in greatly disturbing the ground in the process. When we, therefore, meet with the great carcasses of the mammoths with their most delicate tissue, their eyes, trunks, and feet beautifully preserved and lying several feet underground in hard, frozen, undisturbed gravel and clay, we cannot escape the conclusion that when these carcasses were buried, the ground was soft and yielding. Here then we have a very important and inevitable difficulty from which there is no escape, and which the advocates of Uniformity as that doctrine is currently held, would do well to bravely face. The facts compel us to admit that when the mammoth was buried in Siberia the ground was soft and the climate therefore comparatively mild and genial, and that immediately afterwards the same ground became frozen and the same climate became arctic, and that they have remained so to this day, and this not gradually in accordance with some slowly continuous astronomical or cosmical changes, but suddenly.[172]

Quackenbush, after examining the same phenomenon in the frozen soil of Alaska, made a similar observation. "The existence of bogs amounts to a proof that some portions of the surface were thawed to a considerable depth . . . this is not true today in that it only goes down a few feet. Thus, this suggests a milder climate."[173]

This completes the survey of the remnants of the frozen giants. The evidence seems to bear out the notion that they lived at a time when the climate of northern Siberia was considerably more moderate than today. For some unknown reason all of these animals were destroyed, many of them later frozen into

172. Howorth, *The Mammoth and the Flood*, p. 95.
173. Quackenbush, p. 126.

The Riddle of the Frozen Giants

the tundra muck, and others buried, leaving their skeletal remains behind. How is this continental extinction to be explained? This is "the riddle of the frozen giants." Two schools of thought interpret these data. It is to these contradictory theories that we now turn our attention.

Chapter 11

The Laughter of the Gods

The "Riddle of the Frozen Giants" has yet to be satisfactorily answered. Digby was certainly right when he said, "The Gods must have enjoyed many a hearty laugh over humanity's attempts to account for the remains of the mammoth."[1] It could well be that their mirth will be rekindled as we present a new theory. However, they must have had a twinkle in their eyes when they considered the hypothesis set forth by those schooled in the ways of uniformity, and a hearty chuckle must have erupted when they turned the final pages of Digby's book. In any event, our attention will now be directed toward the question: Was the Pleistocene mammoth extinction sudden or gradual? Needless to say, traditional geology always feels the need to seek a gradualistic solution.

Gradualistic Theories

Recent literature on the mammoth question has gone out of its way to debunk any catastrophic notions of the Pleistocene extinctions. Richard Flint in his excellent work on Pleistocene geology says, "In Siberia alone some 50,000 mammoth tusks have been collected and sold to the ivory trade, and there are rare occurrences of whole animals preserved in frozen ground. The finds have fostered many tales of great catastrophe for which there is no factual support."[2] William Farrand confi-

1. Bassett Digby, *The Mammoth and Mammoth Hunting Grounds in Northeast Siberia*, p. 19.
2. Richard Foster Flint, *Glacial and Pleistocene Geology*, p. 470.

dently assures his readers, "All the evidence now at hand supports the conclusions of previous workers that no catastrophic event was responsible for the death and preservation of the frozen wooly mammoths. The demise of the animals accords with uniformitarian concepts."[3]

Farrand says he wrote his article "to bring the subject up to date and at the same time to supply scientists in general the information with which to refute the current quasi-scientific theories."[4] In point of fact, most "previous workers" interpreted the data catastrophically,[5] and the material discussed above throws serious doubt on whether the demise of these animals could ever "accord with uniformitarian concepts." The discussion to follow should remove any remaining doubts.

A distinction is often drawn between the extermination of an individual mammoth and the extinction of an entire species.[6] This means that one should be cautious about arguing from some seemingly catastrophic aspects concerning the death of a particular mammoth and extrapolating from that a general theory of Pleistocene extinctions. On the other hand, when a number of individual finds have peculiarities about them that do not seem to fit into traditional concepts, we should not continually posit specialized local catastrophes to account for everything when one general catastrophe might equally well, or even more correctly, explain the evidence.

If it were true that the presence of frozen flesh, or of a whole mammoth, in the frozen muck was a rare occasion, then it certainly would be presumptuous to argue for a continental catastrophe. However, as we pointed out in the previous chap-

3. William R. Farrand, "Frozen Mammoths and Modern Geology," *Science* 133 (March 1961):729.
4. Ibid., p. 729, where he refers to articles by Hapgood, Sanderson, and Velikovsky.
5. For example, Howorth, Schrenck, Brandt, Pallas, Buckland, Erman, and many others; see Henry H. Howorth, *The Mammoth and the Flood*.
6. I. P. Tolmachoff, "The Carcasses of the Mammoth and Rhinoceros Found in the Frozen Ground of Siberia," *Transactions of the American Philosophical Society* 23 (1929):65.

ter, the evidence clearly suggests that there are hundreds of thousands, even millions of mammal remains including whole carcasses as well as numerous instances of partial preservation of soft parts. Howorth insists that soft parts are found over a broad area, and he carefully documents his evidence in a way for all to see who care to take the time to check him out.

> Again, as I have said, the instances of the soft parts being preserved are not mere local and sporadic ones, but they form a chain of examples along the whole length of Siberia, from the Urals, to the land of the Chukchis, so that we have to do here with a condition of things which prevails, and with meteorological conditions that extend over a continent. When we find such a series ranging so widely preserved in the same perfect way, and all evidencing a sudden change of climate from a comparatively temperate one to one of great rigour, we cannot help concluding that they all bear witness to a common event. We cannot postulate a separate climatic cataclysm for each individual case and each individual locality, but we are forced to the conclusion that the now permanently frozen zone in Asia became frozen at the same time from the same causes.[7]

Furthermore, this continent-wide distribution of soft parts documented by Howorth and admitted by Tolmachoff requires, according to the latter, that the instances of the preservation of the soft parts be treated exactly the same as the instances of the preservation of an entire carcass. Similar climatic conditions are necessary for both. Tolmachoff insists:

> The preservation of a complete carcass, or of a few ligaments on bones, or of a piece of hide, is exactly the same phenomenon, dependent on the same special conditions, which has to be explained in the same way. For this reason, discoveries of a more or less complete carcass of a mammoth, or of isolated and small remnants of soft parts have been treated alike.[8]

The purpose of the above digression is to anticipate some of the premises behind the development of many of the noncatastrophic theories of extinction and extermination (to use Tolmachoff's distinctions) to be discussed below. By focusing attention on possible gradualistic explanations for the demise of four whole carcasses, some geologists seem to think they have removed the need for catastrophic theories for the mammoth extinctions in general. However, as Tolmachoff pointed out,

7. Howorth, p. 96.
8. Tolmachoff, p. 41.

their same localized theories have to be expanded not to four localities but to hundreds of thousands, wherever soft parts have been preserved. So this common line of argument has little validity.

Finally, the question of the extinction and the preservation of the remains after extinction are intimately related. Too frequently they seem to have been treated separately. For example, Tolmachoff will argue that the Beresovka mammoth must have died in the summer by falling into the mud and suffocating. But elsewhere he argues that the freshly preserved fresh parts of any of these animals can be accounted for by the fact that whales that die in the winter often have fresh fat on them for months. But the Beresovka mammoth did not die in winter. The same mechanism that buried the mammoths must have in some way contributed to their preservation. To posit two separate mechanisms — mud in summer for burial and ice in winter for freezing — overly complicates the problem and, in fact, as we will show in the next section, is for the Beresovka mammoth, at least, thermodynamically impossible. We will show in a later section that drastic and sudden temperature drops are the only possible explanation of at least some of the remains. Since full discussion of that subject is reserved for later, this later evidence will only be alluded to in responses to gradualistic arguments in the discussion to follow.

The present literature on the mammoth question has posited no less than five different theories to account for either the demise of individual mammoths or the extinction of the species. The remnants of well-preserved parts are explained through reference to processes observed today.

EXTINCTION BY MAN

Arguing from the parallels with the human destruction of the American bison, Digby suggests that there is nothing unusual connected with the extermination of the mammoth herds. Apparently flint knives were found near one buried skeleton.[9] Concerning the frozen remains that litter the New Siberian

9. Digby, p. 63.

The Laughter of the Gods 359

Islands north of the Arctic Circle, Digby has proposed that fear of man drove them up there. Then an earthquake occurred that severed these islands from the Asiatic mainland, and the mammoths froze to death in the winter cold.[10] However, if the climate then was as it is today (as Digby insists), why would a mammoth go up there to escape man, only to freeze to death in the intolerable Arctic winter? Furthermore, it really does not seem likely that the human population of northern Siberia could have been sufficient to have put much of a scare into the mammoths. Today's population in this area is less than three people per square mile.[11] Also, there is an equally immense mammoth graveyard far to the south of the New Siberian Islands, indicating that the mammoths never did flee to the north, but were equally distributed all over the area.

Tolmachoff agrees that the notion of extinction by man is quite unlikely. He observes that the human population was then too scarce, ancient men were armed too poorly, and the extermination of the bison was by the *white* man with rifles, not by the Indian who lived peacefully with the bison for thousands of years.[12]

Also, if the New Siberian Islands' climate was the same then as it is today, there is hardly a more improbable place on earth for the mammoths to flee to if they were trying to escape men. Finally, as Howorth pointed out long ago, present-day tribes of men cause absolutely no diminution in the number of easily anguishable herds of reindeer which they attack and slaughter while crossing the rivers, since they return again in equal numbers another year.[13]

EXTINCTION BY DEFECTIVE ADAPTATION TO SURROUNDING
CONDITIONS

Neuville suggested that, due to gradually changing climatic conditions, the mammoths simply ran out of food, and as the

10. Ibid., p. 16.
11. *Hammond World Atlas,* p. 55.
12. Tolmachoff, p. 66.
13. Howorth, p. 170.

food supply diminished, the mammoth herds were exterminated.[14] Digby correctly counters that the mammoths would be rather stupid to simply lie down and starve to death on the icy tundra. It is more likely that they would migrate as other animals do today if they run out of food.[15] Furthermore, there is no evidence to indicate defective adaptation, as the bellies of the animals discovered are always full. In fact, the Adams mammoth was so fat that its belly hung down below its knees.[16] Also, other animals as well died out during the Pleistocene extinction. All of these animals died out more or less simultaneously, and the defective adaptation of one cannot explain the death of the others.[17]

EXTERMINATION BY BURIAL IN MUD FLOWS

During the summer thaws, flows of mud are created in river beds as spring streams swell. Some have suggested that the mammoths got stuck in the sticky "goo" and then fell down. As a result, the mammoth body may have formed a kind of "mud dam," and the mud piled up on it and buried it.[18] Conceivably this could account for the burial of some carcasses. A variation of this is the bog theory. It has been suggested that while grazing near riverbeds the mammoths got caught in swamps and simply sank, or that they fell through flood plain deposits or thin ice and drowned.[19]

14. H. Neuville, "On the Extinction of the Mammoth," *Annual Report Smithsonian Institution*, 1919, p. 335.
15. Digby, pp. 68-69.
16. Tolmachoff, p. 66.
17. Ibid., p. 68.
18. Ibid., p. 57.
19. Harold E. Anthony, "Nature's Deep Freeze," *Natural History* 58 (September 1949):301. See also John Massey Stewart, "Frozen Mammoths from Siberia Bring the Ice Age to Vivid Life," *Smithsonian* 8 (December 1977):64-65, where seven speculative ways of mammoth death are suggested. They are all without evidence and represent a futile attempt to avoid catastrophic interpretations.

As pointed out in the preceding chapter, the evidence clearly suggests that there are thousands of whole carcasses and fresh remains still to be discovered in the frozen muck. The fact that 39 carcasses have been uncovered against incredible odds suggests the presence of thousands more "needles in the haystack." Hence it seems futile to try to explain away a few carcasses on this basis when, in fact, we have to be able to account for thousands like them, which is clearly improbable. Furthermore, on the assumption that the climate then was similar to today's, the presence of permafrost would require that the bog or mud depth could only have been two feet, which is hardly enough mud to make a significant dam or a deep enough bog to bury a mammoth. If the mammoth was buried in mud or bogs, it would require that the climate be much warmer. If it was buried in a mud flow during the present brief summer climate, then the problem of its preservation surfaces again. If the temperature was warm enough for the mud to flow, it was certainly warm enough to decompose the mammoths, yet thousands of whole carcasses are likely to be in the muck and several have already been uncovered. Also, how would this theory account for the common phenomenon of mammoths found buried standing up?[20] We have no known finds in Alaska or Siberia where mammoth remains are buried in peat bogs or mud flows in Siberia. Finally, as Tolmachoff admits, "Everywhere carcasses of the mammoth and rhinoceros were found they had been buried within the frozen ground of the tundra near its upper surface and usually on comparatively elevated points, on the top of bluffs, etc."[21] Long ago Wrangel made the same observation, "The best Mammoth bones, as well as the greatest number, are found at a certain depth below the surface usually in clayhills more rarely in black earth. The more solid the clay, the better the bones are preserved. Experience has also shown that more are found in elevations situated near high hills than along the low coast of the flat tundra."[22]

20. Howorth, p. 61.
21. Tolmachoff, p. 51.
22. Cited by Howorth, p. 181.

This fact seems to be fatal to the thesis that they were caught in bogs or trapped in mud flows, which occur only near the low areas along river banks or along the coast and not near the high hills. Curiously, Farrand rejects this difficulty by insisting that the "best studied" mammoths come from river banks.[23] The relevance of the term "best studied" is ambiguous. Presumably Farrand is referring to the four carcasses that have been treated by modern scientific analysis. What has this to do with the numerous finds of fresh parts and skeletal remains found on high ground all over southern, central, and northern Siberia and Alaska?

CHANGED CLIMATIC CONDITIONS

The idea of mammoth extinction by changed climatic conditions prevailed for many years but is now rejected by many. Howorth, of course, espoused it, as did Neuville and Lydekker in the 20th century. Tolmachoff rejected it on the grounds that it would only account for the extinctions in the New Siberian Islands.[24] However, this objection overlooks the obvious consideration of the *cause* of a change in climate. If a cause for the change in climate in the north Siberian regions (from moderate to severe) could also explain the Pleistocene extinctions in central Siberia and Europe, then that "cause" should be given consideration. Unfortunately, a cause sufficient to produce these kinds of effects requires a continent-wide catastrophe and meteorological phenomena presently unobserved; in other words, it violates the basic principles of uniformity. It is here that we encounter modern geology's real resistance to a suddenly changed climatic condition as an explanation of the Pleistocene extinctions. Tolmachoff admits candidly, "Change of climate could only go on very gradually and slowly, and animals affected by it had plenty of time to become adapted to new conditions, or to migrate southwards and to find conditions corresponding to their former habitat."[25]

23. William R. Farrand, "Letters, Frozen Mammoth — Reply to Lippman," *Science* 137 (August 1962):450.
24. Tolmachoff, p. 68.
25. Ibid.

The Laughter of the Gods 363

Why is it that "change of climate could only go on very gradually and slowly"? As we will demonstrate later, a sudden change of climate provides a reasonable explanation of the evidence.

Neuville was troubled with the same problem:

> If it had been able to flee before the invasion of the cold and to reach temperate or hot regions, perhaps the mammoth would have survived like the present day elephants, of which it shows itself to be in general such a near relative. But it probably did not have the faculty of adaptation which we see existing in the elephants and of which we can analyse some important details. Not having been able, *for reasons which I cannot trace*, to leave the regions which had become particularly inhospitable to it, the mammoth was perhaps subject to the effects of an alimentation made more and more difficult by the gradual depauperization of the vegetation. In any event, it was subjected in a specially inexorable manner to the attacks of the cold against which it was ill protected [italics added].[26]

The reason Neuville cannot trace the rationale for the mammoths' escape could be that he fails to think in terms of catastrophes. Could it be that the mammoth did not escape the change in climate simply because he did not have the time to do so? It was too sudden.

EXTINCTION BY A "WELL-KNOWN PHENOMENON"

After examining and rejecting the above four theories of mammoth extinction, Tolmachoff gives his theory the title, "a well-known phenomenon of extinction."[27] By this he means the same kind of thing that resulted in the extermination of the giant reptiles. He then admits that scientists still have no idea what destroyed these reptiles. He calls the replacement of reptiles by mammals "mysterious."[28] He says that Paleozoic and Mesozoic seas swarmed with trilobites and they died out "without any special reason."[29] He then says that the destruction of the mammoth's contemporaries is so vague that "we

26. Neuville, p. 335.
27. Tolmachoff, p. 69.
28. Ibid.
29. Ibid.

know less about them than about the mammoth and the rhinoceros."[30]

It seems that a kind of "sleight of hand" is going on here. On the one hand, Tolmachoff dismisses catastrophic explanations with a wave of his hand, saying that the mammoth demise can be accounted for by the mechanism of "a well-known phenomenon of extinction"; but then, on the other hand, he admits that this "mechanism" is "mysterious," "without any special reason," and concerning the extinction of the mammoth's contemporaries "we know less about them than about the mammoth." Surely the gods are enjoying a hearty laugh. This natural death by some unknown mechanism contradicts all the evidence. Howorth considered it long ago: "Frequenters of the forest with whom I have conversed, whether Europeans or Singhalese, are consistent in their assurances that they have never found the remains of an elephant which had died a natural death."[31]

If their death was in some way "natural" in an area in which we know hyenas and other carnivorous animals wander about today in the summer, would the corpse be left to the useless duties of decay, as they must have been, since their bones are ungnawed and their flesh uneaten? Today's scavengers are much more diligent. Finally, the fact of finding masses of animal remains of mixed species, all showing the same state of preservation, not only points to a more or less contemporary death, but is quite fatal to the theory that they ended their days peaceably by purely normal causes.

Evidence of a Continental Flood

The inadequacy of gradualistic theories to account for all of the evidence was admitted by Tolmachoff long ago:

> Unfortunately we are unable to replace them by new ones which could harmonize with all accumulated data and stand criticism from different quarters, but must be satisfied with more or less probable suggestions. The problem is extremely difficult. We must explain the extinction of an animal

30. Ibid., p. 71.
31. Howorth, p. 174.

which was living in great numbers, apparently very prosperously, over a large area, in variable physico-geographical conditions to which it was well adapted, and which died out in a very short time, geologically speaking.[32]

Tolmachoff's difficulties would be considerably reduced if he could admit a sudden climatic reversal from moderate to severe accompanied by a flood.

The extinction of the Pleistocene mammals was worldwide. Darwin was impressed with the implications of this when he observed the fossil record in South America, which he visited on the voyage of the *Beagle* in 1845:

> The mind is at first irresistibly hurried into the belief that some great catastrophe has occurred. Thus, to destroy animals both large and small in South Patagonia, in Brazil, in Cordillera, in North America up to the Behring Straits, we must shake the entire framework of the globe. Certainly no fact in the long history of the world is so startling as the wide extermination of its inhabitants.[33]

A contemporary of Darwin, Alfred R. Wallace, made a similar observation:

> We live in a zoologically impoverished world, from which all the hugest, and fiercest, and strangest forms have recently disappeared. ...Yet it is surely a marvelous fact, and one that has hardly been sufficiently dwelt upon, this sudden dying out of so many large mammalia not in one place only but over half the land surface of the globe.... There must have been some physical cause for this great change; and it must have been a cause capable of acting almost simultaneously over large portions of the earth's surface.[34]

Several lines of evidence converge on a possible explanation: the extinction of the Pleistocene mammoths was the result of the pre-Flood atmosphere instabilities, which resulted in the condensation of earth's vapor canopy and the ensuing Flood and climatic reversal that followed.

32. Tolmachoff, p. 65.
33. Charles Darwin, *Journal of Researches*, p. 175, cited by Arthur C. Custance, *Evolution or Creation*, p. 96.
34. Alfred Russell Wallace, *Geographic Distribution of Animals* 1:150-51, cited by Custance, p. 96.

SUFFOCATED ANIMALS

In 1772 Pallas discovered a rhinoceros in Vilyuysk on the Vilyuy River (latitude 64° north), a tributary of the Lena, which had apparently been suddenly overcome and died by suffocation. In the *Proceedings of the Berlin Academy*, Professor Brandt reported, "On careful examination of the head of the Rhinoceros Tichorinus from the Wiljiu, it was further remarkable that the blood vessels and even the fine capillaries were seen to be filled with brown coagulated blood, which in many places still preserved its red color."[35] Dr. Schrenck observed concerning this find that the earth attached to the remains was fresh-water sedimentary deposits. In speaking of its nostrils he says, "They were wide open, and in the case of the one on the right side, which was uninjured, a number of horizontal folds were ranged in rows about it. The mouth was also partly open, whence it may be concluded that the animal died from suffocation, which it tried to avoid by keeping the nostrils wide asunder."[36]

This is exactly the kind of evidence that we look for when we want to know whether an animal has been drowned or suffocated. Asphyxia is always accompanied by the gorging of the capillaries with blood, and the facts justify at all events a probable inference that this particular rhinoceros was the victim of drowning.

Tolmachoff agrees with the above conclusions and adds that death by suffocation was suggested for the specimen of rhinoceros from the Khalbugai Creek as well. The original finders assumed a flood.[37] As reported in chapter 10, the finding of an erect male genital on the carcass of the Beresovka mammoth[38] is normally taken as evidence of death by suffoca-

35. *Proceedings of the Berlin Academy*, (1846), p. 223, cited by Howorth, p. 184.
36. Schrenck, *Memoirs of St. Petersburg Academy* 17:48-49, cited by Howorth, p. 185.
37. Tolmachoff, p. 57.
38. O. F. Herz, "Frozen Mammoths in Siberia," *Annual Report of Smithsonian Institution*, 1903, p. 623.

tion.[39] The death of the above specimens is consistent with the theory of a flood.

UPRIGHT CARCASSES

In several instances, to the surprise of the excavators, mammoth carcasses were found standing erect and facing the north. This fact, first reported by Professor Brandt,[40] certainly conveys the impression of a sudden and immense catastrophe. This makes it improbable that the pachyderms of Siberia sank in mud, but could indicate they were overcome by a vast deluge. "A similar discovery was made by Fisher of a single specimen in the same extraordinary attitude of arrested flight."[41] As previously mentioned, Pfizenmayer describes a mammoth carcass found upright in 1787 near the delta of the Alazeya, which flows into the Arctic Ocean.[42]

THE IMMENSE MAMMAL CACHES

Throughout the deposits of Europe, South America, Siberia, and Alaska, thousands of animals of supposedly different climatic regimes are found mixed together in caches that are so vast as to defy imagination. Before discussing these finds, we should point out that the finding of a dead animal *anywhere*, except on our highways, is not a normal situation. After a wild animal dies, it is quickly eaten by carnivores in 99% of the cases. Hence, to find any animal remains in the frozen muck is rather unusual since it indicates that the animal was buried soon after death *before* the carnivores could get at it or before it could decay in the case of the intact carcasses. We have already referred to these vast cemeteries where horse, bison, lion, tiger, rhinoceros, and mammoth are all mixed together in an immense grave. Scientists noted that in the whole landslide in

39. Digby, p. 132.
40. Cited by Howorth, p. 135; see Lyell's *Principles of Geology*, 1:183.
41. Custance, p. 99.
42. E. W. Pfizenmayer, *Siberian Man and Mammoth*, p. 7.

which the Beresovka mammoth was found, "the richest imaginable storehouse of prehistoric remains,"[43] was discovered. A similar situation prevails in Alaska:

> In many places the Alaskan muck is packed with animal bones and debris in trainload lots. Bones of mammoth, mastodon, several kinds of bison, horses, wolves, bears, and lions tell a story of a faunal population.... The Alaskan muck is like a fine, dark gray sand.... Within this mass, frozen solid, lie the twisted parts of animals and trees intermingled with lenses of ice and layers of peat and mosses. It looks as though in the midst of some cataclysmic catastrophe of ten thousand years ago the whole Alaskan world of living animals and plants was suddenly frozen in midmotion in a grim charade.[44]

This common situation has long been emphasized by catastrophe writers, is admitted by historical geologists, and so need not be expanded on further here.[45] Howorth summarized the implications:

> We must next inquire what the nature of this catastrophe was. Let us, then, focus on the necessary conditions. We want a cause that should kill the animals, and yet not break to pieces their bodies, or even mutilate them, a cause which would in some cases disintegrate the skeletons without weathering the bones. We want a cause that would not merely do this as a widespread murrain or plague might, but one which would bury the bodies as well as kill the animals, which could take up gravel and clay and lay them down again, and which could sweep together animals of different sizes and species, and mix them with trees and other debris of vegetation. What cause competent to do this is known to us, except rushing water on a great scale?[46]

He continued:

> The occurrence of immense caches in which the remains of many species of wild animals are incongruously mixed together pell-mell, often on high ground, seems unaccountable, save on the theory that they were driven to take shelter together on some point of vantage, in view of an advancing flood of water, a position which is paralleled by the great floods which occur occasionally in the tropics, where we find the tiger and its victims all collecting together on some dry place and reduced to common conditions

43. Ibid., p. 106.
44. Frank C. Hibben, *The Lost Americans*, p. 90.
45. See Henry M. Morris and John C. Whitcomb, *The Genesis Flood*, pp. 154-69; Alfred M. Rehwinkel, *The Flood*, pp. 177-87; Custance, pp. 100-6.
46. Howorth, p. 184.

of timidity and helplessness by a flood which has overwhelmed the flat country.[47]

Surely Howorth's conclusions are most reasonable. These vast mammal caches attest to the condensation of earth's pre-Flood vapor canopy and the resulting flood.

MARINE SHELLS MIXED WITH MAMMOTH BONES

The icy waters of the Arctic Ocean cover some of the richest deposits of mammoth remains. Nordenskjold tells how his trawl-net brought up fragments of mammoth tusks and a large number of pieces of wood from the bottom of the sea off the Lyakhov Islands.[48] Farther inland similar deposits have been found in which marine shells abound. For example, near Ust Tatarskoi on the Irtysh River in central Russia numerous shells, mostly fossilized, were found, in some cases retaining traces of the mollusk itself. Bones of elephants and many other animals were found in these same layers. Pallas says, "This undoubtedly has come from a great inundation. . . . We have in it an evident proof that the sea once bathed these countries."[49] He found several remains of both elephants and buffaloes in the same cache, the head of a great fish, and pieces of unrecognized cellular bones all mixed together. Murchison describes Pleistocene marine shells as occurring a long way south of the White Sea. Similar marine shells are found mixed with mammoth remains in the valley of the Lower Somme and in the deposits of the English Channel.[50]

The lesson of these finds is obvious. They indicate that, in some great inundation, sea life and mammoths were buried

47. Ibid., p. 186.
48. N. A. E. Nordenskjold, *The Voyage of the Vega Around Asia and Europe*, 1:420, cited by Howorth, p. 187.
49. Pallas, *Voyages*, 3:124-25, cited by Howorth, p. 188.
50. *Proceedings of the Berlin Academy*, 1846, p. 225, cited by Howorth, p. 188.Thus Farrand's statement that "marine fossils have never been discovered in deposits containing frozen mammoths" (Farrand, p. 732) is apparently incorrect.

together in the same deposits. The only thing that can do this on such a vast scale is a flood.

CAVES AND FISSURES IN EUROPE

Howorth presents extensive confirmatory evidence of a great deluge from the finds of mammoths mixed with hippopotamus and horse remains in caves and fissures all over Europe and the Mediterranean Sea. After documenting this extensively over a broad geographical area, he observes that either these animals withdrew into these caves to die, or they were conveyed into the caves by some other agency.[51] Now it is incredible that a rhinoceros should enter a cave voluntarily. In many of these caves extensive sedimentary deposits are found, indicating that they were flooded.[52] He concluded, "The destruction of a fauna, great and small, old and young, the piling of a mixed medley of its remains upon one another in a state of freshness without sign of weathering or decay, is in the case of the caverns, as in that of the surface beds, only consistent with some widespread flood."[53]

The Duke of Argyll in his address to the Edinburgh Geological Society on its fiftieth anniversary concurred with this analysis: "Chiefly in the countries bordering on the Mediterranean such caves have been found in abundance, containing such a mass of animal remains that it is certain that no agency but that of water could have brought them and huddled them up together in such heaps at one spot."[54]

51. Howorth, pp. 192-224.
52. Ibid., p. 198.
53. Ibid., p. 212.
54. "Address to the Edinburgh Geological Society," 1883, cited by Howorth, pp. 222-23. It is possible that these Pleistocene cave deposits indicate a post-Flood mammoth extinction or catastrophe in that some of them are made of fossiliferous limestones or other rocks which were presumably formed during the Flood.

CONCLUSION

Such is the evidence. After extensive documentation, Howorth summarizes:

> This completes my survey of the evidence furnished by the mammoth itself, and I believe not only is it consistent with the conclusion that that animal and its companions were finally extinguished by a sudden catastrophe, involving a great diluvial movement over all the northern hemisphere from the Pyrenees to the Bering Straits, but it is consistent with no other conclusion. The evidence is not only ample, and there is literally nothing on the other hand so far as my wide reading enables me to judge, save a fantastic attachment to a theory of uniformity which revolts against anything in the shape of a catastrophe. ... It is rather the predicating of one general catastrophe constituted by a wide continental flood, instead of a complicated series of lesser catastrophes, involving violent changes of level, changes of climate, and deluges as well.[55]

Erman, whom many consider to be the greatest of the Siberian explorers in the nineteenth century, said:

> The ground at Yakutsk... consists, to the depth of at least 100 feet, of strata of loam, pure sand, and magnetic sand. They have been deposited from waters which at one time, and it may be presumed suddenly, overflowed the whole country as far as the Polar Sea. ... Everywhere throughout these immense alluvial deposits are now lying the bones of antediluvian quadrupeds along with the vegetable remains. ... So it is clear that at the time when the elephants and trunks of trees were heaped up together, one flood extended from the center of the continent to the furtherest barrier, existing in the sea as it now is.[56]

THE STOMACH CONTENTS OF THE BERESOVKA MAMMOTH

Other writers have extensively documented the case for a global deluge.[57] It is, however, the effect of sudden cooling

---

55. Howorth, p. 189.
56. Cited by Howorth, p. 190. Howorth's extensive documentation of such sedimentary deposits should be of assistance to uniformitarian geologist William Farrand who said, "The specific nature of deposits enclosing the mammoths is not known well enough to be very helpful as an indication of the mode of death or burial" (see Farrand, p. 734).
57. See Morris and Whitcomb, pp. 1-33 and 116-211; Henry Morris, ed., *Scientific Creationism*, pp. 91-130.

caused by the condensation of earth's pre-Flood canopy that is of particular relevance to this discussion. It is clear that the mammoths lived in a warm climate and after a continent-wide catastrophe became buried by the "countless thousands," and were then frozen into the muck of the permafrost. The fact that they were frozen into this muck is generally accepted. What contemporary geologists do not believe is that this freezing of the mammoth was a sudden affair that was accompanied by a general sudden climatic reversal. Not only does the evidence reveal a general climatic reversal described above, but there is evidence of local more drastic climate catastrophes also.

A striking illustration of this turned up in the stomach of the Beresovka mammoth (1901) where about 24 pounds of undigested vegetable matter were uncovered, possibly indicating (as will be discussed below) a sudden deep freeze (that is, in a few hours). The Russian scientist V. N. Sukachev, who examined these remains, was able to identify many different species of plants, some of which no longer grow that far north, and others which grow both in Siberia today and also in Mexico.

IDENTIFICATION OF STOMACH CONTENTS

The following list of stomach contents is compiled from the report of Sukachev, the Russian scientist who first examined them, with his comments,[58] an extensive compilation of the remains by William Farrand,[59] and a list given by Osborn[60] with comments by botanist A. A. Case of the University of Missouri.[61]

58. V. N. Sukachev, "Examination of Plant Remnants Found within the Food of the Mammoth Discovered on the Beresovka River Territory of Yakutsk," 3:1-18, pts. I-IV, 2 figs. cited by Charles Hapgood, *Path of the Pole*, pp. 266-68.
59. Farrand, p. 731.
60. Henry Fairfield Osborn, *Proboscidea*, 2:1127.
61. A. A. Case, botanist associated with College of Veterinary Medicine, University of Missouri, Columbia, Missouri, personal communication, 6 January 1976.

Trees and shrubs

Abies (sibirica?)
Alnus hirsuta
Betula alba
B. nana
Betula sp.
Larix (sibirica?)
Picea (obovata?)
P. sibirica
Salix polaris
Salix sp.
Vaccinium vitis idaea

Herbs, grasses, and mosses[62]

Bryophytes
  Aulacomnium turgidum
  Cladonia ragiferina
  Drepanocladus (Hypnum) fluitans
Caryophyllaceae
  Cerastium sp.
  Dianthus sp.
  Melandrium sp.
  S. (nodosa?)
Chenopodiaceae
  Atriplex (patulum?)
Compositae
  Artemisia dracunculus
  Artemisia sacrorum
  Artemia vulgaris
  Aster sp.
  Gnaphalium uliginosum
  Lactuca (Mulgedium) sibiricum
  Tanacetum vulgare
  Sp. indeterminate

62. Following the usual order, the names from left to right refer to family, genus, and species.

Cruciferae
   Sp. indeterminate
Cyperaceae
   Carex glareosa
   Carex incurva
   Carex lagopina (lachenalii?) — "The remains of this sedge are numerous in the contents of the stomach. The specimens exactly resemble varieties growing today. The measurements show no reduction in size. Its range extends to the shores of the Arctic Ocean. It is found in mountainous regions, including the Carpathians, Alps, and Pyrenees. It is also found in the peat bogs of Western Prussia, in Siberia as far south as Transbaikalia and the southern island of New Zealand."[63]
   Sp. indeterminate (N-2)
Gentianaceae
   Gentiana sp.
Gramineae
   Agropyron cristatûm — "The remains of this plant are very numerous in the contents of the stomach. They are so well preserved that there is no doubt as to the exact species. The individual specimens are slightly smaller than those of the typical more southern variety growing today, but this could be a result of some reduction of size because of pressure in the stomach, which is noted in other cases. The finding of the plants is of very great interest. Not only are they scarcely known anywhere in the Arctic regions, they are even, so far as I have been able to discover, very rare also in the Yakutsk district. . . . Generally speaking the Agropyrum cristatûm L. Bess is a plant of the plains (steppes) and is widespread in the plains of Dauria. . . . The general range of this plant includes southern Europe (in European Russia it is adapted to the plains belt), southern Siberia, Turkestan, Djungaria, Tian-Shan, and Mongolia. Nevertheless, the variety found in the stomach differs slightly from both the European and Oriental-Siberian varieties found to-

---

63. Sukachev, cited by Hapgood, pp. 266-68.

day."[64] It is similar to the crested wheatgrass of the Great Plains and High Plains of North America.[65] This hardly speaks well for the thesis that the climate then was similar to today's. Nor could it help the theory that this mammoth was bogged!

Agrostis borealis

Alopecurus alpinus — "The remains of this grass are numerous in the contents of the stomach. A significant portion of them consists of stems, with occasional remnants of leaves, usually mixed in with other vegetable remains. ... All these remains are so little destroyed that one is able to establish with exactitude to what species they belong."[66]

Beckmannia cruciformis — This is common American slough grass that grows in Missouri.[67] The florets of this plant are numerous in the contents of the stomach and usually are excellently preserved. The detailed description of the remains, with precise measurements in millimeters shows the species to be of the same as that of the present day, only smaller. At the present time the species is widely prevalent in Siberia and in the Arctic generally. It grows in flooded meadows or marshes.[68]

Bromus sibiricus

Elymus sp.

Hordeum jubatum

Hordeum violaccum Boiss, et. Huet — This plant is found in dry grassy areas. It is not found in the Arctic regions. In Siberia this is a meadow plant.[69] It is a variety of barley.[70]

Phragmites communis

Puccinellia (Atropis?) distans

64. Ibid.
65. Case, personal communication, 6 January 1976.
66. Sukachev, cited by Hapgood, pp. 266-68.
67. Case, personal communication, 6 January 1976.
68. Sukachev, cited by Hapgood, pp. 266-68.
69. Ibid.
70. Case, personal communication, 6 January 1976.

Sp. indeterminate (N-8)
Labiatae
  Thymus serpyllum
Leguminosae
  Caragana jubata
  Oxytropis campestris
  Oxytropis sordida — In the contents of the stomach were found several fragments of these beans. . . . In the fragments taken from the teeth there were found eight whole bean pods in a very good state of preservation; they even in places retained five beans. . . . The plant is now found in the Arctic and sub-Arctic regions, but also in the northern forests. It grows in rather dry places.[71] This plant is commonly known as locoweed.[72]
Papaveraceae
  Papaver alpinum
Plantaginaceae
  Plantogo media
Polygonaceae
  Oxyia digyna?
  Rumex acetosella
Polypodiaceae
  Sp. indeterminate (N-2)
Ranunculaceae
  Caltha palustris
  Ranunculus acris L. — This plant is known as the common tall buttercup. Some kind of buttercup may be found from the tundra in the north to near Cape Horn. Case says he has seen them in bloom under the edge of the receding snow at over 12,000 feet altitude in the Colorado Rockies in June and July.[73] The plant grows in rather dry places. It is not at present found growing together with the Beckmannia Cruciformis although both are found in the stomach of the mammoth.[74]

71. Sukachev, cited by Hapgood, pp. 266-68.
72. Case, personal communication, 6 January 1976.
73. Ibid.
74. Sukachev, cited by Hapgood, pp. 266-68.

Rosaceae
  Potentilla sp.
  Rosa sp.
  Sanguisorba officinalis
Umbelliferae
  Aegopodium podagraria?
  Angelica (decurrens?)

We may draw several general conclusions from these data:

(1) The presence of so many varieties that generally grow much to the south indicates that the climate of the region was milder than that of today.

(2) The discovery of the ripe fruits of sedges, grasses, and other plants suggests that "the mammoth died during the second half of July or the beginning of August."[75]

(3) The Beresovka mammoth apparently did not feed primarily on coniferous vegetation, but mainly on meadow grasses.

(4) The mammoth must have been overwhelmed suddenly with a rapid deep freeze and instant death. The sudden death is proved by the unchewed bean pods still containing the beans that were found between its teeth, and the deep freeze is suggested by the well-preserved state of the stomach contents and the presence of edible meat.

Evidence of a Sudden Deep Freeze of Some of the Mammoths

Several lines of evidence seem to converge on the conclusion that at least some of the mammoths were frozen quickly at drastically reduced temperatures. Others, in fact most, froze much more slowly.

THE STATE OF PRESERVATION OF THE STOMACH CONTENTS

When the list of stomach remains cited above was presented to Mahler and Lipscomb, professional botanists at the Southern Methodist University Herbarium, they were amazed. It seemed incredible to them that the remains could have been so well

---

75. Ibid.

preserved that Sukachev was able to distinguish so clearly between the species. They were surprised because of the presence in the stomach of digestive juices, which act quickly to break down the vegetable material of the delicate parts of the plants that were found in the Beresovka mammoth. Since the elephant is not a ruminant (having a multichambered stomach),[76] acid deterioration and enzyme activity would be major factors in breaking down the "cement" that holds together the cellulose in plant fiber. Since the mechanical action of the stomach would break up all vegetable matter within half an hour, the animal must have died within half an hour of swallowing this food.[77] According to the Dallas coroner, acid and enzyme action would completely dissolve the delicate parts of these plants within a matter of hours. He said he would be "shocked" to see them in recognizable form a day after the death of the animal.

Dr. C. W. Foley, a veterinary physiologist, was asked how long the delicate parts of these plants would last in the stomach of a mammoth after death. He responded, "I wouldn't think they would last more than a couple of hours, maybe more in a ruminant."[78]

What precisely did Sukachev find? He discovered that the blossoms of the *Alopecurus alpinus* in the stomach were so well preserved that he could establish the species with exactitude.[79] Apparently, in the case of the *Alopecurus alpinus* the delicate hair-like follicles on the leaves were so well preserved

76. Frances G. Benedict, *The Physiology of the Elephant*, p. 172.
77. Dr. James Garriott, Dallas County (Texas) medical examiner, personal communication, February 1976.
78. Dr. C. W. Foley, department of veterinary medicine and surgery, College of Veterinary Medicine, University of Missouri, personal communication, 22 February 1976.
79. Dr. Klaus Potsch, a theoretical physicist at the Technical University of Vienna, personal communication, 24 February 1979. This observation is based on his translation of Sukachev's article in which the Russian word translated "blossom" is *tsvetok* and means "flower petal."

that Sukachev could relate them to a particular species. Even the color of the leaves — brown — was still intact, indicating that no leaching of the pigment occurred prior to freezing.[80]

How long could such delicate plant remnants last in the stomach juices of a dead mammoth? Garriott and Foley indicated that they could last only a matter of hours and still be in recognizable form. In order to substantiate their estimates, an experiment was conducted with the aid of Dr. Larry Bruce, a gastro-intestinal physiologist with the University of Texas Health Science Center at Dallas. First, a solution of stomach fluid was prepared by mixing 70 micromoles of swine pepsin with a 0.1 normal solution of HCl with a pH of 1 (250 mg of pepsin per 100 ml HCl). To this solution a small amount of NaCl (0.9%) was added as a catalyst. This solution was then poured into four different beakers, each at a different temperature: 4° C, 17° C, 27° C, and 37° C.

After the temperatures had been established, some gladioli and carnations were compacted into the beakers so that the surface level of the solution corresponded to the top of the flower compaction. The stems, leaves, and flowers were all included. On the assumption that it was necessary to have delicate parts of the plants in order to identify them at the species level, these four solutions were left to act on the flowers until they were in each case beyond recognition. Although the observation of this process proved to be highly subjective, four categories of decay were observed:

A = first appearance of dye from the flowers in the solution;
B = the beginning of a loss of flower structure;
C = structural support completely gone, flower petal dissolved beyond recognition; and
D = leaching of flower petal pigment.

Table 11.1 represents the results.

---

80. From the translation of Sukachev by Dr. Klaus Potsch, personal communication, 24 February 1979.

TABLE 11.1
PROGRESSIVE DECAY OF GLADIOLUS FLOWER PETALS IN A SOLUTION OF STOMACH JUICE AT VARIOUS TEMPERATURES (IN HOURS)

	4° C	17° C	27° C	37° C
A	3	1½	1	1
B	4	3	3	2
C	5	3½	3½	3
D	-	25	10	10

It would appear that the gladioli could not have lasted more than five hours in the stomach of a mammoth, even if the initial temperature of the mammoth was 4° C (40° F). The gladiolus is considered to be a very delicate flower. Carnations, however, are somewhat hardier and lasted considerably longer. At the end of 10 hours in the 4° C beaker, the carnations had hardly been touched, whereas they were beyond recognition in the 17° C beaker in 25 hours. Since it is not known for sure what the resistance to attack by acid and enzymes may have been in the blossoms found by Sukachev in the stomach of the Beresovka mammoth, it is risky to draw precise conclusions. However, the above experiment would suggest some limits of perhaps 10 hours for flower petal longevity if the stomach temperature was initially 37° C (98.6° F). If the blossoms in the mammoth had no more resistance than the gladiolus, the stomach temperature would have had to have been lowered to 40° F within 10 hours to have left anything in recognizable form.[81] This may be con-

81. Much has been made of the supposed existence of buttercup flowers in the stomach of the mammoth. I erred in this regard in an earlier publication (see Joseph C. Dillow, "The Catastrophic Deep-freeze of the Beresovka Mammoth," *Creation Research Society Quarterly* 14 [June 1977]:5-13). The author is indebted to Dr. Klaus Potsch for a completed translation of Sukachev's article into English: "In the contents of the stomach only three seeds were found." So only the fruit, the achenes of the buttercup, was actually discovered, not entire flowers. However, the freezing calculations yield similar results in that the flowers of other plants were found in the mammoth.

sidered reasonable because the above experiment did not take into effect the chewing of the food by the mammoth, nor did it account for the continued mechanical activity of the stomach, which persists for up to half an hour after death.[82]

The only way there could have been left any recognizable remains of these delicate flowers would be through the cessation of the digestive activity. The only mechanism that will do this is cooling. The reduction in enzyme activity follows van't Hoff's rule, which says that for every 10° C decrease in temperature, enzyme activity is reduced by 50%.[83]

A professor of veterinary physiology was asked, "Is there any other way than a sudden freezing that flower petals could have survived in such a well-preserved form?" He replied, "I can't think of any other way."[84] Botanist A. A. Case, after examining the list of the remains in the mammoth, concluded, "If the mammoths and other animals were 'quick frozen' in their tracks by minus 100-degree C type of climatic upheaval as suggested by some, the things found today would be logical."[85]

So we may conclude that the remarkable preservation of the vegetable material in the stomach of the Beresovka and other mammoths indicates that at least some of them were frozen rather quickly (that is, in a matter of hours), quickly enough so that their stomach temperatures were reduced to about 40° F in a matter of 10 hours.

THE PRESENCE OF FRESH MEAT

As discussed in chapter 10, reports going back to ancient China indicate that edible flesh has been carved off mammoth carcasses. Even some of the meat on the Beresovka carcass appeared edible, and the excavators were tempted to eat it, but threw it to the dogs instead. We will discuss this in more detail

82. Dr. Melvin J. Swenson, professor of veterinary physiology, Iowa State University, Ames, Iowa, personal communication, 19 December 1976.
83. Ibid.; see "Van't Hoff Equation," in *Van Nostrand's Scientific Encyclopedia*, p. 2273.
84. Foley, personal communication, 22 February 1976.
85. Case, personal communication, 6 January 1976.

below, but here it is sufficient to point out that the temperature must drop far below freezing very quickly or the carcass will rot in 32 to 48 hours.[86] It is clear from the existence of summer flowers in the stomach of the mammoth that the weather was warm when the animal died. It therefore must have suddenly turned cold — very cold — for any of the Beresovka meat to have remained edible.

However, there are some physical constraints in the freezing process that must be maintained if any of the meat could ever be described as "wholesome" or "delicious." This circumstance rules out the possibility of extremely rapid freezing (a matter of minutes) because the temperatures necessary to produce that in an animal the size of a mammoth are impossible (they would have to be colder than liquid nitrogen). If the cells are frozen rapidly, but not rapidly enough, then intracellular crystals form, which will burst the cells and ruin the flavor of the meat.

According to Harold Meryman, the coldest temperature to which tissue can be frozen without cell damage is $-5°$ C.[87] Furthermore, this must occur by slow freezing (hours), not rapid (minutes). Apparently what damages the cells and ruins the flavor of the meat is dehydration, which is caused by the withdrawal of water from the cells to be incorporated into the surrounding ice crystals. This process goes on after the initial freezing. "The principal cause of injury from slow freezing is not the physical presence of extracellular ice crystals, but the denaturation incurred by the dehydration resulting from the incorporation of all free water into the ice."[88]

The only way this denaturation could be stopped in a natural setting would be for the tissue to be first frozen to $-5°$ C, then, after it was frozen, to have the temperature reduced immediately to very low stabilizing temperatures of near $-70°$ C (which is dry ice temperature, or $-94°$ F).[89] So if portions of the

86. Armour, Inc., Greyhound Tower, Phoenix, Arizona, personal communication, June 1976.
87. Harold T. Meryman, "Mechanics of Freezing in Living Cells and Tissues," Science 124 (21 September 1956):519.
88. Ibid.
89. Ibid.

The Laughter of the Gods

mammoth were initially frozen to about −5° C, then quickly reduced to dry ice temperature, the things found today would be logical. As we will discuss in the thermodynamic models later in the chapter, this could easily happen if the outside temperatures were below −150° F. In that case, tissue several inches in from the outer skin of the mammoth would only "see" a temperature of −5° C while it was freezing, and after the outer few inches were completely frozen, the temperature would rapidly drop to that of dry ice.

The Sudden Deep Freeze of the Beresovka Mammoth

It should be evident from the above discussion that we are faced with a situation most foreign to uniformitarian geology. The stomach contents indicate that it was mid-summer when the mammoth died, yet the state of preservation of the stomach remains require that, shortly after death, the stomach temperature must have been lowered to temperatures near 40° F in order to stop the activity of the digestive juices. The question now is: What degree of outside temperature drop is necessary to reduce the stomach temperature to around 40° F in 10 hours? In consultation with Dr. Roger Simpson of the Department of Civil and Mechanical Engineering at Southern Methodist University, two thermodynamic models of the mammoth were constructed.

THE THERMOPHYSICAL PROPERTIES OF MAMMOTH MEAT

In order to set up a physical model from which the above question may be answered, we must make certain assumptions about the thermophysical properties of the mammoth. Since this specific information is impossible to obtain, it will be assumed that these thermodynamic properties are similar to those of contemporary elephants. For the calculations below, we must first determine four properties: the thermal conductivity of beef, the specific heat of beef, the density of the mammoth, and the film conductance of the mammoth.

(1) *Thermal conductivity of beef.* This quantity, k, is a measure of the time rate of transfer of heat by conduction, through a unit of thickness, across unit area for unit difference of temperature.[90] The dimensional units are commonly in BTU per hour per foot per degree F in the British Engineering System, which is used here. This property of the mammoth meat varies with the temperature of the mammoth. An approximate range of variation is given in Table 11.2.

TABLE 11.2

VARIATIONS OF THERMAL CONDUCTIVITY (WITH TEMPERATURE) OF MAMMOTH

Temperature Range ° F	Thermal Conductivity, k, in BTU/hr-ft-° F
100 - 32	0.257[91]
32 - −10	0.65[92]
−10 - −27	0.75[93]
−27 - −150	0.919[94]

(2) *Specific heat of beef.* This quantity, c, is a measure of the amount of heat necessary to raise the temperature of a unit mass of a substance one degree F. The dimensional units are commonly in BTU per pound per degree F. Like thermal conductivity, specific heat also varies with temperature. Table 11.3 gives an approximate variance over a wide temperature range.

90. Leonard R. Ingersoll, Otto J. Zobel, and Alfred C. Ingersoll, *Heat Conduction,* p. 3.
91. J. E. Hill, J. D. Litman, and J. E. Sunderland, "Thermal Conductivity of Various Meats," *Food Technology* 21 (1967):1143-1408.
92. R. W. Dickerson, *The Freezing Preservation of Foods* 2:35.
93. Approximation from "Semiannual Report on TPRC Activities on Preparation of Tables on the Thermal Conductivity of Foods," 15 December 1969.
94. J. H. Awberry and E. Griffiths, "Thermal Properties of Meat," *J. Soc. Chem. Ind. (London)* 52 (1933):326-28 T.

TABLE 11.3

VARIATION OF SPECIFIC HEAT (WITH TEMPERATURE) OF MAMMOTH

Temperature Range °F	Specific Heat, c, in BTU/lb-°F
100 - 32	0.84[95]
32 - −40	0.6[96]
−40 - −60	0.49[97]
−60 - −110	0.44[98]
−110 - −170	0.24[99]

(3) *Density of beef.* We will assume that the density of the mammoth (the mean or average density) is the same as that of a human being or a cow today. The mean density of a cow has been computed to be 66.14 lb/cu.ft.[100] The Aerobics Center in Dallas has computed by specific measurements involving water displacement that the mean density of a human being is 66.68 lb/cu.ft.[101] The density of beef has been placed at 72.4 lb/cu.ft.[102] Armour[103] and Birds Eye[104] both use a value of 62.4 lb/ft³ for their freezing calculations. A value of 66.14 lb/ft³ will be assumed in the calculations below.

95. Dickerson, p. 39.
96. Approximation from Dickerson, p. 39.
97. Ibid., p. 35.
98. Ibid.
99. Ibid.
100. "Semiannual Report on TPRC Activities."
101. Dr. Michael L. Pollock, et al., "Prediction of Body Density in Young and Middle-Aged Women," *Journal of Applied Physiology* 38 (April 1975):745.
102. Dickerson, p. 40.
103. Armour, Inc., personal communication, October 1975.
104. Ivor Morgan, Birds Eye engineer with General Foods Corporation, personal communication, 7 October 1975.

(4) The film conductance of the mammoth. This quantity, h, is the coefficient of heat transfer between a surface and its surroundings, or "emissivity" or "exterior conductivity." It is a measure of the energy radiated from a unit area of a surface in unit time for unit difference of temperature between the surface in question and surrounding bodies. The units are BTU per hour per foot^2 per degree F. For forced convection heat transfer produced by a cold wind, this coefficient depends on the geometry of the freezing specimen, kinematic viscosity, wind velocity, and other factors. For modeling purposes, the mammoth will first be assumed to be a cylinder. The formula for the film conductance for flow over a cylinder is then:[105]

$$h = \frac{(C)(Re)^m k}{d},$$

where C = 0.024 and m = 0.8, (constants for a cylinder).[106] The diameter, d, of the mammoth will be assumed to be 5 feet. This value was suggested to the Birds Eye engineers by a curator of the American Museum of Natural History.[107] The thermal conductivity, k, of air is 0.015 BTU/ft-hr °F (at 0° C).[108] The equation for the Reynolds number, Re, is given by:[109]

$$Re = \frac{(\text{wind velocity})(\text{diameter})}{(\text{kinematic viscosity})}$$

The kinematic viscosity is the ratio of the dynamic viscosity (1.11 × 10^{-5} lb/ft-sec for air at 0° C), to the density (0.086 lb/ft^3

---

105. Shao Ti Hsu, *Engineering Heat Transfer*, pp. 227, 328.
106. Ibid., p. 328.
107. Ivor Morgan, personal communication, 7 October 1975.
108. Hsu, p. 577. Also see *Thermal Conductivity of Nonmetallic Liquids and Gases* in *Thermophysical Properties of Matter, The TPRC Data Series*, ed. Y. S. Touloukian, P. E. Liley, S. C. Saxena, 3:512, where a value of k (at 290° K) = 0.2538 mW/cm-° K or 0.0147 BTU/ft-hr-°F. At 270° K, k = 0.0138 BTU/ft-hr-°F. To convert from mW/cm-°K to BTU/ft-hr-°F, divide the former by 0.01731 × 10^3; see William H. McAdams, *Heat Transmission*, p. 444, for conversion tables.
109. Hsu, p. 328.

for air at 0° C) or 1.29 × 10⁻⁴ft²/sec.[110] Assuming that the cold front that overcame the mammoths moved across the tundras at 100 mph (147 ft/sec), the Reynolds number would then be 5.68 × 10⁶. This gives a value of h = 18.24 BTU/hr·ft²·°F.

In 1961 Birds Eye was asked to check the credibility of an article on the mammoths to be published by *Reader's Digest*. The Birds Eye engineer, Ivor Morgan, who made the calculations, assumed a wind velocity of 40 mph, a temperature of −50° F, and a value of h = 10.5 BTU/hr-ft²-°F. In the calculations below, we will assume a value of 18.24.[111]

With these approximate assumptions, it is possible to predict with fair certainty the magnitude of the outside (ambient) temperature necessary to have left the Beresovka mammoth in its present state of preservation. Two different geometries will be used for a physical model of the mammoth: an infinite cylinder and an equivalent sphere.

Model 1 — an infinite cylinder. Birds Eye originally modeled the mammoth as an infinite cylinder. Luikov has presented graphical solutions for the problem of the rate of cooling of an infinite cylinder that render tremendously complex calculations relatively simple.[112] Figure 11.1 shows a $\theta = \frac{T-T_a}{T_i-T_a}$ as a function of the Fourier number. T is the temperature of a certain point in the cylinder, in this case 40° F at six inches into the mammoth. It is assumed that if the temperature of a point six inches into the mammoth has been brought to 40° F, that diges-

110. *Handbook of Chemistry and Physics*, p. F-56 gives a value of 170.8 micropoises for viscosity of air at 0° C = (170.8 × 10⁻⁶ poises) (0.0672) = 1.15 × 10⁻⁵lb/ft-sec. The density of moist air was computed from tables on p. F-9.
111. Using the *Handbook of Chemistry and Physics* value of k = 0.0138 BTU/ft-hr-°F (at 0° C), air density = 0.08 lb/ft³, and air viscosity = 1.15 × 10⁻⁵ lb/ft-sec (from the TPRC Data Series), a value of h = 15.42 results. Using this value instead of the above value of 18.24 yields as negligible difference in the outcome of both the graphical and computer solutions. So 18.24 is maintained.
112. A. V. Luikov, *Analytical Heat Diffusion Theory*, p. 146.

tive action will have been sufficiently retarded so that the mammoth could freeze over the next few weeks without significant further damage to the stomach contents. Needless to say, this is a very generous assumption. The stomach begins at about six inches into the mammoth.[113] T_a is the ambient temperature of the surrounding air; a value of $-50°$ F (a more moderate value consistent with today's observations) and values $-100°$ to $-250°$ will be used (radical values beyond present day experience). T_i is the initial temperature of the mammoth. It will be assumed that the mammoth was suddenly overcome by intense cold so that he immediately stopped whatever he was doing (including chewing), and began slowly to freeze to death. Death will occur at $75°$ F (body temperature) in a mammal.[114] So at $-50°$ F, $(1-\theta) = 0.274$, at $-175°$ F, $(1-\theta) = 0.137$, and at $-200°$ F, $(1-\theta) = 0.124$.

The ratio r/R is the ratio of the distance a point r in inches is from the center of the mammoth to the radius of the mammoth. In this problem a value for $r = (30'' - 6'') = 24''$ is assumed. So r/R = 0.8.

The dimensionless Fourier number is given by $Fo = \frac{at}{R^2}$, where $a = \frac{k}{(den.)(c)}$. From the above discussion of the thermophysical properties of mammoth meat, values of k = 0.257 BTU/hr·ft·°F, den. = 66.14 lb/ft³, and c = 0.84 BTU/lb·°F produce a = 0.00462 ft²/hr. In the above, t = time in hours, and R = the radius of the mammoth = 2.5 ft.

---

113. Estimate given by a curator of the American Museum of Natural History to Ivor Morgan, engineer with Birds Eye, February 1960.
114. Vernon B. Mountcastle, ed., *Medical Physiology* 2:557.

The Laughter of the Gods

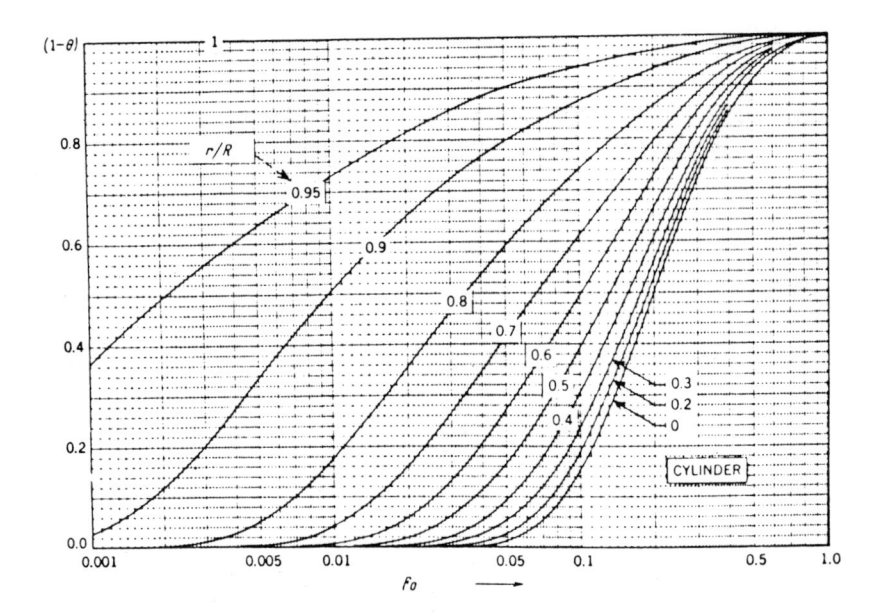

Fig. 11.1 — Plot of Dimensionless Excess Temperature $(1-\theta)$ Versus the Fourier Number, Fo, for Various Values of the Coordinate for a Cylinder.

By reference to Figure 11.1, it can be seen, therefore, that when $T_a = -50°$ F, the Fourier number is 0.274 and t = 19.6 hours. If $T_a = -175°$ F, then the Fourier number is 0.137 and t = 10.8 hours. Due to the fact that the outer few inches of the mammoth will plunge far below freezing in the first few minutes, the rate of heat removal will be somewhat faster than the above calculations allow for. This is because the thermal conductivity of the outer shell will increase threefold with the sudden freezing of the outer shell, whereas the specific heat will drop by nearly 30%. So we may safely conclude that, if the outside temperature is dropped suddenly to $-175°$ F, a point six inches into the mammoth would be brought down to 40° F within 10 hours.

Assuming the above parameters, the time necessary to bring a point six inches into the cylinder down to 40° F is displayed in Table 11.4 (graphical solution).

TABLE 11.4

TIME IN HOURS TO BRING THE TEMPERATURE OF THE STOMACH CONTENTS DOWN TO 40° F

Air temp. $T_{a'}$ °F	Computer Solution (spherical geometry)				Graphical Solution (cylindrical geometry)
	Time in hours to bring mean temp. of mammoth to 40° F.		Time in hours to bring a point 7.27" in to 40° F.		Time in hours to bring a point 6" in to 40° F.
	$T_i=100$	$T_i=74$	$T_i=100$	$T_i=74$	$T_i=74°$ F
−50	45.6	23.3	31.4	23.3	19.6
−100	21.3	13.0	20.0	15.0	14.2
−129	16.5	11.0	17.5	13.3	13.5
−150	13.3	9.5	15.2	12.0	11.9
−175	11.6	7.6	14.2	10.1	10.8
−200	10.0	6.5	12.8	9.0	10.4
−225	8.3	6.5	11.2	8.8	9.9
−250	7.8	5.3	10.8	7.8	9.6

If the temperature was anything like observed temperatures today (−50° F), the bath of acids and enzymes would have nearly 19 hours to dissolve the stomach contents and there would be little left preserved in the stomach to distinguish the species. This calculation establishes that the mammoth must have been overcome suddenly by temperatures approaching −175° F.

Model 2 – an equivalent sphere. In order to validate the above equation, an inquiry was directed to the Birds Eye Frozen Food Corporation in New York. In a popular science article it had been reported that "Birds Eye frozen food experts, in examining the mammoth tissue, have deduced that they were 'thrown into the cooler' suddenly, into temperatures below −150° F."[115] The writer contacted the Birds Eye engineer, Ivor Morgan, who actually did the calculations on the mammoth in February 1960. Apparently Birds Eye had been asked by Reader's Digest to check the credibility of an article they were proposing to publish in 1960 on the catastrophic deep freeze of mammoths.

115. Donald Patten, "The Pre-flood Greenhouse Effect," Symposium on Creation, II, p. 21.

They did not, as was erroneously reported, "examine mammoth tissue."[116]

However, Morgan supplied the writer a computer program which he designed for Birds Eye to determine freezing rates in spheres of different diameters.[117] This program is quite rigorous and takes into consideration the variation of specific heat and thermal conductivity with temperature, and also considers the effects of freezing and the extraction of the latent heat of fusion. In order to adapt the program specifically to the mammoth question, we consulted a computer programmer, Bert Dollahite, who works with the United States Army in Washington, D.C. The program assumes the mammoth is composed of ten concentric spheres. It is an approximate solution of the Fourier heat conduction equation for small increments of time and small finite increments of spherical radius. Heat flow into each of the ten concentric spheres less heat flow out equals the residual heat, which manifests itself as a change of state and as a temperature change. The program has the ability to compute the mean or average temperature of the mammoth at any given time as a function of the outside temperature. Morgan, who designed the program, and Dollahite, who adapted it, said that the mean temperature would give an accurate representation of the temperature of the stomach contents of the mammoth at any given time.

In order to determine the equivalent volume of the sphere, we had to make an approximation of the size of the main body of the mammoth. Based on the suggestion made to Birds Eye by a curator of the American Museum of Natural History, the radius of the mammoth was set at 2.5 feet. The length of the main body was estimated to be about eight feet.[118] So the mammoth's torso

116. Ivor Morgan, personal communication, 7 October 1975.
117. Computer program for determining the time necessary to bring various parts of a sphere to various temperatures given a certain outside temperature, supplied courtesy of Ivor Morgan, personal communication, 7 October 1975.
118. This estimate is based on scale drawings and specific measurements given in Bjorn Kurten, *Pleistocene Mammals of Europe*, pp. 137-38; Osborn, 2:1139; Robert Silverberg, *Mammoths, Mastodons, and Man*, pp. 88, 135.

is modeled as a cylinder. This yields a volume of the cylinder of:

$$v = \pi r^2 L = 3.1416(2.5)^2(8)$$
$$= 157 \text{ ft}^3 = 271,296 \text{ in}^3$$

The radius of a sphere of this volume is given by:

$$r = (0.2387 \text{ v})^{1/3}$$
$$= 40 \text{ inches.}$$

So in the program a sphere with a radius of 40 inches is equivalent to the mammoth carcass. The assumed film conductance is the same as that of the cylinder, 18.24 BTU/hr·ft²·°F, and the density is 66.14 lb/ft³. Assuming these parameters, the Birds Eye program yields the data in Table 11.4 for the time necessary to bring the mean temperature of the mammoth to 40° F as a function of the ambient temperature (see Table 11.4 computer solution).

The Birds Eye program and the Luikov graphical solution for a cylinder demonstrate general agreement for slightly different assumptions on the geometry. It is obvious from Table 11.4 that temperatures well below −150° F are necessary in order to bring the temperature of the stomach contents down to the required 40° F within the 10-hour limit specified by the botanists and gastro-intestinal physiologists who were consulted.

It is interesting to note that this temperature (−150° F) was the same as that reported by Ivan Sanderson. Referring to a report that indicated the cells of the mammoth had not burst, Sanderson argued that frozen food experts concluded that the mammoth under examination had been frozen at temperatures below −150° F.[119] So the same figure was determined from two entirely different approaches.

Probably these numbers are quite conservative. To say that ten hours is the limit and 40° F the required temperature is beyond what the actual situation must have been. It is more

119. Ivan T. Sanderson, "Riddle of the Frozen Giants," *Saturday Evening Post*, 16 January 1960, pp. 39 and 82 ff. Unfortunately, Sanderson does not cite the primary source of this report. In an inquiry to his agent in New York on 27 July 1978, I learned that he is now deceased.

likely that the temperature had to be brought to 35° F within six or seven hours. Furthermore, if the Beresovka mammoth was killed instantly, as the evidence seems to indicate, then $T_i = 100°$ F and air temperatures of below $-200°$ F would have been necessary. The value of $T_i = 74°$ F assumes that the animal gradually froze to death.

In the computer solution the reason that the mean temperature closely approximates the temperature of a point 7.27 inches into the mammoth is that 42.6% of the volume of the mammoth is outside of a point 7.27 inches from the surface. The temperature outside that point is much lower and almost half of the volume of the mammoth is located there.

For comparison purposes a cow was also modeled as an equivalent sphere with a radius of 20 inches. The thermal-physical properties of the inner shells of the cow were assumed to be the same as those of the mammoth. However, the outer shell of the cow was considered to be fat, and the density was, therefore, 59 lb/ft³.[120] The thermal conductivity of the outer shell, k, was set at 0.0762 BTU/hr-ft-°F for temperatures above 32° F and 0.1 for temperatures below freezing.[121] The specific heat of this fat layer was set at 0.6 BTU/lb-°F for temperatures above 28° F and 0.35 for temperatures below 28° F. Table 11.5 presents a comparison of the cooling and freezing in a cow and in a mammoth according to the Birds Eye program. Beef freezes at 29° F. It is clear that a cow placed in a blast freezer for 12 to 24 hours could be cooled to 40° F.

Finally, we examined the possibility of the mammoth's being frozen in ice. For the purposes of the model we assumed that the mammoth was entombed in ten feet of ice. How this could have happened in the middle of the summer remains a mystery. The

120. *Handbook of Chemistry and Physics*, p. F-1.
121. "Semiannual Report on TPRC Activities," Purdue University Thermal Research Center, 15 December 1969; Y. S. Touloukian et al., eds., *Thermophysical Properties Research Center Data Series*, 2:1072. Actually, the value of k = 0.1 BTU/lb·ft·°F is low. It should be 0.1→0.2 BTU/lb·ft·°F. Thus the cow will cool even more quickly than the data in Table 11.5 indicate. See Dickerson, p. 36.

variation of k, c, and D of ice with temperature was included in the program.[122] A value of h = 7 BTU/hr-ft²-°F was assumed. This more moderate value (but still high) is more consistent with the theory of ice entombment and no drastic temperature drop. Furthermore, due to the enormous insulation provided by the ice, it makes no difference in the calculation whether h = 18.24 or 7. The initial temperature of the mammoth was assumed to be 100° F. Table 11.6 presents the comparison between a blast-frozen mammoth modeled above and the ice-entombed mammoth posited by some. Even at −250° F, it will take 275 hours (11 days) to reduce the temperature of a point eight inches into an ice-entombed mammoth to 40° F. At more realistic temperatures consistent with the ice theory, for instance, −100° F — it would take 363 hours (15 days) compared with only 21 hours for the blast-frozen mammoth. The delicate flower parts would not be recognizable if they remained in the mammoth's stomach at temperatues above 40° F for 15 days.

TABLE 11.5

COMPARISON OF COOLING AND FREEZING RATES IN A COW AND A MAMMOTH

Air temp. °F	Time in hours to bring mean temp. of cow to 40° F, T_i=101° F	Time in hours to freeze mammoth at 29° F, T_i=100° F	Time in hours to freeze cow at 29° F, T_i=101° F h=7BTU/hr-ft²-°F
0	64.3	—	223.0
−30	32.3	—	163.2
−50	23.0	523.6	142.2
−100	12.0	351.3	112.4
−129	9.0	298.0	102.0
−150	7.3	269.1	96.1
−175	6.0	241.6	90.4
−200	5.0	220.5	85.7
−225	4.3	202.2	81.7
−250	3.8	187.6	78.3

122. See Dickerson, p. 37.

TABLE 11.6

COMPARISON OF COOLING AND FREEZING OF A MAMMOTH "BLAST FROZEN" AND A MAMMOTH BURIED IN ICE

Air temp. °F	Blast Frozen $T_i = 100°$ F		Buried in Ice T_i-mammoth = 100° F	
	Time in hours to bring a point 7.27 inches in to 40° F	Time in hours to freeze mammoth at 29° F	Time in hours to bring a point 8 inches in to 40° F	Time in hours to freeze mammoth at 29° F
−50	45.6	523.6	445.7	1740.0
−100	21.3	351.3	363.0	1236.4
−129	16.5	298.0	337.2	1076.9
−150	13.3	269.1	326.7	988.4
−175	11.6	241.6	306.0	904.5
−200	10.0	220.5	295.6	837.2
−225	8.3	202.2	285.3	782.4
−250	7.8	187.6	275.0	736.5

Also the likelihood of any fresh meat being left on a mammoth carcass under such conditions is quite small. If burial in ice can be considered approximately similar to burial in frozen mud, then it is clear that the temperature of the outer 8 inches of the mammoth would be well above 40° F for 300 to 400 hours, assuming the gradualistic and noncatastrophic theory of mammoth extinction. In this time the meat would spoil. Only by a blast freeze can the reports of fresh meat be accounted for; mud or ice burial is insufficient.

All these calculations are based on the premise that it was necessary that the delicate parts were essential for identification of the plant remains. However, even if it were possible to have identified these plants without reference to their vegetable parts, the fact that edible meat has been carved off mammoth carcasses also requires a drastic temperature drop to 40° F within a day or so to have left meat edible. Unfrozen meat will begin to spoil in a refrigerator after about 100 hours.

Conclusion

It is clear that for the Beresovka mammoth, at least, some violent climatic upheaval is the only explanation for these remains. The animal was peacefully grazing in late July, and suddenly within a half hour of ingestion of his last lunch he was overcome by temperatures colder than $-150°$ F., and froze to death in the middle of the summer. Furthermore, he never completely unthawed *until* he fell out of a riverbank in 1901. So whatever climatic upheaval caught him, it permanently changed the climatic conditions of the Siberian tundra.

We did not undertake this extensive discussion of the Beresovka mammoth to prove that the entire northern continents were swept by $-175°$ F blizzards. At best, it simply argues for a local catastrophe of horrendous proportions. As we will discuss in the next chapter, it is possible that this blast freeze could have been connected with the vapor canopy's condensation.

The major purpose of this chapter has been to demonstrate the weaknesses in uniformitarian theories of mammoth extinction. They certainly cannot account for the case of the Beresovka mammoth. Neither can they explain the evidence of a great flood and sudden climate reversal.

Chapter 12

The Catastrophic Freeze

The evidence that the northern hemisphere was suddenly overcome by a terrible climatic catastrophe converges from several sources. We will summarize them in this chapter.

SUMMARY OF EVIDENCE FOR CONTINENTAL CLIMATIC CATASTROPHE

STOMACH CONTENTS OF THE BERESOVKA MAMMOTH

As discussed in the previous chapter, the state of preservation of the stomach contents of the Beresovka mammoth requires a sudden deep freeze in mid-summer. We discussed our analysis of the freezing rates necessary to leave the stomach remains in their present condition with A. F. Christensen, an engineer with the Oscar Mayer meat company. From his experience in freezing meats and entire cows he found the present analysis to be substantially correct:

> Heat removal from a 10,000-pound animal at a rate sufficiently great to freeze stomach contents before digestion could commence would require a very low temperature. The presence of flower petals would require a very sudden application of that low temperature. This could not have been a seasonal weather change, for summer flowers would be long gone before low arctic temperatures could prevail.[1]

1. A. F. Christensen, general utilities engineer, Oscar Mayer and Company, personal communication, 14 April 1976.

INABILITY TO FLEE THE CLIMATE CHANGE

Among the growing number of geologists who recognize that the climate of northern Siberia was once much more moderate than today, there is still some perplexity as to why the mammoths did not simply flee to the south when the climate gradually changed from moderate to severe. As mentioned in chapter 11, Neuville says they failed to leave the area "for reasons which I cannot trace."[2] Assuming a sudden instead of gradual change in temperature would remove Neuville's perplexity. The mammoths did not leave because they did not have time to leave; they were overwhelmed by a sudden catastrophe. This assumption adequately explains why countless thousands of mammoths were frozen all over the northern hemisphere. How else could they freeze to death in mid-summer?

FRESH MEAT

As documented in the previous chapter, for centuries reports of eating mammoth meat have filtered out of the north. Joseph Barnes, a *New York Herald Tribune* journalist, testified to the delicious flavor of a mammoth steak served to him at the Russian Academy of Sciences in the 1930s.[3] Although the reports of humans eating mammoth flesh are frequently rejected as mythological by uniformitarian geologists, it is universally admitted that various carnivores regularly eat mammoth flesh. Furthermore, on the Beresovka expedition the fresh-looking meat that was rejected by the explorers was thrown to the dogs who devoured it with glee.[4] This single fact establishes beyond doubt that this meat was in some sense "fresh" and also edible to humans. The basis for this is that even though dogs will eat

2. H. Neuville, "On the Extinction of the Mammoth," *Annual Report Smithsonian Institution*, 1919, pp. 327-38.
3. Reported by Charles Hapgood in a personal conversation with Barnes in Charles H. Hapgood, *The Path of the Pole* (Philadelphia: Chilton, 1970), p. 261.
4. Basset Digby, *The Mammoth and Mammoth Hunting Grounds in Northeast Siberia*, p. 129.

rotten meat, they will *always* become ill. When this situation was described to a local veterinarian, he observed that if the meat had been rotten, the dogs would never have made it back home. This, of course, would have crippled the expedition and would certainly have been reported if it had occurred. So there were portions, at least, of the Beresovka mammoth flesh that had not rotted prior to freezing.

Any American housewife will tell you that she will not chance serving her family hamburger that has been in the refrigerator for more than three or four days. It begins to spoil in five to seven days. For humans to have eaten this meat and considered it "delicious" (Joseph Barnes) or "wholesome"[5] suggests that if the temperature was lowered to about 40° F shortly after death, the animal must have been preserved in a "fresh" condition. Assuming the outside temperature was -50° F and the constants described in chapter 11, the time necessary to freeze 10 inches into the mammoth would be 97.3 hours or 4.0 days. If the ambient temperature was -150° F, it would take 47 hours. In order to freeze the mammoth solid all the way to the center, it would take 522 hours at -50° F and 269 hours at -150° F, assuming h = 18.24 BTU/hr·ft^2·°F.[6] Since unfrozen meat kept in a refrigerator will not begin to spoil for about 100 hours, it appears that an animal the size of a mammoth, even under today's conditions could lie down in the midst of the tundra in the middle of winter, freeze to death, and still leave behind some remains that would be edible. However, even in this case unless the storage temperature was rapidly reduced to -70° C, if the meat did not spoil, it surely would not have been "delicious" or "wholesome."[7]

So there seems to be no inherent difficulty in assuming that men might have eaten mammoth flesh. But "today's condi-

5. Cited by H. H. Howorth, "The Mammoth in Siberia," *The Geological Magazine,* September 1880, p. 411.
6. These figures result from the Birds Eye program referred to in the preceeding chapter.
7. Harold T. Meryman, "Mechanics of Freezing in Living Cells and Tissues," *Science* 124 (21 September 1956):519. Also note the discussion of this point in the preceding chapter.

tions" clearly did not prevail during the mammoth age, when it was much warmer (not -50° F). To find fresh meat on an animal that cannot survive in temperatures below 32° F would prove that the surrounding air temperature suddenly dropped from warm to at least -50° F, and that very quickly. (Armour Meat Company says that the animal would rot in 32 to 48 hours unless the temperature was dropped far below freezing.) Hence the presence of fresh meat is clear proof of a sudden temperature drop. The presence of summer flowers in the stomach of the Beresovka mammoth confirms this.

Tolmachoff, on the one hand, denies the reports of mammoth flesh being eaten, yet, on the other hand, cites evidence that whales have been found frozen, partially covered with drift, with fat on them good enough to be used for food.[8] The problem is, of course, that these whales died in winter, hence could have been immediately exposed to the cold air and frozen; but the mammoths, in order to have been buried in soft mud, must have been buried when it was warm. Both the Adams' and Beresovka mammoths had stomachs full of food, evidencing that they died and froze to death in mid-summer.

Sensing this difficulty, Tolmachoff tries to circumvent it with the assertion that the decay of organic matter in the Arctic is very slow due to the purity of the air and the absence of insects. He argues, "In such conditions, sometimes a carcass of an animal could stay over the warm season without becoming very much decayed."[9] Seemingly aware of what he had denied earlier — that relatively "fresh" meat has been found on the carcasses of mammoths that evidently died in the summer — he tries to find a way for these carcasses to make it through the summer sun (which averages from 32° F to 68° F today[10]). He finds evidence for this possibility from a mountain trip he took in southern Siberia. During the trip the natives took slabs of

8. I. P. Tolmachoff, "The Carcasses of the Mammoth and Rhinoceros Found in the Frozen Ground of Siberia," *Transactions of the American Philosophical Society* 23 (1929):56.
9. Ibid., p. 61.
10. *Hammond World Atlas*, p. 56.

meat out of their knapsacks to expose them to the freezing mountain air. Apparently by this procedure they were able to maintain the meat in a fresh condition for extended periods of time during the summer months.

It appears that Tolmachoff confuses the thermodynamic differences between a mammoth on the hoof and a one-inch slab of steak. It is one thing to preserve a slab of meat by regular exposure to the night air, but an entirely different matter to keep a complete carcass from rotting. A steak, for example, can be blast frozen in about 30 minutes, but to freeze an entire mammoth carcass would take over 500 hours. Furthermore, the mammoths of Siberia were not exposed in the summer to mountain air; they were in the highlands, plains, and lowlands, but not mountains. It does not normally dip below freezing during the summer months there even today, and it never did during the mammoth age, or they would have died due to the lack of oil-producing glands in their skin (as discussed in chapter 10).

Also we find many mosquitoes in the tundras during the summer. On his way to excavate the Beresovka mammoth in August of 1901, Pfizenmayer had to give up sleep and sit by the fire all night to get protection from them.[11] If that is true, then the rate of decay of mammoth flesh during the summer in the tundra is probably even more pronounced, not less, than it is in other areas.

Perhaps the most disadvantageous aspect of Tolmachoff's theory of summer survival is that wild animals would certainly have immediately destroyed the mammoth if it had died in summer and lain there on the tundra. The carcass of a similarly exposed animal today would be picked clean by carnivores within two days.

The theory that mammoths were preserved in this fashion by bog chemicals was argued from parallels in Starunia, Poland, where specimens of the wooly rhinoceros have been preserved from glacial times in a silt impregnated with salt and crude oil. However, as has been noted, this results in an embalming process, and no such evidence is present in the mammoth

11. E. W. Pfizenmayer, *Siberian Man and Mammoth*, p. 41.

remains. Neither is there any evidence of salty soil or crude oil.[12]

In view of the evidence presented from the thermodynamic model (chapter 11) and the data now under discussion, Farrand's statement, "There is no direct evidence that any wooly mammoth froze to death,"[13] may be disregarded as uninformed. He says that the full stomachs of these animals argues against death by slow freezing. This is true in that a full stomach indicates a plentiful food supply, which does not exist in the winter when an animal would die and slowly freeze to death. Furthermore, he insists, the large size of the animal argues against sudden freezing. Both of these observations are valid if one is assuming the impossibility of a sudden catastrophic temperature drop, which is the very point in question. The evidence requires a sudden deep freeze (as shown in chapter 11).

Farrand also objects to the sudden freeze theory on the grounds that the animals rotted and were eaten prior to freezing, "as many firsthand accounts attest."[14] Farrand cites Tolmachoff, who argues that the strong smell of the ground in the mammoth localities proves that the animals must have rotted prior to freezing.[15] It should be obvious, however, that this could equally well indicate the observed phenomenon of thawing and refreezing of numerous carcasses seen today. Furthermore, even under the catastrophic conditions predicated in the canopy model, it is not necessary to believe that the permafrost was formed instantly for hundreds of feet down. Rather, it was undoubtedly the result of a gradual process over a number of years. Animals caught in the sediments of the Deluge, which was later turned to permafrost, may have rotted as the warm ground cooled during the following years. Also, it is undoubt-

12. I. P. Tolmachoff, "Note on the Extinction of the Mammoth in Siberia," *American Journal of Science* 14 (July 1927):297.
13. William R. Farrand, "Frozen Mammoths and Modern Geology," *Science* 133 (March 1961):733.
14. Ibid., p. 733.
15. Tolmachoff, "The Carcasses of the Mammoth," p. 60.

edly true that many of the animals *did* rot after dying but prior to freezing during pre-Flood or early Flood atmospheric disruptions.

SOFT PARTS IN FROZEN GROUND

The question is: How did they get there? Across the whole length of Siberia, from the Bering Strait to the Ural Mountains, we find soft parts buried and preserved in the permafrost.[16] If the ground was frozen then as it is now, these remains could never have penetrated the rock-hard earth. On the other hand, if the ground was soft, which their burial requires, then the temperature must have been warm. However, if the temperature at burial was warm, then the soft parts would have rotted away and not been preserved. This requires us to believe that immediately after burial the ground was frozen and has remained so ever since. Such was the conclusion of Howorth:

> The facts compel us to admit that when the mammoth was buried in Siberia the ground was soft, and the climate therefore comparatively mild and genial, and that immediately afterwards the same ground became frozen and the same climate became Arctic, and that they have remained so to this day, and this not gradually in accordance with some slowly continuous astronomical or cosmical changes, but suddenly and per saltem.[17]

In reference to the Adams' mammoth, Dr. Buckland made a similar observation:

> One thing, however, is certain as to this mammoth, i.e., Adams', that whether it was embedded in a matrix of pure ice or of frozen earth, it must have been rapidly and totally enveloped in that matrix before its flesh had undergone decay, and that, whatever may have been the climate of the coast of Siberia in antecedent times, not only was it intensely cold within a few days after the mammoth perished, but it has also continued cold from that time to the present hour.[18]

Such an extensive series of finds, preserved in the same perfect way, all evidencing a sudden change of temperature from warm to cold, requires us to posit meteorological conditions that must have extended over an entire continent.

16. Henry H. Howorth, *The Mammoth and the Flood*, p. 96.
17. Ibid., p. 96.
18. Cited by Howorth, p. 97.

FRESH MAMMOTH BONE

Ezra and Cook made a histological examination of a fragment of compact bone taken from the mammoth skeleton discovered in 1907 by L. S. Quackenbush at Eschscholtz Bay, Alaska. To their surprise it had all the appearances of fresh bone, which suggests sudden freezing:

> The routine histology of the section thus confirmed our initial observation that the fragment had all the appearances of fresh bone. ... The outer surface resembled fresh bone in that it was smooth and shiny. It had the characteristic odor of fresh bone but was yellowish and brown in color. ... There was no evidence of loss by leaching, and the typical bone pattern was remarkably intact. As a further check on the condition of the mammoth bone, we analyzed the bone for total nitrogen and acid-extractable carbonate. The mean value of nitrogen, by the Kjeldahl method, was 4.2% by weight; for the carbonate, 3.4%. These values fall definitely within the range to be expected in fresh, compact mammalian bone.[19]

This particular carcass had been mostly rotted and eaten by carnivores by the time the scientists arrived. Apparently, this particular fragment of bone never thawed out. Beside the mouth of this carcass, a bright green, partially chewed plant was found, indicating a sudden deep freeze.

WELL-PRESERVED MAMMOTH IVORY

As discussed previously, in order for ivory to be suitable for carving, it must be carved soon after the death of the animal, before the animal matter in it has rotted and stained it. Yet 25% of all the mammoth ivory tusks in Siberia are in good enough condition for ivory turning.[20] This condition requires that 25% of the nearly 50,000 tusks dug out so far must have been suddenly frozen and never thawed out.[21]

19. H. C. Ezra and S. F. Cook, "Histology of Mammoth Bone," Science 129 (February 1959):465-66.
20. Digby, p. 177.
21. Richard Lydekker, "Mammoth Ivory," Smithsonian Reports, 1899, 361-66.

Hence we are confronted with countless thousands of tusks spanning the entire length of Siberia, all indicating a rapid freeze and evidencing meteorological conditions of unparalleled ferocity. What could have caused this deep freeze?

THE MAMMOTH AND THE CANOPY

The cause of the Pleistocene extinctions has long been an enigma to historical geology. "Some 70 percent of all native North American mammals with an adult body weight of 100 pounds or more died out during a 1,000 year period at the end of the Pleistocene."[22] Harold Anthony candidly admits, "It is not known why so many animals of the late Pleistocene and early Recent fauna became extinct. Climatic change is often evoked to account for the disappearances of this sort."[23]

A STRATIGRAPHICAL RECLASSIFICATION

At this point a problem in definitions arises. What do we mean by the word *Pleistocene*? For historical geology this refers to strata that is dated as being between 1 and 2 million to about 10,000 years of age. It was the era of the Ice Age, when as much as 27% of the earth's surface was covered by glacial ice to a depth of up to 10,000 feet.[24] However, these designations cannot be used fairly by those espousing the kind of Deluge geology advocated here or by Whitcomb and Morris. It should be obvious that if the earth is only 6,000 years old, then all the geological designations are meaningless within that framework, and it is deceptive to continue to use them. If, as many creationist geologists believe, the majority of the geologic column represents Flood sediments and post-Flood geophysical activity, then the mammoth, the dinosaur, and human be-

22. Daniel Cohen, "The Great Dinosaur Disaster," *Science Digest* 65 (March 1969):45-52.
23. Harold E. Anthony, "Nature's Deep Freeze," *Natural History* 58 (September 1949):300.
24. *Hammond World Atlas*, p. E-10.

ings all existed simultaneously.[25] Furthermore, the "Pleistocene" then could have come *before* the Permian. For the Flood geologist, Pleistocene strata may mean simply strata that indicates cold temperatures, glacial ice, and mammoth extinctions. Some limited attempts have been made by creationist geologists to reclassify the entire geological column within this framework, but the task is immense. Uniformitarian geology has had 150 years to construct its system of strata, a system that needs to be redone from the assumptions of Flood geology.[26]

25. There *is* good evidence that these species existed at the same time. In 1973 two human skeletons were discovered in Cretaceous strata; see Clifford L. Burdick, "Discovery of Human Skeletons in Cretaceous Formation," *Creation Research Society Quarterly* 10 (September 1973):109-10. Footprints of saber-toothed tigers, dinosaurs, and men were all found in Cretaceous strata in Glen Rose, Texas, A. E. Wilder Smith, *Man's Origin and Man's Destiny*, pp. 135-39, where pictures of human footprints are reproduced along with dinosaur prints; also see Roland T. Bird, *Natural History*, May 1939, pp. 225, 261, 302. At Antelope Springs, 43 miles from Delta, Utah, a human sandal print with a trilobite fossil embedded in the heel was found in a Cambrian formation; see William J. Meister, "Discovery of Trilobite Fossils in Shod Footprint of Human in Trilobite Beds — A Cambrian Formation, Antelope Springs, Utah," *Why Not Creation*, pp. 186-93. Of special interest in this regard is the discovery of a size 13 human sandal print in Triassic rock, which showed a double line of stitches, see *Journal of the Transactions of the Victoria Institute* 80:21-22. For extensive documentation of similar finds, see Erich A. von Fange, "Time Upside Down," *Creation Research Society Quarterly* 11 (June 1974):13-27.
26. For a tentative outline see Henry Morris, ed., *Scientific Creationism*, p. 129; also Alfred M. Rehwinkel, *The Flood*, pp. 257-75; and Henry Morris and John C. Whitcomb, *The Genesis Flood*, pp. 132-36; 212-330. Two helpful articles arguing for a different reconstruction than the above:

(Continued on following page)

We suggest that the general designations for this new classification of strata be as given in Table 12.1. In the discussion following the table the term "Pleistocene extinctions" will be used to indicate the extermination of many mammals by drastic climate that occurred during the "FLOOD STRATA, *Initial*" period. The "Pleistocene extinctions" coincided with the dinosaur extinctions. When historical geologists refer to these extinctions and to the volcanic activity that was associated with them as occurring at the *close* of the Pleistocene, in the scheme to be described below we posit that these extinctions mostly occurred in the initial phases of the Deluge and were caused by sudden climatic reversals and floods.

The notion of a changed climate as a partial explanation for dinosaur and mammoth extinction is not new. In fact, *sudden* changes of climate have even been suggested. A major reason that these kinds of theories have never received general acceptance is that the necessary mechanism to generate a sudden and permanent climatic revolution is inconceivable. Howorth summarized the difficulty years ago: "A change so complete and so sudden in the climatic conditions of any district presents problems for the meteorologist and physicist to ponder over, which have hardly been present to the minds of those tutored in the easygoing ways of Uniformity."[27]

However, those tutored in the "easygoing ways of Uniformity" have indeed pondered the necessary meteorological conditions and for this reason have attempted to interpret the data in a noncatastrophic way. Howorth was criticized for offering no theory of what could have produced the climatic reversal. In a review of Howorth's book in *Nature*, the root objection

---

Stuart E. Nevins, "Post-flood Strata of the John Day Country, Northeastern Oregon," *Creation Research Society Quarterly* 10 (March 1974):191-204, and an article by Northrup in the same issue, pp. 205-7. However, all of these approaches labor under the impossible burden of assigning Flood geology dates to historical geology's strata designations. The designations of historical geology need to be completely abandoned.

27. Howorth, p. 96.

to the catastrophic interpretation of the data emerges: "Mr. Howorth, as an alternative, offers the hypothesis of a deluge, followed by a sudden change of temperature, but, apart from the difficulties attending the former part of this, by what physical or astronomical catastrophe does he account for the latter? Wisely, he makes no attempt to indicate this."[28]

Once we grant the fact of the ancient vapor canopy, a plausible explanation is forthcoming. The condensation of this canopy would result in a flood, burial, and a sudden deep freeze, and it would explain the permanence of the climatic change.

Whatever overcame the mammoths and other animals of that fateful era must have been able to accomplish several things:

(1) It rapidly froze many animals and preserved them intact up to the present day.

(2) It unleashed a massive flood, which subsequently buried these creatures under tons of tundra muck.

(3) It permanently changed the climate of the tundras from their formerly subtropical climate to today's severe Arctic climate.

These are the minimum requirements for a theory of "Pleistocene extinctions" as argued in chapters 10 and 11. In the condensation of the earth's ancient vapor canopy and the ensuing flood we find a mechanism that may adequately account for those facts.

Obviously it is impossible to describe exactly what may have happened, but following is an attempt to outline the broad strokes of a theory of the "Pleistocene extinctions." It may not have happened this way; in fact, it probably did not. The variables are numerous and other sequences could have occurred. However, we have outlined a possible sequence under three phases.

---

28. "Review of *The Mammoth and the Flood*," Nature 37 (8 December 1887):123-25.

TABLE 12.1

RECLASSIFICATION OF GEOLOGICAL STRATA ALONG THE LINES OF FLOOD GEOLOGY

PRE-FLOOD STRATA

This represents the world under the vapor canopy. Strata that reveal warm polar temperatures and abundant animal life would be included. It is to be expected that very little of these strata are to be found in their original position since they were largely washed away and redeposited during the Flood. Much of what historical geology terms "Precambrian" would define these deposits.

FLOOD STRATA

Initial These strata would constitute the geological activity that may have constituted the months just prior to the Flood and in its initial phases. It is here that the so-called Pleistocene extinctions occurred. Some of the mammoths may have been buried and quick-frozen during this time.

Middle These strata constitute the erosional material washed from the pre-Flood world and redeposited by the hydraulic mechanisms of the Deluge. They constitute the majority of the geologic column.

Final Here post-Flood geophysical activity and residual catastrophism would have continued for many years before the earth returned to a new equilibrium. It therefore constitutes a redeposition of *Initial* and *Middle* strata.

TABLE 12.1 continued

POST-FLOOD STRATA
> During this era, the Ice Age occurred (if it occurred at all).[29] Very little fossilization went on, and the animals redistributed themselves over the globe. It constitutes the "Recent" strata of historical geology, except that it dates from around 2000 B.C.

PHASE I: DEVELOPMENT OF STORM CENTERS

In chapter 8 we proposed that about a year prior to the Flood a number of volcanoes began to erupt and spewed many cubic miles of volcanic dust into the atmosphere, where some of it was carried by the canopy convection cells to the top of the canopy. This would immediately have begun to reduce the solar input into the atmosphere. In order to model this effect we will arbitrarily assume that the presence of this dust will reduce the solar input into the earth by 50% (instead of the 35% without it). Using the approximations outlined in Equations (7.7) to (7.24), a canopy base temperature of 80° C and a surface temperature of 4.85° C (40° F) results.[30]

On the opening day of the Flood, we assume that the mountain uplifts began to occur, along with the volcanic activity. These two factors will cause tremendous rainfall to develop, especially over the areas of uplift. This rainfall, in turn, would reduce the surface pressure because the weight of the canopy over that area would have been reduced. As a result, the warmer

29. Douglas Cox cites the evidence commonly adduced for an Ice Age and argues that this constitutes no evidence at all. Furthermore, he suggests that the physics of ice precludes a glacial age from ever occurring: Douglas E. Cox,"Problems in the Glacial Theory," *Creation Research Society Quarterly* 13 (June 1976):25-34.
30. The cooler the cloud becomes the sooner the fine mist droplets will grow to rain drops by coalesence.

The Catastrophic Freeze

air on the outer fringes of this low-pressure area would immediately begin to rush in to equalize the pressure differential. When that happened, a circular rotating system of great winds would have been generated due to the coriolis force. Hence terrible low pressure systems with wind velocities of over 200 miles per hour would surely have developed.

These low pressure systems would be composed of icy cold air, freezing hail, frozen mud (as explained below), and would leave vegetable matter, smaller animals, and other debris behind.

HIGH PRESSURE
(2.18 atm)

LOW PRESSURE

Area of continental uplift and volcanism

(1.68 atm)

HIGH PRESSURE
(2.18 atm)

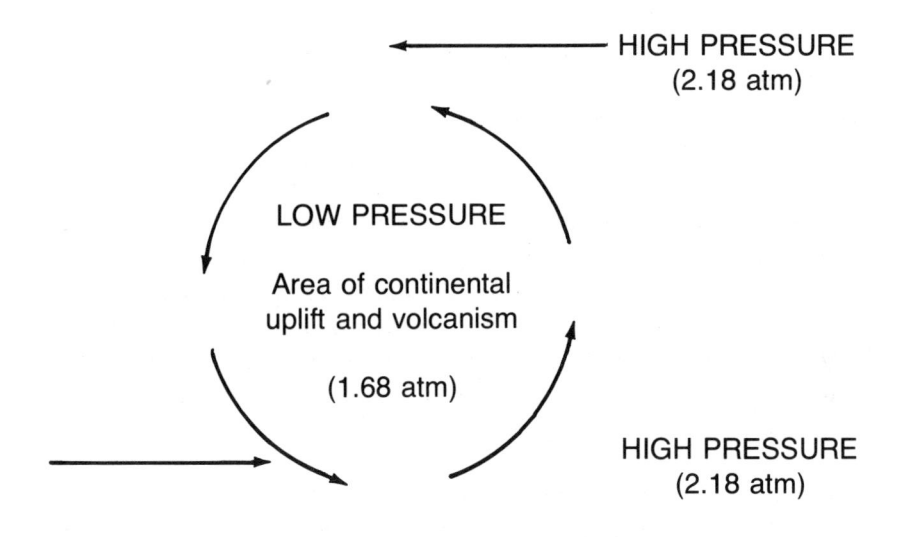

Fig. 12.1 — Development of Low Pressure Centers Prior to the Flood.

A number of cooling mechanisms could conceivably have resulted in immense cold in these hurricane winds.

The cloud cover. As outlined in chapter 8, the volcanic cloud cover and the water droplet cloud cover would result in the cooling of the canopy and a drastic reduction of the surface temperature to somewhere between 32° F and 60° F.

Pressure drop. Assuming violent rain over the areas of volcanic activity and mountain uplift, a sudden drop of pressure would result. If the rain fell at eight inches per hour for the first 48 hours, the surface pressure would drop from 2.18 atm to 1.18 atm. Assuming that the surface temperature was 40° F (4.4°C) over the area of the pressure drop, the reduction in surface temperature can be computed from:[31]

$$T_2 = T_1(P_2/P_1)^{0.286} \qquad (12.1)$$

where T_2 = the temperature at the end of the 48 hours in °K; T_1 = the initial surface temperature, 4.4° C = 277.4° K; P_2 = the pressure at the end of the 48 hours of rainfall, 1.18 atm; and P_1 = the initial surface pressure, 2.18 atm. This change in surface pressure in 48 hours will drop the surface temperature to -40° F in the middle of the storm center. This approximation is very rough because it assumes an adiabatic expansion that is not strictly accurate. Heat from the friction of the rain and from the warmer areas at the side of the storm center would be transmitted by advection and convective turbulence into the area of the pressure drop. But the pressure drop effect will predominate over a short time in a localized area, and a pseudo-adiabatic expansion may be assumed.

Air updrafts. As warmer than -40° F air rushed into the areas of the lower pressure, it would have slid over the colder air and been forced upward. Furthermore, the presence of mountain uplifts in the vicinity of the storm center would have resulted in the updraft of immense quantities of air at high velocity. Also, any newly upthrust mountains in the path of this front would cause the inrushing air to accelerate upward as it traveled over these hills. As this cold air was thrust upward, it was cooled even more by atmospheric expansion. The canopy over these areas would have been completely unstable and the temperature inversion reversed so that air could penetrate into the base of the canopy with relative ease. As this cold, dry air went

31. Byers, p. 79.

The Catastrophic Freeze 413

upward, vast amounts of moist warm air would be entrained (captured) within it as it ascended. The temperature in this expanding air would drop according to (12.1). Assuming that the initial temperature of the air was 10° F and that it rose through a pressure drop of about 1 atm (from 1.18 atm to 0.18 atm), the air temperature when it reached that altitude would have been -185° F. So it would have been cooler above than below and the temperature inversion in this area removed. As a result, vast amounts of hail would have formed and begun to fall to the surface of the earth. The presence of such extremely cold (-185° F) ice on the surface of the planet would cool the air quickly as it blew over it. How much cooling would have occurred is difficult to predict, but it is clear that terrible blizzards and freezing wind would result.

Drastically cooled volcanic gases. Assuming that volcanism was becoming general on a global basis in the weeks prior to the Flood, vast amounts of volcanic gases and water vapor would be hurled up into the canopy and beyond it into the cold of space (150 miles). Volcanic ash and water would be caught in these updrafts and cooled due to the cold of space (-250° C) and the expansion of the air medium that carried them upward. This may have occurred far to the south of the Arctic. As this extremely cold material was carried poleward by the canopy convection currents, it would have crashed through the atmosphere at tremendous velocity; ash, gases, hail, and cold air would have swept down across the tundras with terrible force.

We propose that a combination of these four drastic cooling mechanisms could easily have produced the kinds of temperatures necessary to have left fresh meat on a mammoth carcass and to preserve flower petals in an elephant's stomach. Two of these mechanisms grow naturally out of the existence of the canopy (pressure drop and cloud cover).

PHASE II: GLOBAL RAINFALL AND DELUGE

At the conclusion of Phase I of the mammoth extinctions, the earth was assumed to be dotted with toroidal storm systems created by volcanism and rapid precipitation. These mechanisms, in turn, caused a chain reaction to set in, triggering global atmospheric instabilities. Central among these was the global cloud cover from which the rain of Genesis would precipitate. As the day of the Deluge approached, the earth was already in growing instability, and in some areas, violent storms with blizzards having temperatures lower than -40° F were present. Other parts of the earth, however, were relatively peaceful and, except for the growing cloud cover and apparent cooling, sheltered from the violence of other geographical areas. In view of the fact that mammoths seem to have been feeding on summer buttercups when they were overwhelmed, it may be presumed that northern Siberia was free from these storms. Suddenly, after the northern temperatures had already dipped into the low 40s due to the cloud cover, as the Beresovka mammoth was having his last chilly lunch, a 200-mile-per-hour storm front drove raging blizzards of ice, vegetable matter, mud, rain, and snow across the tundras as the "windows of heaven were opened." Thus the mammoths were caught in a terrible catastrophe during the beginning phase of the Flood.

Burial of the mammoths. Thus, on the opening day of the Flood, the atmospheric instabilities that had been building up for a year or more suddenly precipitated into a global instability, and the "windows of heaven were opened." Simultaneously, the fountains of the deep spewed forth, and the earth was overwhelmed with rainfall and deluge. Some of the mammoths were caught in raging blizzards at -175° F temperatures and frozen in their tracks. Other "Pleistocene" animals were swamped in a rain of freezing mud and buried in tons of frozen vegetable material along with trees, shrubs, and gravel that was driven in front of the great winds. Others, after freezing in the blizzards, were buried in unfrozen muck (35° F) swept over them by flood waves. To the south other animals were buried in the turbid mud flows and were not exposed at this time to freezing conditions. Even in the north it is not necessary to posit a freezing storm for the entire area; many of the remains would simply be buried in the mud and mixed with other animals in what is now the Siberian muck.

Some of the animals may have been literally frozen in ice. The existence of these ice lenses with frozen animals in them that are readily edible after thousands of years is well known. Others frozen in ice would tumble out of glaciers later on and become buried in the mud flows generated by the glacial thaws. Many would rot after their initial burial because they were not buried in freezing conditions. Others would begin to rot after the Flood as the sediments in which they were entombed began to warm up due to the warmer temperatures of the southern European climate. Gradually, however, in the northern areas this entire mass of mud, trees, shrubs, and animals became frozen to depths of hundreds of feet into what is called the permafrost today.

The evidence of a violent atmospheric disturbance in the northern regions has been graphically presented by Professor Frank C. Hibben in his book *The Lost Americans*. Since his description of the evidence is firsthand, it will be useful to quote him extensively.

> In many places the Alaskan muck is packed with animal bones and debris in trainload lots. Bones of mammoth, mastodon, several kinds of bison, horses, wolves, bears and lion tell a story of a faunal population. . . .
> The Alaskan muck is like a fine, dark gray sand, . . . Within this mass, frozen solid, lie the twisted parts of animals and trees intermingled with lenses of ice and layers of peat and mosses. It looks as though in the midst of some cataclysmic catastrophe of ten thousand years ago the whole Alaskan world of living animals and plants was suddenly frozen in mid-motion in a grim charade. . . .
> Throughout the Yukon and its tributaries, the gnawing currents of the river had eaten into many a frozen bank of muck to reveal bones and tusks of these animals protruding at all levels. Whole gravel bars in the muddy river were formed of the jumbled fragments of animal remains.[32]

In another portion of the book Hibben continues:

> The Pleistocene period ended in death. This is no ordinary extinction of a vague geological period which fizzled to an uncertain end. This death was catastrophic and all-inclusive. . . . The large animals that had given their name to the period became extinct. Their death marked the end of an era.
> But how did they die? What caused the extinction of forty million animals? This mystery forms one of the oldest detective stories in the world. A good detective story involves humans and death. These conditions are met at the end of the Pleistocene. In this particular case, the death was of such colossal proportions as to be staggering to contemplate.

32. Frank C. Hibben, *The Lost Americans*, pp. 90-92.

The "corpus delecti" of the deceased in this mystery may be found almost everywhere . . . the animals of the period wandered into every corner of the New World not actually covered by the ice sheets. Their bones lie bleaching on the sands of Florida and in the gravels of New Jersey. They weather out of the dry terraces of Texas and protrude from the sticky ooze of the tar pits of Wilshire Boulevard in Los Angeles. Thousands of these remains have been encountered in Mexico and even in South America. The bodies lie as articulated skeletons revealed by dust storms, or as isolated bones and fragments in ditches or canals. The bodies of the victims are everywhere in evidence.

It might first appear that many of these great animals died natural deaths; that is, that the remains that we find in the Pleistocene strata over the continent represent the normal death that ends the ordinary life cycle. However, where we can study these animals in some detail, such as in the great bone pits of Nebraska, we find literally thousands of these remains together. The young die with the old, foal with dam and calf with cow. Whole herds of animals were apparently killed together and overcome by some common power.

We have already seen that the muck pits of Alaska are filled with the evidences of universal death. Mingled in these frozen masses are the remains of many thousands of animals killed in their prime. The best evidence that we could have that this Pleistocene death was not simply a case of the bison and the mammoth dying after their normal span of years is found in the Alaskan muck. In this dark gray frozen stuff is preserved, quite commonly, fragments of ligaments, skin, hair, and even flesh. We have gained from the muck pits of the Yukon Valley a picture of quick extinction. The evidences of violence there are as obvious as the horror camps of Germany. Such piles of bodies of animals or men simply do not occur by any ordinary natural means.[33]

After describing the extensive deposits of volcanic dust interspersed throughout the Alaskan muck, Hibben argues that the evidence suggests a violent atmospheric disturbance as a plausible explanation of the remains.

A volcanic eruption would explain the end of the Alaskan animals all at one time, and in a manner that would satisfy the evidences there as we know them. The herds would be killed in their tracks either by the blanket of volcanic ash covering them and causing death by heat or suffocation, or, indirectly, by volcanic gases. Toxic clouds of gas from volcanic upheavals could well cause death on a gigantic scale.

Throughout the Alaskan muck, too, there is evidence of atmospheric disturbances of unparalleled violence. Mammoth and bison alike were torn and twisted as though by a cosmic hand in a Godly rage. In one place, we can find the foreleg and shoulder of a mammoth with portions of the flesh and the toenails and the hair still clinging to the blackened bones. Close by is the neck and the skull of a bison with the vertebrae clinging together with

33. Ibid., pp. 168-70.

tendons and ligaments and the chitinous covering of the horns intact. There is no mark of a knife or cutting instrument. The animals were simply torn apart and scattered over the landscape like things of straw and string, even though some of them weighed several tons. Mixed with the piles of bones are trees, also twisted and torn and piled in tangled groups and the whole is covered with fine sifting muck, then frozen solid.

Storms, too, accompany volcanic disturbances of the proportions indicated here. Differences in temperature and the influence of the cubic miles of ash and pumice thrown into the air by eruptions of this sort might well produce winds and blasts of inconceivable violence. If this is the explanation of the end of all this animal life, the Pleistocene period was terminated by a very exciting time indeed.[34]

Global flood. As the storms of the pre-Flood period and of the early phases of the Flood completed their work of burial and freezing of the Pleistocene animals, they also unleashed a growing flood. By the end of 40 days of rain, the entire canopy had condensed and, due to continental shifts and the spewing forth of subterranean waters, the entire earth was covered with water. The geological activity that went on during this period involved more deposits laid down on top of the mammoth burial grounds and extensive global sedimentation.

Crucial to this theory of mammoth extinction is the claim that buried under tons of muck, which in turn was covered by the flood waters, these mammoths could have remained at temperatures below 40° F or could have, in some cases, remained frozen. Would not the warmer flood waters warm up the muck and as a result thaw and rot the mammoths?

Without a doubt, this must have happened in many cases. However, it would not have happened in every instance. In fact, preservation could have been quite common. In order to quantify this problem we consulted Professor Richard A. Schapery of the civil engineering department at Texas A & M University.[35] Dr. Schapery employed graphical solutions suggested by Carslaw and Jaeger.[36] He assumed the following thermal prop-

34. Ibid., pp. 176-78.
35. Richard A. Schapery, Ph D., professor of mechanical, civil, and aeronautical engineering, civil engineering department, Texas A & M University, personal communication, 5 November 1977.
36. H. S. Carslaw and J. C. Jaeger, *Conduction of Heat in Solids.*

erties for frozen tundra muck:[37] density = 94 lb/ft², specific heat, c = 0.25 BTU/lb·° F; and thermal conductivity, k = 0.7 BTU/hr·ft·° F. For unfrozen tundra muck the thermal properties are:[38] k = 0.5 BTU/hr·ft·° F; density = 94 lb/ft²; and c = 0.6 BTU/lb·° F. He assumed that the mammoth was blast frozen (or cooled) in a blizzard and subsequently buried either in frozen mud and vegetable matter (32° F) blown over him by the blizzard, or in 35° F muck that was washed over him by flood tidal waves. Also he assumed that the flood waters were 75° F, and that the initial temperature of the mammoth was 35° F. Finally, he assumed that the animal was buried in 20 feet of this material.

With these assumptions if the mammoth was buried in 20 feet of frozen muck, it would take 155 days for the temperature of the mammoth to be raised from 32° F to 40° F. If the initial temperature of the mammoth was 35° F and unfrozen muck buried him at 35° F, it would take 438 days for the temperature of the mammoth to rise from 35° F to 40° F. In the case of the frozen muck, it takes a shorter time because the thermal conductivity of frozen muck is much higher than that of unfrozen muck. However, this calculation does not take into consideration the heat of melting or the fact that as the muck thawed out its thermal conductivity would go up. So the 155-day figure for frozen muck is much too low, and it could easily have taken over a year for a mammoth buried in frozen muck to thaw out.

It is clear then that there is no problem in preserving at least some of the mammoth remains in a relatively fresh state throughout the year of the Flood, securely preserved, fresh frozen under tons of tundra muck, which subsequently froze into today's permafrost.

Buried and frozen under tons of muck, the Pleistocene animals would be well protected from the thawing effects of the warmer flood waters. Some may have been ripped up and

37. Suggested by Barry Dempsy, Ph. D., professor of civil engineering, University of Illinois, personal communication, 12 July 1977.
38. Leonard R. Ingersoll, Otto J. Zobel, and Alfred C. Ingersoll, *Heat Conduction*, p. 244.

redeposited by the raging Deluge. So fossiliferous sedimentary strata would be found under the mammoths in many cases. Some were buried by sedimentation during early phases of the Flood. As the mountains rose (Psalm 104:4-8), the sediments in which the mammoths were buried rose out of the waters. As they did, tons of muck would have washed down on them from the continental slopes that were at higher elevation.

PHASE III: POST-FLOOD CLIMATE REVERSAL

A common problem encountered with all previous theories of Pleistocene extinction is that while the evidence seemed to demand a sudden and permanent climate change, no known mechanism existed that could accomplish both. Volcanic activity could conceivably unleash the storm necessary to freeze the animals and trigger the floods, but after the volcanism had ceased and the storm quieted, what maintained the temperature at its present lowered levels?

An easy answer is supplied from the biblical model of the vapor canopy. Once the canopy had condensed, the universal greenhouse effect was destroyed and the climate quickly and permanently stratified into its present latitudinal zones. Furthermore, it is likely that at the end of the Flood there was extensive freezing in localized areas all over the globe (perhaps explaining the evidence of glaciation found in the tropics?) due to the pressure drop from 2.18 atmospheres under the canopy to our present 1 atmosphere of pressure. Since this would be even more pronounced in the polar regions, this would have expedited the freezing of the permafrost to great depths.

But what about the mammoth and dinosaur extinctions? What is the connection between them? Obviously the theory presented here suggests that the mammoths and dinosaurs lived at the same time and were destroyed by the same global catastrophe. The reason that dinosaur and mammal bones are not commonly found in the same deposits can be largely explained by "ecological zonation." Animals that live together in the same geographical locales would have tended to have been buried together in the Flood. Apparently the mammals and the reptiles tended to associate with their own kind and live more or less in separate areas.[39]

But what caused the dinosaur extinctions? Interestingly enough, many have theorized sudden climate change as the explanation. In answer to the question, "The Great Dying: Why Did It Occur?" John Ostrom, curator of vertebrate paleontology at the Peabody Museum of Natural History at Yale University, says, "No one knows what did the dinosaurs in, but I favor the cooling-environment hypothesis, whether the cold was caused by shifting continents or by an exploding supernova — or a combination of both."[40] Or the condensation of earth's pre-Flood vapor canopy? The problem with many climate reversal theories for dinosaur extinction has been succinctly stated by Professor Ostrom himself: "But why didn't the dinosaurs simply migrate to more hospitable environs as the climates deteriorated? Tropical conditions must have persisted somewhere at low altitudes."[41]

The answer, of course, is that the dinosaurs did not have time to migrate. Like the mammoths, they were overwhelmed with a sudden and global flood. The representatives of the dinosaurs that Noah presumably took with him on the ark were simply not able to survive in the changed post-Flood climate with its cooler temperatures and severe winters.

Conclusion

Such is our theory of the Pleistocene extinctions. It attempts to correlate the data of a sudden freeze and a permanent climate reversal, even if the precise sequence of events is quite debatable. With one assumption (the existence of the vapor canopy) we can account for the evidence of moderate northern climate, a sudden deep freeze, the burial of thousands of mammoths, and permanent climate reversal.

39. Harold G. Coffin, *Creation — Accident or Design*, pp. 174-83.
40. John Ostrom, "A New Look at Dinosaurs," *National Geographic* 154 (August 1978):184.
41. Ibid., p. 178.

Chapter 13

How It All Fits Together

The objective of this book has been to establish the exegetical and scientific plausibility of a vapor canopy model implied in a normal exegesis of Genesis 1:6-8. This demonstration is the product of a general argument involving several categories.

SUMMARY OF THE ARGUMENTS

EXEGETICAL BASIS

A normal exegesis of Genesis 1:6-8 suggests that at the end of the second creative day God had placed a literal liquid ocean of water above the ancient troposphere. Since there is no indication in the text of Genesis that miracles reigned from the Fall to the Flood, we assumed that natural laws as we understand them today were in operation. In view of this we argued from the significance of the text for modern science that the liquid ocean must have been sustained in a way that would not require miraculous intervention — that is, in vapor form.

EVIDENCE FROM MYTHOLOGY

As would be expected, since the Bible speaks of a water heaven, the ancient myths would also. This is because these myths often reflect racial memories of the way things were in prehistory. The factual reality on which the biblical data are based and which has been preserved in the writing of Moses is reflected in a distorted way in the pagan myths of the water heaven. This circumstantial evidence suggests that the source of these myths was the narration by the sons of Noah to their descendants of the nature of the pre-Flood world.

EVIDENCE FROM SCIENCE

A helpful way of analyzing events beyond human observation is to construct a model, then make predictions based on the model as to what would naturally follow if the model is correct. Based on an exegesis of Scripture and the plausible significance of such exegesis, we structured a tentative model of the pre-Flood vapor canopy. Then we stated ten separate predictions drawn from the model. We found that each of these predictions has some confirmation in the rock record. Although the historical geologist has quite adequate explanations for some of these predictions on grounds other than that of a vapor canopy, we saw that with this one assumption, many seemingly unrelated facts were correlated. The efficiency of any theory is verified by the number of facts correlated divided by the number of assumptions made. So the vapor canopy model may be a helpful theory within which to structure further investigation of prehistory.

THE VAPOR CANOPY MODEL

No model, no matter how many facts it correlates, is worthy of consideration unless the model itself is based on sound physical principles. The water heaven could have existed in four forms: water, ice, clouds, or vapor. We showed that only a vapor canopy model can satisfactorily meet the requirements of the necessary support mechanism. Even though such a model is not specifically taught in Scripture, it is the only form in which the water heaven could have been maintained without appeal to special miracle.

THE MAMMOTH EXTINCTIONS

The most obvious prediction of such a vapor canopy is of a universal greenhouse and subsequent climate reversal when the vapor shield precipitated. Because of the crucial nature of the prediction, we presented extensive documentation that indeed the polar regions once enjoyed warm temperatures. Furthermore, it is evident that the most satisfactory explanation of the extinction of the giant elephants as well as thousands of other tropical animals is that of a sudden deep freeze, followed by a permanent climate change from warm to severely cold — one of the predictions of the canopy model.

Some Spiritual Implications

The reader who has followed the thesis thus far has managed to wade through extensive documentation, argumentation, and scientific discussion. After this many pages of much technical data it is appropriate to ask in accordance with the mood of the modern age, "So what?" Why are books such as this one written, and what relevance does it all have to us today? What does it all prove?

The main thrust of what has been said, of course, has been to demonstrate the truthfulness of the Bible in its statements on creation and the Flood. Through a direct revelation from God we are able to peer into the ancient past. Although the validity of the Bible's claim to be the revelation from God has not been established by the discussions in this book, it is certainly confirmed by them. If the Bible can be trusted on this issue (of the world before the Flood), then perhaps it can be trusted when it speaks of the ultimate issues of life — personal meaning and life after death.

Many are not aware that Jesus Christ accepted the literal truth of the biblical Flood account. At the conclusion of one of His greatest sermons, the so-called Olivet Discourse, He connected the discussion of the Flood in Noah's day with the practical issues of everyday life. His comments on this subject will serve as a fitting conclusion. Jesus began the last part of His discussion on His second coming with a warning, "But of that day and hour no one knows, not even the angels of heaven, nor the Son, but the Father alone. For the coming of the Son of Man will be just like the days of Noah" (Matt. 24:36-37).

Today we have an expression that is sometimes used to describe steadfastness under difficult circumstances. We say that we will hold fast "come hell or high water." In other words, no matter what happens we will not be budged when trials and difficulties assail us. In the words of Jesus on Mount Olivet we have the biblical basis behind that phrase "hell and high water." In the Bible we have an intimate connection between the two: the eternal judgment of hell is compared to the temporal judgment of the high water of the Flood of Noah's time. The condensation of the vapor canopy and the ensuing Flood was a judgment by God on an unbelieving world.

Furthermore, God has left evidence of that judgment in the rock record as a warning to us of the judgment to come. When we look at the rock record, what do we see? Does it not reveal a testimony of death, decay, devastation, and destruction? Does it not speak of a judgment on the earth? It has been estimated that 70% of the geological record is sedimentary rock, material that has settled out of water. The very existence of fossils indicates sudden destruction and rapid burial.

The geologic column, which is often turned against the literal truth of the Bible, testifies of the Flood the Bible describes. The Flood in the days of Noah tells us clearly through the rock record that God has dealt with man in justice. He is a just God. Those who sin (which includes *all* of us) will pay the penalty for their sins both in this life and in the life to come. But what has man done with this warning? Instead of seeing God's warning of eventual judgment in the geologic column, man has twisted this clear evidence into the fabeled evolutionary development of life onward and upward to a utopia and the greatness of man.

Jesus said there would be a similarity between the days of Noah and the days of the coming of the Son of Man. What was it like in the days of Noah? "For as in those days which were before the flood they were eating and drinking, they were marrying and giving in marriage, until the day that Noah entered the ark, and they did not understand until the flood came and took them all away; so shall the coming of the Son of Man be" (Matt. 24:38-39). The force of this passage seems to be that prior to the Flood the philosophy that predominated was the priority of the "here and now," of such things as eating, drinking, and marrying. The attitude that seemed to prevail was one of indifference to eternal verities. The people did not know or care if there was a judgment to come; all they cared about was the moment.

Certainly no better description can be found of the thinking of many people today. For them the coming judgment of the second advent will be similar to that of the Flood in its unexpectedness. "Then there shall be two men in the field; one will be taken, and one will be left. Two women will be grinding at the mill; one will be taken, and one will be left. Therefore be on the alert, for you do not know which day your Lord is coming" (Matt. 24:40-42).

Noah's generation had ample warning. He had been proclaiming the judgment to come for 120 years. The people chose not to believe him. Similarly, we have had ample warning too. For nearly 2,000 years Christ's promise "I will come again" has stood firm. The eternal consequences of sin and self-will have been clearly explained in the Scriptures. The testimony that God has and will deal in the affairs of men is clear in the geologic record. Yet in spite of all of this Jesus said many would not believe and would be caught unexpectedly.

Fortunately the last word of the Bible is not that of God's justice but that of His love. The good news is that the judgment that was due to fall on us fell instead on a substitute. The claim of the Bible is that God became a man, and as Man He went to the cross and there paid the penalty that His own justice required. The penalty of sin is eternal separation from God. But in that one moment at Calvary, when Jesus screamed, "My God, My God, why hast Thou forsaken Me?" (Matt. 27:46), all the sin of the world was poured on Him and He was separated from the Father. According to Paul (Gal. 3:13), God turned His back on Jesus and cursed Him for our sakes. So it is now possible to avoid the personal payment of the penalty for our sins by receiving God's payment in the person of Jesus Christ on our behalf. When we do that, we can indeed be steadfast, "come hell or high water."

How is this payment received? By faith. The word *faith* simply means "trust." As presented in the Bible it is the rational decision of the will based on sufficient historical evidence. It is not a blind leap like that of the uniformitarians, as the preceding chapters of the book have labored to show. It means coming to God and deciding to trust in Jesus Christ for the forgiveness of sins and entrance into heaven rather than continuing to trust in ourselves.

Many sincere Christians who are scientists would not agree with the vapor canopy theory presented in this book. Many others would accept most of it. What all would agree on, however, is the vital need to receive Jesus Christ as personal Savior and Lord. Although it would be nice if all who read this book were convinced of this theory, what is of greater importance is that all who read this book understand and personally embrace the truth that is presented in these closing paragraphs. If the writing of this book results in but one reader's entering into a personal relationship with Jesus Christ, the time will have been well spent.

BIBLIOGRAPHY

I. BOOKS

Albright, William. *Archaeology and the Religion of Israel.* Baltimore: Johns Hopkins, 1942.

Alford, Henry. *The Greek Testament: with a Critically Revised Text, A Digest of Various Readings, Marginal References to Verbal and Idiomatic Usage, Prolegomena, and a Critical and Exegetical Commentary.* Revised by Everett F. Harrison, vol. 4, Hebrews to Revelation. Chicago: Moody, 1958.

Allis, Oswald T. *God Spake by Moses.* Philadelphia: Presbyterian and Reformed, 1951.

Archer, Gleason L., Jr. *A Survey of Old Testament Introduction.* Chicago: Moody, 1964.

Arndt, William F., and Gingrich, F. Wilbur. *A Greek-English Lexicon of the New Testament and Other Early Christian Literature.* Chicago: U. of Chicago, 1957.

Asimov, Isaac, and Dobzhansky, Theodosius. *The Genetic Effects of Radiation.* Oak Ridge, Tenn.: U. S. Atomic Energy Commission, 1973.

Barnett, Lincoln. "The Arctic Barrens." In *The World We Live In*, edited by Lincoln Barnett. New York: Time Inc., 1955.

Battan, Louis J. *Weather.* Englewood Cliffs, N. J.: Prentice-Hall, 1974.

Baumgartner, Walter. *Lexicon in Veteris Testamenti Libros*, edited by Ludwig Köhler. 2 vols. Grand Rapids: Eerdmans, 1953.

Benedict, Frances G. *The Physiology of the Elephant.* Washington: Carnegie Institute, 1936.

Berkhof, Louis. *Principles of Biblical Interpretation.* Grand Rapids: Baker, 1966.

Berry, F. A.; Bollay, E.; and Beers, Norman R., eds. *Handbook of Meteorology*. New York: McGraw-Hill, 1945.

Bertin, Leon. *Larousse Encyclopedia of the Earth*. New York: Prometheus Press, 1967.

Brasseur. *Sources de l'histoire Primitive du Mexico*.

Breasted, James Henry. *A History of Egypt*. New York: Bantam Classics, 1964.

Briggs, Charles. *The Book of Psalms*. The International Critical Commentary. New York: Scribner's, 1909.

Bronner, Leah. *The Stories of Elijah and Elisha*. Leiden: E. J. Brill, 1968.

Brown, Francis; Driver, S. R.; and Briggs, Charles A., eds. *A Hebrew and English Lexicon of the Old Testament*, based on the lexicon of William Gesenius as translated by Edward Robinson. Oxford: At the Clarendon Press, 1907.

Bullard, Fred M. *Volcanoes*. Austin, Tex.: U. of Texas, 1962.

Bullinger, E. W. *Figures of Speech Used in the Bible*. 1898. Reprint. Grand Rapids: Baker, 1968.

Burdick, Clifford. "Is Erosion Undermining the Geologic Column?" In *A Challenge to Education*. Caldwell, Ida.: Bible Science Association, 1972.

Bush, George. *Notes on Genesis*. 2 vols. 1860. Reprint. Minneapolis: James & Klock, 1976.

Butzer, Karl W. *Environment and Archaeology*. Chicago: Aldine, 1964.

Byers, Horace Robert. *General Meteorology*. 4th ed. New York: McGraw-Hill, 1974.

Calvin, John. *Calvin's Commentaries*. 8 vols. Grand Rapids: Assoc. Publishers and Authors, n.d. vol. 1, *The Pentateuch*.

Carslaw, H. S., and Jaeger, J. C. *Conduction of Heat in Solids*. Oxford: U. Press, 1948.

Cassuto, U. *A Commentary on the Book of Genesis*. Translated by Israel Abrahams. 2 vols. Jerusalem: Magnes, The Hebrew University, 1961.

Chandrasekhar, S. *Hydrodynamic and Hydromagnetic Stability*. Oxford: At the Clarendon Press, 1961.

Chapman, Dean R. *Technical Report R-11, An Approximate Analytical Method for Studying Entry into Planetary Atmospheres.* NASA TR-11. Washington, D.C.: National Aeronautics and Space Adm., 1961.

Chapman, Dean R., and Kapphahn, Arline K. *Tables of Z Functions for Atmospheric Entry Analyses.* NASA TR-106. Washington, D.C.: National Aeronautics and Space Adm., 1961.

Charlesworth, J. K. *The Quaternary Era.* 2 vols. London: Edward Arnold, 1957.

Clark, Harold W. *Fossils, Flood, and Fire.* Escondido, Calif.: Outdoor Pictures, 1968.

Cockrum, E. Lendell. *Introduction to Mammalogy.* New York: Ronald, 1962.

Coffin, Harold G. *Creation – Accident or Design?* Washington: Review and Herald Publishing Ass'n., 1969.

Cohen, A. *The Socino Chumash.* The Socino Books of the Bible. London: Socino, 1970.

Colbert, Edwin H. *The Age of Reptiles.* New York: Norton, 1965.

_____. "When Reptiles Ruled." In *Our Continent, A Natural History of North America,* edited by Edwin H. Colbert. Washington: National Geographic, 1976.

Conant, Thomas J., and Moll, Carl Bernhard. "The Psalms." In *Lange's Commentary on the Holy Scriptures,* edited by John Peter Lange, translated from the German with additions by J. Isidor Mombert, vol. 5. Reprint. Grand Rapids: Zondervan, 1960.

Cook, Melvin A. *Prehistory and Earth Models.* London: Max Parish, 1966.

Coulson, Kinsell L. *Solar and Terrestrial Radiation: Methods and Measurements.* New York: Academic, 1975.

Courville, Donovan A. *The Exodus Problem and Its Ramifications.* 2 vols. Loma Linda, Calif.: Challenge Books, 1971.

Cousins, Frank W. "The Alleged Evolution of Birds." In *A Symposium on Creation, III,* edited by Donald W. Patten. Grand Rapids: Baker, 1971.

Cunningham, J. T. *Reptiles, Amphibia, Fishes, and Lower Chordata.* London: Methuen, 1912.

Custance, Arthur C. *Evolution or Creation?* The Doorway Papers. Grand Rapids: Zondervan, 1976.

_____. *Genesis and Early Man.* The Doorway Papers. Grand Rapids: Zondervan, 1975.

_____. *The Virgin Birth and the Incarnation.* The Doorway Papers. Grand Rapids: Zondervan, 1976.

Cuvier, Baron G. *Essay on the Theory of the Earth*, translated from the French by Baron G. 5th ed. London: William Blackwood, 1827.

de'A. Bellairs, Angus. *Reptiles.* London: Hutchinson, 1957.

_____. *Reptiles: Life History, Evolution, and Structure.* New York: Harper, 1950.

Dahood, Mitchell. *The Psalms.* 3 vols. The Anchor Bible. Garden City, N. Y.:Doubleday, 1970.

Daly, Reginald. *Earth's Most Challenging Mysteries.* Grand Rapids: Baker, 1972.

Darwin, Charles. *Journal of Researches.* New York: Ward Lock, 1845.

Davidson, A. B. *Old Testament Prophecy*, edited by J. A. Paterson. Edinburgh: T. & T. Clark, 1903.

Delitzsch, Franz. *The Book of Job*, translated by Francis Bolton. Biblical Commentary on the Old Testament. Reprint. Grand Rapids: Eerdmans, n.d.

_____. *A New Commentary on Genesis*, translated by Sophia Taylor. 2 vols. Edinburgh: T. & T. Clark, 1899.

_____. *Psalms*, translated by Francis Bolton. 3 vols. Biblical Commentary on the Old Testament. Reprint. Grand Rapids: Eerdmans, n. d.

Dhorme, E. *A Commentary on the Book of Job*, translated by Harold Knight. Camden, N. J.: Nelson, 1967.

Dickerson, R. W. *The Freezing Preservation of Foods.* 2 vols. 4th ed. Westport, Conn.: AVI Publishing, n. d.

Digby, Bassett. *The Mammoth and Mammoth Hunting Grounds in Northeast Siberia.* New York: Appleton, 1926.

Dixon, Roland B. *Oceanic Mythology.* Vol. 9, *The Mythology of All Races*, edited by John MacCulloch. New York: Cooper Square, 1964.

Driver, S. R. *The Book of Genesis*. London: Methuen, 1904.

Dunbar, Carl O., and Waage, Karl M. *Historical Geology*. New York: Wiley, 1969.

Durant, Will. *Caesar and Christ*. Vol. 3, *The Story of Civilization*. New York: Simon and Schuster, 1944.

_____. *The Life of Greece*. Vol. 2 *The Story of Civilization*. New York: Simon and Schuster, 1966.

Eichrodt, Walther. *Theology of the Old Testament*, translated by J. A. Baker. 2 vols. The Old Testament Library. Philadelphia: Westminster, 1967.

Fausset, A. R. "The Book of Job." In *A Commentary, Critical and Explanatory, on the Old and New Testaments*, by Robert Jamieson, A. R. Fausset, and David Brown. Vol. 3, *Old Testament*. Reprint. Grand Rapids: Eerdmans, 1967.

Ferguson, John. *The Religions of the Roman Empire*. Ithaca, N. Y.: Cornell U., 1970.

Fermor, John H. "Paleoclimatology and Infrared Radiation Traps: Earth's Antediluvian Climate." In *A Symposium on Creation, VI*, edited by Donald W. Patten. Grand Rapids: Baker, 1977.

Ferry, James F., and Ward, Henry S. *Fundamentals of Plant Physiology*. New York: Macmillan, 1959.

Fields, Weston. *Unformed and Unfilled*. Nutley, N. J.: Presbyterian and Reformed, 1976.

Filby, Frederick A. *The Flood Reconsidered*. Grand Rapids: Zondervan, 1971.

Flammarion, Gabrielle Camille, ed. *The Flammarion Book of Astronomy*, translated by Annabel and Bernard Pagel. New York: Simon and Schuster, 1964.

Flint, Richard Foster. *Glacial and Pleistocene Geology*. New York: Wiley, 1957.

Flower, William Henry, and Lydekker, Richard. *An Introduction to the Study of Mammals*. London: Adam and Charles Black, 1891.

Fox, C. S. *Water*. New York: Philosophical Library, 1952.

Frankfort, H.; Frankfort, H. A.; Wilson, John A.; Jacobsen, Thorkild; and Irwin, William A. *The Intellectual Adventure of*

Ancient Man. Chicago: U. of Chicago, 1946.

Frazer, Sir James George. *Folk-lore in the Old Testament.* 3 vols. London: Macmillan, 1919.

Frigerio, Norman A. *Your Body and Radiation.* Oak Ridge, Tenn.: U. S. Atomic Energy Commission, 1973.

Gaster, Theodore H. *Myth, Legend, and Custom in the Old Testament.* New York: Harper, 1969.

Goody, R. M. *Atmospheric Radiation I, Theoretical Basis.* Oxford: U. Press, 1964.

Goody, R. M., and Walker, James C. G. *Atmospheres.* Englewood Cliffs, N. J.: Prentice-Hall, 1972.

Gordon, Cyrus H. *Ugaritic Textbook.*

Grant, Michael, and Hazel, John. *Gods and Mortals in Classical Mythology.* Springfield, Mass.: Merriam, 1973.

Gray, Dwight, ed. *American Institute of Physics Handbook.* New York: McGraw-Hill, 1963.

Green, John C. *Darwin and the Modern World View.* Baton Rouge, La.: La. State U., 1961.

Green, William Henry. "Primeval Chronology." In *Classical Evangelical Essays in Old Testament Interpretation,* edited by Walter C. Kaiser, Jr. Grand Rapids: Baker, 1974.

Guirand, Felix. *Greek Mythology,* translated by Delano Ames. London: Paul Hamlyn, 1963.

Hammond's World Atlas. Maplewood, N. J.: Hammond, 1971.

Hapgood, Charles H. *The Path of the Pole.* Philadelphia: Chilton, 1970.

Heide, Fritz. *Meteorites,* translated by Edward Anders and Eugene R. DuFresne. Chicago: U. of Chicago, 1964.

Heidel, Alexander. *The Babylonian Genesis.* Chicago: U. of Chicago, 1963.

————. *The Gilgamesh Epic and Old Testament Parallels.* Chicago: U. of Chicago, 1963.

Hengstenberg, E. W. *Commentary on the Psalms.* 3 vols. Edinburgh: T. & T. Clark, 1854.

Herskowitz, Irwin H. *Genetics.* Boston: Little, Brown, 1962.

Hesiod Theogony. In *Hesiod, the Homeric Hymns and*

Bibliography

Homerica, translated by Hugh G. Evelyn-White. The Loeb Classical Library. Cambridge, Mass.: Harvard U., 1936.

_____ . Works and Days. In Hesiod, the Homeric Hymns and Homerica, translated by Hugh G. Evelyn-White. The Loeb Classical Library. Cambridge, Mass.: Harvard U., 1936.

Hess, Seymour L. Introduction to Theoretical Meteorology. New York: Holt, Rinehart and Winston, 1959.

Hibben, Frank C. The Lost Americans. New York: Crowell, 1946.

Higgins, Arnold E. The Effects of Alcohol at Three Simulated Aircraft Cabin Conditions. Washington, D.C.: U.S. Clearinghouse of Federal Scientific and Technical Information, 1968.

Hirsch, E. D., Jr. Validity in Interpretation. New Haven: Yale U., 1967.

Holman, J. P. Heat Transfer. 4th ed. New York: McGraw-Hill, 1976.

Hooker, Dolph E. Those Astounding Ice Ages. New York: Exposition, 1948.

Hoskyns, Edwin, and Davey, Noel. The Riddle of the New Testament. London: Faber and Faber, 1936.

Howorth, Henry H. The Glacial Nightmare and the Flood.

_____ . Ice or Water? 2 vols.

_____ . The Mammoth and the Flood.: An Attempt to Confront the Theory of Uniformity with the Facts of Recent Geology. London: Sampson Low, Marston, Searle, & Rivington, 1887.

Hsu, Shao Ti. Engineering Heat Transfer. Princeton, N. J.: Van Nostrand, 1963.

Humphreys, W. J. Physics of the Air. New York: McGraw-Hill, 1940.

Ingersoll, Leonard R.; Zobel, Otto J.; and Ingersoll, Alfred C. Heat Conduction. New York: McGraw-Hill, 1948.

Ions, Veronica. Indian Mythology. London: Paul Hamlyn, 1967.

Jacob, B. The First Book of the Bible, abridged, edited, and translated by Ernest I. Jacob and Walter Jacob. New York: Ktav Publishing, 1974.

Jacob, Edmond. *Theology of the Old Testament,* translated by Arthur W. Heathcote and Philip J. Allcock. New York: Harper, 1958.

Jamieson, Robert. "Genesis." In *A Commentary, Critical and Explanatory, on the Old and New Testaments,* by Robert Jamieson, A. R. Fausset, and David Brown. Vol. 1, *Old Testament.* Reprint. Grand Rapids: Eerdmans, 1967.

Jeans, Sir James. *Astronomy and Cosmogony.* Cambridge: U. Press, 1928.

Johnson, John C. *Physical Meteorology.* New York: Wiley, 1954.

Josephus, Flavius. *The Antiquities of the Jews.* In *The Complete Works of Flavius Josephus,* translated by William Whiston. Reprint. Grand Rapids: Kregel, 1960.

Kaiser, Walter C. "The Literary Form of Genesis 1-11." In *New Perspectives on the Old Testament,* edited by J. Barton Payne. Waco, Tex.: Word, 1970.

Kauzmann, Walter. *Kinetic Theory of Gasses.* 2 vols. New York: W. A. Benjamin, 1966.

Keil, C. F., and Delitzsch, F. *The Pentateuch,* translated by James Martin. 3 vols. Biblical Commentary on the Old Testament. Reprint. Grand Rapids: Eerdmans, n. d.

Kellogg, Howard W. *The Canopied Earth.* Los Angeles: American Prophetic League, n. d.

_____. *The Coming Kingdom and the Re-Canopied Earth.* Los Angeles: American Prophetic League, 1936.

Kidner, Derek. *Genesis.* Tyndale Old Testament Commentaries, D. J. Wiseman, general editor. Downers Grove, Ill.: InterVarsity, 1969.

Koelle, Heinz Herman, ed. *Handbook of Astronautical Engineering.* New York: McGraw-Hill, 1961.

Kondratyev, K. Ya. *Radiation in the Atmosphere.* New York: Academic, 1969.

_____. *Radiative Heat Exchange in the Atmosphere.* New York: Pergamon, 1965.

Kramer, Samuel Noah. *Sumerian Mythology.* Ann Arbor, Mich.: Edwards, 1947.

_____. *The Sumerians.* Chicago: U. of Chicago, 1970.

Bibliography

Krause, Hans. *The Mammoth – in Ice and Snow?* Stuttgart: Im Selbstverlag, 1978.

Kruse, W., and Dieckuoss, W. *The Stars*. Ann Arbor, Mich.: U. of Michigan, 1957.

Kurten, Bjorn. *Pleistocene Mammals of Europe*. London: Weidenfeld and Nicolson, 1968.

Lagler, Karl F.; Bardach, John E.; and Miller, Robert R. *Ichthyology*. New York: Wiley, 1962.

Langdon, Stephen Herbert. *Semitic Mythology*. Vol. 5, *The Mythology of All Races*, edited by John MacCulloch. New York: Cooper Square, 1964.

Lange, John Peter. "Genesis," translated by Taylor Lewis and A. Gosman. In *Lange's Commentary on the Holy Scriptures*, edited by John Peter Lange, translated from the German with additions by J. Isidor Mombert, vol. 1. Reprint. Grand Rapids: Zondervan, 1960.

Leupold, H. C. *Exposition of Genesis*. 2 vols. Grand Rapids: Baker, 1942.

Libby, Willard F. *Radiocarbon Dating*. 2nd ed. Chicago: U. of Chicago, 1955.

Liddell, Henry George, and Scott, Robert. *A Greek-English Lexicon*. Oxford: At the Clarendon Press, 1925.

Linsley, Ray K.; Kohler, Max A.; and Paulhus, Joseph L. H. *Hydrology for Engineers*. New York: McGraw-Hill, 1958.

Livingston, G. Herbert. *The Pentateuch in Its Cultural Environment*. Grand Rapids: Baker, 1974.

Loeb, Leonard B. *The Kinetic Theory of Gasses*. New York: Dover, 1961.

Longenecker, Richard. *Biblical Exegesis in the Apostolic Period*. Grand Rapids: Eerdmans, 1975.

Luikov, A. V. *Analytical Heat Diffusion Theory*. New York: Academic, 1968.

McAdams, William H. *Heat Transmission*. 3rd ed. New York: McGraw-Hill, 1954.

MacDonald, Gordon A. *Volcanoes*. Englewood Cliffs, N. J.: Prentice-Hall, 1972.

McDowall, R. J. S. *Handbook of Physiology*. 43rd ed. Philadelphia: Lippincott, 1960.

Macquarrie, John. *Principles of Christian Theology*. New York: Scribner's, 1966.

Mason, Brian. *Meteorites*. New York: Wiley, 1962.

Maunder, E. Walter. *The Astronomy of the Bible*. London: T. Sealy Clark & Co., n. d.

Maximov, Nicolai A. *Plant Physiology*. New York: McGraw-Hill, 1935.

Michael, H. M., and Ralph, E. K. *Eighth International Congress on Radiocarbon Dating*.

Miller, Albert. *Meteorology*. Merrill Physical Science Series. Columbus, O.: Charles E. Merrill, 1966.

Mixter, Russell L., ed. *Evolution and Christian Faith*. Grand Rapids: Eerdmans, 1959.

Montgomery, John Warwick. *The Quest for Noah's Ark*. Minneapolis: Bethany Fellowship, 1972.

Morris, Henry M. *Biblical Cosmology and Modern Science*. Nutley, N. J.: Craig, 1970.

_____. *Studies in the Bible and Science*. Grand Rapids: Baker, 1966.

Morris, Henry M., ed. *Scientific Creationism*. San Diego: Creation-Life Publishers, 1974.

Morris, Henry M., and Whitcomb, John C. *The Genesis Flood*. Philadelphia: Presbyterian and Reformed, 1965.

Mountcastle, Vernon B., ed. *Medical Physiology*. 12th ed. 2 vols. St. Louis: C. V. Mosby Company, 1968.

Nairn, A. E. M. *Descriptive Paleoclimatology*. New York: Interscience Publishers, 1961.

Nelson, Byron. *The Deluge Story in Stone*. Grand Rapids: Baker, 1968.

Neugebauer, O. *The Exact Sciences in Antiquity*. 2nd ed. Providence, R. I.: Brown U., 1957.

Nevins, Stuart E. "Stratigraphic Evidence of the Flood." In *A Symposium on Creation, III*, edited by Donald W. Patten. Grand Rapids: Baker, 1971.

Newman, Robert C., and Eckelman, Herman J., Jr. *Genesis One and the Origin of the Earth.* Downers Grove, Ill.: InterVarsity, 1977.

New Scofield Reference Bible. New York: Oxford U., 1967.

Nordenskjold, N. A. E. *The Voyage of the Vega Around Asia and Europe,* translated by Alexander Leslie. 2 vols. London: Macmillan, 1881.

Olcott, William Tyler, and Putnam, Edmund W. *Field Book of the Skies.* 3d ed. New York: Putnam's, 1936.

Olsson, I. U., ed. *Radiocarbon Variation and Absolute Chronology.* New York: Wiley, 1969.

Osborn, Henry Fairfield. *Proboscidea.* 2 vols. New York: American Museum of Natural History, 1942.

Ovid *Metamorphoses,* translated by Henry T. Riley. Philadelphia: David McKay, 1899.

Paltridge, G. W., and Platt, C. M. R. *Radiative Processes in Meteorology and Climatology.* New York: Elsevier Scientific Publishing, 1976.

Parrot, André. *The Tower of Babel.* London: SCM, 1955.

Patten, Donald W. *The Biblical Flood and the Ice Epoch.* Seattle: Pacific Meridian Publishing, 1966.

──────── . "The Pre-Flood Greenhouse Effect." In *A Symposium on Creation, II,* edited by Donald W. Patten. Grand Rapids: Baker, 1970.

Patten, D. W.; Hatch, R. R.; and Steinhauer, L. C. *The Long Day of Joshua and Six Other Catastrophes.* Seattle: Pacific Meridian Publishing, 1973.

Payne, D. F. *Genesis One Reconsidered.* London: Tyndale, 1964.

Payne, J. Barton. *The Theology of the Older Testament.* Grand Rapids: Zondervan, 1962.

Payne-Gaposchkin, Cecilia. *Introduction to Astronomy.* Englewood Cliffs, N. J.: Prentice-Hall, 1954.

Perowne, J. J. Stewart. *The Book of Psalms.* 4th ed. 2 vols. Reprint. Grand Rapids: Zondervan, 1966.

Peters, Walter G. "Bible and Earth History." In *A Challenge to*

Education II, Technical Essays on Creationism. Caldwell, Ida.: Bible-Science Ass'n., 1974.

Petterson, Sverve. *Weather Analysis and Forecasting.* 2d ed. 2 vols. New York: McGraw-Hill, n. d.

Pfeiffer, Charles F. *Old Testament History.* Grand Rapids: Baker, 1973.

Pfizenmayer, E. W. *Siberian Man and Mammoth,* translated from the German by Muriel D. Simpson. London: Blackie & Son, 1939.

Pitts, David. *A Computer Program for Calculating Model Planetary Atmospheres.* NASA TN-4292. Washington, D. C.: National Aeronautics and Space Administration, 1968.

Plummer, William. *Studies in the Book of Psalms.* Philadelphia: Lippincott, 1867.

Pope, Marvin H. *Job.* The Anchor Bible. Garden City, N. Y.: Doubleday, 1965.

Pritchard, J. B. *Ancient Near Eastern Texts.* Princeton, N. J.: Princeton U., 1969.

Ramm, Bernard. *The Christian View of Science and Scripture.* Grand Rapids: Eerdmans, 1954.

_____. *Protestant Biblical Interpretation.* Boston: W. A. Wilde, 1956.

Rehwinkel, Alfred M. *The Flood in the Light of the Bible, Geology, and Archaeology.* St. Louis: Concordia, 1951.

Reid, James. *God, the Atom and the Universe.* Grand Rapids: Zondervan, 1968.

Rhodes, F. H. T.; Zim, H. S.; and Shaffer, P. R. *Fossils.* New York: Golden Press, 1962.

Rimmer, Harry. *Modern Science and the Genesis Record.* 2 vols. Grand Rapids: Eerdmans, 1943.

Robinson, J. Hedley. *Astronomy Data Book.* New York: Wiley, 1972.

Robinson, N. *Solar Radiation.* New York: Elsevier Scientific Publishing, 1966.

Romer A. S. *Vertebrate Paleontology.* 3d ed. 2 vols. Chicago: U. of Chicago, 1966.

Rouse, Hunter. *Engineering Hydraulics.* New York: Wiley, 1950.

Rowley, H. H. *The Book of Job.* Camden, N. J.: Nelson, 1970.

Rupke, N. A. "Prolegomena to a Study of Cataclysmal Sedimentation." In *Why Not Creation?* edited by Walter E. Lammerts. Grand Rapids: Baker, 1970.

Saggs, H. W. F. *The Greatness That Was Babylon.* New York: Mentor, 1962.

Schlichting, Hermann. *Boundary-Layer Theory,* translated by J. Kestin. 6th ed. New York: McGraw-Hill, 1968.

Schwarze, C. Theodore. *The Harmony of Science and the Bible.* Grand Rapids: Zondervan, 1942.

_____. *The Marvel of Earth's Canopies.* Westchester, Ill.: Good News Publishers, 1957.

Scott, W. B. *A History of Land Mammals in the Western Hemisphere.* New York: Macmillan, 1937.

Shortley, George, and Williams, Dudley. *Elements of Physics.* 3d ed. 2 vols. Englewood Cliffs, N. J.: Prentice-Hall, 1961.

_____. *Principles of College Physics.* 2 vols. Englewood Cliffs, N. J.: Prentice-Hall, 1959.

Sikes, Sylvia K. *The Natural History of the African Elephant.*

Silverberg, Robert. *Mammoths, Mastodons, and Man.* New York: McGraw-Hill, 1970.

Skinner, John. *A Critical and Exegetical Commentary on Genesis.* The International Critical Commentary. Edinburgh: T. & T. Clark, 1910.

Smith, A. E. Wilder. *Man's Origin and Man's Destiny.* Wheaton, Ill.: Harold Shaw, 1968.

Solzhenitsyn, Aleksandr I. *The Gulag Archipelago.* 3 vols. New York: Harper, 1978. Vol. 1, translated by Thomas P. Whitney.

Speisor, E. A. *Genesis.* The Anchor Bible. Garden City, N. Y.: Doubleday, 1964.

Steam Tables. New York: St. Martin's Press, 1967.

Stern, Curt. *Principles of Human Genetics.* 2d ed. San Francisco: W. H. Freeman and Co., 1960.

Steyermark, Julian A. *Flora of Missouri*. Ames, Ia.: Iowa State U., 1963.

Stigers, Harold G. *A Commentary on Genesis*. Grand Rapids: Zondervan, 1976.

Tan, Paul Lee. *The Interpretation of Prophecy*. Winona Lake, Ind.: BMH Books, 1974.

Thomas, W. H. Griffith. *Genesis, A Devotional Commentary*. Grand Rapids: Eerdmans, 1946.

Touloukian, Y. S. et al, eds. *Thermophysical Properties*. Research Center Data Series. 13 vols. New York: IFI/Plenum. Vol. 2, *Thermal Conductivity: Nonmetallic Solids*, 1971.

Unger, Merrill F. *Archaeology and the Old Testament*. Grand Rapids: Zondervan, 1954.

_____. *Unger's Bible Handbook*. Chicago: Moody, 1967.

Vail, Isaac Newton. *The Deluge and Its Cause*. Chicago: Suggestion Publishing, 1905.

_____. *The Waters Above the Firmament*. Philadelphia: Ferris & Leach, 1902.

Valley, Shea L., ed. *Handbook of Geophysics and Space Environments*. Cambridge, Mass.: Air Force Research Laboratories, 1965.

Vander, Arthur J.; Sherman, James H.; and Luciano, Dorothy S. *Human Physiology: The Mechanisms of Body Function*. New York: McGraw-Hill, 1970.

Velikovsky, Immanuel. *Worlds in Collision*. Laurel Edition. Garden City, N. Y.: Doubleday, 1967.

Ville, Claud. *Biology*. 2d ed. Philadelphia: Saunders, 1954.

Von Rad, Gerhard. *Genesis*. Rev. ed., translated by John H. Marks. The Old Testament Library. Philadelphia: Westminster, 1972.

Wagner, R. *Environment and Man*. New York: W. W. Norton, 1971.

Wakeman, Mary K. *God's Battle with the Sea Monster, A Study in Biblical Imagery*. Leiden: E. J. Brill, 1973.

Wallace, Alfred Russell. *Geographic Distribution of Animals*. New York: Horner, 1876.

Bibliography 441

Wallace, Bruce. *Genetic Load, Its Biological and Genetic Aspects.* New York: Prentice-Hall, 1970.

Wallace, Bruce, and Dobzhansky, Theodosius. *Radiation, Genes, and Man.* New York: Holt, 1959.

Waltke, Bruce K. *Creation and Chaos.* Portland, Ore.: Western Conservative Baptist Seminary, 1974.

Warfield, Benjamin B. *Biblical and Theological Studies,* edited by Samuel G. Craig. Philadelphia: Presbyterian and Reformed, 1968.

Weast, Robert C., ed. *Handbook of Chemistry and Physics.* 56th ed. Cleveland: CRC, 1965.

Webb, Willis L. *Structure of the Stratosphere and Mesosphere.* New York: Academic, 1966.

Weigert, A., and Zimmerman, H. *A Concise Encyclopedia of Astronomy.* New York: Elsevier Scientific Publishing, 1968.

Weiser, Arthur. *The Psalms,* translated by Herbert Hartwell. The Old Testament Library. Philadelphia: Westminster, 1962.

Welsh, Stanley L. *Anderson's Flora of Alaska.* Provo, Utah: Brigham Young U., 1974.

Westberg, V. L. *The Master Architect.* Napa, Calif.: V. L. Westberg, n. d.

Whipple, Fred. *The New Astronomy.* New York: Simon and Schuster, 1955.

Whitcomb, John C., Jr. *The Early Earth.* Grand Rapids: Baker, 1972.

Wigram, George V. *The Englishman's Hebrew and Chaldee Concordance of the Old Testament.* Reprint. Grand Rapids: Zondervan, 1970.

Wilson, Clifford. *Ebla Tablets: Secrets of a Forgotten City.* San Diego: Master Books, 1977.

Wilson, John A. *The Culture of Ancient Egypt.* Chicago: U. of Chicago, 1951.

Wiseman, D. J. *New Discoveries in Babylonia about Genesis.* 2d ed. revised. London: Marshall, Morgan, and Scott, 1936.

Witt, C. *Myths of Hellas,* translated by Frances Younghusband. London: Longmans, Green, 1883.

Wright, W. B. *The Quarternary Ice Age*. London: Macmillan, 1914.

Yapp, W. B. *An Introduction to Animal Physiology*. Oxford: At the Clarendon Press, 1960.

Young, Edward J. *Studies in Genesis One*. Philadelphia: Presbyterian and Reformed, 1973.

Young, Robert. *Analytical Concordance to the Bible*. 22d ed. revised. Grand Rapids: Eerdmans, n. d.

Zockler, Otto, "The Book of Job," translated by L. J. Evans. In *Lange's Commentary on the Holy Scriptures*, edited by John Peter Lange, translated from the German with additions by J. Isidor Mombert, vol. 4. Reprint. Grand Rapids: Zondervan, 1960.

II. Encyclopedia and Dictionary Articles

Anderson, B. W. "Creation." In *The Interpreter's Dictionary of the Bible*, edited by George Arthur Buttrick, 1:725-32. Nashville: Abingdon, 1962.

Bertram, Georg. "Stereos, stereoō, stereōma." In *Theological Dictionary of the New Testament*, edited by Gerhard Kittel, translated and edited by Geoffrey W. Bromiley, 7:609-14. Grand Rapids: Eerdmans, 1971.

Blank, S. H. "Age, Old." In *The Interpreter's Dictionary of the Bible*, edited by George Arthur Buttrick, 1:54-55. Nashville: Abingdon, 1962.

"Brahmanic Charma, India, The." In *New Larousse Encyclopedia of Mythology*.

"Electron Theory." In *Van Nostrand's Scientific Encyclopedia*, edited by Douglas M. Considine. 5th ed. New York: Van Nostrand Reinhold, 1976. p. 930.

"Elephant." In *Van Nostrand's Scientific Encyclopedia*, edited by Douglas M. Considine, p. 939.

"Fermentation." In *Van Nostrand's Scientific Encyclopedia*, edited by Douglas M. Considine, p. 1014.

Gaster, T. H. "Cosmogony." In *The Interpreter's Dictionary of the Bible*, edited by George Arthur Buttrick, 1:702-9. Nashville: Abingdon, 1962.

Bibliography

_____. "Firmament." In *The Interpreter's Dictionary of the Bible*, edited by George Arthur Buttrick, 2:270. Nashville: Abingdon, 1962.

_____. "Heaven." In *The Interpreter's Dictionary of the Bible*, edited by George Arthur Buttrick, 2:551-52. Nashville: Abingdon, 1962.

Gelb, Ignace J. et al. "Edu." In *The Assyrian Dictionary of the Oriental Institute of Chicago*, edited by Ignace J. Gelb et al., p. 35. Chicago: Oriental Institute, 1958.

Goppelt, Leonhard. "Hudōr." In *Theological Dictionary of the New Testament*, edited by Gerhard Kittel, translated and edited by Geoffrey W. Bromiley, 8:314-33. Grand Rapids: Eerdmans, 1972.

Jewett, Paul K. "Neo-Orthodoxy." In *Baker's Dictionary of Theology*, edited by Everett F. Harrision, p. 377. Grand Rapids: Baker, 1950.

McGraw-Hill Encyclopedia of Science and Technology. New York: McGraw-Hill, 1970.

Maunder, E. W. "Astronomy." In *The International Standard Bible Encyclopedia*, edited by James Orr, 1:315. Reprint. Grand Rapids: Eerdmans, 1939.

"Obversion." In *The Lexicon Webster Dictionary*, edited by Dana F. Kellerman, 1:655.

"Ocean." In *Van Nostrand's Scientific Encyclopedia*, edited by Douglas M. Considine, p. 1670.

Orr, James. "World." In *The International Standard Bible Encyclopedia*, edited by James Orr, 5:3108. Reprint. Grand Rapids: Eerdmans, 1939.

Ottosson, Magnus. " 'eres." In *Theological Dictionary of the Old Testament*, edited by G. Johannes Botterweck and Helmer Ringgren, translated by John T. Willis, 1:388-405. Grand Rapids: Eerdmans, 1974.

Page, R. M. "Science in the Bible." In *The Zondervan Pictorial Encyclopedia of the Bible*, edited by Merrill C. Tenney, 5:294-96. Grand Rapids: Zondervan, 1975.

Patrick, James. "Rainbow." In *Hastings' Dictionary of the Bible*, edited by James Hastings, 4:196.

Peck, Harry Thurston, ed. *Harper's Dictionary of Classical Literature and Antiquities.* New York: Harper, 1911.

Petrie, W. M. Flinders. "Cosmogony and Cosmology (Egyptian)." In *Encyclopedia of Religion and Ethics,* edited by James Hastings, 4:145.

"Photosynthesis." In *Van Nostrand's Scientific Encyclopedia,* edited by Douglas M. Considine, p. 1776.

Poussin, Vallée. "Cosmogony and Cosmology (Buddhist)." In *Encyclopedia of Religion and Ethics,* edited by James Hastings, 4:131.

"Saturn." In *New Larousse Encyclopedia of Mythology.*

Thewlis, J., ed. *Encyclopaedic Dictionary of Physics.* 9 vols. New York: Pergamon, 1962.

Traub, Helmut. "Ouranos, ouranios, epouranios, ouranothen." In *Theological Dictionary of the New Testament,* edited by Gerhard Kittel, translated and edited by Geoffrey W. Bromiley, 5:497-543. Grand Rapids: Eerdmans, 1967.

"Van't Hoff Equation." In *Van Nostrand's Scientific Encyclopedia,* edited by Douglas M. Considine, p. 2273.

White, W., Jr. "Astronomy." In *The Zondervan Pictorial Dictionary of the Bible,* edited by Merrill C. Tenney, 1:394-99. Grand Rapids: Zondervan, 1975.

_____. "Firmament." In *The Zondervan Pictorial Dictionary of the Bible,* edited by Merrill C. Tenney, 2:540. Grand Rapids: Zondervan, 1975.

Whitehouse, Owen C. "Cosmogony." In *Hastings' Dictionary of the Bible,* edited by James Hastings, 1:505.

III. JOURNAL AND MAGAZINE ARTICLES

Albright, William F. "The Predeuteronomic Primeval." *Journal of Biblical Literature* 58 (1939):91-103.

Anthony, Harold E. "Nature's Deep Freeze." *Natural History* 58 (September 1949):296-301.

Armstrong, Harold. "An Attempt to Correct for the Effects of the Flood in Determining Dates by Radioactive Carbon." *Creation Research Society Quarterly* 2 (January 1966):28-32.

_____. "Comments on Scientific News and Views." *Creation Research Society Quarterly* 6 (December 1969):139.

_____. "Comments on Scientific News and Views." *Creation Research Society Quarterly* 9 (September 1972):134-35.

Asimov, Isaac. "14 Million Tons of Dust Per Year." *Science Digest* 45 (January 1959):34 ff.

A. S. W. "The New Mammoth at St. Petersburg." *Nature* 68 (30 July 1903):297-98.

Awbery, J. H., and Griffiths, E. "Thermal Properties of Meat." *Journal of the Society of Chemical and Industrial Engineers* 52 (1933):326-8T.

Bakker, Robert T. "Dinosaur Renaissance." *Scientific American* 232 (April 1975):58-78.

Barnes, Thomas G. "Decay of the Earth's Magnetic Moment and the Geochronological Implications." *Creation Research Society Quarterly* 8 (June 1971):24-29.

Berglund, B. E.; Hakansson, S.; and Lagerlund. "Radiocarbon-dated Mammoth (Mammuthus Primigenius Blumenbach) Finds in South Sweden. *Boreas* 5 (March 1976):177-91.

Bjorksten, Johan. "Aging, Primary Mechanism." *Gerontologia* 8 (1963):179-92.

_____. "The Crosslinkage Theory of Aging." *Finska Kemists. Medd.* 80 (1971):23-38.

_____. "The Crosslinkage Theory of Aging: Clinical Implications." *Comprehensive Therapy* 2 (February 1976):65-74.

Bramwell, Cherrie D., and Whitfield, G. R. "Biomechanics of Pteranodon." *Philosophical Transactions of the Royal Society of London, B. Biological Series* 267 (11 July 1974):503-81.

Bridge, B. J. *African Wild Life* 8 (March 1954):37.

Bright, John. "Has Archaeology Found Evidence of the Flood?" *The Biblical Archaeologist* 4 (December 1942):56-59.

Brown, R. H. "Radiocarbon Dating." *Creation Research Society Quarterly* 3 (September 1968):65-68.

Brueggeman, Walter. "Kingship and Chaos." *The Catholic Biblical Quarterly* 33 (July 1971):317-32.

_____. "Weariness, Exile, and Chaos." *The Catholic Biblical Quarterly* 34 (January 1972):19-38.

Budyko, M. J. "The Effect of Solar Radiation Variations on the Climate of the Earth." *Tellus* XXI, no. 5 (1969):611-19.

Bunte (20 October 1977):138.

Burkhalter, J. E., and Koschmieder, E. L. "Steady Supercritical Taylor Vortex Flow." *Journal of Fluid Mechanics* 58 (1973):547-60.

_____. "Steady Supercritical Taylor Vortices after Sudden Starts." *Physics of Fluids* 17 (November 1974):1929-35.

Cassel, J. Frank. "The Origin of Man and the Bible." *Journal of the American Scientific Affiliation* 12 (June 1960):15 ff.

Cess, Robert D. "Radiative Transfer Due to Atmospheric Water Vapor: Global Considerations of the Earth's Energy Balance." *Journal of Quantitative Spectroscopy and Radiative Transfer* 14 (1974):861-71.

Clark, John, and Kietzke, Kenneth K. "Paleoecology of the Lower Nodular Zone, Brute Formation in the Big Badlands of South Dakota." *Fieldiana: Geology Memoirs* 5 (1967):114-40.

Coakley, James A., Jr. "An Efficient Numerical Approach to Radiative-Convective Equilibrium." *Journal of the Atmospheric Sciences* 34 (September 1977):1402-7.

Cohen, Daniel. "The Great Dinosaur Disaster." *Science Digest* 65 (March 1969): 45-52.

Colbert, Edwin H. "Evolutionary Growth Rates in the Dinosaurs." *Scientific Monthly* 69 (August 1949):71.

_____. "The Weights of Dinosaurs." *American Museum Novitates* 2076 (28 February 1962):1-16.

Collier, A. J.; Hess, F. L.; Smith, P. S.; and Brooks, A. H. "The Gold Placers of Part of Seward Peninsula, Alaska." *U. S. Geological Survey Bulletin* 328 (1908).

Cook, Melvin A. "Radiological Dating and Some Pertinent Applications of Historical Interest, Do Radiological Clocks Need Repair?" *Creation Research Society Quarterly* 5 (September 1968):69-77.

Courville, Donovan A. "The Use and Abuse of Astronomy in Dating." *Creation Research Society Quarterly* 12 (March 1976):201-10.

Cox, Douglas E. "Problems in the Glacial Theory." *Creation Research Society Quarterly* 13 (June 1976):25-34.

Crow, James F. "Ionizing Radiation and Evolution." *Scientific American* 201 (September 1959):138-60.

Curtis, Howard. "What Science Knows About Aging." *Think,* March-April 1964, pp. 15-17.

Daly, Reginald. "The Cause of the Ice Age." *Creation Research Society Quarterly* 9 (March 1973):210-17.

_____. "Was the Ice Age Caused by the Flood?" *Creation Research Society Quarterly* 11 (March 1975):213-17.

Dillow, Joseph C. "The Catastrophic Deepfreeze of the Beresovka Mammoth." *Creation Research Society Quarterly* 14 (June 1977):5-13.

Doumani, George A., and Long, William E. "The Ancient Life of the Antarctic." *Scientific American* 207 (September 1962):169-84.

Elsasser, Walter M., and Culbertson, Margaret F. "Atmospheric Radiation Tables." *Meteorological Monographs* 4 (August 1960):43.

Emden, R. "Strahlungsgleichgewicht und Atmosphärische Strahlung." *Sitz. K. Bayer. Akad. Wissensch.* (1913).

Ezra, H. C., and Cook, S. F. "Histology of Mammoth Bone." *Science* 129 (February 1952):465-66.

Farrand, William R. "Frozen Mammoths and Modern Geology." *Science* 133 (March 1961):729-35.

_____. "Letters, Frozen Mammoth — Reply to Lippman." *Science* 137 (August 1962):450-51.

Ferguson, E. E., and Fehsenfeld, F. E. Article in *Journal of Geophysical Research* 74 (May 1969):2217.

Fetner, Robert H. "Ozone-induced Chromosome Breakage in Human Cell Cultures." *Nature* 194 (May 1962):793-94.

Geological Magazine 8 (1881):505.

Gow, Anthony J. "Glaciological Investigations in Antarctica." *Antarctic Journal of the United States* 7, no. 4 (1972):100-101.

Hapgood, Charles H. "The Mystery of the Frozen Mammoths." *Coronet* 48 (September 1960):75-82.

Harris, R. Laird. "The Bible and Cosmology." *Bulletin of the Evangelical Theological Society* 5 (March 1962):12 ff.

_____ . "The Mist, the Canopy, and the Rivers of Eden." *Bulletin of the Evangelical Theological Society* 11 (Fall 1968):177-79.

Hasel, Gerhard F. "The Fountains of the Great Deep." *Origins* 1 (1974):67-72.

_____ . "The Polemic Nature of the Genesis Cosmology." *The Evangelical Quarterly* 46 (April-June 1974):81-103.

Hensen, Joseph et al. "Book Review of *The Biblical Flood and the Ice Epoch*." *Creation Research Society Quarterly* 4 (March 1968):129-32.

Herz, O. F. "Frozen Mammoths in Siberia." *Annual Report of Smithsonian Institution*, 1903, pp. 611-25.

Heylmun, Edgar B. "Should We Teach Uniformitarianism?" *Journal of Geological Education* 19 (January 1971):36.

Hill, J. E.; Litman, J. D.; and Sunderland, J. E. "Thermal Conductivity of Various Meats." *Food Technology* 21 (1967):1143-48.

Hoff, Philip. "Roche's Limit and the Patten Epic." *Creation Research Society Quarterly* 8 (June 1971):62-63.

Hollander, Willard F. "Lethal Heredity." *Scientific American* 187 (July 1952):58-61.

Hongi, H. "A Maori Cosmogony." *Journal of Polynesian Studies* 16 (1907):113-17.

Howe, George F. "Seed Germination, Sea Water, and Plant Survival." *Creation Research Society Quarterly* 5 (December 1968):105-12.

Howorth, H. H. "The Mammoth in Siberia." *The Geological Magazine*, September 1880, pp. 408-14. See series of articles from 1880 to 1881 for finds and conditions of burial of the mammoths.

Hrdlicka, Alex. "Anthropology and Medicine." *American Journal of Physical Anthropology* 10 (1926).

Humphreys, D. Russell. "Is the Earth's Core Water? Part One: The Biblical Evidence." *Creation Research Society Quarterly* 15 (December 1978):141-47.

Iberall, A. S. "Quantitative Modeling of the Physiological Factors in Radiation Lethality." *Annals of the New York Academy of Sciences* 147 (October 1967):1-81.

Ingersol, Andrew P. "The Runaway Greenhouse: A History of Water on Venus." *Journal of the Atmospheric Sciences* 26 (November 1969):1191-98.

Johanneson, A. D. et al. "Detention of Water Cluster Ions at the High Latitude Summer Menopause." *Nature* 235 (1972):212-17.

Johnson, G. L. "The Genesis Flood and the Geological Record." *Creation Research Society Quarterly* 11 (September 1974):108-10.

Kidner, Derek. "Genesis 2:5, 6: Wet or Dry?" *Tyndale Bulletin* 17 (1966):109-14.

Kigoshi, Kunihiko, and Hasegawa, Hiroich. "Secular Variation of Atmospheric Radiocarbon Concentration and Its Dependence on Geomagnetism." *Journal of Geophysical Research* 121 (15 February 1966):1065-71.

The Kingston Whig-Standard. (Kingston, Ontario, Canada) 21 September 1970, p. 3.

Kline, Meredith G. "Because It Had Not Rained." *Westminster Theological Journal* 20 (May 1958):146-55.

Kofahl, Robert E. "Critique of Canopy and other Models." *Creation Research Society Quarterly* 13 (March 1977):202-6.

Korff, Serge A. "Effects of the Cosmic Radiation on Terrestrial Isotope Distribution." *Transactions, American Geophysical Union* 35 (February 1954):105.

Kuiper, F. B. J. "The Basic Concept of Vedic Religion." *History of Religions* 15 (November 1975):107-20.

LaSor, William Sanford. "Further Information About Tell Mardikh." *Journal of the Evangelical Theological Society* 19 (Fall 1976):265-70.

_____. "Notes on Genesis 1:1-2:3." *Gordon Review* 2 (1965).

Lawson, Douglas A. "Pterosaur from the Latest Cretaceous of West Texas: Discovery of the Largest Flying Creature." *Science* 187 (14 March 1975):947-48.

Lee, David G. "Wind Power." *National Wildlife* 13 (August-September 1975):31 ff.

Lewis, Arthur H. "The Localization of the Garden of Eden." *Bulletin of the Evangelical Theological Society* 11 (Fall 1968):169-75.

Libby, W. F. "Accuracy of Radiocarbon Dates." *Science* 140 (19 April 1963):278-80.

Lippman, Harold E. "Letters, Frozen Mammoths." *Science* 137 (August 1962):449-50.

Long, Ronald D. "The Bible, Radiocarbon Dating, and Ancient Egypt." *Creation Research Society Quarterly* 10 (June 1973):19-30.

Lydekker, Richard. "Mammoth Ivory." *Smithsonian Reports* (1899):361-66.

McClellan, W. H. "The Newly Proposed Translation of Genesis 2:5-6." *The Catholic Biblical Quarterly* 1 (1939):106-14.

"Mammoth Find." *New Scientist*, 4 August 1977, p. 277.

Manabe, Syukuro, and Möller, Fritz. "On the Radiative Equilibrium and Heat Balance of the Atmosphere." *Monthly Weather Review* 89 (December 1961):503-32.

Manabe, Syukuro, and Strickler, Robert F. "Thermal Equilibrium of the Atmosphere with a Convective Adjustment." *Journal of the Atmospheric Sciences* 21 (July 1964):361-84.

Manabe, Syukuro, and Wetherald, Richard T. "Thermal Equilibrium of the Atmosphere with a Given Distribution of Relative Humidity." *Journal of the Atmospheric Sciences* 24 (May 1967):241-59.

Martin, Paul. "Stay Young with Hyperbaric Oxygen." *Piedmont Airlines Inflight Magazine*, March-April 1977, pp. 27-29.

Meryman, H. T. "Mechanics of Freezing in Living Cells and Tissues." *Science* 124 (21 September 1956):515-21.

Morton, Glen. "Can the Canopy Hold Water?" *Creation Research Society Quarterly* 16 (December 1979):164-70.

"Much About Muck." *Pursuit* 2 (October 1969):68-69.

Muller, H. J. "Radiation and Human Mutation." *Scientific American* 193 (November 1955):58-68.

Bibliography

Murray, Bruce et al. "Venus: Atmospheric Motion and Structure from Mariner 10 Pictures." *Science* 183 (29 March 1974):1307-14.

"Mysteries of Mars — Finally Some Clues; Meanwhile on Venus...." *U. S. News and World Report,* 18 October 1976, p. 88.

"Neanderthals Had Rickets." *Science Digest* 69 (February 1971):35.

Neuville, H. "On the Extinction of the Mammoth." *Annual Report Smithsonian Institution,* 1919, pp. 327-38.

Nevins, Stuart E. "Post-Flood Strata of the John Day Country, Northeastern Oregon." *Creation Research Society Quarterly* 10 (March 1974):191-204.

_____. "Reply to Critique by Daniel Wonderly." *Creation Research Society Quarterly* 10 (March 1974):241-44.

Noll, Richard B., and McElroy, Michael B. "Engineering Models of the Venus Atmosphere." *Journal of Spacecraft and Rockets* 11 (January 1974):21-28.

Northrup, Bernard E. "Comments on the Stuart E. Nevins Paper (Post-Flood Strata of the John Day Country, Northeastern Oregon)." *Creation Research Society Quarterly* 10 (March 1974):205-7.

Ostrom, John. "A New Look at Dinosaurs." *National Geographic* 154 (August 1978):152-85.

Peters, Walter G. "Field Evidence for Rapid Sedimentation." *Creation Research Society Quarterly* 10 (September 1973):89-96.

Pettersson, Hans. "Cosmic Spherules and Meteoritic Dust." *Scientific American* 202 (February 1960):132 ff.

Plass, Gilbert N. "Carbon Dioxide and Climate." *Scientific American* 201 (July 1959):41-47.

Pollock, Michael et al. "Prediction of Body Density in Young and Middle-aged Women." *Journal of Applied Physiology* 38 (April 1975):745-49.

Porter, Warren P., and Gates, David M. "Thermodynamic Equilibria of Animals with Environment." *Ecological Monographs* 39 (Summer 1969):227-44.

Price, G. B., and Makinodan, T. "Aging: Alteration of DNA-Protein Information." *Gerontologia* 19 (1973):58-70.

Quackenbush, L. S. "Notes on Alaskan Mammoth Expeditions of 1907 and 1908." *Bulletin of the American Museum of Natural History* 25 (1909):87-130.

Ramanathan, V. "Radiative Transfer within the Earth's Troposphere and Stratosphere: A Simplified Radiative-Convective Model." *Journal of the Atmospheric Sciences* 33 (July 1976):1330-46.

Ramanathan, V., and Coakley, J. A., Jr. "Climate Modeling through Radiative-Convective Models." *Reviews of Geophysics and Space Physics* 16 (November 1978):465-89.

"Review of *The Mammoth and the Flood*." *Nature* 37 (8 December 1887):123-25.

Rogers, C. D., and Walshaw, C. D. "The Computation of Infrared Cooling Rates in Planetary Atmospheres." *The Quarterly Journal of the Royal Meteorological Society* 92 (1966):67-92.

Russell, Dale, and Tucker, Wallace. "Supernova and the Extinction of the Dinosaurs." *Nature* 229 (19 February 1971):553-54.

Russell, W. L. "Shortening of Life in the Offspring of Male Mice Exposed to Neutron Radiation from an Atomic Bomb." *Proceedings of the National Academy of Science* 43 (1957):324-49.

Ryder, M. L. "Hair of the Mammoth." *Nature* 249 (10 May 1974):190-92.

Sanderson, Ivan T. "Riddle of the Frozen Mammoths." *Saturday Evening Post*, 16 January 1960, pp. 39 ff.

Schenk, R. V., and Bjorksten, J. "The Search for Microenzymes: The Enzyme of Bacillus Cereus." *Finska Kemists. Medd.* 82 (1973):26-46.

Scholander, P. F. et al. "Body Insulation of Some Arctic and Tropical Mammals and Birds." *Biological Bulletin* 99 (1950):226.

Seely, Paul H. "The Three-Storied Universe." *Journal of the American Scientific Affiliation* 21 (March 1969):1.

Shor, George G., Jr. "Letters, Could Pterosaurs Fly?" *Science* 188 (16 May 1975):677.

Smith, Maynard. "Biology of Aging." *Nature* 178 (24 November 1956):1154.

Speisor, E. A. "'ed in the Story of Creation." *Bulletin of the American Schools of Oriental Research* 140 (December 1955):9-11.

Spotila, James R. et al. "A Mathematical Model for Body Temperatures of Large Reptiles: Implications for Dinosaur Ecology." *The American Naturalist* 107 (May-June 1973):391-404.

Springstead, William A. "The Creationist and Continental Glaciation." *Creation Research Society Quarterly* 10 (June 1973):47-53.

_____. "Monoglaciology and the Global Flood." *Creation Research Society Quarterly* 8 (December 1971):175-82.

Stair, Ralph. "Tektites and the Lost Planet." *Scientific Monthly* 83 (July 1956):11 ff.

Steinhauer, Loren C. "The Relevancy of Roche's Limit to the Flood-Ice-Dump Theory." *Creation Research Society Quarterly* 8 (June 1971):63-65.

Stevenson, Peter A. "Meteoritic Evidence for a Young Earth." *Creation Research Society Quarterly* 12 (June 1975):23-25.

Stewart, John Massey. "Frozen Mammoths from Siberia Bring the Ice Age to Vivid Life." *Smithsonian* 8 (December 1977):61-68.

Strickling, James E. "A Quantitative Analysis of the Life Spans of the Genesis Patriarchs." *Creation Research Society Quarterly* 10 (December 1973):149-54.

_____. "The Waters Above the Firmament." (Letters to the Editor). *Creation Research Society Quarterly* 12 (March 1976):221.

Sukachev, V. N. "Examination of Plant Remnants Found within the Food of the Mammoth Discovered on the Beresovka River Territory of Yakutsk." Petrograd (1914):1-18. Translated from the Russian by Dr. Klaus Potsch, Technical University of Vienna.

_____."Examination of Plant Remnants Found within the Food of the Mammoth Discovered on the Beresovka River Territory of Yakutsk." Petrograd (1914, in Russian):1-18. Resultats scientifigues de l'expedition organisee par l'Academie Impericle des Sciences pour la pouilee du Mammouth, trouve sur la vuiere Berezovka en 1901. Translated by Mrs. Norman Hapgood, cited by Charles Hapgood, *Path of the Pole,* p. 266.

Taber, Stephen. "Perennially Frozen Ground in Alaska: Its Origin and History." *Geological Society of America Bulletin* 54 (1943):1433-1548.

Tolmachoff, I. P. "The Carcasses of the Mammoth and Rhinoceros Found in the Frozen Ground of Siberia." *Transactions of the American Philosophical Society* 23 (1929):11-71.

_____. "Note on the Extinction of the Mammoth in Siberia." *American Journal of Science* 14 (July 1927):66-69.

Trudinger, Paul. "'Not Yet Made' or 'Newly Made,' a Note on Genesis 2:5." *The Evangelical Quarterly* 47 (April-June 1975):67-69.

Tucker, W. H., and Terry, K. D. "Biologic Effects of Supernovae." *Science* 159 (26 January 1968):421-23.

_____. "Cosmic Rays from Nearby Supernovae: Biological Effects." *Science* 168 (7 June 1968):1138-39.

Tyler, H. T. et al. "Venus: Mass, Gravity Field, Atmosphere, and Ionosphere as Measured by the Mariner 10 Dual-Frequency Radio System." *Science* 183 (29 March 1974):1297-1301.

Udd, Stanley V. "The Canopy of Genesis 1:6-8." *Creation Research Society Quarterly* 12 (September 1975):90-93.

Upton, A. C. "Ionizing Radiation and the Aging Process, A Review." *Journal of Gerontology* 12 (1957):306-13.

Vawter, Bruce. "Fuller Sense." *Catholic Biblical Quarterly* 26 (January 1964):85-96.

Warren, Shields. "Longevity and Causes of Death from Irradiation in Physicians." *Journal of the American Medical Association* 162 (29 September 1956):464-68.

_____. "Radiation and the Human Body." *The Scientific Monthly* (January 1957):3-5.

Weare, Bryan C., and Snell, Fred M. "A Diffuse Thin Cloud Atmospheric Structure as a Feedback Mechanism in Global

Climate Modeling." *Journal of the Atmospheric Sciences* 31 (October 1974):1725-34.

"What Happens When the Sun Turns Off?" *Design News*, 5 May 1977, p. 15.

White, A. J. "Radio Carbon Dating." *Creation Research Society Quarterly* 9 (December 1972):155-58.

Whitelaw, Robert L. "Time, Life and History in the Light of 15,000 Radiocarbon Dates."*Creation Research Society Quarterly* 7 (June 1970):56-71.

Willis, E. H.; Tauber, H.; and Munnich, K. O. "Variations in the Atmospheric Radiocarbon Concentration over the Past 1,300 Years." *American Journal of Science Radiocarbon, Supplement* 2 (1960):1.

Wyngaarden, Martin J. "Phenomenal Language According to Dr. Bernard Ramm." *Bulletin of the Evangelical Theological Society* 2 (Fall 1959):10-14.

Yamauchi, Edwin M. "Stones, Scripts, and Scholars." *Christianity Today* 8 (1969): 432-37.

IV. UNPUBLISHED MATERIAL

Allen, Ron. "The Leviathan-Rahab-Dragon Motif in the Old Testament." Th.M. thesis, Dallas Theological Seminary, 1968.

Bjorksten, Johan. "Some Therapeutic Implications of the Crosslinkage Theory of Aging." Paper presented at the American Chemical Society, San Francisco, California, 2 September 1976.

Burkhalter, John E. "Experimental Investigation of Supercritical Taylor Vortex Flow." Ph.D. dissertation, The University of Texas at Austin, August 1972.

Clark, H. David. "The Genealogies of Genesis Five and Eleven." Th.D. dissertation, Dallas Theological Seminary, 1967.

Clough, Charles Albert. "A Calm Appraisal of *The Genesis Flood*." Th.M. thesis, Dallas Theological Seminary, 1968.

Dallas Times Herald, 24 April 1978.

Gooding, Bob. Report on Channel 8 News, Dallas, Texas, 9 February 1976.

Kaiser, Walter C., Jr. "Legitimate Hermeneutics." Essay given at the International Conference on Biblical Inerrancy, Wheaton, Ill., November 1978.

Morgan, Ivor. Calculations supplied to *Reader's Digest* to check the credibility of a 1960 article published by them on the frozen mammoths; the article was a condensation of one published by the *Saturday Evening Post,* 16 January 1960, by Ivan Sanderson, "Riddle of the Frozen Giants." He is an engineer with Birds Eye of the General Foods Corporation, White Plains, New York.

_____. Computer program for determining the time necessary to bring various parts of a sphere to various temperatures given a certain outside temperature.

Newman, Robert. "The Biblical Teaching on the Firmament." Th.M. thesis, Biblical School of Theology, Hatfield, Pennsylvania, 1972.

O'Keefe, John, and Ahrens, Thomas J. "Impact-Induced Energy Partitioning, Melting and Vaporization on Terrestrial Planets." Contribution Number 2907, Division of Geological and Planetary Sciences, California Institute of Technology, Pasadena, California.

Rusk, Roger. Cassette tape, "The Flood," 1971. Physics professor at the University of Tennessee.

"Semiannual Report on TPRC Activities on Preparation of Tables on the Thermal Conductivity of Foods." Thermophysical Properties Research Center, Purdue University, West Lafayette, Ind., 15 December 1969. Mimeographed.

Udd, Stanley V. "The Early Atmosphere." Th.M. thesis, Grace Theological Seminary, Winona Lake, Ind., 1974.

Wagner, A. James. "Some Geophysical Aspects of Noah's Flood." Private research paper, Department of Meteorology, Massachusetts Institute of Technology, 1961.

"Warm-Blooded Dinosaurs." A "Nova" television program of WGBH, Boston, Mass.

Bibliography

V. Personal Communications

Ahrens, Thomas J., Ph. D., research associate Seismology Laboratory, California Institute of Techonology, Pasadena, Calif., personal communication, 13 July 1977.

Anderson, Kirby, M. S. in evolution, Yale University. Research associate with Probe Ministries, Dallas, Texas, personal communication, 22 August 1977.

Armour Inc., Greyhound Tower, Phoenix, Ariz., personal communications, October 1975 and June 1976.

Army Cold Regions Laboratory, Hanover, N. H., personal communication, 10 July 1977.

Barker, Kenneth, Th.D., professor of Old Testament, Dallas Theological Seminary, personal communication, May 1977.

Baumgardner, John R., M. S., optical physicist in laser physics with the U. S. Air Force, personal communication, May 1976.

Bjorksten, Johan, director of the Bjorksten Research Foundation, Madison, Wis., personal communications, 12 October 1976 and 27 October 1976.

Blick, Edward, Ph.D., professor of aeronautical engineering, University of Oklahoma, Norman, Okla., 17 February 1977.

Brown, Robert Henry, Geoscience Research Institute, Berrien Springs, Mich., personal communication, 22 March 1979.

Bruce, Larry, M.D., gastro-intestinal physiologist with the University of Texas Health Science Center, Dallas, Tex., personal communication, June 1976.

Burkhalter, John E., Ph.D., assistant professor of aerospace engineering, School of Engineering and Engineering Experiment Station, Auburn University, Auburn, Ala., personal communication, 26 February 1976.

Case, A. A., botanist associated with the College of Veterinary Medicine, University of Missouri, Columbia, Mo., personal communication, 6 January 1976.

Christensen, A. F., general utilities engineer, Oscar Mayer & Company, Madison, Wis., personal communication, 14 April 1976.

Clark, Frank, professor of astronomy, department of physics, University of Kentucky, personal communication, February 1976.

Dempsy, Barry, Ph.D., professor of civil engineering, University of Illinois, personal communication, 12 July 1977.

Foley, C. W., D.V.M., department of veterinary medicine and surgery, College of Veterinary Medicine, University of Missouri, Columbia, Mo., personal communication, 22 February 1976.

Garriott, James, M.D., Dallas County (Texas) medical examiner, personal communication, February 1976.

Goody, Richard M., professor of dynamic meteorology, Harvard University, personal communication, 25 February 1977.

Hess, Seymour, Ph.D., department of meteorology, Florida State University, Tallahassee, Fla., 3 November 1975.

Holroyd, Ed, III, Ph.D. in atmospheric physics, Bureau of Reclamation, Denver, Colo., personal communication, 26 February 1977.

McKnight, Clyde, Ph.D. in atmospheric physics, department of meteorology, University of Nevada, personal communication, April 1977.

Meyer, John, Ph.D., assistant professor of physiology and biophysics, University of Louisville, Ky., personal communication, 7 September 1976.

Morgan, Ivor, Birds Eye engineer with the General Foods Corporation, personal communication, 7 October 1975.

Morton, Glen, senior geophysicist with the Atlantic Richfield Company, Dallas, Tex., personal communication, 14 July 1979.

Newman, Robert, Ph.D. in theoretical astrophysics, professor, Biblical School of Theology, Hatfield, Pa., personal communication, May 1976.

Patten, Donald W., personal communications, 18 October 1975 and 3 April 1977.

Pleticha, Dale, Ph.D., astrophysics department, Cornell University, Ithaca, N. Y., personal communication, 23 February 1976.

Bibliography

Potsch, Klaus, Ph.D., theoretical physicist at the Technical University of Vienna, Austria, personal communication, 24 February 1979.

Schapery, Richard A., Ph.D., professor of mechanical, civil, and aeronautical engineering, civil engineering department, Texas A & M University, personal communication, 5 November 1977.

Simpson, Roger L., Ph. D., department of civil and mechanical engineering, School of Engineering and Applied Science, Southern Methodist University, Dallas, Tex., personal communication, 1 November 1976.

Smith, A. E. Wilder, F.R.I.C., London, professor of pharmacology and consultant, Roggern, CH-3646 Einigen am Thunersee, Switzerland, personal communication, 12 September 1979.

Snell, Fred M., Ph.D. in atmospheric physics, department of biophysical sciences, State University at Buffalo, N. Y., personal communication, December 1976.

Swenson, Melvin J., D.V.M., professor of veterinary physiology, Iowa State University, Ames, Ia., personal communication, 19 December 1976.

Udd, Stanley V., professor of Old Testament, Calvary Bible College, Kansas City, Mo., personal communication, 12 March 1976.

Vardiman, Larry, Ph.D. in meteorology, Bureau of Reclamation, Denver, Colo., personal communications, May 1976 and 13 January 1977.

Voss, Henry, Ph.D., research associate in atmospheric science, University of Illinois, Champaign, Ill., personal communication, October-November 1976.

Whitelaw, Robert, department of mechanical engineering, Virginia Polytechnic Institute, "The Canopy Theory and the Rift-Drift-Shift Theory in the Light of Scripture and Physical Facts," personal communications, 16 February 1976, 29 February 1976, 25 May 1976.

Wiggans, Don, Ph.D. in biochemistry, professor of biochemistry, University of Texas Health Science Center, Dallas, Tex., personal communication, December 1976.

Subject Index

'Adamah, 82
'Ed, 79, 81, 82, 90, 91
'Eres, 82
Adams's mammoth. See Mammoth finds
Aerodynamic heating, 203, 206
Ahura-Mazda, 122, 305
Al'pene, 54
Alaska
  animals buried in tundra muck, 347, 416
  former climate, 348
  mammoth find, 327
Alcohol, 103
Allegory. See also Interpretation, biblical
  in New Testament, 33
Alopecurus Alpinus, 343, 378
Altitude of canopy, 233, 239
Ammon-Re (Sun god of Egypt), 305
Apostrophe, 106
Apsu, 116
Archaeology, and interpretation, 34
Aruba, 67
Astrology. See also Mythology
  origins of, 191, 307, 310
  Tower of Babel, 307, 309
Atahasis Epic, 20
Atmospheric pressure
  calculation of, 233
  fermentation rate, 103
  flight of pteranodon, 147
  gigantism, 152
  oxygen delivery, 153
  pre-Flood, 146
Attenuation of starlight. See also Starlight
  Beer's Law, 292
  pre-Flood, 302
  Rayleigh scattering, 292, 295
Authorial intent, 13, 14, 15, 28

Babel, tower of. See Tower of Babel
Babylon
  Apsu, 116
  Gilgamesh Epic, 117
  Tiamat, 116
Bara, 19
Battle myths
  differences from Genesis, 40
  stars, 20
Beer's Law. See Attenuation of starlight
Beresovka mammoth. See also Mammoth finds
  animals buried with, 368
  Bird's Eye calculations, 387
  deep freeze of, 377
  discovery of, 318
  erect male genital, 320
  flesh on, 319
  food in mouth of, 319
  modeled as an equivalent sphere, 390
  modeled as infinite cylinder, 387
  month of death, 344
  stomach contents, 319, 343, 371, 397
  sudden deep freeze of, 383
Bible. See also Interpretation, biblical
  conflict with science, 5
  cultural setting of, 12
  dual authorship of, 30
  interpretation of, 4

language of, 11
phenomenal language, 11
and science, 29
textbook of science, 1-2
Bird's Eye computer model, 390
Black body temperature (outer space), 194
Blackbirds, sebaceous glands in, 340
Blue light, 293
Bog chemicals, 401. See also Mammoth deep freeze
Buoyant force, 249
Buttercup flowers. See Beresovka mammoth; Mammoth

Canal water, 86
Canopy
  altitude of, 233, 239
  average temperature of, 236
  Babylon, 116
  biblical evidence for, 43
  Buddhism, 117
  calculation of cooling, 275
  carbon 14 production, 175
  cloud model, 215
  condensation, cooling effect, 412
  decay of, theological implications, 263
  diffusion rate of, 262
  diffusion to surface of, 219-20
  dry adiabatic lapse rate of, 232
  dynamics of, 283
  eastern Asia, 116
  Egypt, 118
  Greece, 119
  Greek and Hebrew, 121
  heat load of, 269
  ice model, 195
  ice shell, 197
  India, 121
  India and Israel, 123
  infrared cooling, 284
  liquid model, 193, 297
  mammoth extinction, 405
  model description of, 136-37
  molecular diffusion, 259
  mythology, 113
  nighttime visibility, 245
  Persia, 124
  Polynesia, 124
  pre-Flood atmosphere, 242
  pre-Flood cooling of, 273
  precipitation of, 267-68
  predictions, 138
  Rayleigh optical depth of, 296
  Rome, 125
  spiritual implications of, 423
  stability of, 249
  sudden climate change, 419
  Sumer, 127
  surface temperature of, 240
  temperature inversion of, 241, 244, 247
  temperature profile of, 237, 243
  total optical depth of, 296
  water vapor model, 217
  without clouds, 235
Carbon 14
  dating method, 176
  disequilibrium ratio, 177
  longevity, 173
Catastrophic burial, mammoths, 324
Centrifugal force, support mechanism, 196
Chaos
  battle myths, 18
  seasons, 99
  Yahweh's control over, 101
Circumcision, 96
Climate
  Alaska, 347-48
  change of, 164, 187
  Cretaceous, 143
  Pleistocene, 348
  polar, 142
  pre-Flood, 78, 93, 141, 280
  Siberia, 336, 346-47, 349
  sudden change, 363, 397
  wind systems, 281
Climate change, 352, 419. See also Climate
  argued from tundra muck, 352
  old explanation, 407
  pre-Flood, 277
Cloud canopy. See also Canopy
  Patten model, 215
  surface temperature, 216
Cloud cover, pre-Flood, 411
Clouds
  black body radiation, 241
  dissipation at night, 245

Subject Index

firmament, 44
  formation of, 234, 236, 238
  Genesis 1:6-8, 48
  location of, 243
  nighttime visibility, 245
  polemic intent, 58
  waters above, 48
  year before Flood, 277
Constants, radiation calculations, 228
Convection cells, 234, 283
Convective adjustment, 238
Cooling. See Canopy
Cosmology
  critical view, 7
  definition, 7
  pictorial view, 9
Cosmos, 100
Couette flow, 254
Cow, freezing of, 393
Cross-linkage theory, longevity, 171
Cultural conventions
  and interpretation, 38
Culture, 12

Dalton's Law, 218
Dating methods
  and canopy. See Canopy
Day, Genesis 2:5, 80
Deceleration forces, on ice particles, 205
Decompression. See nitrogen narcosis
Deep
  'ed, 82
  Tiamat, 18
Density
  equation of, 253
  of mammoth meat, 385
Deuterium, concentration of, 146
Diet and longevity, 174
Diffusion. See also Canopy
  calculation of, 259
  canopy problem, 247
  canopy support, 219
  Fick's Law, 259
  model of, 261
  rate of, 262
Diffusivity, 260
Dima, 317
Dinosaurs
  contemporaneous with men, 406
  extinction of, 363, 419
Distance factor, 230
Dry adiabatic lapse rate, 232
Dual Authorship
  implications of, 30
  and prophecy, 31
Dynamic viscosity, 386

E-sag-ila, 308
E-temem-an-ki, 308
Earth's radiation, 227
Ecological zonation, 419
Eddington Approximation, 216, 226
Eddy diffusion, 248, 259
Electromagnetic spectrum, 165
Elephant
  Indian, 313
  Indian and mammoth, 351
Elephant Point, mammoth found, 347
Emden Approximation, 226
Enuma Elish, 20
Equation of state, 253
Equivalent sphere, model of. See Beresovka mammoth
Eschscholtz Bay, mammoth find, 327
Eseb, 81, 84
Existentialism, 14
Expansional cooling, 238, 270
Exponential decay curve, Genesis 11, 158. See also Longevity
Extinction zenith angle. See Starlight

False obversion, 1
Fermentation rate, 103
Fick's Law, 259
Figures of speech. See also Interpretation, biblical
  apostrophe, 106
  hypocatastasis, 66
Film conductance, 386
Firmament
  and battle myths, 45
  literal, 25
  meaning of, 43
  and pillar support, 47

and Septuagint, 46
Flood
　date of, 163
　evidence for, 183, 364, 370
　mammoth preservation during, 417
　month it began, 345
Food supply
　inadequate for mammoth, 348
　required for elephant, 350
　in Siberia, 346
Foreknowledge, of God, 264
Fourier number, 388
Foxtail grass, 343

Garden of Eden
　extent of, 81
　rivers of, 81
Gasham, 93
Genesis, book of
　days, 24
　nature myths, relation to, 17
Genesis 1
　structure, 23
　and typology, 31
Genesis 2
　contradiction in, 78, 91
　situation in life, 92
Geologic column, testimony to judgment by God, 424
Gigantism, 152
Gilgamesh epic, 117
Gladiolus flowers, decay of
　action of gastric juices, 380
　experiment, 380
　Van Hoff's Rule, 381
Global circulation, pre-Flood, 281
Gods, Egypt, 118
Gray model atmosphere, 230
Greece, 119
Greenhouse
　climate, 78
　prediction of, 139
Gulag Archipelago, 311

Heat balance, Venus parallel, 283
Heat load reduction, 272, 276-77
Heaven, meaning of, 115
Heavens, change in appearance, 191
Helios, 305

Hydrological cycle, pre-Flood, 282
Hydrostatic
　equation, 225, 248
　equilibrium, 247
Hyperbaric oxygen and senility, 156
Hyperion, 305
Hypocatastasis, 66

Ice canopy. See also Canopy
　aerodynamic heating, 206
　Issac Vail, 196
　kinetic energy dissipation, 212
　mechanical energy, 212
　mechanical energy analysis, 198
　oceanic heat sink, 214
　terminal velocity, 215
Infinite cylinder model. See Beresovka mammoth
Instability, 255
Interpretation, biblical
　allegory, 32
　and archaeology, 34
　authorial intent, 13
　battle myths, 22
　cultural conventions, 38
　and culture, 12
　dual authorship, 30
　existentialism, 14, 16
　extremes of, 10
　figures of speech, 40
　implications of text, 27
　and language, 11
　literalism, 25
　and literary form, 39
　meaning, 27
　mechanistic science, 29
　polemic intent, 16
　and prophecy, 31
　sharability, 27
　significance of text, 30, 35, 221
　subject matter, 27
　and typology, 31
Inundation, by mist, 86
Ivory. See Mammoth finds
Ixtililxochitl, 306

Jet streams, 283

Ki, 79-80, 92

Subject Index

Kinematic viscosity, 386
Kinetic energy
  dissipation of, 211
  ice canopy, 200
  re-entry analysis, 201
  temperature increase, 212
Kolyma River, 317

Laminar flow, 250
Lapse rate, 232
Latent heat, 269
Leningrad University, 317, 321
Liquid canopy. See Canopy
Liquid ocean. See Waters above
Literary form. See Interpretation,
  biblical
Longevity
  carbon 14, 174
  and climate, 102
  cross-linkage, 171
  diet, 174
  enzyme for, 173
  exponential decay curve, 161
  linear regression, 159
  oxygen partial pressure, 156
  radiation, 170
  radiation shielding, 157
Luminances, light sources, 291

Mabbul, 83
Mammals, caches of, 367
Mammoth
  adaptation to cold, 336
  anal flap, 342
  caribou and moose, 342
  dimensions of, 391
  extinction, 356
  fat layer, 337
  food supply, 350
  frozen in ice, 393
  names of, 315
  not a ruminant, 378
  physical dimensions of, 313
  sebaceous glands, 339
  similarity to Indian elephant, 351
  stomach contents, experiment
    on, 379-80
  wooly coat, 338
Mammoth bones
  histology of, 404
  marrow, fresh, 322

Mammoth deep freeze
  Bird's Eye calculations, 387
  compared to cow, 393-94
  in ice, 393, 395
  initial phases of Flood, 411
  preservation during Flood, 417
  time in hours (chart), 390
  uniformitarian objections, 402
Mammoth extinction
  by burial in mud flows, 360
  by changed climate, 362, 398
  by defective adaptation, 359
  by man, 358
  preservation during Flood, 417
  related to vapor canopy, 405
  requirements for theory on, 408
  same cause as dinosaur, 363
  suffocated animals, 366
  time of burial, 414
Mammoth finds. See also
  Beresovka mammoth
  Adams's mammoth, 314, 403
  Alaska, 327, 347
  Chinese records and reports,
    314-15
  date 1972, 316
  date 1977, 317
  drowned animals, 366
  Europe, 324
  ivory, 329, 331, 404
  located on high ground, 361
  marine shells mixed with, 369
  North America, 325
  number of remains, 328
  Quackenbush find, 327
  Siberia, 315
  Siberian Islands, 330
  soft parts in frozen ground, 403
  Stenbock-Fermor's mammoth,
    314
  upright carcasses, 367
  upright condition, 316
Mammoth meat
  Chinese reports, 322
  density of, 385
  edible by dogs, 319
  edible by humans, 312, 315,
    323, 381, 398
  film conductance, 386
  fox bait, 312
  freezing rate, 382

fresh, 321
Joseph Barnes's report, 323
report in Manchu dictionary, 322
thermophysical properties, 383-84
uniformitarian explanations, 399
Marduk, 306, 308
Mass absorption coefficients, 228
Masuq, 47
Matar, 93
Me'al, 51
Melting ice, 208
Meteorites, 188
Micropotease MPB, 173
Mist
  canal water, 86
  greenhouse effect, 78
  in Genesis 2:5, 77
  meaning of, 88-89
  pre-Flood watering, 280
  resupply of river systems by, 282
  traditional meaning, 87
Mist formation, location of, 243
Mithras, 122, 305
Model of canopy. See Canopy
Moisture, pre-Flood. See Mist
Moon, magnitude of light, 290
Mount Etna, 72
Mountains, 246
Mud flows, 360
Mummu, 116
Mythology
  Ahura-Mazda, 305
  Ammon-Re, 305
  analysis of, 128
  Buddhism, 117
  eastern Asia, 116
  Egypt, 118
  Greece, 119
  Helios, 305
  Hyperion, 305
  India, 121
  Marduk, 306
  origin of astrology, 310
  origins of sun-worship, 305
  Persia, 124
  Polynesia, 124
  Rome, 125
  Sumer, 127

  sun, 305
  sun ages, 306
  Varuna, 305
Myths
  Babylon, 20
  characteristics of, 21
  nature, 17 (see also Genesis)

Nahar, 83
Neanderthal man, rickets in, 179-80
Nighttime visibility, 245, 288, 298, 304. See also Starlight; Stars
Nitrogen narcosis, 279
Noah
  days of, 424
  drunkenness, 102
Noah's wood, 347

Oceans
  absorption of canopy heat, 277
  absorption of kinetic energy, 214
  mass of, 214
Optical depth, 227, 296. See also Canopy
Orbital entry, ice, 209
Osar, 62
Oscar Mayer and Company, 397
Ovid, 125
Oxygen
  atmospheric pressure, 279
  toxicity, 278
Oxygen delivery
  astronauts, 155
  atmospheric pressure, 153
  gigantism, 153
  longevity, 156
Ozone, at canopy top, 285

Partial pressure
  nitrogen, 279
  oxygen, 154, 279
Patten epic
  ice epic, 201
  kinetic energy, 213
Permafrost, 315, 350-51
Permian glaciation, 143
Persia, 124
Phenomenal language. See Bible

Subject Index

Photosynthesis. *See* Plant growth and ultraviolet light
Pillar, 47
Plank Function, 226, 228-29
Plant growth and ultraviolet light, 180
Pleistocene extinctions
  animals drowned, 366
  animals in tundra muck, 326, 352
  caused by climate change, 362, 397, 407, 419
  cave and fissures in Europe, 370
  mammal caches, 367
  marine shells with mammoth bones, 369
  phases of, 410
  problem of, 312
  requirements for theory on, 408
  uniformitarian geology, 326, 355
Poisson's Equation, 232, 412
Polar climate
  frozen fruit trees, 142
  pre-Flood, 283
  sudden change, 187
Polynesia, 124
Polystrate fossils, 183
  tree trunk, 328
Potential energy, ice canopy, 200. *See also* Kinetic energy
Pre-Flood storm centers, 410
Prediction
  canopy, 138
  fewer meteorites, 188
  Flood, 182
  greenhouse effect, 139
  He_3, 145
  higher atmospheric pressure, 146
  new appearance of sky, 310
  new heavenly appearance, 191
  radiation shielding, 157
  stratospheric water vapor, 190
  sudden polar temperatue drop, 187
  volcanic ash in ice, 186
Pressure, 233
Primeval sea, mist, 86
Pteranodon
  lift/drag ratio, 147
  west Texas, 149

Q factor, 207
Quackenbush. *See* Mammoth finds

Radiation
  balance, 242
  biological effects, 166
  Earth's surface, 165
  effect on rats, 169
  exposures in United States, 167
  longevity, 168
Radiative equilibrium, 236
Radiative heat transfer, 223, 228
  constants, 228
  window region, 244
Radius ratio, ice entry, 210
Rain
  amount in Flood, 63, 65
  before Flood, 93
  global average today, 281
  raindrop size, 268
  rainfall rate, 69
  source of, 71-72
Rainbow
  covenant, 93
  droplet size, 94
  first appearance, 95
Raqa, 44
Raqia, 44
Rayleigh optical depth. *See* Canopy
Rayleigh scattering. *See also* Attenuation of starlight
  calculation of optical depth, 294
  coefficient of, 293
  sunsets and clear skies, 293
Re-entry analysis. *See also* Ice canopy
  aerodynamic heating, 203
  ice particles, 201
  kinetic energy dissipation, 211
  orbital entry, 209
  Q factor, 207
  terminal velocity, 215
  thermal stress, 206
Revelation, 17
Reynolds' number, 386

Rhinoceroses, 318
River systems, 280
Roche's Limit, 201

Sabbath, 100
Saber-toothed tiger, Siberia, 346
Sadeh, 84
Saturation vapor pressure, 219, 231, 237, 248
Saturn, canopy, 126
Sedimentation, rapid, 328
Science
  assumptions, 3
  models, 135
  reproducibility, 3
  uniformity of nature, 99
Seasons, pre-Flood, 98
Second Law of Thermodynamics, canopy decay, 264. See also Canopy
Shahaq, 44
Shamash, 306
Shaqah, 83
Shrub, 79, 84
Siah, 79, 84
Siberia
  animals, ancient times, 347
  caribou and moose, 342
  climate, 335, 344-45
  food supply today, 349
  mammoth finds, 315
  permafrost, 315
  scarcity of food, 346
  sudden climate change, 362, 397
Solar input, 227
Somatic mutation, 166
Spectral albedos, 228
Spherical shell canopy. See Canopy; Ice canopy
Stability
  criteria for, 233
  diffusion rate, 262
  Taylor Stability, 255
  and temperature inversion, 249
Starlight
  attenuation, canopy, 297
  extinction of, 302
  extinction zenith angle, 300
  intensity, calculation of, 289, 300
  portion of sky visible, 303
  pre-Flood intensity, 299
Stars
  battle myths, 20
  light to eye, 291-92
  magnitude of light, 288
  number, 289, 303-4
  pre-Flood, 191, 287
  relative intensities of, 289
  worship of, 307
Stenbock-Fermor's mammoth. See Mammoth finds
Stephan-Boltzman Constant, 229
Storehouses, 61
Strata reclassification of, 405, 409
Stratospheric water vapor, 190
Subterranean water
  mist of Genesis 2:5, 86
  pre-Flood, 282
Sumer, 127
Sun. See also Mythology
  magnitude of light, 290
  pre-Flood appearance, 304
  worship of, 305
Sun ages, 306
Sunsets, 293
Support mechanism, 218
Surface temperature,
  calculation of, 232, 240, 242. See also Temperature; Temperature profile

Tanninim, 19
Taylor Instability, 255, 257
Taylor number, 251, 257
Taylor Stability
  definition, 250
  model of, 252
Tefnut, 118
Tehom
  and 2 Peter 3, 61
  deep, 83
  Tiamat, 18
Temperature. See also Surface temperature
  cloud canopy, 216
  coldest reported, 336
  at equator and poles, 283
  lapse rate, 237
  surface, 232
  at time of Flood, 410

Subject Index

Temperature increase, by kinetic energy input, 212
Temperature inversion. See Canopy
Temperature profile
  average temperature, 236
  calculation of, 229
  convective adjustment, 238
  dry adiabatic lapse rate, 232
  Emden Approximation, 226
  inversions, 241
  pre-Flood, 243
  surface temperature, 240, 242
  without clouds, 235, 237
Terem, 79
Terrestrial output, 227
Thermal conductivity, 384
Thermal stresses on ice particles, 206
Thermophysical properties, 383
Thorns, 84
Tiamat, 18, 21, 116, 117
Tohu and Bohu, 24
Tower of Babel, 191, 307, 308, 309
Transcultural, 13
Transmissivity, 242
Tundra
  animals buried in, 416
  mosquitoes, 401
  odor of, 330
Tundra muck
  depth of, 351
  proof of formerly warm climate, 351
Typology. See Interpretation, biblical

Unconformities, 184
Uniformity
  objections to mammoth freeze, 402
  and providence of God, 99
  science, 3

Van Hoff's Rule. See Gladiolus flowers, decay of
Vapor canopy. See also Canopy
  exegetical basis, 222
  interpretation, 222
  objections, 218
Varuna, 123, 305
Vegetation
  growth under canopy, 180
  order of creation, 91
  pre-Flood, 78, 79, 80, 84, 85
  shrub, 84
Visual magnitudes, standard light sources, 291
Vitamin D, 179
Volcanic ash, 186, 268, 274
  canopy precipitation, 268
  Pleistocene extinctions, 416
Volcanoes, canopy precipitation by, 268
  glacial ice, 186
  heat load of, 74
Vritra, India, 122

Water vapor
  optical depth, 230
  support mechanism, 218
Watering of earth, 280
Waters above. See also Canopy; Vapor canopy
  duration of, 107
  liquid ocean, 51
  meaning of, 48, 104, 108
  not clouds, 50, 55, 57
  Psalm 148, 104
  present today, 104
Wave numbers, 228
Wind systems, pre-Flood, 281
Window, 244
Windows of heaven
  chaos, 22
  hypocatastasis, 66
  meaning of, 66, 68
Wine, rate of fermentation, 102
Without form, 24
Wooly coat, mammoth, 338

Yarah, 94

Zaqaq, 90
Zenith angle, 301
Ziggurats, 307
Zodiac, origin of, 309

Index of Persons

Ahrens, Thomas J., 211, 212
Albright, William F., 86, 88, 130
Alexander, 306
Alford, Henry, 59
Allen, Ron, 38
Allis, Oswald T., 5
Anderson, B. W., 18
Anderson, Kirby, 155
Anthony, Harold E., 328, 343, 360, 405
Archer, Gleason, 137
Armstrong, Harold, 174, 177, 190
Arndt, W. F., 59
Asimov, Isaac, 165, 166, 167, 168, 169, 170
Awberry, J. H., 384

Bakker, Robert T., 155
Bardach, John E., 279
Barker, Kenneth, 92
Barnes, Joseph, 399
Barnes, Thomas G., 177
Barnett, Lincoln, 336
Barth, Karl, 16
Battan, Louis J., 248, 255, 274, 281
Baumgardner, John R., 294
Baumgartner, Walter, 51, 116
Beers, Norman R., 148, 231
Bellairs, Angus de 'A., 147, 157
Benedict, Francis G., 378
Berglund, B. E., 325
Berry, F. A., 148, 231
Bertram, G., 46
Bird, Roland T., 406
Bjorksten, Johan, 170, 171, 172, 173
Blick, Edward, 204, 207, 215
Bollay, E., 148, 231
Bramwell, Cherrie D., 143, 147, 148, 149, 150, 151, 152

Brandt, 356
Brasseur, 306
Breasted, James Henry, 118
Bridge, B. J., 337
Briggs, Charles A., 44, 51, 53, 54, 55, 62, 67, 80, 84, 85, 87, 90, 92, 97, 106, 107
Bright, John, 133
Bronner, Leah, 67
Brooks, A. H., 348
Brown, David, 51, 87, 92
Brown, Francis. See Briggs, Charles A.
Brown, Robert Henry, 62, 80, 87, 90, 176, 240
Brueggeman, Walter, 99, 100
Buckland, 356, 403
Budyko, M. J., 144
Bullard, Fred M., 74
Bullinger, E. W., 41, 66, 106
Burdick, Clifford L., 406
Burkhalter, J. E., 253, 254, 255, 258
Bush, George, 78, 87, 98
Butzer, Karl W., 338, 346
Byers, Horace Robert, 63, 217, 218, 232, 233, 239, 241, 248, 253, 259, 268, 269, 292, 293, 296, 297, 412

Calvin, John, 48, 87
Carslaw, H. S., 417
Case, A. A., 343, 344, 372, 375, 376, 381
Cassel, J. Frank, 5
Cassuto, U., 37, 48, 54, 57, 68, 78, 79, 84, 95, 308, 345
Cess, Robert D., 224
Chandrasekhar, S., 250, 251
Chapman, Dean R., 207, 208

471

Charlesworth, J. K., 351
Christensen, A. F., 397
Clark, Frank, 299
Clark, H. David, 137, 162
Clark, Harold W., 144
Clark, John, 330
Clough, Charles A., 6, 94, 132, 162
Coakley, James A., 223, 224, 238
Cockrum, E. Lendell, 350
Coffin, Harold G., 104, 420
Cohen, A., 116
Cohen, Daniel, 405
Colbert, Edwin H., 141, 149, 152, 246
Collier, A. J., 348
Conant, Thomas J., 62
Cook, S. F., 351, 404
Coulson, Kinsell L., 165, 166, 179
Courville, Donovan A., 163
Cox, Douglas E., 145, 410
Culbertson, Margaret F., 229
Cunningham, J. T., 156
Curtis, Howard, 170
Custance, Arthur C., 365, 367, 368
Cuvier, Baron G., 315

Dahood, Mitchell, 106
Daly, Reginald, 72
Darwin, Charles, 365
Davey, Noel, 32
Delitzsch, Franz, 62, 66, 69, 80, 87, 90, 345
Dempsy, Barry, 418
Dhorme, E., 90
Dickerson, R. W., 384, 385, 393, 394
Dieckuoss, W., 288, 289, 290
Digby, Bassett, 142, 315, 318, 320, 321, 330, 332, 338, 340, 343, 345, 346, 349, 355, 358, 359, 360, 367, 399, 404
Dixon, Roland B., 124, 307
Dobzhanksy, Theodosius, 165, 166, 167, 168, 169, 170
Doumani, George A., 142
Dunbar, Carl O., 314, 318, 326
Durant, Will, 118, 125

Eckelman, Herman J., Jr., 30, 32
Eichrodt, Walther, 8
Elsasser, Walter M., 229
Emden, R., 226

Evelyn-White, Hugh G., 119
Ezra, H. C., 351, 404

Farrand, William R., 313, 314, 315, 329, 334, 338, 344, 356, 362, 369, 371, 372, 402
Fausset, A. R., 62, 87, 90
Fehsenfeld, F. E., 190
Ferguson, E. E., 190
Ferguson, John, 122, 305, 306
Fermor, John H., 180
Ferry, James F., 180, 181
Fields, Weston, 197
Filby, Frederick, 114, 134, 345, 350
Flint, Richard Foster, 326, 355
Foley, C. W., 378, 381
Fox, C. S., 70
Frankfort, A., 17
Frankfort, H., 17, 128
Frankfort, H. A., 128
Frazer, James George, 114, 116, 124, 130, 131, 133
Frigerio, Norman A., 166

Garriott, James, 378
Gaster, T. H., 8, 66, 44, 115
Gaster, Theodor H., 114
Gates, David M., 153
Gelb, Ignace J., 88
Gingrich, F. W., 59
Gooding, Bob, 312
Goody, R. M., 216, 225, 226, 230, 256, 268, 283
Goppelt, Leonhard, 57
Gordon, C. H., 91
Gow, Anthony J., 186
Grant, Michael, 119, 120, 126
Gray, Dwight E., 200
Green, John C., 5
Green, William Henry, 137
Griffith-Thomas, W. H., 23
Griffiths, E., 384
Guirand, Felix, 129, 305

Hakansson, S., 325
Hapgood, Charles H., 142, 324, 329, 336, 337, 341, 344, 356, 374, 375, 376, 377, 399
Harris, R. Laird, 81, 86
Hasel, Gerhard F., 18, 19, 20, 21, 308

Index of Persons

Hazel, John, 119, 120, 126
Heide, Fritz, 188, 189
Heidel, Alexander, 18, 117, 308, 309
Hengstenberg, E. W., 106, 108
Hensen Joseph, 201
Herz, O. F., 314, 321, 337, 338, 366
Hesiod, 120
Hess, F. L., 348
Hess, Seymour L., 217, 233, 239, 245, 248, 269, 272
Heylmun, Edgar B., 144
Hibben, Frank C., 186, 368, 415, 416, 417
Higgens, Arnold E., 104
Hill, J. E., 384
Hirsch, E. D., 28, 29
Hirsch, E. D., Jr., 13, 35
Hoff, Philip H., 202
Holman, J. P., 259
Holroyd, Edmond W. III, 78
Hongi, H., 125
Hoskyns, Edwyn, 32
Howorth, Henry H., 145, 313, 314, 316, 318, 322, 323, 324, 325, 326, 338, 347, 348, 349, 352, 356, 357, 359, 361, 364, 366, 367, 368, 369, 370, 371, 399, 403, 407
Hsu, Shao Ti, 386
Humboldt, 306
Humphreys, D. Russell, 282
Humphreys, W. J., 73, 268, 274
Hunt, Barrie, 268, 275
Huxley, T. H., 5

Iberall, A. S., 169
Ingersol, Andrew P., 217
Ingersoll, Alfred C., 384, 418
Ingersoll, Leonard R., 384, 418
Ions, Veronica, 121, 122
Irwin, William A., 128

Jacob, B., 96
Jacob, Edmond, 7
Jacobsen, Thorkild, 128
Jaeger, J. C., 417
Jamieson, Robert, 67, 87, 90, 96
Jeans, James, 202
Jewett, Paul K., 16
Johanneson, A. D., 190

Johnson, John C., 94

Kaiser, Walter, 13, 14, 34, 41
Kapphahn, Arline K., 208
Keil, C. F., 66, 69, 78, 81, 84, 87, 98, 345
Kellogg, Howard W., 115, 195, 196, 197
Kidner, Derek, 23, 49, 54, 64, 82, 83, 86, 87
Kietzke, Kenneth K., 330
Kline, Meredith G., 80
Koehler, Ludwig, 51
Koelle, Heinz Herman, 204
Kofahl, Robert E., 278
Kohler, Max A., 69, 70
Kondratyev, K. Ya., 225, 229
Korff, Serge A., 146
Koschmieder, E. L., 253
Kramer, Samuel Noah, 127, 128
Krause, Hans, 317, 337, 338, 342
Kruse, W., 288, 289, 290
Kuiper, F. B. J., 122
Kurten, Bjorn, 313, 314, 391

LaSor, William Sanford, 131
Lagerlund, E., 325
Lagler, Karl F., 279
Lammerts, Walter E., 132, 183
Langdon, Stephen Herbert, 114
Lange, John Peter, 78, 87, 98
Lawson, Douglas A., 149
Lee, David G., 148
Leupold, H. C., 49, 87, 91
Lewis, Arthur, 79
Lewis, Taylor, 95
Libby, Willard F., 176
Liddell, Henry George, 46, 100, 115
Liley, P. E., 386
Linsley, Ray K., 69, 70
Litman, J. D., 384
Loeb, Leonard B., 297
Long, William E., 142
Longenecker, Richard, 33
Luciano, Dorothy S., 154
Luikov, A. V., 387
Lydekker, Richard, 312, 332, 404

MacCulloch, John, 114
MacDonald, Gordon A., 73, 74

Macquarrie, John, 16
Makinodan, T., 171
Manabe, Syukuro, 224, 244
Martin, Paul, 156
Mason, Brian, 189
Maunder, E. W., 10, 46, 66
Maximov, Nicolai A., 181
McAdams, William H., 386
McClellan, W. H., 80, 86, 87, 89
McDowall, R. J. S., 179
McElroy, Michael B., 140
McKnight, Clyde, 194, 236
Meister, William J., 406
Merrill, Eugene, 88
Meryman, Harold T., 382, 399
Meyer, John R., 280
Michael, H. M., 179
Miller, Albert, 165
Miller, Robert R., 279
Mixter, Russel L., 5
Moll, Carl Bernhard, 62
Möller, Fritz, 224
Morgan, Ivor, 385, 386, 391
Morris, Henry M., 6, 77, 81, 129, 132, 133, 137, 140, 144, 145, 157, 158, 183, 184, 185, 186, 218, 368, 371, 405, 406
Morton, Glen, 230, 234, 245
Mountcastle, Vernon B., 278, 280, 388
Muller, H. J., 166
Murray, Bruce, 236, 284

Nairn, A. E. M., 141
Nelson, Byron, 133
Neugebauer, O., 162
Neuville, H., 339, 340, 341, 342, 344, 351, 359, 360, 363, 398
Nevins, Stuart E., 183, 407
Newman, Robert, 34, 52, 54, 218
Newman, Robert C., 30, 32, 47, 49, 57
Noll, Richard B., 140
Nordenskjold, N. A. E., 336, 369
Northrop, Bernard E., 100, 407

O'Keefe, John D., 211
Olcott, William Tyler, 290, 291, 300
Olsson, I. U., 179
Orr, James, 10
Osborn, Henry Fairfield, 316, 320, 331, 372
Ostrom, John, 420
Ottosson, Magnus, 81

Page, R. M., 29
Pallas, 356
Paltridge, G. W., 225, 226, 229, 236, 238, 241
Parrot, Andre, 309
Patrick, James, 94
Patten, Donald Wesley, 70, 71, 94, 100, 142, 158, 180, 183, 201, 202, 203, 204, 210, 211, 213, 215, 216, 390
Paulhos, Joseph L. H., 69, 70
Payne, D. F., 23
Payne, D. R., 101
Payne-Gaposchkin, Cecilia, 288, 292
Peck, Harry Thurston, 119
Perowne, J. J. Stewart, 61, 62, 105, 158
Peters, Walter G., 183
Petrie, W. M. Flinders, 118
Pfeiffer, Charles F., 118
Pfizenmayer, E. W., 320, 322, 323, 332, 333, 334, 342, 346, 347, 351, 367, 368, 401
Pitts, David E., 225
Plass, Gilbert, 139
Platt, C. M. R., 140, 225, 226, 229, 236, 238, 241
Pleticha, Dale, 290
Plummer, William, 106
Pollock, Michael L., 385
Pope, Marvin H., 89
Porter, Warren P., 153
Potsch, Klaus, 378, 379, 380
Poussin, L. la Vallee, 118
Price, G. B., 171
Putnam, Edmund W., 290, 291, 300

Quackenbush, L. S., 327, 328, 347, 352

Ralph, E. K., 179
Ramanathan, V., 223, 238
Ramm, Bernard, 11, 32, 33, 45, 218
Rehwinkel, Alfred M., 72, 102, 368, 406
Reid, James, 29
Rhodes, F. H. T., 183

Index of Persons

Riley, Henry T., 126
Rimmer, Harry, 218
Rogers, C. D., 224
Romer, A. S., 147
Rouse, Hunter, 70
Rowley, H. H., 90
Rupke, N. A., 132, 182, 183
Russell, W. L., 169
Ryder, M. L., 340, 342

Saggs, H. W. F., 309
Sanderson, Ivan T., 321, 329, 347, 356, 392
Saxena, S. C., 386
Schapery, Richard A., 417
Schenk, R. U., 173
Schlichting, Hermann, 251, 256
Scholander, P. F., 338
Schrenck, 356, 366
Schwarze, C. Theodore, 197, 200
Scott, Robert, 46, 100, 115
Seely, Paul H., 44
Shaffer, P. R., 183
Sherman, James H., 153
Short, George G., Jr., 149
Shortley, George, 136, 198, 219, 290, 292
Sikes, Sylvia K., 342
Silverberg, Robert, 391
Simpson, Roger L., 209
Skinner, John, 79, 84
Smith, A. E. Wilder, 174, 406
Smith, P. S., 348
Snell, Fred M., 284
Solzhenitsyn, Aleksandr, 311
Speisor, E. A., 86, 88, 89
Spotila, James R., 153
Springstead, William A., 73
Stair, Ralph, 189
Stauton, George, 316
Steinhauer, Loren C., 202
Stern, Curt, 168
Stevenson, Peter A., 189
Stewart, John Massey, 317, 360
Stigers, Harold G., 78
Strickler, Robert F., 224, 244
Strickling, James E., 25, 160
Sukachev, V. N., 344, 345, 372, 374, 375, 376, 377, 378, 379
Sunderland, J. E., 384
Swenson, Melvin J., 381

Taber, Stephen, 347, 349
Tan, Paul Lee, 33
Terry, K. D., 171
Toll, Edward, 142
Tolmachoff, I. P., 312, 313, 314, 316, 318, 320, 321, 322, 323, 329, 330, 332, 333, 334, 336, 341, 342, 343, 345, 356, 357, 359, 360, 361, 362, 363, 364, 365, 366, 400, 402
Touloukian, Y. S., 386, 393
Traub, Helmut, 115, 116, 119
Trudiner, L. Paul, 79, 80
Tucker W. H., 171
Tyler, H. T., 284

Udd, Stanley V., 45, 55, 58, 61, 193, 194, 287
Unger, Merrill F., 94, 131
Upton, A. C., 171

Vail, Isaac Newton, 77, 115, 118, 140, 157, 195, 196, 198, 200
Valley, Shea L., 288, 289, 292
Vander, Arthur J., 154
Vardiman, Larry, 259, 260, 263, 280
Velikovsky, Immanuel, 100, 306, 307, 356
Von Fange, Erich A., 406
Von Rad, Gerhard, 20
Voss, Henry, 269, 280

Waage, Karl M., 314, 318, 326
Wagner, A. James, 78, 98
Wakeman, Mary K., 19, 22, 32, 116, 118, 122
Walker, James C. G., 256, 268, 283
Wallace, Alfred Russell, 365
Wallace, Bruce, 167
Walshaw, C. D., 224
Waltke, Bruce K., 17, 21, 23, 24, 38, 131
Ward, Henry S., 180, 181
Warfield, Benjamin B., 137
Warren, Shields, 166, 169, 306
Webb, Willis L., 190
Weiser, Arthur, 106
Westberg, V. L., 157, 195, 197, 200, 212
Wetherald, Richard T., 224
Whipple, Fred, 189

Whitcomb, John C. Jr., 77, 81, 129, 132, 133, 140, 144, 145, 157, 158, 183, 218, 368, 371, 405, 406
White, A. J., 176
Whitehouse, Owen C., 117, 118, 120
Whitelaw, Robert, 25, 30, 72, 218, 240, 280, 281
Whitfield, G. R., 143, 147, 148, 149, 150, 151, 152
Wiggans, Don, 156
Wigram, George V., 58
Williams, Dudley, 136, 198, 219, 290, 292

Wilson, Clifford, 131
Wilson, John A., 17, 128

Yamauchi, Edwin M., 163
Yapp, W. B., 153
Young, E. J., 51
Young, Robert, 159

Zim, H. S., 183
Zobel, Otto J., 384, 418
Zockler, Otto, 90

Index of Scripture

Genesis		2	221	7:12	62, 72, 138
1	193, 221	2:2-3	100	7:16	67
1:1	22, 30, 82	2:4	82, 83	7:19-24	64
1:1-2	32, 196, 282	2:4-6	77	7:22 ff	100
1:2	18, 23, 21, 29, 50, 54, 55, 56, 57, 62, 63, 64, 82, 83, 86, 109, 110, 282	2:5	78, 79, 80, 81, 82, 84, 85, 93, 280, 282	8:1	62, 72, 103, 117, 160
		2:5-6	91, 92, 110, 282	8:2	68
		2:6	78, 79, 80, 81, 82, 83, 86, 88, 91, 111	8:14	304
1:4	29			8:20	103
1:6	216			8:22	98, 99, 100, 108, 127
1:6-7	43, 44, 62, 71, 137	2:7	80, 93	9:2-4	180
		2:7-8	84	9:3	85, 174
1:6-8	21, 22, 23, 29, 45, 48, 59, 60, 63, 106, 108, 421	2:7-10	81	9:9-17	103
		2:8	82, 93	9:12	95
		2:10-14	282	9:12-16	94
1:7	24, 26, 35, 50, 52, 53, 55, 56, 57, 58, 64, 105, 110	2:19	85	9:13	93, 95, 97
		3:8	79	9:20-21	102
		3:18	79, 84, 85	9:21	102
		3:24	175	10	163
1:7-8	25, 26	4:15	96, 97	11	102, 157, 158, 160, 163, 191
1:9	59	4:25-26	162		
1:11	81, 84, 85, 93	5	60, 102, 162, 163, 288	11:10	160
1:12	85			15:10	55
1:14	11, 26, 96, 97, 99	6:5-9	102	19:28	105
		7:1	102	21:15	84
1:14-17	25, 288	7:4	93	24:19	83
1:14-18	19, 217	7:6	160	30:37-39	40
1:14-19	20, 245	7:6-7	83	31:7-12	40
1:15	25, 26	7:10	83	49:25	282
1:16	287	7:11	8, 10, 22, 38, 46, 63, 64, 65, 66, 67, 68, 117, 138, 186, 246, 267, 273, 282, 345		
1:20	51, 53			Exodus	
1:21	19			9:22	52, 53, 85
1:25	19, 85			9:22-23	52
1:28-29	20			9:25	85
1:29	85			10:12	84
1:30	85	7:11-12	43, 51, 69, 137	10:21-22	52
1:31	101, 102			12:3	67

13:21-22	47	2 Chronicles		33:7	63, 110
20:4	7, 282	2:6	26	37:29	108
39:3	44	6:18	26	68:33	26
				62:16	85
Numbers		Nehemiah		77:17	10, 38, 44,
14:4	97	9:6	26		49, 55
16:39	44			78:23	46
		Job		78:23-25	8
Deuteronomy		5:25	85	90:10	158
5:8	282	9:8	8	92:8	85
10:14	26	19:24	108	104:2	10, 37
11:10	83	20:4	108	104:3	8
11:15	85	22:14	37	104:4-8	419
28:12	62, 63	22:16	83	104:8	246, 273
29:22	84	26:7	9, 37	104:14	85
32:2	84	26:8	49, 57	104:29	36
34:7	158, 159	26:11	8, 46	105:35	85
		28:1	90	106:20	84, 85
Joshua		28:25	36	119:83	105
14:10	158	30:4	84	135:6	282
		30:7	84	135:7	63
Judges		31:26	11	148	104
5:4	10, 38, 55	36:27	89, 90, 91	148:1	108
20:40	47	36:27-78	10, 89	148:1-12	105
		36:27-29	49	148:2-3	108
1 Samuel		36:28	55	148:4	26, 52, 106,
2:8	47	36:29	38		107, 108
		37:11	49	148:5	108
2 Samuel		37:18	8, 44	148:6	107, 108
1:24-25	107	38:6-11	282	148:8	108
22:8	46	38:9	50		
22:12	44	38:22	8, 62, 63	Proverbs	
22:43	44	38:35	29	1:7	6
				3:20	267
1 Kings		Psalms		8:24-28	282
2:35	97	9:5	108	8:27	37
7:15-22	47	16	32	9:10	6
8:27	26	18:7-15	138, 186,	27:25	85
18:41	69		273		
		18:8	8	Ecclesiastes	
2 Kings		19:4	8	10:20	29
7:1	67	19:5-6	11	12:3	68
7:1-3	67	19:6	8		
7:2	67, 68	21:5	108	Isaiah	
7:19	67, 68	21:7	108	24:18	67, 68
19:26	85	24:1-2	282	27:3	83
		29:5	8	28:17	8
1 Chronicles		33:1	63	30:30	8
2:4	159	33:29	63	31:5	29
2:4-11	159	33:6-9	61	34:4	10

Index of Scripture

37:27	85	Amos		1:21-23	310
40:22	8, 10, 27, 37	7:2	85	1:28	6
42:15	84			8:20	181
44:24	8	Micah		8:20-21	264
45:8	44	3:7	14	9:14-19	264
60:2	50	5:7	36, 85, 222		
60:8	8, 67, 68			1 Corinthians	
		Habakkuk		9:8-10	33
Jeremiah		3:6	108		
10:9	44	3:11	8	2 Corinthians	
10:13	49, 55, 62, 63			12:2	26
12:4	84	Zephaniah			
13:16	50	1:15	50	Galatians	
14:6	84			3:13	425
51:16	49, 62, 63	Zechariah		4:19-26	33
		10:1	84	4:20	34
Ezekiel		14:4	267	4:24	34
1:22	45				
1:23	45	Malachi		Ephesians	
1:25	45	3:10	46, 67, 68	1:11	263
1:26	45				
6:11	44	Matthew		Philippians	
10:1	45	2:15	31	2:10	107
13:11	107	5:17-18	6, 38		
25:6	44	24:36-37	423	2 Timothy	
30:18	50	24:38-39	424	3:16-17	14, 38
31:14-16	282	24:40-42	425		
32:6	83	27:46	425	Hebrews	
32:7	50			11:3	4, 29
34:12	50	Mark			
		13:4	31	1 Peter	
Daniel				1:11	31
9:25	2	John			
		10:34-35	6	2 Peter	
				1:21-22	38
Hosea		Acts		3:3-13	59, 109
11:1	32	2:22-23	264	3:4	3
13:3	32	2:25-28	31	3:5-6	282
				3:6	60
		Romans			
Joel		1:18-32	307	Jude	
2:2	50	1:21	310	14	162